September 2, 1997
Rutgers University

Traditional Japanese Poetry

人まつ江べを
あけいずれば

紀貫之
きのつらゆき

それゆふしほの
魚?鳥?るる

Traditional Japanese Poetry

AN ANTHOLOGY

Translated, with an Introduction, by
Steven D. Carter

Stanford University Press
Stanford, California

Stanford University Press
Stanford, California
© 1991 by the Board of Trustees of the
Leland Stanford Junior University

Printed in the United States of America

Original printing 1991
Last figure below indicates year of this printing:
01   00   99   98   97   96   95   94

CIP data appear at the end of the book

For Mother

Acknowledgments

For their assistance in bringing this book into being I must first thank several generations of students at Brigham Young University. Their questions and comments have done much to improve my translations. Gratitude is also due my research assistant Edward Peng, who helped me with poems in Chinese, and my colleagues in the Department of Asian and Near Eastern Languages, Brigham Young University, for various other kinds of assistance. In particular I wish to thank Professor Masakazu Watabe for years of steadfast support, moral and otherwise. I am also grateful to Gail Oman King for bibliographic assistance; to Melvin Smith for help in computer formatting; to my editors Helen Tartar of Stanford University Press and Barbara Mnookin for their patience in revising a very complicated manuscript; and to my wife, Mary, who has been my most valuable critic. Any errors that remain are of course mine alone.

Permission to reprint material has been kindly granted by Columbia University Press for my translations from *Waiting for the Wind: Thirty-six Poets of Japan's Late Medieval Age*. Except for a few prepared specifically for this anthology, all translations by Helen Craig McCullough appeared originally in her *Brocade by Night: 'Kokin Wakashū' and the Court Style in Japanese Classical Poetry* or *Kokin Wakashū: The First Imperial Anthology of Japanese Poetry*, both published by Stanford University Press.

S.D.C.

Contents

Translator's Note

All genres of classical Japanese poetry involve combinations of five- and seven-syllable lines: 5-7-5-7-7 for the *tanka* or *uta*, 5-7-5 for the *haiku* or *hokku*, etc. The translations in this collection attempt to reflect this pattern by using alternating long and short English lines, albeit with careful attention paid to English rhythm. Likewise, the translations attempt to retain the order of images as they appear in the original poems, whenever syntactic patterns make that possible in English.

In these two respects the translations represent nothing new. In punctuation and line format, however, I have attempted to find new ways to suggest the variety of pauses and stops in the original poems. To this end, I begin flush left each new poem and generally every new line following any punctuation mark, then indent two spaces the next one or two lines when those lines constitute one complete sentence or phrase, with the restriction that this "jogging" of lines will never continue for more than three lines. The most common pattern is thus,

> 202. SUMMER. Topic unknown
>
> A barge of timber
>   floating down a logging stream
>   makes a sad pillow—
> but in summer it's a cool place
>   to lie down for the night.
>
> somagawa no / ikada no toko no / ukimakura / natsu wa
> suzushiki / fushido narikeri

But there are several variations, as in the following examples:

> 314. WINTER. "Leaves Falling at Dawn"
>
> Raindrops, I first thought
> ·   as I lay awake in my bed—
> but what I heard
>   was the unbroken patter
>   of leaves overcome by storm winds.

shigure ka to / nezame no toko ni / kikoyuru wa / arashi
ni taenu / ko no ha narikeri

515. WINTER. Written on the first day of the Tenth
Month

> Autumn's gone away.
> The wind has blown from the trees
>   every single leaf;
> and the mountains are forlorn
>   now that winter has come.

aki wa inu / kaze ni konoha no / chirihatete / yama
sabishikaru / fuyu wa kinikeri

958. SPRING

> Term of duty done,
> he stops, umbrella in hand—
>   gazing at dusk rain.

dekawari ya / karakasa sagete / yūnagame

1058. SPRING

> Snow starts melting
>   and the village overflows—
> with children.

yuki tokete / mura ippai no / kodomo kana

All together, this approach succeeds, I hope, in suggesting the syntax of the
original Japanese poems in ways that the uniform formats used by many
other translators cannot.

   Poems are introduced with information taken from the original sources
—the topical book of an imperial anthology, headnotes, and so forth—as
in this example.

662. SUMMER. A verse on "Cooling Down," writ-
ten for a thousand-verse sequence at the house of the
governor of Ise

> Oh, for some blossoms—
> to bid storm winds to visit
>   this summer garden!

hana mogana / arashi ya towan / natsu no niwa

Titles or topics written in Japanese (as opposed to headnotes) are set in quotation marks; titles on poetry in Chinese are italicized. Sources for the poems are given in a separate section at the back of the book, keyed to the anthology numbers. A list of abbreviations used there and in the text appears on pp. 468–70.

Whenever possible, I have kept notes with the poems, but a handful of long notes containing important but sometimes complex information seemed better cast as supplementary notes. These notes, referred to as s.n. 1, s.n. 2, and so forth, are keyed to the footnotes and appear in a separate section at the back of the book. For convenience, on poems of five lines or less, the romanized versions of the originals are printed beneath the translations, with slashes separating five- and seven-syllable units for the benefit of those accustomed to the parsing used in standard indexes. Longer romanizations are given in sequence as supplementary notes. I have followed the practice of most translators in providing romanizations based on current native Japanese pronunciations rather than attempting to reconstruct the pronunciations of the various historical periods.

In choosing poems, I have assumed that the anthology will be used in the college classroom, and I have therefore given priority to authors and works well recognized as of artistic and/or historical importance by Japanese scholars. For this reason major poets such as Kakinomoto no Hitomaro, Izumi Shikibu, Saigyō, and Matsuo Bashō are particularly well represented, as are important collections such as *Man'yōshū*, *Kokinshū*, and *Shin kokinshū*. In addition, the volume contains generous samplings from poets and works representing other genres and sensibilities—from Chinese verse written by Zen monks to comic poetry. In particular, it gives more attention to the late medieval age (1333–1600) than other anthologies, reflecting the new interest in the poets and poems of that age now being shown in Japan and the West. Introductory material and explanatory notes have been included to assist the first-time student in approaching the poems, with particular attention given to historical context, aesthetic ideals, and rhetorical techniques. The organization of material is by historical period, beginning with the earliest native poems and ending with a few samples of traditional forms still being used in the twentieth century.

An asterisk on a poem heading indicates that the poem was translated by Helen Craig McCullough. All other translations are my own.

Traditional Japanese Poetry

Introduction

What is poetry? Shelley called it "the record of the best and happiest moments of the happiest and best minds."[1] But for readers acquainted with T. S. Eliot or Robert Lowell or Allen Ginsberg, that definition simply will not do. A happier and better definition, as well as one more useful for introducing an anthology of traditional Japanese poetry, comes from Ezra Pound, who saw great literature as "simply language charged with meaning to the utmost possible degree," and poetry, his own chosen art form, as "the most concentrated form of verbal expression."[2] Certainly, this is particularly appropriate for students—as Pound was himself—of the great poets of Japan, who wrote poems as charged and compressed as poems can be.

The reasons why traditional Japanese poetry should so clearly fit Pound's definition are various. The most obvious no doubt derives from the nature of the Japanese language, whose sound system, with its few consonants and even fewer vowels and diphthongs, did not lend itself to expansive forms, making small seem better and perhaps more powerful. There is also the historical context in which Japanese poetry as we know it today first developed—the highly refined society of the early courts of Nara and Kyōto. In this setting, for complex psychological and sociological reasons, poetry came to be used as much for communication between lovers or friends as for artistic expression, and a tradition of cryptic statement evolved, with notes passed from sleeve to sleeve or conundrums exchanged furtively in the night. Add to this the high sense of decorum that dominated court society for centuries, and you get the conditions in which developed the classical *uta* (also referred to

1. "A Defence of Poetry," in G. B. Harrison, ed., *Major British Writers* (New York: Harcourt, Brace), 1: 314.

2. Ezra Pound, *An ABC of Reading* (New York: New Directions, 1934), p. 36.

as *tanka* or *waka*), the thirty-one-syllable poem that is the foundation of virtually all poetry written in Japanese between 850 and 1900.

The success of the uta meant that traditional Japanese poetry came to be characterized by certain phenomena resulting from or reacting against the short verse form: first, a strong emphasis on internal alliteration and assonance, which provided the poet with his only musical tools; second, an absence of rhyme, which inevitably would have produced tedious, sing-song rhythms; third, the use of ellipsis and various forms of compressed syntax; and fourth, a reliance on the concrete image as the primary vehicle of expression. That many of these same features characterize much modern poetry in English—whether in short forms or long—is an accident of history that goes far in explaining why the poetry of so remote a culture held such an attraction for Pound and his modernist cohorts at the turn of the century.

To be sure, some possibilities were lost to Japanese poetry by its reliance on short verse forms. There is no epic poetry in the Japanese tradition, nor any dramatic form akin to the plays of the Elizabethan stage. Instead, the Japanese poets stayed within the bounds of a quiet lyricism that explored a few privileged topics, chief among them the beauties of the natural world and the obsessions of the human heart.

If one is looking for a Milton or a Browning, then, one will not find him in the poetry of Japan's classical age. And although one is more likely to find there lines reminiscent of Wordsworth or Keats, one should probably put even such comparisons aside in order to be fair to the Japanese poets. The poems of Japan's classical ages have virtues of their own, unique to their own situation, and it is for those virtues that the poems deserve to be read. For if one does not find the grandeur of Hamlet's soliloquies in classical Japan, neither does one find in Shakespeare's sonnets the careful understatement of a lyric like this one (poem 57, below):

> Our life in this world—
> to what shall I compare it?
> It is like a boat
>   rowing out at break of day,
> leaving not a trace behind.

yo no naka o / nani ni tatoemu / asabiraki / koginishi
fune no / ato naki ga goto

Of Sami Mansei, the author of this poem, we know almost nothing except that he was active in the early eighth century. Yet we do not need to know anything about Mansei or his time to respond to the simple but moving image that he creates in just a few lines. It was the ability to create such an image under the great linguistic stress of a short verse form that was respected above all else among poets of Mansei's time; and it is the ability to respond to such an image that should be the goal of a study of Japanese poetry.

After the end of the classical tradition as such in the sixteenth century, some changes did take place. But, contrary to what one might expect, the verse form got shorter with the emergence of the *hokku*, known as haiku in the West. And although some fresh topics were treated in the new genre, the old boundaries were still generally respected, and the focus continued to be primarily on the natural world for imagery and on the impressionistic portrayal of human perception and emotion.

Of course this should not be taken to mean that the premodern tradition of Japanese poetry is all of a piece; from age to age there were changes in thematics, rhetorical devices, topics, and so on. But these matters are best treated in relation to specific poets and poems, as I have attempted to do in the introductions to the authors and works represented in this book. Here what is needed is a more precise definition of the genres of the Japanese poetry and how they relate to each other in time.

We must begin with an exception to much of what has been said above. For the earliest genre of the Japanese tradition is not the uta, but the *chōka*, which translated literally is "long poem." Although it too was a courtly genre, the chōka was clearly a longer and more complex form, as a famous example shows (poems 36–37):

ametsuchi no	5	Since that ancient time
wakareshi toki yu	7	when heaven and earth were sundered,
kamu sabite	5	like a god soaring
takaku tōtoki	7	in high-towering majesty
suruga naru	5	over Suruga
fuji no takane o	7	has stood Fuji's lofty peak.
ama no hara	5	Turn your eyes upward
furisakemireba	7	to heaven's high plain and see
wataru hi no	5	how it hides from sight
kage mo kakurai	7	the sun in its constant course
teru tsuki no	5	and obstructs our view
hikari mo miezu	7	of the moon in its shining,

shirakumo mo	5	blocking even clouds
iyukihabakari	7	from going on their way—
toki jiku so	5	and how always on its peak
yuki wa furikeru	7	snow is falling, ever falling.
kataritsugi	5	We praise it now, and ever more—
fuji no takane wa	7	the lofty peak of Fuji.

Envoy

tago no ura yu	6	At Tago Bay
uchiidete mireba	8	I came out, and looked afar—
mashiro ni so	5	to see the pure white
fuji no takane ni	7	of Mount Fuji's lofty peak,
yuki wa furikeru	7	amidst a flurry of snow.

A simple paean? Perhaps; but this poem, written by Yamabe no Aka-hito sometime in the early eighth century, does much that its descendant the uta could not, employing parallelism and repetition for a grand effect that would be impossible in the shorter form. Akahito's deli-cately articulated structure—moving from the beginning of time to the present moment of the poet's vision, while at the same time tracing the timeless arc of the sun, the moon, the stars, and the mountain itself—was something later uta poets could admire but never reproduce.

But the fact is that the chōka did not survive. *Man'yōshū* (A Col-lection of Ten Thousand Leaves; ca. 759), our first sourcebook for Japanese poems, contains only 266 examples of the form, as opposed to over 4,000 uta. Whether for reasons that have to do with the sound structure of the language or with literary developments at court, the chōka was a dying genre even before the end of the Ancient Age (fifth century–794). With it died the possibility of sustained poetic narrative.

Nevertheless, the chōka bequeathed much to the new tradition form-ing at court, including the spirit of aesthetic celebration so apparent in Akahito's poem and the gentle humanism so important in defining Japanese standards of taste. In formal terms, it also bequeathed to later poets the basic 5-7-5-7-7 prosodic structure that appeared in its envoys (Akahito's poem presents a slight deviation) and the use of so-called "pillow-words." These *makura kotoba* were fixed imagistic epithets ("night, black as leopard-flower seeds"; "Nara, where the earth is rich"; "Kara, the cape of wave-chatter like Cathay speech") that would per-form an economic function for poets into the centuries to come. Con-sequently, lines by Kakinomoto no Hitomaro (fl. ca. 680–700; from poem 15),

> Thus the courtiers,
> men of the *stone-built* palace,
> align their vessels
>   to cross the morning river . . .

momoshiki no / ōmiyabito wa / fune namete / asakawa
watari

are echoed by Retired Emperor Juntoku (1197–1242), writing in the
1200's (poem 514):

> In the *stone-built* palace
>   the old eaves are overgrown
>   with Memory Fern—
> but ah, what a past is here
>   still left to be remembered!

momoshiki ya / furuki nokiba no / shinobu ni mo / nao
amari aru / mukashi narikeri

This is not direct allusion; the Emperor is drawing on a whole tradi-
tion, not on a single poem. Yet for those who know its long history, the
image presented in the epithet "stone-built" (*momoshiki no*) gains extra
power and authority borne by its rhetorical connection to the past.

So the chōka poets left behind them a specific body of images and
epithets that went far toward defining the focus of Japanese poetry.
More important, they left behind a heritage of lyricism that would in-
spire generations of poets to come. It is largely because of the chōka, in
fact, that the Japanese still think of the seventh and eighth centuries as
an optimistic, happy time when Japanese culture had its first flowering.

The Classical Age (794–1185), often referred to as Heian after the
capital (Heian Kyō; modern Kyōto), was more elegant but less open.
With the remove of the nation's capital from Nara in the broad Yamato
plain to the hill-lined valley of the Kyōto basin, poetry too took an
inward turn, becoming a more strictly courtly art, with elaborate con-
ventions and strict rules on proper imagery and themes that allowed
for no more "vulgar" influences. And no longer was its inspiration the
Japanese state or Mount Fuji. Now the model looked to by poets was
Chinese—a tradition that poets of *Man'yōshū* had been aware of, but
less obviously influenced by.

As it happened, the Chinese looked to by the Japanese at the time
were not those of the *Shi jing* (The Book of Poetry) or the great Tang

poets closest to them in time, such as Li Bo (701–62), Du Fu (712–70), and Bo Juyi (772–846). Instead, in a sort of "time-lag" that would characterize much of Japan's cultural borrowing from the continent for ages to come, Japanese poets of the Classical Age read the poets of the fourth, fifth, and sixth centuries—the period known as the Six Dynasties. These poets, who had fallen into relative obscurity in China itself, were known less for philosophical profundity than cleverness, charm, color, and wordplay. "Breaking the Willows," by Xiao Gang (503–51), shows the style at its height:[3]

> The willows tangle like silken threads;
> people pull and break them at the beginning of spring.
> The leaves are dense: bird flight is impeded;
> the breeze is light: flower fall is languid.
> In lofty castles short flutes begin to sound;
> in lonely groves painted flutes echo sadly.
> There is no difference in the songs;
> all express thoughts of long separation.

Little exegesis is needed to point out the basic qualities of this style: lyricism and a reliance on parallelism as a basic organizing principle. Xiao's poem is an extension of earlier Chinese traditions, but his elegant conceits make for a density of expression and an indirect rhetorical stance that mark his work as the product of a new kind of verbal perception.

Some of this newness had already been experienced by Japanese poets in the eighth century. It was in the mid-ninth century, however, that the Six Dynasties style became a defining factor of the uta, whose rhetorical stance and thematics can often be traced directly to models by Chinese courtiers writing several hundred years before. One need only compare the following poem (223) by the courtier Ōshikōchi no Mitsune (d. ca. 925?) with Akahito's envoy quoted above to see the effect of the new sensibility on the poetry of the Japanese court.

> Its effort is vain,
> the darkness of this spring night:
> true, we cannot see

---

3. Translation from Helen Craig McCullough, *Brocade by Night: 'Kokin Wakashū' and the Court Style in Japanese Classical Poetry* (Stanford, Calif.: Stanford University Press, 1985), p. 62.

> the color of the plum blossoms—
> but how can it hide their scent?

haru no yo no / yami wa ayanashi / ume no hana / iro
koso miene / ka ya wa kakururu

In Akahito's description of "Fuji's lofty peak, amidst a flurry of snow" we have only one major metaphor, no syntactic hesitations, and no questioning of perceptions. Mitsune, by contrast, is more tentative and more cerebral—producing a clever conception, using personification and a plea to the reader's reasoning powers to complicate what could have been a simple exclamation on the wonderful scent of the plum blossoms.

It was this somewhat convoluted, highly rhetoricized approach that became the foundation of court poetry in the uta form, enshrined first of all in *Kokinshū* (Collection of Early and Modern Japanese Poetry; 905). This was a work compiled by imperial order and intended to represent the poetic accomplishment of the courtly classes, for whom poetry had become a constant feature of life—whether informally in conversation or formally in poem contests or at banquets. In its pages we find many poems like Mitsune's, appealing to studied logic or courtly taste for their effects. Others poems use similar devices. For instance, in the following poem (430) we confront a *kakekotoba*—a "pivot-word," or pun involving one word used in two senses at once, and often in two syntactic positions.

> I must depart now
> for the pines that await me
> at Mount Inaba—
> but should I hear that you too pine,
> I will hurry back to you.

tachiwakare / inaba no yama no / mine ni ouru / matsu
to shi kikaba / ima kaerikon

Composed by Ariwara no Yukihira (818–93) before leaving for his post as provincial governor in Inaba, this poem was probably intended to convey his steadfastness to a lover. Rather than announce his devotion openly, however, he has chosen to cloak it in a poem that employs two puns, the first involving *inaba*, functioning as both a place-name and an inflection of the verb *inu*, "to go," and the second *matsu*, or "pine," a word that fortunately can mean both the tree and "to wait" in English as well—although to actually render them as a single word without repetition is impossible in translation.

The list of devices could go on; what is important is that all of them owe something to the Chinese poetry of the Six Dynasties period—a tradition that, after *Kokinshū*, became part of the heritage of Japan. In coming years, twenty-one such anthologies were compiled by imperial order, the last appearing fully five centuries after the first. In all but a few cases, the compilers were courtiers whose allegiance was to their past. Quibble though they might about some matters, their basic agreements defined poetry and resisted fundamental change in genre, basic subject matter, and so forth.

This does not mean that there were no developments in later years, as the introductory material to various later poets and works below should make clear. For instance, one definitely finds a new seriousness of tone in the Early Medieval Age (1185–1330; often referred to as the Kamakura Period), represented most fully by the eighth imperial anthology, *Shin kokinshū* (The New *Kokinshū*; 1205), which features poems like these by Monk Saigyō (1118–90) and Fujiwara no Teika (1162–1241); poems 302 and 401, respectively):

> That spring long ago
>   at Naniwa in Tsu:
> was it all a dream?
> Now only dead leaves on the reeds
>   rustle in the passing wind.

tsu no kuni no / naniwa no haru wa / yume nare ya / ashi
no kareba ni / kaze wataru nari

> The years have gone by,
>   with my prayers still unanswered—
> as Hase's bell
>   signals evening from its peak,
> sounding somehow far away.

toshi mo henu / inoru chigiri wa / hatsuseyama / onoe no
yama no / yoso no yūgure

These poems—presenting a stark autumn scene that seems a Buddhist contemplation of the law of change and the forlorn complaint of a rejected lover—have little of the lightheartedness of *Kokinshū* days, to be sure. And in general the poems of this later period follow the same pattern, with more direct means of expression, as is even clearer in another famous example, by Monk Jakuren (1139?–1202; poem 324):

> Ah, solitude—
> it is not the sort of thing
>   that has a color.
> Mountains lined with black pine
>   on an evening in autumn.

> sabishisa wa / sono iro to shi mo / nakarikeri / maki
> tatsu yama no / aki no yūgure

In its appeal to the natural world for an image to express a state of mind, Jakuren's poem reveals its continuity with the court tradition, but it does so in a quieter, more straightforward way than the *Kokinshū* poets would have chosen.

Yet it is important to note that Jakuren's poem was written not as true natural description but as one of a group of one hundred poems submitted to a patron upon request[4]—that is, it was a product of imagination mediated by traditional conventions and expectations. And this is true of Saigyō's and Teika's poems as well, the first because it refers directly to an earlier poem, by Monk Nōin (998–1050?), that described the beauty of spring at the same location (poem 247), the second because it relies partially for its effect on the pivot-word Hatsuse, which functions both as a place-name associated with a famous temple and the verb *hatsu*, "to come to an end."

Upon study, then, seeming breaks with tradition prove often to be merely shifts within it. Moreover, the influence of China continued. For example, the somber, contemplative qualities of many poems in *Shin kokinshū* derive partly from the profound impact on Japanese courtiers of the poets of the Tang Dynasty. Thus the tradition begun in the early days of Heian culture continued on through most of the Late Medieval Age (1333–1600; often referred to as the Muromachi Period)—through the civil wars of the mid-1300's to the final collapse of aristocratic society in the 1500's. Changes were occurring, but always within the limits of a conservative tradition. The form of the uta continued, although with new developments in syntax and caesura. The basic themes of the *Kokinshū* poets—the four seasons, love, felicitations, travel, and

---

4. The poem (SKKS 361) originally appeared in a hundred-poem sequence submitted to Fujiwara no [Go-Kyōgoku] Yoshitsune (1169–1206) in 1191.

so on—remained the same, even as newer and more complex topics within those themes were introduced and subgenres were developed to organize anthologies in new ways. Pillow-words and pivot-words were still employed. And, above all, the tradition remained a courtly one, with courtiers—though now sharing their art with men of the military families—still its primary poets and court tastes always at its foundation.

Yet some other changes did take place. One was that the composition of Chinese poetry became popular again, this time in Zen monasteries. More important, though, was the growth that took place in *renga*, or "linked uta." At first the new form was nothing more than an elegant verse-capping game, in which one poet provided the first half of an uta (the 5-7-5), and a companion the conclusion (the final 7-7). But in time the game became a serious business, with the art of "linking" at its heart. By the age of *Shin kokinshū*, poets like Fujiwara no Teika were composing one-hundred-verse sequences.

It is a testament to the power of courtly attitudes, that the new child in most ways responded positively to the discipline of its parent—working within the thematic bounds of the imperial anthologies, for instance, and demanding the same standards of decorum. For, as an example from the fifteenth century shows, renga—at least the renga that have been preserved for us—represent nothing more than an extension of uta aesthetics.[5]

1. Takayama Sōzei [d. 1455]

> The green underleaves
> of wisteria in bloom:
> seaweed on the waves.

saku fuji no / uraba wa nami no / tamamo kana

2. Monk Ninsei [mid-15th century]

> Borrowing color from spring,
> the pines are a deeper hue.

haru ni iro karu / matsu no hitoshio

5. Translation from Steven D. Carter, "A Lesson in Failure: Linked-Verse Contests in Medieval Japan," *Journal of the American Oriental Society*, 104.4 (Fall 1984): 733–34.

3. His Holiness Gyōjō [1405–69]

> In this morning's rain
> the snow on the mountain peaks
> starts to melt away.

mine yo yuki / kesa furu ame ni / kiesomete

4. Venerable Senjun [1411–76]

> Shining faintly in the haze,
> the moon before break of day.

kasumi ni usuku / nokoru tsukikage

5. Bishop Shinkei [1406–75]

> The warbler still sleeps
> as I bed down in the fields,
> travel my pillow.

uguisu mo / mada nuru nobe no / tabimakura

6. Sōzei

> The house-paths cannot be seen,
> so dark is the gloom before dawn.

tare ka ieji mo / mienu akegure

7. Ninsei

> Despite the fields
> of clinging kudzu vines,
> autumn takes its leave.

makuzuhara / kaeru aki mo / tadoruran

8. Gyōjo

> On last year's bush clover
> blossoms are fragrant once more.

furue no kohagi / nao niou koro

These verses were composed by monks and men of warrior back-
ground who might have been expected to do something entirely new.
And at first glance their work does appear to hark back to the chōka,
with a longer, more complex prosodic form. But, in fact, these verses
were neither composed nor interpreted as a whole; rather they were
treated as individual links, with rules that made for constant change
and variety—although only within the thematic limits of the uta tra-
dition that would classify the first verse as in the spring category, the
sixth as miscellaneous, and the last two as autumn. Once again, the
poetry of the court stood as the authority, which the major renga poets
seem to have treated as an absolute, adopting a neoclassical attitude in
both their poetry and their critical writings.

Real change could come only when the old authority structure was
displaced, which started just after the above sequence (dated 1453) was
composed, with the wars that began in the capital in the late 1460's
and continued on until the great unification of 1600. In the world of
poetry, these were years of great contrasts. Ironically, courtiers of this
time were often joined in their meetings and contests by warrior barons
eager to obtain the trappings of culture. But the fragmentation that was
fundamental to linked verse (a signal of changes to come sent out by
that genre, almost despite itself) was more true to the trend of the age.
For poetry too was undergoing a reorientation—moving away from
the capital as the center of culture, into the provinces, the castle towns
and trade centers.

It was in this atmosphere that *haikai renga* (also referred to as *haikai
renku*), the last major genre of premodern poetry, evolved. In essence
still another development from within the tradition, the new form main-
tained classical form but allowed for broader thematic range. A link
from around 1500 illustrates the point (poem 787):

> Is there any hair, or not?
> He feels around, to make sure.

> With no disciple,
> the monk has shaved his head
>   all by himself.

ke no aru naki wa / sagurite zo shiru; deshi motanu /
bōzu wa kami o / jizori shite

One can easily imagine such a bawdy verse being composed earlier
in Japanese history, in a formal linking session; but in those days such

lapses in decorum had not generally been recorded. Not until the sixteenth century, a time of great upheaval and change in Japanese society, would such work be preserved. This alone signals a change in the values of the poetic world. As the aristocratic classes lost their wealth and, along with it, their privileged place in Japanese culture, their elegant tastes were replaced by those of the new classes—the samurai, the artisans, and the merchants.

These changes continued on into the Early Modern Age (or the Edo Period, 1600–1868), an era that can be seen as either the end of an old tradition or the beginning of a new one. Formally speaking, it was clearly the former, since the basic 5-7-5 syllable scheme remained intact; but in terms of thematics, haikai represented a new and plebeian trend. For while poets of the new linked verse still seem to have conceived of their work in terms of the old categories of the seasons, love, and so on, they felt free to work all sorts of material into those categories that earlier poets would never have allowed. Hence Matsuo Bashō (1644–94) and a few friends were able to create a series of scenes never even considered possible by *Kokinshū* or *Shin kokinshū* poets.

823. Tsuboi Tokoku [d. 1690]

    White briar-rose:
    frost on a horse's bones,
    in second bloom.

hana mubara / bakotsu no shimo ni / sakikaeri

824. Okada Yasui [1648–1743]

    I saw a crane from that window—
    and now that faint dawn moon.

tsuru miru mado no / tsuki kasuka nari

825. Matsuo Bashō [1644–94]

    A day with no
      autumn wind—a day with no
      sake in my pot!

kaze fukanu / aki no hi kame ni / sake naki hi

These verses can be fitted into the categories of orthodox renga—winter for the first, autumn for the last. Not so, however, their images of a horse's bones or a *sake* pot. Indeed, what the verses seem to present is a parody. This was the case with much work in the last two-and-a-half centuries of premodern Japan. Uta were written, but either parodying *Kokinshū* and *Shin kokinshū* poets or looking for inspiration further back, to the age of *Man'yōshū*; finally, even haikai itself was poked fun at by *senryū*, a madcap form that reacted against Bashō's relative seriousness.

In the end, then, one can claim that even the poetry of the Early Modern Age owed its allegiance to past tradition, although it paid its tribute obliquely, through comic imitation. And more: clearly, the most prestigious forms of the period, Chinese verse and the hokku, or haiku—a subgenre deriving from the "first verse" of a haikai sequence—can be seen as extensions of the past in every way. For is not this verse (poem 965) by Yosa Buson (1716–83)

> Fuji all alone—
> the one thing left unburied
> by new green leaves

> fuji hitotsu / uzuminokoshite / wakaba kana

more than vaguely reminiscent of Akahito's chōka, just as a Chinese couplet (from poem 1065) by Monk Ryōkan (1758–1831)

> In the blue heavens, cold geese calling.
> On the empty hills, leaves flying.

reminds us of Saigyō or of the Chinese poems by Zen monks? For all their irreverence, most Early Modern poets were still working within the strictures of a tradition they had inherited as a state of mind.

More fundamental change, in formal and philosophical terms, came with the introduction of Western culture into Japan in the late nineteenth century. Now poets had true alternatives, from Shakespeare and Wordsworth to, eventually, Eliot, Lowell, and Ginsberg. It was these new influences that made it possible for the contemporary poet Yoshioka Minoru (b. 1919) to title a work "Paul Klee's Dining Table" and use words like these:

> Forks grow like feeble weeds
> Glasses that have lost lips tilt in the air

And a sour drink flows
Sausage skins and fish bones go under
In the city of water that can't be surveyed from above[6]

In such lines, obscure in reference and unfettered by any strict sense of form, almost nothing of the premodern world remains. Thus, with true clarity, the reader of Japanese poetry at last confronts something almost absolutely new.

Yet, to conclude, most of the old forms have survived. This is especially true of haiku, which still supports a large poetic community, and, to a lesser extent, even of uta—now referred to by its practitioners as tanka. What has continued on in these traditions is form rather than subject matter, perhaps because not all poets feel comfortable with free verse and find some sense of security in the rhythms of their own heritage. And even linked verse, the most difficult of classical genres to master, is receiving new attention both in Japan and abroad by those who find something very modern in its fragmented vision.[7]

What all of this will ultimately mean is something we cannot know at present, of course; but the one thing affirmed by such developments is that classical poetry of Japan, like that of China or Greece, is still very much a living force in the modern world—as the twentieth-century examples included in this "classical" anthology attest.

6. Translation of Hiraoka Sato, in Howard Hibbett, ed. and comp., *Contemporary Japanese Literature: An Anthology of Fiction, Film, and Other Writing Since 1945* (New York: Knopf, 1977), p. 340.

7. See, for instance, a Western renga (in English, French, Italian, and Spanish, no less) in Octavio Paz et al., *Renga, a Chain of Poems* (New York: Braziller, 1971). Another sign of interest in the form is indicated by William H. Gass's reference to it in *Habitations of the Word* (New York: Simon and Schuster, 1985), p. 272.

The
Ancient Age

Our earliest written records of Japan are Chinese chronicles that note the existence in southern and central Japan of a tribal society with some central authority structures by about A.D. 400. These tribes went through a series of conflicts during the next two hundred years, culminating in the triumph of a ruling clan that championed the introduction into Japan of Chinese culture, with its religions, superstitions, political thought, bureaucratic systems, and, of course, literature.

One measure of the success of these efforts toward the definition of Japanese culture is evident in the appearance in 712 of Kojiki (A Record of Ancient Matters), a compendium of mythological tales put together with the intent of establishing the claims of the reigning imperial house. Around that same time, the government established on the Yamato plain the capital city of Nara—then known as Heijō. Naturally, the capital also became a center of literary culture, with courtiers as its primary participants. It was there that ceremonial poems were composed by laureates at court, liturgies were recited by priests of the Shinto sect, and more informal poems were composed by the lords and ladies of the great families. When officials of the government went to outposts as provincial governors, they took the new culture with them, provid-

ing a stimulus toward cultural synthesis equal to the impetus toward political unity that their offices had as their chief goal.

As noted in the Introduction, our primary record for this activity is Man'yōshū (A Collection of Ten Thousand Leaves), an immense work of over four thousand poems compiled around 759, probably by Ōtomo no Yakamochi. Organized in some sections by author and in others by topic, Man'yōshū presents poems in three main categories— Love, Elegies, and Miscellaneous themes, particularly poems of cele- bration. In this respect, it is a mirror of its age, which other records show to be dominated by just such concerns. But in its pages we have a record of earlier ages, too, and of folk culture as well as the highbrow culture of the court. Yet even the poems of frontier guards collected by Yakamochi have clearly been reworked to fit the conventions of a later time. In this sense, Man'yōshū is a book that shows the first flowering of a poetry whose sophistication, highly refined rhetorical techniques, and even imagery were largely Chinese-inspired. The chōka and the uta were the genres of the day, with the latter clearly dominant by the time of Yakamochi himself, whose audience was a court influenced in its tastes as much by the example of the Chinese bellestristic tradition and the world-denying doctrines of Buddhism as by primitive song and the pantheistic and life-affirming sentiments of the native Way of the Gods. The combination of these forces made for some of the grandest poetry the tradition would ever produce.

Poets of the Early Courts

The first Japanese poets we know anything about are the royal figures of Yamato culture in the earliest eras of recorded history, whose work—edited by later hands—is to be found in *Kojiki* (A Record of Ancient Matters; 712) and *Man'yōshū* (A Collection of Ten Thousand Leaves; ca. 759).[1] These early poems, from a warrior's paean on the majesty of the Yamato plain (poem 1) to the more sophisticated declarations of high men and ladies of the imperial clan, provide only a hint of the nature and variety of song in those ancient times. But the glimpse they do show is of a society in which the composition of poetry played a conspicuous public role on state occasions and in religious rites, while also serving as a means of the personal expression of the joys of love and the sorrows of rejection, parting, and death. Later generations have appreciated the poems of this time for their simplicity of expression and sincerity, particularly so in the case of their evocations of erotic love and lyric descriptions of the beauty of the Japanese landscape.

Of the eight poets presented here, the first two, the land-subduer Yamato Takeru and Prince Kinashikaru, are figures more of legend than of history. The third, Emperor Yūryaku, is depicted in the chronicles as a man of fierce disposition that belies the gentle words of the poem attributed to him. The rest all come from the seventh century, when the native tradition reached its first flowering at the Japanese court.

1. Yamato is the early name for the site of the first courts on the plain surrounding what would later be the capital at Nara (modern Nara Prefecture). The term was later used to refer to Japan as a whole, as in "the poetry of Yamato."

1. Attributed to Yamato Takeru. [Written after his return from a successful campaign against the barbarians of the East Country]

> Great Yamato, of all lands most supreme!
> Enclosed by ranks of verdant banks

on surrounding hills,
Great Yamato—unmatched for beauty!

yamato wa kuni no mahoroba / tatanazuku aokaki /
yamagomoreru / yamato shi uruwashi

2–3. Attributed to Prince Kinashikaru. [Both writ-
ten when he had been captured after revolting
against those who had denied him the throne be-
cause of an illicit romance with his sister, the
Maiden of Karu]

[2]   O heaven-soaring Maiden of Karu:
        if I weep aloud,
        people will know our secret—
        so like the doves
            of Hasa Mountain,
        I will weep, but weep quietly.

amadamu karu no otome / ita nakaba / hito shirinu beshi /
hasa no yama no / hato no / shitanaki ni naku

[3]   The heaven-coursing birds are couriers:
        each time you hear
            the call of a passing crane,
        ask what has become of me.

ama tobu tori mo tsukai so / tazu ga ne no / kikoemu toki
wa / wa ga na towasanu

*4. Attributed to Emperor Yūryaku [5th century]

        O maiden
            with a basket,
        a pretty basket,
        with a scoop,
        a pretty scoop,
        maiden picking greens
            on this hillside:
        I want to ask about your house;

I want to be told your name.
In the sky-filling land of Yamato,
it is I
    who rule everyone,
it is I
    who rule everywhere,
and so I think you will tell me
    where you live,
what you are called.[1]

1. For the romanized text, see s.n. 1.

*5. Emperor Jomei [593–641; r. 629–41]. A poem written by the Emperor when he climbed Kaguyama to survey the land[2]

Many are the hills,
the mountains of Yamato,
yet when I ascend
    heavenly Kaguyama,
the peerless mountain,
when I look down on the land:
where the land stretches,
hearth smoke rises everywhere;
where the water stretches,
water birds fly everywhere.
Ah, a splendid country,
this land Yamato
    of bounteous harvests!

2. This poem, along with Yamato Takeru's (poem 1), represents an ancient rite called *kunimi*—"surveying the land" from a high peak to praise the richness of the ruler's domain and the prosperity of his subjects. For the romanized text, see s.n. 2.

6. Emperor Tenji [626–71; r. 668–71]

At the broad sea's edge
    the setting sun casts its gleam
        on banners of cloud:
this night, the moon of this night—
so clearly may its rays too shine!

watatsumi no / toyohatakumo ni / irihi sashi / koyoi no
tsukuyo / sayakekari koso

3. For a later ver-
sion of this poem, see
poem 415.

7. Emperor Tenji[3]

> In autumn paddies
>   I make myself a makeshift hut—
> for a short stay:
> and how cold are my sleeves,
> burdened so with beads of dew!

akita karu / kariho o tsukuri / waga oreba / koromode
samuku / tsuyu zo okinikeru

*8. Princess Nukada [7th century]

> When springtime arrives,
> breaking free of winter's bonds,
> birds that had been still
>   come singing their melodies;
> flowers that had not bloomed
>   burst out into blossom;
> yet the hills are too lush:
> we cannot enter and pick;
> the growth is too dense:
> we cannot pick and behold.
> When we gaze upon
>   foliage in autumn hills,
> we can pick the leaves,
> red and yellow, to admire.
> As for the green ones—
> lamenting, we let them stay.
> Green leaves must be regretted,
> but I choose the autumn hills![4]

4. For the romanized
text, see s.n. 3.

9. A poem written by Princess Nukada when she
was longing for Emperor Tenji

> Waiting for you,
> I languish, full of longing—
> and then the blinds
>   of my house flutter slightly,
> blown by the autumn wind.

kimi matsu to / a ga koi oreba / wa ga yado no / sudare
ugokashi / aki no kaze fuku

10. Princess Kagami [7th century]. [A response to
poem 9]

> If even the wind . . .
> I think, in envy of you.
> If even the wind
>> would answer my vain waiting—
> of what could I complain?

kaze o dani / kouru wa tomoshi / kaze o dani / komu to
shi mataba / nani ka nagekamu

*11. Emperor Temmu [d. 686; r. 673–86]

> At Mimiga peak
>> soaring in fair Yoshino,
> unending, they say,
> is the falling of the snow,
> unceasing, they say,
> is the falling of the rain.
> Even unending
>> as the falling of that snow,
> even unceasing
>> as the falling of that rain,
> my thoughts continued
>> as I followed every turn
>>> on that path through the mountains.[5]

5. For the romanized
text, see s.n. 4.

Kakinomoto no Hitomaro (fl. ca. 680-700)

Early records indicate that Hitomaro, the first major figure in the Japanese poetic tradition, may have been born into a family of ceremonial reciters whose vocation was to present to the court important stories passed down in oral form from ancient times. Beyond that we know only that he served during the reigns of three sovereigns as an official of some sort, and that he also spent time in government service in several places away from the capital, including Iwami (modern Shimane Prefecture), a lonely province on the rugged shores of the Japan Sea, where the headnote to one poem (29) says he died. His reputation is based solely on his poetry.

In some ways, Hitomaro stands at the beginning of a long tradition of courtly poets, who would look to him as mentor for the next millennium and more. For one thing, he spoke to and for a court audience, who shared with him a common vocabulary, customs, and basic world view. Several of his most famous poems were in fact composed on formal occasions in which he acted as laureate—such as those lamenting the death of a princess (23–25) and celebrating a new palace in Yoshino (15–18). Furthermore, his sense of the ephemerality of human existence and of the loneliness of the individual in the forward march of time argues that he was much affected by the continental thought that was transporting his land from an era of myth to an era of history.

Yet in other respects Hitomaro stands at the end of an older era: first, because he nearly always speaks, as would a reciter, in a public voice that was seldom heard again in later court history; and second, because he is, despite his excellence in the shorter tanka form, one of the last and certainly the best master of the chōka, or "long poem," which fact may in itself be one of the reasons for his success as a "public" poet. A true expert in this demanding genre, he brought to perfection all of its rhetorical resources: a parallelism that often excels the more obvious use of that device by Chinese poets writing in shorter verse forms; well-conceived and evocative pillow-words, many of which he himself seems to have created; and intricate patterns of imagery that give his poems a symphonic scope. (See 20–22, in which the images move from sea, to land, to sky, with the last two reprised in the envoys via the image of the scattering autumn leaves; and 26–28, in which the movement is from large to small, abstract to concrete—the gods, nature, men in their boat, one man in endless slumber on the rocky beach.) And yet, whether in his grand public declarations or his more personal statements, he reveals an awareness of the sadness of the human situation with an ironic touch that is as gentle as it is unmistakable. It is this humanity that is his most important asset as a poet, giving the expansive rhetorical structures of his ancient genre a power that still registers today.

*12–14. On passing the ruined capital at Ōmi[1]   1. See s.n. 5.

[12]   Ever since the day
     of the august Emperor[2]
who made his abode
     at Kashihara where rises
holy Mount Unebi,
every sovereign born to us
     had exercised sway
       over all beneath the skies,
each one in his turn,
from the land of Yamato.
But for a reason
     beyond our understanding,
there was a ruler[3]
     who left the sky-filling land,
crossed the mountains
     of Nara where the earth is rich,
and exercised sway
     over all beneath the skies
       at Ōtsu Palace,
the place of rippling wavelets
     in Ōmi
       where the water breaks on rocks,
rural though it was,
and distant as the heavens.
But though we are told
     here rose the palace compound
       where dwelt the sovereign,
the godlike Emperor,

2. Emperor Jimmu, legendary founder of the Yamato clan, whose traditional dates are 660 B.C.–585 B.C.

3. Emperor Tenji; see s.n. 5.

and though people say
    here soared the mighty halls,
now haze veils the sky
    above luxuriant growths
        of springtime grasses,
and the spring sun shines weak
    on the site where stood
        the great stone-built palace—
the place I sorrow to see.[4]

4. For the romanized
text, see s.n. 6.

Envoys

[13]   It remains unchanged—
Cape Karasaki in Shiga
    of rippling wavelets—
but it will await in vain
    the courtiers in their boats.

sasanami no / shiga no karasaki / sakiku aredo / ōmiya-
hito no / fune machikanetsu

[14]   They lie quietly,
the shore waters at Shiga
    of rippling wavelets:
but will they ever meet again
    those whom they knew in the past?

sasanami no / shiga no ōwada / yodomu to mo / mukashi
no hito ni / mata mo awame ya mo

5. The precise date
of this excursion is
unknown.

6. Yoshino was of
special significance
to the Empress as the
place where the then-
consort of the future
Emperor Temmu had
stayed in seclusion just
prior to the Jinshin
Disturbance.

*15–16. Composed when the Sovereign journeyed
to the Yoshino Palace[5]

[15]   Many are the lands
    in the realm under heaven
        where our Empress reigns,
where holds sway our great Sovereign
    who governs in peace;
yet her august heart inclines
    toward Yoshino,[6]

holding it to be a place
   where the mountain stream
      courses into pure clear pools;
and there in the fields
   where flowers fall at Akizu,
she has erected
   firm pillars of a palace.
Thus the courtiers,
men of the stone-built palace,
align their vessels
   to cross the morning river,
and race their vessels
   to cross the evening river.
Though I gaze and gaze,
never shall I have enough:
palace eternal
   as the flow of the river,
palace soaring high
   as the towering mountains,
beside the seething cascade.[7]

7. For the romanized text, see s.n. 7.

Envoy

[16]   I shall come again
      to see it—come ceaselessly
   as grows velvet moss
      in the Yoshino River,
   of which my eyes never tire.

miredo akanu / yoshino no kawa no / tokoname no /
tayuru koto naku / mata kaerimimu

*17–18. Composed when the Sovereign journeyed
to the Yoshino Palace[8]

8. The precise date of this excursion is unknown.

[17]   Our great Sovereign
      who rules the nation in peace,
   a very goddess,
   thinking to act as a god,
   has built splendidly

                    a hall towering on high
                  by the seething pools
                    of the Yoshino River;
                  and when she climbs up
                    and standing surveys the land,[9]
                  the green-wall mountains
                    ranging in their serried ranks,
                  wishing to present
                  (tribute from the mountain gods,)
                  deck their heads with flowers
                    if the season be springtime,
                  and wear colored leaves
                    with the coming of autumn.
                  And eager to give
                    food for the august table,
                  the gods of the stream
                    flowing beside the mountains
                  send out cormorants
                    to fish the upper shallows,
                  send men with scoop nets
                    to fish the lower shallows.
                  Ah, this is the reign
                    of a god in whose service
                      mountains and rivers unite![10]

          Envoy

  [18]   A very goddess
            whom the mountains and rivers
              unite in serving,
          she is rowed forth in her boat,
          rowed forth to the seething pools.

        yama kawa mo / yorite tsukauru / kamu nagara / tagitsu
        kōchi ni / funade sesu ka mo

9. On "surveying the land," see the note to poem 5.

10. For the romanized text, see s.n. 8.

11. The future Emperor Mommu (683–707; r. 696–707).

19. A poem written by Kakinomoto no Hitomaro when Prince Karu[11] took lodging in the fields of Aki

Off to the eastward,
the first shimmer of daylight
     rises on the fields—
and when I turn round to see,
the moon is sinking away.

himugashi no / no ni wa kagiroi / tatsu miete / kaerimi
sureba / tsuki katabukinu

*20–22. Written on parting from his wife when
he went from Iwami Province to the capital

[20]   In Iwami Sea,
     minding of rock-creeping vines,
     at Kara, the cape
          of wave-chatter like Cathay speech,[12]
     upon rocky reefs
          grows the sea-pine of the deep,
     upon stony strands
          grows seaweed fair as gems.
     Deep as the sea-pine
          was my love for a dear girl,
     one who lay yielding
          as fair gemweed yields to waves,
     yet only a few
          were the nights of our sweet sleep,
     and then I set off;
     we parted like creeping vines.
     Pain ravaged the heart
          that sits within my breast,
     made me turn my head,
     look back in ceaseless yearning,
     yet only faintly
          could I see her waving sleeve,
     glimmering among
          falling leaves in autumn hues
               at Crossing Mountain,
     minding of journeying ships.
     It grieved me as when
          the moon hides herself from view

12. *Koto saeku kara,*
here referring to the
"foreign" dialects of
the provinces.

as she journeys on
    through cloud rifts at Yakami,
hill of cloistered wives.
As my love's sleeve disappeared,
the sky-coursing sun
    declined shining toward day's end,
and then I, the man
    who thought himself stouthearted,
wept into my sleeve—
robe-sleeve spread for sheet at night—
cried until the tears soaked through.[13]

13. For the romanized
text, see s.n. 9.

Envoys

[21] Too swift is the stride
        of the dapple-gray stallion.
    I have left behind
        as distant as the heavens
            the place where my love dwells.

aogoma ga / agaki o hayami / kumoi ni zo / imo ga atari
o / sugite kinikeru

[22] You colored leaves falling
        among autumn mountains:
    for just a moment
        stop scattering and let me see
            the place where my love dwells.

akiyama ni / otsuru momichiba / shimashiku wa / na
chirimagai so / imo ga atari mimu

14. A daughter of
Emperor Tenji who
died in 700. As was the
case with most royalty,
she was laid in a shrine
before final entomb-
ment. Her husband
was Prince Osakabe
(d. 705).

*23–25. Written at the time of the temporary en-
shrinement of Princess Asuka[14]

[23] At Asuka,
        the river of birds in flight,
    there are stepping stones
        crossing the upper reaches,

there is a wood bridge
  crossing the lower reaches.
The gemmed water weed
  growing tall, waving its fronds
    by the stepping stones,
grows again when it is cut;
the river weed too,
growing tall, putting forth shoots
  by the lower bridge,
sprouts again when it withers.
Why, then, should it be
  that you, O great Princess,
have quite forgotten
  the palace of the morning,
have quite forsaken
  the palace of the evening
    of your fair husband—
you who when you stood erect
  resembled gemweed,
you who when you lay with him
  bent your limbs to his,
as pliant as river weed?
Your meetings have ceased,
and there is an end to speech
  exchanged between you
now that you have determined
  to dwell forever
    at the Kinoe Palace—
you who while you lived
  in this transitory world,
plucked flowers in spring
  to decorate your tresses,
and when autumn came
  decked your head with colored leaves;
you who now and then
  came to take your pleasure there,
came in company—
walking sleeve beside sleeve
  spread for sheet at night—
with the husband you gazed on
  as on a mirror,

gazed and never had enough,
loved more ardently
   than men admire a full moon.
For my aching heart
   there is no hope of solace,
while I see the Prince
   who was wont to visit you
     like a morning bird,
the grieving widower,
like a tiger thrush,
sorrowing beyond measure
(and surely for this?)—
while I behold him drooping
   like summer grasses,
going yonder, coming here
   like the evening star,
unsteady as a great ship.
And since it is thus,
I cannot tell what to do.
Yet throughout all time,
through ages longer lasting
   than heaven and earth,
we will hold ever in mind
   the sound at least, the name:
for countless generations,
the River Asuka,
stream bearing your honored name,
will be a keepsake
   preserving the memory
     of our beloved Princess.[15]

15.   For the romanized
text, see s.n. 10.

Envoys

[24]   If we were to stop
   the flow of the Asuka
     by making a weir,
surely the coursing waters
   would stay quietly in place.

asukagawa / shigarami watashi / sekamaseba / nagaruru
mizu mo / nodo ni ka aramashi

[25]   Though there is no hope
            of seeing her tomorrow
        (*asu*, recalling Asuka's flow),
        I shall hold in memory
            the name of our great Princess.

asukagawa / asu dani mimu to / omoe ya mo / waga
ōkimi no / mina wasure senu

*26–28. On seeing a dead man among the rocks
at Samine Island in Sanuki

[26]   Land of Sanuki,
        rich in gemlike seaweed:
        is it the land's nature
            that attracts our tireless gaze?
        Is it the god's nature[16]
            that inspires us with such awe?
        This is the visage
            of a god who will flourish
        together with
            heaven and earth, sun and moon:
        thus we have been taught.
        Arrived at Naka harbor,
        we set out to sea,
        and as we rowed onward,
        a seasonal wind
            began to blow in the sky.
        In the offing,
        surging waves towered high;
        on the shoreline,
        white waves came thundering in.
        In dread of the sea,
        that awesome place where men hunt whales,
        we bent the oars
            on our journeying boat.
        There were many isles
            scattered in this place and that,
        but we made our shelter,
            our rude hut, by the rocky strand
            of Samine,

16.   According to
native beliefs, the
islands were created by
the gods Izanagi and
Izanami.

fair-named island of renown.
And there I saw you
    fallen face down on a rough bed,
with only the shore
    where the waves sound ceaselessly
to serve as pillow
    on which to rest your head.
If I knew your house,
I would go there with tidings;
if your wife but knew,
she would come to seek you out.
But not knowing
    even the way to follow,
she must be waiting
    with anxious, yearning heart—
she, your beloved wife.[17]

17. For the romanized
text, see s.n. 11.

Envoys

[27]   Had your wife been here,
    the two of you might have eaten
      starwort from the fields
    of Mount Sami—that starwort
      whose season is now past.[18]

18. Starwort, or
uhagi, a perennial
related to the aster,
produces edible shoots.

tsuma mo araba / tsumite tagemashi / sami no yama / no
no ue no uhagi / suginikerazu ya

[28]   Alas, poor man,
    that you have lain down to sleep,
    taking as pillow
      the rocky, wind-swept shore,
    battered by waves from the sea!

okitsunami / kiyoru ariso o / shikitae no / makura to
makite / naseru kimi ka mo

29. Written when he was about to die, in the province of Iwami

> On Kamo hill
>   I make ready for my sleep
>   on a slab of stone;
>   will my wife, unknowing,
>   be awaiting my return?

kamoyama no / iwane shi makeru / ware o ka mo / shira
ni to imo ga / machitsutsu aruramu

30. Written on the occasion of an imperial procession to Thunder Hill[19]

> Our Sovereign great,
>   a very god is she,
>   making her abode
>   among the clouds of heaven
>   on Thunder Hill!

ōkimi wa / kami ni shi maseba / amakumo no / ikazuchi
no ue ni / iora seru ka mo

19. The precise date of this procession is unknown, but it was probably made by Empress Jitō (645–702; r. 690–97).

31–32. [Two travel poems][20]

[31]   Down into the straits
>   of Akashi, land of torchlight,
>   the sun will soon sink:
>   and I—must I row away,
>   beyond sight of my home?

tomoshibi no / akashi ōto ni / iramu hi ya / kogiwaka-
renamu / ie no atari mizu

20. From a group of eight that take the Inland Sea between the main island, Kyūshū, and Shikoku as their setting.

[32]   The sea at Kehi
>   must be a good place to harvest:
>   for like reeds cut free
>   they float in confused array—
>   those boats of the fishermen.

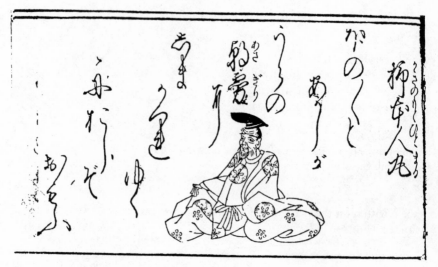

Kakinomoto no Hitomaro. Inscription: "In the dim, dim light / of the early morning mist / on Akashi Bay, / a boat fades behind the isles— / my heart following in its wake." (KKS 409)

kehi no umi no / niwa yoku arashi / karikomo no / midarete izumiyu / ama no tsuribune

33. A poem written by Kakinomoto no Hitomaro when he arrived at the Uji River on his way from Ōmi to the capital

21. *Mononofu no yaso uji.* Applied to the Uji River because of its many tributaries. A fishing weir (*shigarami*) was composed of wooden stakes placed in a river to catch fish on their way downstream.

Like waves that ripple
   around the stakes of weirs
set in Uji, river
   of the emperor's mighty men[21]—
so I wander on my way.

mononofu no / yaso ujikawa no / ajiroki ni / isayou nami no / yukue shirazu mo

34.

> You wave-plovers
>> of dusk on the Ōmi Sea[22]—
> each time you cry out
>> my heart withers within me,
> set on things of long ago.

ōmi no umi / yūnami chidori / na ga nakeba / kokoro mo
shino ni / inishie omôyu

22. *Yūnami chi-dori* (lit., "dusk-wave plovers") is a compound created by Hito-maro.

35. Travel. Topic unknown

> In the dim, dim light
>> of the early morning mist
>>> on Akashi Bay,
> a boat fades behind the isles—
> my heart following in its wake.[23]

honobono to / akashi no ura no / asagiri ni / shimaga-
kureyuku / fune o shi zo omou

23. Authorship un-certain, although tra-ditionally attributed to Hitomaro.

Yamabe no Akahito (early 8th century)

One indication of the gradual decline of the chōka after Hitomaro is the dominance of the shorter tanka form in the work of Yamabe no Akahito, the most outstanding poet of the early eighth century. Active in the court of Emperor Shōmu (701–56; r. 724–49), where he held some minor posi-tion, Akahito composed chōka memorializing official journeys and other occasions. However, his long poems are relatively brief affairs that lack Hitomaro's intricate designs and subtle but powerful statements of emotion—so much so that their finely crafted envoys often seem to overshadow them (poems 36–37, 39–40). His tanka too show an aloof sensibility, but make up for what they lack in sentiment with vivid natural descriptions that go far toward explaining his reputation among poets of later eras as the equal of Hitomaro.

36–37. Written upon seeing Mount Fuji

[36]   Since that ancient time
            when heaven and earth were sundered,
        like a god soaring
            in high-towering majesty
                over Suruga
        has stood Fuji's lofty peak.
        Turn your eyes upward
            to heaven's high plain and see
        how it hides from sight
            the sun in its constant course
        and obstructs our view
            of the moon in its shining,
        blocking even clouds
            from going on their way—
        and how always on its peak
            snow is falling, ever falling.
        We praise it now, and ever more—
        the lofty peak of Fuji![1]

1. For the romanized text, see s.n. 12.

Envoy

[37]   At Tago Bay
            I came out, and looked afar—
        to see the pure white
            of Mount Fuji's lofty peak,
        amidst a flurry of snow.

tago no ura yu / uchiidete mireba / mashiro ni zo / fuji no takane ni / yuki wa furikeru

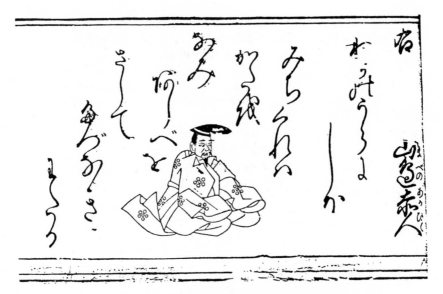

Yamabe no Akahito. Inscription: "At Waka Bay/ the beach is hidden now, / with the waters high: / heading off toward the reeds, / cranes go, crying out in flight." (MYS 924)

38.

> At Waka Bay
>   the beach is hidden now,
> with the waters high:
> heading off toward the reeds,
> cranes go, crying out in flight.[2]

waka no ura ni / shio michikureba / kata o nami / ashihe o sashite / tazu nakiwataru

2. An envoy to MYS 917, although often quoted independently.

39–40. [Written when the Sovereign visited Yoshino][3]

[39]   Our great Sovereign
>   who rules the nation in peace
>   comes to fair Yoshino,
>   to the meadows of Akizu,

3. The precise date of this excursion is unknown. For the romanized text, see s.n. 13.

and there in the fields
    puts trackers to their task,
there on the hillsides
    builds game-blinds all around;
on the morning hunt
    they start deer and boar for chase,
on the evening hunt
    they start fowl into flight—
lined up on horseback,
men set out on the noble hunt
    in the thick growth of spring fields.

Envoy

[40]   When in the meadows
        and the foot-wearying hills
    the noble huntsmen
        hold arrows at the ready—
    ah, what a clamorous sight!

ashihiki no / yama ni mo no ni mo / mikarihito / satsuya
tabasami / sawakite ari miyu

41.

4. *Masurao*, "men of brawn," a general term for the men of the imperial court.

The emperor's men [4]
    embark on a noble hunt;
ladies of the court
    trail their red skirts as they go—
walking down a clean ocean strand.

masurao wa / mikari ni tatashi / otomera wa / akamo
susobiku / kiyoki hamabi o

42.

Into the spring fields
    I came, intending only
        to pick violets.

But so appealing were the fields
    that I stayed to spend the night.

haru no no ni / sumire tsumi ni to / koshi ware zo / no o
natsukashimi / hitoyo nenikeru

43.

    When morning came
        I had planned to pick spring greens
    out in these fields
        where yesterday, and now today,
    the snow just keeps on falling.

asu yori wa / haruna tsumamu to / shimeshi no ni / kinō
mo kyō mo / yuki wa furitsutsu

Ōtomo no Tabito (665-731)

Though never of the greatest political significance, the name Ōtomo was
prominent in the world of poetry throughout the first century of the court
tradition, beginning with Ōtomo no Tabito, whose son would go on to
compile *Man'yōshū*. Modern literary historians have stressed Tabito's im-
portance as the primary figure of one of the court tradition's first great
salons of uta poets, which he led for a brief time while serving as governor-
general of Kyūshū at Dazaifu early in the eighth century. Yet he was equally
well known in his own time as a poet in Chinese, and even in his Japa-
nese poems, he owes much to the continent, as is evident in his poems on
drinking and plum blossoms, both perennial topics in China.

44. [Written when he was serving at Dazaifu]

> The full bloom of youth—
> might it still come back to me?
> Or must I suppose
> that I will never again see
> the capital at Nara?

waga sakari / mata ochime ya mo / hotohoto ni / nara no
miyako o / mizu ka narinamu

45–47. [Three poems in praise of *sake*]

[45]   Instead of fretting
> over things that can't be changed,
> how much better
> to swallow down a full cup
> of cloudy *sake*!

shirushi naki / mono o omowazu wa / hitosuki no /
nigoreru sake o / nomu beku arurashi

[46]   What an ugly bunch—
> those who in pretended wisdom
> will not drink *sake*.
> The closer you look at them,
> the more they look like monkeys!

ana miniku / saka shira o su to / sake nomanu / hito o
yoku miba / saru ni ka mo nimu

[47]   If in this world
> I can only enjoy myself,
> then in the next world
> let me be a bug or a bird[1]—
> it will not matter to me!

1. A reference to the
Buddhist doctrine of
the transmigration of
souls, or reincarnation.

kono yo ni shi / tanoshiku araba / komu yo ni wa / mushi
ni tori ni mo / ware wa narinamu

48. Written in the Twelfth Month of the second
year of the Tempyō era [730], just before he left
Dazaifu to return to the capital

> That juniper tree
>> my woman saw long ago
> at Tomo Bay
>> stands here still, ever green—
> though the one who saw it is gone.[2]

wagimoko ga / mishi tomo no ura no / muronoki wa /
tokoyo ni aredo / mishi hito zo naki

2. The *muronoki*,
modern Japanese *nezu*,
is a needle juniper.

49. Written at a banquet held at his house on the
thirteenth day of the second year of the Tempyō
era [730]

> Out in my garden
>> plum blossoms are scattering.
> Or might it be snow
>> floating down from the sky—
> those distant heavens?

waga sono ni / ume no hana chiru / hisakata no / ama yori
yuki no / nagarekuru ka mo

"elegant
confusion":
from Chinese verse

Yamanoue no Okura (660?-733?)

One of the most distinguished members of Ōtomo no Tabito's Kyūshū salon was a scholar named Yamanoue no Okura. Some scholars contend that he was born on the continent to a scholarly father who emigrated to Japan and eventually became physician to several Japanese emperors. Whatever the case, Okura was raised in Japan, although with a Chinese-style education in the classics and, of course, in poetry. After serving in various scholarly capacities at court, he was appointed governor of the province of Chikuzen (the western half of modern Fukuoka Prefecture) in northern Kyūshū. There he became part of Tabito's group. His poems, though written in Japanese, show a didacticism and knowledge of Buddhist thought that bespeak their creator's thorough schooling in Chinese letters.

*50–51. A lament on the evanescence of life

[50]   What we must accept
            as we journey through the world
        is that time will pass
            like the waters of a stream;
        in countless numbers,
        in relentless succession,
        it will besiege us
            with assaults we must endure.
        They could not detain
            the period of their bloom,
        when, as maidens will,
        they who were then maidens
            encircled their wrists
                with gemmed bracelets from Cathay,
        and took their pleasure
            frolicking hand in hand

with their youthful friends.
So the months and years went by,
and when did it fall—
that sprinkling of wintry frost
  on glistening hair
    as black as leopard flower seeds?
And whence did they come—
those wrinkles that settled in,
marring the smoothness
  of blushing pink faces?
Was it forever,
the kind of life those others led—
those stalwart men,
who, as fine young men will do,
girded at their waists
  sharp swords, keen-bladed weapons,
took up hunting bows,
clasped them tight in their clenched fists,
placed on red horses
  saddles fashioned of striped hemp,
climbed onto their steeds,
and rode gaily here and there?
They were not many,
those nights when the fine young men
  pushed open the doors,
the plank doors of the chamber
  where the maidens slept,
groped their way close to their loves,
and slept with their arms
  intertwined with gemlike arms.
Yet already now
  those who were maidens and youths
    must use walking sticks,
and when they walk over there,
others avoid them,
and when they walk over here,
others show distaste.
Such is life, it seems, for the old.
Precious though life is,
it is beyond our power
  to stay the passing of time.[1]

1. For the romanized text, see s.n. 14.

Envoy

[51]   Would that I might stand
              a rock through eternity,
         unchanged forever—
         but life does not allow us
              to halt the passing of time.

tokiwa nasu / kaku shi mo ga mo to / omoedomo / yo no
koto nareba / todomikanetsu mo

*52–53. Dialogue between Poverty and Destitu-
tion

feature of
Chinese verse

[52]   [Poor Man]

         On nights when rain falls
              mingling with the blowing wind,
         on nights when snow falls
              mingling with the pouring rain,
         I have no choice
              but to endure the cold.
         I eat lumpy salt,
         keep nibbling away at it,
         drink *sake* dregs,
         keep sipping away at them,
         keep clearing my throat,
         snuffle the snot in my nose,
         keep running my hand
              over my skimpy beard,
         boast to myself,
         "Where is there to be found
              a better man?"
         But I'm cold all the same.
         I pull over me
              my bedding of coarse hemp,
         pile on as clothing
              layers of sleeveless cloth coats—
         every one I own—
         and still the night is bitter.
         The mother and father
              of someone whose lot

is worse than my own
    must be starving and freezing;
his wife and children
    must cry in weak voices.
At times like this,
how is it that you manage
    to keep going at all?

[Destitute Man]

Heaven and earth
    are said to be far-ranging,
yet they have become
    too narrow to fit me in.
The sun and the moon
    are said to be radiant,
yet they do not deign
    to cast their light upon me.
Is it like this
    for everyone, or just for me?
Although by good luck
    I have been born a human[2]
and though I till fields
    like any other human,
upon my shoulder
    I wear nothing but rags—
a sleeveless jacket
    not even stuffed with cotton,
hanging in tatters
    like strands of deep-pine seaweed.
Inside my crooked hut,
my hut with its leaning walls,
I lie on bare ground
    spread with a little loose straw.
My father and mother
    are beside my pillow,
my wife and children
    are at the foot of my bed;
all sit around me
    complaining and groaning;
at the cooking-place
    nothing sends up any steam;

2. According to Buddhist doctrine, one had to pass through the human stage to attain enlightenment and be released from the chain of rebirth.

in the rice steamer
   a spider has spun its web.
We have forgotten
   how rice is supposed to be cooked.
And as we wail there,
voices thin as tiger thrushes,
to make matters worse
(cutting, as the saying goes,
the end of something
   that is already too short),
the village headman
   seeks me out, holding his whip,
comes with his summons
   right up to my sleeping-place.
Must it be like this,
so utterly without hope—
a man's journey through the world?[3]

3. For the romanized
text, see s.n. 15.

Envoy

[53]   Though we think of life
      as a vale of misery,
   a bitter trial,
      it is not as if we were birds
         who can simply fly away.

yo no naka o / ushi to yasashi to / omoedomo / tobitachi-
kanetsu / tori ni shi araneba

*54–56. Longing for his son Furuhi

[54]   What value to me
      the seven kinds of treasures[4]
         by which others set store—
the precious things coveted
      by the run of men?
My son Furuhi,
the child fair as a white pearl,
born of the union
      between his mother and me,

4. The seven treasures
referred to in Buddhist
texts—gold, silver,
pearls, etc.

used to play with us
   when the morning star announced
      the dawn of each new day—
to stay close to the bedside
   where our sheets were spread,
to frolic with us
   standing and sitting.
And when evening
   came with the evening star,
he used to take us
   by the hand and say to us,
"Let's go to bed now,"
and then, in his pretty way,
"Father and Mother,
don't go where I can't see you.
I want to sleep
   right here in the middle."
And we thought, trusting
   as people trust a great ship,
"May the time come soon
   when he becomes an adult;
for good or for ill,
may we behold him a man."
But then suddenly
   a mighty storm wind blew up,
caught us from the side,
overwhelmed us with its blast.
Helpless, distraught,
not knowing what to do,
I tucked back my sleeves
   with paper-mulberry cords,
I took in my hand
   a clear, spotless mirror.[5]
With upturned face,
I beseeched the gods of the sky;
forehead to the ground,
I implored the gods of the earth.
"Whether he be cured
   or whether he die—
that is for the gods to say."
But though I begged them

5. Exactly what is indicated here is not clear, but mirrors—representing the light of the Sun Goddess Amaterasu, the founder of the Japanese nation—were used in many primitive Shinto rituals.

in frantic supplication,
there resulted
    not the briefest improvement.
His body wasted,
changing little by little;
he uttered no more
    the words he had spoken
        with each new morning;
and his life came to its end.
I reeled in agony,
stamped my feet, screamed aloud,
cast myself down,
looked up to heaven, beat my breast.
I have lost my son,
the child I loved so dearly.
Is this what life is about?[6]

6. For the romanized
text, see s.n. 16.

Envoys

[55]   He is still so young
            that he won't know the way to go.
        I will give you something—
        only carry him on your back,
        messenger from the netherworld![7]

7. A messenger was
believed to guide souls
on their way in the
next world.

wakakereba / michiyuki shiraji / mai wa semu / shita e no
tsukai / oite tōrase

[56]   Making offerings,
        I utter this petition:
        tempt him not afield,
        but lead him straight ahead—
        show him the way to heaven.

fuseokite / are wa koinomu / asamukazu / tada ni iyukite /
amaji shirashime

Other Poets of the Ancient Age

Although they do not enjoy the same reputation today as Hitomaro or Akahito, there were many other poets of the same age whose contribution to *Man'yōshū* and all it represented was considerable. Some, such as Sami Mansei (poem 57) are known for only a few poems; others, especially Kasa no Kanamura (63–64), rival their more famous contemporaries in the number of their poems included in the anthology.

Other than what headnotes to poems tell us, we have only a few facts about these poets, all of whom seem to have been active during the period of the late 600's to the early 700's. Sami Mansei was the priestly name of Kasa no Ason Maro, who, while on assignment to a temple in northern Kyūshū, was a member of Ōtomo no Tabito's Kyūshū salon; Takechi no Kurohito is an obscure figure who is now known as one of the tradition's first travel poets; Takahashi no Mushimaro and Kasa no Kanamura were minor court officials whose careers may have overlapped; and Lady Ōtomo of Sakanoue was the younger sister of Ōtomo no Tabito.

57. Sami Mansei [early 8th century]

> Our life in this world—
> to what shall I compare it?
> It is like a boat
>   rowing out at break of day,
> leaving not a trace behind.

yo no naka o / nani ni tatoemu / asabiraki / kogiinishi
fune no / ato naki ga goto

58. Takechi no Kurohito [early 8th century]

Toward Sakurada
    cranes go, crying out in flight.
At Ayuchi Strand
    the tide must have gone out—
cranes go, crying out in flight.

sakurada e / tazu nakiwataru / ayuchigata / shio hinikera-
shi / tazu nakiwataru

59. Kurohito

Where will I go now
    to find a place for lodging—
as day is ending
    on the fields of Katsuno
    in Takashima?

izuku ni ka / waga yadori semu / takashima no / katsuno
no hara ni / kono hi kurenaba

60. Kurohito

If only sooner
    I had come here to see them:
now the leaves are gone
    from the groves of zelkova
    at Taka, in Yamashiro.

haya kite mo / mitemashi mono o / yamashiro no / taka
no tsukimura / chirinikeru ka mo

61–62. Takahashi no Mushimaro [fl. 730–35].
Written when all the men of the court were de-
parting for Naniwa, in spring, during the Third
Month[1]

1. Probably writ-
ten when his patron
Fujiwara no Umakai
(d. 737) visited Naniwa
in the spring of 732.
For the romanized text,
see s.n. 17.

[61]   At Mount Tatsuta
            where white clouds ever trail,

above the cascade
   on the Peak of Ogura,
the cherry blossoms
   are blooming everywhere;
but so high is the peak,
so unending the winds,
and so constant
   the falling of the spring rain,
that the upper branches
   are already bare.
You blossoms clinging
   to the lower branches—
wait awhile, please,
before scattering away;
at least until
   our lords return from travel,
from nights spent on grass pillows.

Envoy (in reply)

[62] Our journey will end
      before seven days have passed.
    Tatsuta Goddess,[2]
    do not allow the blossoms
      to scatter on the wind.

2. Tatsuta-hiko, worshipped at Tatsuta Shrine in Yamato.

waga yuki wa / nanuka wa sugiji / tatsuta hiko / yume
kono hana o / kaze ni na chirashi

63–64. Kasa no Kanamura [early 8th century].
Written in autumn, the Ninth Month of the fifth
year of the Jingi era [728]

[63] To be born a man
      is a thing hard to obtain,[3]
    but by good fortune
      I received this body of mine—
    living or dying,
    I had always told myself,
    only for you.

3. A condition for attaining enlightenment and release from the cycle of rebirth.

But now it has happened:
since even you
    are a man of this transient world,
you must be obedient
    to our great Sovereign's command
and go to govern
    a land remote as the sky—
like a morning bird
    flying off in the morning,
with your flock of birds
    gathered to go with you,
while I stay behind.
Please do think of the one
    you will not see so long a time!⁴

4. For the romanized
text, see s.n. 18.

Envoy

[64]   On the day you cross
            over the snowy mountains
                on the Koshi Road,
        remember me, won't you—
        the one who stayed behind?

mikoshiji no / yuki furu yama o / koemu hi wa / tomareru
ware o / kakete shinohase

65. Lady Ōtomo of Sakanoue [early 8th century].
[Sent in response to poems from Fujiwara Umakai]

        You say, "I will come"—
        but then often you don't come.
        If you say you won't,
            why should I wait for you to come—
        when you said you wouldn't come?

komu to iu mo / konu toki aru o / koji to iu o / komu to
wa mataji / koji to iu mono o

66. Lady Ōtomo. A poem on the moon

> Black as leopard-flower seeds
>   is the night-mist spreading round;
> and through it all
>   the moonlight comes shining down—
> a moving sight to look upon!

nubatama no / yogiri no tachite / ooshiku / tereru tsukuyo
no / mireba kanashisa

67. Lady Ōtomo

> Let's set plum blossoms
>   afloat in our *sake* cups.
> And who will care
>   if they must scatter in the end,
> after our drinking is done?

sakazuki ni / ume no hana ukabe / omoudochi / nomite
no nochi wa / chirinu to mo yoshi

Anonymous Poems from 'Man'yōshū'

One indication of the importance of poetry in the general society of the Ancient Age is that over half of the poems of *Man'yōshū* are anonymous. To be sure, even these poems were mostly written—or in some cases, re-written from folk materials—by people of relatively high social status. Yet the diversity of topics, themes, and imagery in these poems still shows a breadth of participation in literary culture that would be lacking in the more strictly court poetry of the next half millennium.

Internal evidence reveals that most of these anonymous poems were composed in the second half of the seventh century or the first half of the eighth. Some of them are recorded in groups by theme or origin, as in the case of the famous pseudo-primitive *azuma uta,* or "East Country Songs" (poems 78–81), and *sekimori no uta,* or "Songs by Frontier Guards" (82–83). Most are simply poems of disparate subject matter and derivation that were lumped together for convenience by the compilers, who in the process no doubt drew on sources—folk or otherwise—now lost to us. As one would expect, the finest of them are in the short tanka form that had become the dominant genre by that time. And many of them employ such techniques as the *jo,* or metaphorical preface (79–81), that mark them as at least partly a product of a courtly sensibility.

68. Lamenting Prince Kashiwade

> That the world of men
>   is a place of constant change—
> that's what it must mean:
> the way the radiant moon
>   first waxes and then wanes.

yo no naka wa / munashiki mono ni / aramu to zo / kono teru tsuki wa / michikake shikeru

69.

> The day is breaking,
> a night-crow seems to cry—
> while in the treetops
>   at the top of this mountain
>   everything is quiet still.

akatoki to / yogarasu nakedo / kono oka no / konure no ue wa / imada shizukeshi

70.

>   Whose is that woman—
>   the one trailing her red skirts
>   as she walks away
>   along the bay at ebb tide
>   on Kuroushi strand?

kuroushigata / shiohi no ura o / kurenai no / tamamo
susobiki / yuku wa ta ga tsuma

71.

>   It was all for you—
>   for you that I drenched the skirts
>   of my long robes,
>   picking bulbs near hill paddies
>   in water from melted snow.

kimi ga tame / yamada no sawa ni / egu tsumu to / yukige
no mizu ni / mo no suso nurenu

72.

>   The men of the court—
>   of the stone-built palace—
>   must have lots of time:
>   to gather together so,
>   plum garlands in their caps.

momoshiki no / ōmiyabito wa / itoma are ya / ume o
kazashite / koko ni tsudoeru

73.

>   Winter passes by
>   and then spring comes around,
>   and thus time goes on,
>   always beginning anew—
>   while men alone keep growing old.

fuyu sugite / haru shi kitareba / toshitsuki wa / arata nare-
domo / hito wa furiyuku

74.

> In everything
>   it's new things that are the best,
> except for in men:
> only men just get better
>   after they've grown old.

mono mina wa / atarashiki yoshi / tadashiku mo / hito wa
furinishi / yoshikaru beshi

75.

> That autumn wind
>   swaying leaves on kuzu vines—
> each time it blows by,
> blossoms from bush-clover
>   scatter over Ada Moor.

makuzuhara / nabiku akikaze / fuku goto ni / ada no ōno
no / hagi no hana chiru

76.

> Like Naniwa folk
>   sooty from the smoke of reeds
>   burned in the hearth—
> that's that woman of mine!
> But still she catches my eye.

naniwahito / ashihi taku ya no / sushite aredo / ono ga
tsuma koso / tsune mezurashi

77.

> More peace would I have
>   if I could die and be gone;

for as it is now
    I can't tell dawn from dusk—
so pained am I by love.

nakanaka ni / shinaba yasukemu / izuru hi no / iru waki-
shiranu / ware shi kurushi mo

78–81. Poems from the East Country

[78]   If I go off now
        to the haze covered slopes
            of Mount Fuji,
how will she know where to look—
my wife, when she longs for me?

kasumi iru / fuji no yamabi ni / waga kinaba / izuchi
mukite ka / imo ga nagekamu

[79]   Like the whitecaps
        rising always in the sea
            off the Izu shore,
let's go on loving like this,
tossing, turning recklessly!

izu no umi ni / tatsu shiranami / aritsutsu mo / tsuginamu
mono o / midareshimeme ya

[80]   On Musashi Moor
        the grasses bend where they will—
this way or that way:
but in every little thing
    I have yielded to you.

musashino no / kusa wa moromuki / ka mo kaku mo /
kimi ga ma ni ma ni / a wa yorinishi o

[81]   Though at Jewel Point
        your boat out in the offing
may face winds so strong

that they break your mooring ropes—
don't break off writing to me.

sakitama no / tsu ni oru fune no / kaze o itami / tsuna wa
tayu to mo / koto na tae so ne

82–83. Poems by frontier guards

[82]   That dawn when I left
            to serve as a frontier guard,
        going out my gate
            she would not let go my hand—
        and how she wept, that wife of mine!

sakimori ni / tachishi asake no / kanatode ni / tabanare
oshimi / nakishi kora wa mo

[83]   When in the reed leaves
            the evening mist is spreading
                and the drakes call out—
        in the cold of those evenings
            I will be yearning for you.

ashi no ha ni / yūgiri tachite / kamo ga ne no / samuki
yūhe shi / na o ba shinowamu

Lady Kasa (mid-8th century)

Though her name has led some to conclude that she might be a daughter of
Kasa no Kanamura, nothing certain is known about Kasa no Iratsume—
Lady Kasa—except that she was one of Ōtomo no Yakamochi's lovers
(see next section). All of her twenty-eight poems, including those pre-
sented here, are addressed to Yakamochi. Their wit and intensity were an
inspiration to later poets, particularly those who sought to emulate her
"passionate" style.

84.

> Faintly I saw you—
> a man spied for an instant
>   as through morning mist.
> And yet I fear I may die,
> so clear is the love I feel.

asagiri no / ōni aimishi / hito yue ni / inochi shinu beki /
koiwataru ka mo

85.

> In a dream I saw you
>   girding to your manly form
>   a great long-sword.
> What might such a thing portend—
> if not that I must meet you?

tsurugitachi / mi ni torisou to / ime ni mitsu / nani no
sagaso mo / kimi ni awamu tame

86.

> The bell is tolling,
>   telling all the time has come
>   to go off to bed.
>   But, yearning for you so,
>   how could I hope to sleep?

minahito no / neyo to no kane wa / utsu naredo / kimi o
shi omoeba / ine katenu ka mo

87.

> To love someone
>   who won't love you in return—
>   that's like kowtowing
>   at a great Buddhist temple
>   from back behind the fence.

aiomowanu / hito o omou wa / ōtera no / kaki no shirie
ni / nukazuku gotoshi

Ōtomo no Yakamochi (718?-785)

Exactly when *Man'yōshū* was compiled we do not know. But the last poem
in the work is a banquet verse dated 759, written by Ōtomo no Yakamo-
chi, whom most scholars believe to be the collection's chief compiler. This
conclusion is supported by the fact that its last four books are a poetic
memoir of that same man.

Ōtomo no Yakamochi

The son of Ōtomo no Tabito, Yakamochi spent his youth surrounded by the poets of his father's salon and his own extended family, both in Dazaifu and in the capital. He began composing poems, mostly of courting, while still a youth. It was while he was away from the capital as governor of the remote province of Etchū (modern Toyama Prefecture), however, that he came into his own artistically. There, gathering around him others with literary interests, he found escape from the loneliness of his outpost in poetry, producing much of his finest work in both the chōka and the tanka form.

Yakamochi ended his six-year assignment in Etchū in 751 (see poems 101–2) and returned to Nara, where he continued to be active as a poet. For a time he was at the center of court culture, but political intrigues worked against him, and in 758 he was demoted and sent to Inaba (modern Tottori Prefecture). Even though he was able to return to the capital and resume his official career about a decade later, this blow left a permanent scar—on his poetry if not in other ways. He left no poetic record whatsoever of his last twenty-seven years.

Yakamochi would be an important figure in poetic history if for no other reason than that *Man'yōshū* contains over 450 of his poems, by far the most of any poet. But his reputation rests on more than numbers, for it is with his work that the tradition takes a definite turn toward the reflective and wistful tones that would characterize it for the rest of the classical era. Some of his poems adopt a public stance (as in 92, on the death of Prince Asaka) or employ lofty diction (105); and he makes good use of rhetorical devices of the earlier tradition, such as the preface (92) and the pillow-word. But, in all, the grand vistas of Hitomaro and Akahito are lacking in his work, replaced often—in the earlier poems especially—with the wittiness of the Six Dynasties style that he learned from his father, Yamanoue no Okura, and the Chinese poets themselves.

Yakamochi's most enduring contribution is a gentle, understated lyricism that nearly always focuses on the poet's own personal reaction to the world and its events. It is this quality, perhaps seen best in a few masterpieces of delicate impressionism written at the end of his career (95–96, 103–4), that was so influential in later ages. Similarly, his world-weariness (especially in 88–91, 98–100) and nostalgia (107) represent attitudes that were to become fundamental to Japanese aesthetics.

1. Identity unknown.

88–91. [A lament for his dead mistress[1]]

[88] In my courtyard
        the flowers are blooming now,
      but the sight of them
        still leaves my heart unmoved.
      Were my wife with me,
      she whom I loved so dearly—
      were we side by side
        like drakes out on the water,
      we would gather sprigs
        and then show one another:
      but all in this world

2. *Utsusemi*, a pillow-word used as a metaphor for the ephemerality of human life.

        are shells of the cicada[2]—
      like glistening dew
        all too soon to fade away;
      thus she has vanished
        like the light dying
      as the sun sets on a path
        in foot-wearying hills;
      and to think of her
        brings me pain deep in my heart
          beyond any words,
      beyond power to describe—
      in this world of ours

3. For the romanized text, see s.n. 19.

        where all fade without a trace
          and all effort is in vain.[3]

Envoys

[89] It is a season
        that can come at any time.
    But still my heart aches
        for my wife, who went away
            leaving behind a young child.

toki wa shi mo / itsu mo aramu o / kokoro itaku / iyuku
wagimo ga / midoriko o okite

[90] Had I known the path
        that she is traveling now,
    I would have gone ahead
        to put up a barrier-gate[4]—
    and stopped her going away.

idete yuku / michi shiramaseba / arakajime / imo o
todomemu / seki mo okamashi o

4. *Sekisho*, toll gates
placed along roads
for surveillance and
taxation.

[91] Flowers are blooming
        in the courtyard she gazed upon—
    thus time wends its way.
    But still my eyes are not dry
        of the tears I have shed.

imo ga mishi / yado ni hana saki / toki wa henu / waga
naku namida / imada hinaku ni

92. Written when Prince Asaka passed away, in
spring, the Second Month of the sixteenth year of
the Tempyō era [744][5]

5. The Prince died
young, at seventeen,
poisoned by rivals.

    Like the bright blossoms
        that make the foot-wearying hills
    shine forth with color
        but then scatter and are gone—
    so it is with our great lord.

ashihiki no / yama sae hikari / saku hana no / chirinuru
gotoki / waga ōkimi ka mo

93. [Sent to a woman]

> Riding my horse
>   across the sparkling shallows
>   at Saho River Ford,
>   where plovers ever cry—
>   I will come, if you say when.

chidori naku / sao no kawato no / kiyoki se o / uma uchi-
watashi / itsu ka kayowamu

94. [Sent to the elder daughter of the Sakanoue
house] [6]

> What anguish it is
>   to meet you only in dreams—
>   when I wake at night
>   and reach out to touch you,
>   but my hand finds nothing!

ime no ai wa / kurushikarikeri / odorokite / kakisagure-
domo / te ni mo fureneba

95. Written on viewing peach and damson blos-
soms in a spring garden, on the evening of the first
day of the Third Month of the second year of the
Tempyōshōhō era [750]

> The spring garden
>   is aglow with the deep pink
>   of peach blossoms:
>   and below, in their soft light—
>   a girl pausing on her way.

haru no sono / kurenai niou / momo no hana / shitaderu
michi ni / idetatsu otome

96. A poem on picking dogtooth violets [7]

> Like the serried ranks
>   of the emperor's warriors

are these young maidens
    jostling buckets in the temple well
—after dogtooth violets.

mononofu no / yaso otomera ga / kumimagau / terai no
ue no / katakago no hana

97. A poem written when he heard a boatman
singing as he went up the river

    At morning, in bed
        I hear something far away.
    On Imizu River,
        rowing off in the morning,
        a boatman is singing.

asatoko ni / kikeba harukeshi / imizukawa / asa kogishi-
tsutsu / utau funabito

*98–100. A lament on the ephemerality of life

[98]   The life a man leads
            is but a transient affair:
        so it has been said
            through all the generations
        since the ancient time
            when heaven and earth began.
        Observed from afar
            on the broad plain of heaven,
        the radiant moon
            sometimes waxes, sometimes wanes;
        so, too, with treetops
            in the foot-wearying hills:
        when springtime arrives
            they glow with blossoms' beauty,
        and in the autumn
            their leaves of many colors
        are touched by dew and frost
            and scatter before the wind.
        The life of a man
            seems to be no different.

The pink flush of youth
    fades from the complexion;
the raven tresses,
black as leopard-flower seeds,
take on a new hue;
the morning smile dies at dusk.
I am powerless
    to hold back the tears that fall
like a flooding rain
    when I think of man's transience,
of how he declines
    with changes invisible
        as a blowing wind,
with changes unremitting
    as the flow of a river.[8]

8.   For the romanized
text, see s.n. 20.

Envoys

[99]   It is precisely
        because all is transient
    that even mute trees
        put forth blossoms in springtime
    and in autumn shed brown leaves.

koto towanu / ki sura haru saki / akizukeba / momichi
jiraku wa / tsune o nami koso

[100]   When I contemplate
        the brevity of man's life,
    I am indifferent
        to worldly things: how many
            are the days I spend in thought!

utsusemi no / tsune naki mireba / yo no naka ni / kokoro
tsukezute / omou hi zo ōki

101–2. On the seventeenth day of the Seventh
Month, he was promoted to minor counselor. Thus

he wrote two farewell poems and sent them to the house of Kume no Hirotsuna, imperial collector[9]

Already my term of six years is complete, and I confront my time of transfer. The sadness of parting from old friends chokes my breast; I wonder if ever my tear-drenched sleeves will be dry. And so I have written these two laments, leaving them in token of a friendship I shall never forget.

[101]   For years that stretch back
               like a string of rough-cut gems,
          we were together.
          How could I ever forget
               the tie that binds our hearts?

aratama no / toshi no o nagaku / aimiteshi / sono kokoro-
biki / wasuraeme ya mo

[102]   And must I go, then—
               before the first hawking,
          when on horseback
               we would push through bush-clover,
          side by side on Iwase Moor?

iwaseno ni / akihagi shinogi / uma namete / hatsutogari
dani / sezu ya wakaremu

103. Written when the mood took him, on the third day of the Second Month [753]

          Out in the spring fields
               the haze is trailing along;
          and I am sad somehow—
          listening in evening light
               to a bush warbler calling.

haru no no ni / kasumi tanabiki / uraganashi / kono
yûkage ni / uguisu no naku mo

9. Yakamochi was promoted in the summer of 751, while still serving as an official in Etchū. His new position at court required his attendance back in the capital.

104. Written on the fifth day of the Second Month
[753]

> Into the soft light
>   of a tranquil day in spring
>   a lark rises high—
>   leaving my heart saddened
>   as I muse on all alone.

uraura ni / tereru harubi ni / hibari agari / kokoro kanashi
mo / hitori shi omoeba

105. [Written when slander led to the removal of a
relative from his position as governor of Izumo] [10]

> Now the name you bear
>   must be honed to a bright edge—
>   for like a great sword
>   it has come to us in splendor
>   from an age long ago.

tsurugitachi / iyoiyo togubeshi / inishie yu / sayakeku
oite / kinishi sono na zo

10.   His cousin Ōtomo
no Koshibi, who was
accused of slandering
Empress Kōken (718–
70; r. 749–58, 764–70)
and her lover, Fuji-
wara no Nakamaro
(706–64).

106. A plea for long life

> Full well do I know
>   that this passing form of mine
>   is foam on the water:
>   yet all the more what I want
>   is to live a thousand years!

mitsubo nasu / kareru mi zo to wa / shireredomo / nao shi
negaitsu / chitose no inochi o

11.   Mid-8th century;
lineage unknown.

107. A poem written at a banquet held at the
home of Prince Mikata [11] on the twenty-third day

of the Sixth Month of the ninth year of the Shōhō
era [757]

> Each time I behold
>   the seasons slipping away,
> I am pained within—
>   my mind thinking of those
>   I knew once, so long ago.

utsuriyuku / toki miru goto ni / kokoro itaku / mukashi
no hito shi / omōyuru ka mo

The
Classical Age

In the late eighth century, the capital of Japan was moved from Heijō to Heian Kyō, the city of peace and tranquility. Again the model for the city was to be found in China, with which the Japanese court was carrying on an active correspondence through ambassadors, traders, artists, and Buddhist priests. For the first years of the new era, continental models dominated poetry as well. But by the mid-800's the Tang dynasty was in collapse, and for this and other reasons the Japanese began to turn away from the continent. In the past they had assimilated Chinese models in almost every area of cultural life; now the time had come to refine them, to make them more distinctly Japanese.

This inward turn resulted in one of the greatest flowerings of court culture in Japanese history. Made wealthy by their sinecures and private estates, the aristocratic classes—meaning particularly the Fujiwara clan, which dominated the court for most of the Classical Age—adorned themselves in fine silks and the costliest appurtenances, from ornamental swords to carts and carriages. Competing among themselves, they built grand mansions, which they surrounded with gardens and lakes and decorated with paintings and furnishings commissioned from thriving craftsmen and artists. Even their chapels were decorated

with fine statuary and furnishings whose bright colors failed to strike
them as out of keeping with the innate somberness of the Buddha's
message.

Poetry figured large in this efflorescence. In fact, throughout the
Classical Age, or the Heian period (794–1185), poetry was at the very
heart of court life, used in witty conversation at court, for correspon-
dence between friends, and—perhaps most importantly—for messages
between lovers. Along with calligraphy and musical talent, the ability
to compose a good poem was considered an essential accomplishment
of the highborn and their minions. As mentioned in the Introduction,
Chinese influences in diction and imagery, theme and tenor, were again
prominent: composing poetry was no idle pastime, but a serious busi-
ness involving the mastery of rhetorical techniques and knowledge of
a canon.

Much of the poetry of the period, nearly all of which was in the uta
form, was of course never recorded. But tales such as Murasaki Shi-
kibu's Genji monogatari (The Tale of Genji) make it clear that it was
indeed a constant feature of court life. Diaries and memoirs of the time
are also filled with it; seldom do even historical works fail to spend a
good deal of time recording their subject's poems.

It was at this time that poetry contests (uta-awase) became a con-
stant feature of aristocratic life, providing one means of "publication"
for avid poets. And these contests in turn became raw material for im-
perial anthologies, six of which were compiled by imperial order during
the years between 905 and 1151. Recorded on the finest paper by the
finest hands of the day and then stored in elegant boxes of the same sort
used to store Buddhist sutras, these collections came to symbolize the
heritage of court society. Along with the personal collections of family
members, handwritten copies of Kokinshū (Collection of Early and
Modern Japanese Poetry; 905) and its successors became the central
holdings of aristocratic libraries, whose owners cherished the ambition
of one day having some of their works memorialized in the same way.

Among these poets, the finest came from the middle classes of court
society—ladies in waiting and middle-ranking officials who could win
through poetry the sort of fame denied them by family background and
rank. It is a tribute to their energy and perseverance that what they
deemed appropriate in the way of subject matter, vocabulary, and senti-
ments for their own poems remained the standard for several centuries
to come. If Man'yōshū had left any doubt about the matter, men like
Ki no Tsurayuki (ca. 872–945) made it clear that poetry in Japanese—

or, for that matter, in Chinese, when it was still being produced—was a product of court culture meant for a courtly audience. Others could be allowed into the circle of the higher culture the uta represented only by mastering its strictly defined conventions and standards of taste.

Ariwara no Narihira (825-880)

For nearly a hundred years after the compilation of *Man'yōshū*, the Japanese court continued to show intense interest in those things Chinese that had first attracted Ōtomo Tabito and his circle. Unlike the members of the Kyūshū salon, however, the emperors and courtiers of the capital composed their works almost exclusively in Chinese. Meanwhile, poetry in Japanese, although remaining a medium of informal communication, languished. Not surprisingly, then, even when the native tradition did reassert itself in the mid-800's, it was with preoccupations that showed the influence of the Chinese poems of the Six Dynasties, which were characterized by witty expression involving the use of elaborate metaphor and wordplay, an emphasis on intellect and often convoluted reasoning, and a preoccupation with problems of perception—in all, an approach that departed from the directness of Hitomaro and Akahito.

One of the first great figures of this new tradition was Ariwara no Narihira, a man who could trace his genealogy back to the imperial family but who remained a minor figure in a hierarchy increasingly dominated by the powerful Fujiwara clan. His highest office was that of head chamberlain, a post to which he was appointed just months before he died. The records of the time are fairly specific in their delineation of Narihira's traits, saying that he was a handsome man of passionate disposition who had little Chinese learning but excelled in the poetry of his own land. He was much involved in the poetic life of his age, leaving behind occasional poetry (poems 109, 119) that displays a total mastery of technique—but with serious overtones that set much of his work apart from the mere playfulness of many of his contemporaries. Thus even in what first appears to be a straightforward declaration on the beauty of the cherry blossoms (see 108)—an old topic even by his time—he manages to hint at a truth that one might call the aesthetic paradox: yes, we might be more at peace without the blossoms; but without their beauty, would spring be spring?

This introspective bent is particularly obvious in his love poems. Himself a legendary lover whose exploits are partially chronicled in *Ise monogatari* (Tales of Ise), Narihira can play the rake (116–17, 120–21), using all the tools of the language. But for him love is more than a conventional topic; it is a feeling of losing control, and hence a fitting example of what it means to be a human being—to have powers of reason that the stronger forces of emotion refuse to obey. Time and again he asks questions. Why can I not argue my way out of feeling (111)? Is it the waking world that is reality, or the world of dreams (113–14)? As the objective world changes, why doesn't my heart? Or vice versa (115)? In the end, he has no sure answers, choosing (as in 114) to let other men make such pronouncements. He is content merely to express, albeit with great artistry, what he feels.

108. SPRING. On seeing cherry blossoms at the Nagisa no In[1]

> Ah, if in this world
>   there were only no such thing
>   as cherry blossoms—
> then perhaps in the springtime
>   our hearts could be at peace.

yo no naka ni / taete sakura no / nakariseba / haru no
kokoro wa / nodokekaramashi

1. A palace anciently located in what is now Hirakata City, Ōsaka Municipality.

* 109. FELICITATIONS. Composed when there was a fortieth-year celebration for the Horikawa Chancellor at the Kujō Mansion[2]

> Scatter at random,
> O blossoms of the cherry,
> and cloud the heavens,
> that you may conceal the path
>   old age is said to follow.

sakurabana / chirikaikumore / oiraku no / komu to iu
naru / michi magau ga ni

2. The Horikawa Chancellor was Fujiwara no Mototsune (836–91).

* 110. TRAVEL. Once Narihira was traveling toward the East Country with one or two friends. . . . When they reached the bank of the Sumida River, which flows between the provinces of Musashi and Shimōsa, they were miserably homesick for the capital. They dismounted and stood for a time on

the bank, thinking, "How very far we have come!" The ferryman interrupted their laments. "Come aboard quickly; it's getting late." They got into the boat and prepared to cross, all in wretched spirits, for there was not one among them who had not left someone dear to him in the city. A white bird with a red bill and red legs chanced to be frolicking near the river. Since it was of a species unknown in the capital, none of them could identify it. "What kind of bird is that?" they asked the ferryman. "A capital-bird,[3] of course," he replied with an air of surprise. Then Narihira recited this poem.

3. *Miyakodori*, a small gull, probably the same as the modern *yurikamome*.

> If you are in truth
> 　　what your name seems to make you,
> I will put to you,
> 　　capital-bird, this question:
> 　　do things go well with my love?

na ni shi owaba / iza koto towamu / miyakodori / waga omou hito wa / ari ya nashi ya to

*111. LOVE. On the day of an archery meet at the riding grounds of the Bodyguards of the Right, Narihira glimpsed a lady's face through the silk curtains of a carriage opposite. He sent her this poem.

> How very foolish!
> Shall I spend all of today
> 　　lost in pensive thought,
> my heart bewitched by someone
> 　　neither seen nor yet unseen?

mizu mo arazu / mi mo senu hito no / koishiku wa / aya naku kyō ya / nagamekurasamu

* 112. LOVE. Composed during a drizzle and sent to a lady whom he had been secretly wooing since early in the Third Month

> Having passed the night
>   neither waking nor sleeping,
> I have spent the day
>   brooding and watching the rain—
> the unending rain of spring.

See McCallough p. 41

oki mo sezu / ne mo sede yoru o / akashite wa / haru no mono tote / nagamekurashitsu

113–14. LOVE. When Narihira went to Ise Province, he met in great secrecy with the lady who was serving as Ise Virgin.[4] The next morning, while he was wondering how to manage a message without a messenger, he received this poem from the Virgin.

4. See s.n. 21.

[113]　Did you come to me?
　　　Was it I who went to you?
　　　I am beyond knowing.
　　　Was it dream or reality?
　　　Was I sleeping or awake?

kimi ya koshi / ware ya yukikemu / omōezu / yume ka utsutsu ka / nete ka samete ka

His reply:

[114]　I have wandered lost
　　　in the gloomy darkness
　　　　that is my heart.
　　　Whether dream or reality,
　　　let someone else decide.

kakikurasu / kokoro no yami ni / madoiniki / yume utsu-tsu to wa / yohito sadame yo

5. Legend identifies the lady as the daughter of the powerful Fujiwara no Yoshifusa (804–72) who later (as Kōshi; 842–910) became a consort to Emperor Seiwa (850–80; r. 858–76). The Gojō Empress refers to Junshi, a daughter of Fujiwara no Fuyutsugu (775–826).

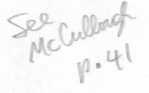

*115. LOVE. Once, quite without premeditation, Narihira began to make love to a lady who lived in the western wing of a palace belonging to the Gojō Empress.⁵ Shortly after the tenth of the First Month, the lady moved away with no word to him. He learned where she had gone, but it was impossible to communicate with her. In the spring of the following year, when the plum blossoms were at their finest, memories of the preceding year drew him back to the western wing on a beautiful moonlit night. He lay on the floor of the bare room until the moon sank low in the sky.

> Is this not the moon?
> And is this not the springtime,
>   the springtime of old?
> Only this body of mine
>   the same body as before . . .

tsuki ya aranu / haru ya mukashi no / haru naranu / wa ga mi hitotsu wa / moto no mi ni shite

6. Dates 815–77; a middle-ranking courtier of the Ki family.

*116–17. LOVE. While Narihira was married to the daughter of Aritsune,⁶ he once became displeased with her. After a period of some length, during which he called in the daytime but always left in the evening, someone wrote this poem and sent it to him.

[116]   Like a proper spouse,
>   you have remained visible—
>   but for what reason
>   might you be growing distant
>   as a cloud in the heavens?

amakumo no / yoso ni mo hito no / nariyuku ka / sasuga ni me ni wa / miyuru mono kara

His reply:

[117] That I spend my days
　　　going and then returning,
　　ever in the sky,
　　is the fault of the harsh wind
　　　on the hill where I would stay.

yukikaeri / sora ni nomi shite / furu koto wa / waga iru
yama no / kaze hayami nari

* 118. LAMENTS. Composed when he was ill and
failing

　　Upon this pathway,
　　I have long heard others say,
　　man sets forth at last—
　　yet I had not thought to go
　　　so very soon as today.

tsui ni yuku / michi to wa kanete / kikishikado / kinō kyō
to wa / omowazarishi o

* 119. MISCELLANEOUS. Once Narihira accompa-
nied Prince Koretaka on an excursion.[7] Back at
their lodgings, the Prince's party drank and talked
all through the night. When the eleven-day-old
moon was about to set,[8] the Prince, somewhat be-
fuddled, prepared to retire, and Narihira composed
this poem.

　　Must the moon vanish
　　　in such great haste, leaving us
　　　　still unsatisfied?
　　Retreat, O rim of the hills,
　　and refuse to let it set.

akanaku ni / madaki mo tsuki no / kakururu ka / yama no
ha nigete / irezu mo aranamu

7. Dates 844–97;
a son of Emperor
Montoku (827–58;
r. 850–58). Narihira
served in the Prince's
entourage.

8. According to the
lunar calendar, the full
moon comes at mid-
month, on the fifteenth.
Thus the moon would
be near full on the
eleventh.

*120–21. MISCELLANEOUS. Sent to someone at Fukakusa—"Village of Deep Grass"—as he prepared to return to the capital after having lived there

[120] This Fukakusa,
  my home for so long a time—
   if I go away,
  will it become a wild field,
  "Deep Grass" deeper than ever?

toshi o hete / sumikoshi sato o / idete inaba / itodo fuka-kusa / no to ya narinamu

Her reply:

[121] If it be a field,
  I will spend the years crying
   like a calling quail—
  and surely you will at least
   come briefly for some hunting.

no to naraba / uzura to nakite / toshi wa hemu / kari ni dani ya wa / kimi ka kozaramu

Ono no Komachi (fl. ca. 850)

Her poetic exchanges with several other ninth-century poets provide most of our information about Ono no Komachi, who ranks alongside Ariwara

Ono no Komachi

no Narihira as one of the greatest poets of the Early Classical period. Those same poems indicate that she was a lady-in-waiting at court in the 850's and 860's. However, nowhere is there evidence to account for the legend, most fully articulated in a number of medieval Nō plays, that portrays her as a beautiful but coldhearted lover who, in symbolic recompense for her cruel treatment of men, ended life as an impoverished old hag living on the outskirts of the capital.[1]

Legends aside, her poetry does evince a passionate temperament that may have provided the impetus for later storytellers. A number of her works (poems 122, 127, for example) state a preference for the world of dreams, which in her case is a realm free of social restraints on romantic and erotic fulfillment. And one of her most famous poems (131) is also one of the most open avowals of passionate physical desire in the classical canon. It should be added, however, that Komachi is also a consummate craftsman, whose use of pivot-words, prefaces, and associative technique makes her poems some of the most rhetorically complex and yet wholly successful in the language.

1. The most famous of the plays are *Kayoi Komachi* (Komachi and the Hundred Nights) and *Sotoba Komachi* (Komachi on the Stupa).

*122. LOVE. Topic unknown

> Did you come to me
>   because I dropped off to sleep,
> tormented by love?
> If I had known I dreamed,
> I would not have awakened.

omoitsutsu / nureba ya hito no / mietsuramu / yume to shiriseba / samezaramashi o

*123–24. LOVE. Abe no Kiyoyuki [825–900]. Suggested by the monk Shinsei's sermon during a memorial service at the Lower Izumo Temple;[1] sent to Ono no Komachi

[123]   They are only tears
>   shed for one I cannot see—
>   those fair white jewels

1. Located in the Yamashina area, in the Eastern Hills of Kyōto.

that will not stay in my sleeve
    when I seek to wrap them up.

tsutsumedomo / sode ni tamaranu / shiratama wa / hito o
minu me no / namida narikeri

Her reply:

[124] Tears that do no more
        than turn into beads on sleeves
            are formal indeed.
    Mine flow in a surging stream,
    try though I may to halt them.

oroka naru / namida zo sode ni / tama wa nasu / ware wa
sekiaezu / takitsuse nareba

*125. LOVE. Topic unknown

    There is no seaweed
        to be gathered in this bay.
    Does he not know it—
        the fisher who comes and comes
        until his legs grow weary?[2]

mirume naki / waga mi o ura to / shiraneba ya / karenade
ama no / ashi tayuku kuru

2. This poem is an example of complex rhetorical technique involving pivot-words (*mirume naki* meaning both "there's no seaweed" and "you cannot see me") and a string of associated words: seaweed, bay, fisher, and so on.

*126. SPRING. Topic unknown

    Autumn nights, it seems,
    are long by repute alone:
        scarcely had we met
        when morning's first light appeared,
    leaving everything unsaid.

aki no yo mo / na nomi narikeri / au to ieba / koto zo to
mo naku / akenuru mono o

*127. LOVE. Topic unknown

> Yielding to a love
>   that recognizes no bounds,
> I will go by night—
>   for the world will not censure
>   one who treads the path of dreams.

kagiri naki / omoi no mama ni / yoru mo komu / yumeji o
sae ni / hito wa togameji

*128. LOVE. Topic unknown

> Though I go to you
>   ceaselessly along dream paths,
> the sum of those trysts
>   is less than a single glimpse
>   granted in the waking world.

yumeji ni wa / ashi mo yasumezu / kayoedomo / utsutsu
ni hitome / mishi goto wa arazu

129. LOVE. Topic unknown

> What is it that fades
>   without a change in color?
> It is the flower
>   in the heart of those who love
>   in this world of ours.

iro miede / utsurou mono wa / yo no naka no / hito no
kokoro no / hana ni zo arikeru

130. MISCELLANEOUS. Composed in reply when
Fun'ya no Yasuhide,[3] who had been named a third-
ranking official in Mikawa, sent her a message say-
ing, "How about coming to have a look at my new
duty post?"

> In my forlorn state
>   I feel like a floating reed[4]

3. Dates unknown;
another prominent
poet of the time (see
poem 436).
4. *Ukikusa* (lit.,
"floating grass"), or
duckweed, is a plant
that floats on the sur-
face of ponds and
inlets but is rooted to
the bottom. Used in
Chinese poetry as a
metaphor for travel.

ready to break free
  at the roots and drift away—
if the waters would but tempt me.

wabinureba / mi o ukikusa no / ne o taete / sasou mizu
araba / inamu to zo omou

131. MISCELLANEOUS FORMS. Topic unknown

When I cannot see him
  in the dark of a moonless night,
fire rises in me—
leaping in my burning breast,
charring my heart with its flames.

hito ni awamu / tsuki no naki ni wa / omoi okite / mune
hashiribi ni / kokoro yake ori

Archbishop Henjō (816-890)

If Ariwara no Narihira is a poet full of questions, his contemporary Yoshi-
mine Munesada, known by his religious name Henjō, seems to be a man
with only answers. Born to an imperial prince, he spent the first several
decades of his career in various posts at court, and then took the tonsure
after the death of a chief benefactor, going on eventually to become an
archbishop and the abbot of an important temple. He was fully involved
in the poetic affairs of his time, numbering several emperors, a prince, and
many important courtiers among his companions.

  Henjō is a master of poetry as a medium of courtly expression—whether used to praise a patron (poem 135), to make a witty and flattering request (136), or simply to impress with imagination, verbal skill, and descriptive power (132–34; see also poem 426). In other words, it seems fair to characterize Henjō's work as an artful display of Six Dynasties style. Although lacking the philosophical depth or psychological insight of Narihira and Komachi, his elaborate metaphors (see especially 132–33) cannot fail to impress with their ingenious conception and imagery.

1. Located opposite Tōji at the south end of Suzaku Avenue in Kyōto.

* 132. SPRING. A willow near Nishi no Ōtera [1]

> It twists together
>   leafy threads of tender green
> and fashions jewels
>   by piercing clear, white dewdrops—
> the willow tree in springtime.

asamidori / ito yorikakete / shiratsuyu o / tama ni mo nukeru / haru no yanagi ka

2. The lotus, a plant that rises through the muddy water of a pond to blossom on the surface, is often used as a metaphor for those who rise through the filth of the world toward Buddhist enlightenment.

* 133. SUMMER. Seeing dew on a lotus [2]

> How puzzling it seems
>   that lotus leaves untainted
> by impurity
>   should nonetheless deceive us,
> displaying dewdrops as gems.

hachisuba no / nigori ni shimanu / kokoro mote / nani ka wa tsuyu o / tama to azamuku

3. The garden was no doubt a grand affair, and certainly no rustic mountainside. Henjō's description is an attempt at "modest" praise. Kōkō (830–87) reigned from 884 till his death.

* 134. AUTUMN. While Emperor Kōkō was a prince, he stopped at the house of Henjō's mother on his way to view Furu Waterfall. The garden had been redesigned to suggest autumn fields. [3] Henjō recited this poem at an opportune moment in the conversation.

> The house is decayed
>   and its mistress has grown old:

perhaps that is why
    garden and fence have vanished,
leaving only autumn fields.

sato wa arete / hito wa furinishi / yado nare ya / niwa mo
magaki mo / aki no nora naru

*135. FELICITATIONS. While Emperor Kōkō was a
prince, he sent his grandmother a silver-trimmed
staff to commemorate her eightieth year. When
Henjō saw the staff, he composed this on the
grandmother's behalf.

    Might it have been cut
        by one of the mighty gods?
    With its assistance,
    I can climb the hill of age
        for a thousand happy years.

chihayaburu / kami ya kirikemu / tsuku kara ni / chitose
no saka mo / koenubera nari

*136. PARTING. Composed under the cherry blos-
soms as the Urin-in Prince was returning home
after having visited Mount Hiei for a Sarira Ser-
vice[4]

    Blow, cherry blossoms,
    in the wind from the mountains;
    blow in swirling clouds
        and make our guest tarry here,
        lost amid flying petals.

yamakaze ni / sakura fukimaki / midarenamu / hana no
magire ni / kimi tomarubeku

4. The Urin'in Prince
was Tsuneyasu (d. 869).
The Sarira (Skt. *sharie*)
Service was held in
honor of a temple's
Buddhist relics.

Anonymous Poems from 'Kokinshū'

As was the case with *Man'yōshū*, the next great anthology of Japanese poetry, *Kokinshū* (Collection of Early and Modern Japanese Poetry; 905), contains a great many poems assigned to no particular author—460 of the total 1,100. Traditionally, scholars have assumed that most of these come from the period between Ōtomo no Yakamochi and Ariwara no Narihira, continuing anonymously the native tradition that had been abandoned in favor of Chinese poetry in the public context of the court. And, indeed, some of the anonymous poems selected by the compilers of *Kokinshū* do seem to continue the old traditions of earlier days in directness of expression (poems 140, 147), reliance on prefaces involving simple natural metaphors (141–42) and so on. But it is equally true that many employ the more sophisticated techniques of ninth-century court poetry, such as personification (137), clever hypothesis (146), the conceit (144), and witty humor (150–52), suggesting that they may date from a later period, or that there are more continuities between the ancient and classical traditions than is usually supposed.

* 137. SPRING. Topic unknown

> I pray you, warbler,
>   address your reproachful cries
>   to the blowing breeze.
>   Have I so much as ventured
>   to lay a hand on the blossoms?

fuku kaze o / nakite urami yo / uguisu wa / ware ya wa
hana ni / te dani furetaru

*138. SUMMER. Topic unknown

Scenting the fragrance
   of orange blossoms that wait
      the Fifth Month's coming,
I recall a perfumed sleeve
   worn by someone long ago.

satsuki matsu / hanatachibana no / ka o kageba / mukashi
no hito no / sode no ka zo suru

*139. SUMMER. Topic unknown

O cuckoo singing
   amid the summer mountains:
if you have feelings,
   do not harrow with your voice
      one whose heart already aches.

natsuyama ni / naku hototogisu / kokoro araba / mono
omou ware ni / koe na kikase so

*140. WINTER. Topic unknown

As night settles in,
the cold finds its way through sleeves.
Snow will be falling
   at fair Yoshino, falling
      in the hills of Yoshino.

yū sareba / koromode samushi / miyoshino no / yoshino
no yama ni / miyuki fururashi

*141. LOVE. Topic unknown

Although there are days
   when waves fail to rise
near Suruga's shore
   at Tago, there are no days
when I do not yearn for you.

suruga naru / tago no uranami / tatanu hi wa / aredomo
kimi o / koinu hi wa nashi

* 142. LOVE. Topic unknown

> Mine is not a love
>   as plain to see as rice ears
>   in the autumn fields,
> but never is there a time
>   when you are not in my heart.

aki no ta no / ho ni koso hito o / koizarame / nado ka
kokoro ni / wasure shi mo semu

* 143. LOVE. Topic unknown

> But little better
>   than the vivid dream I dreamt
> was our encounter
>   in reality's darkness,
>   black as leopard-flower seeds.

mubatama no / yami no utsutsu wa / sadaka naru / yume
ni ikura mo / masarazarikeri

* 144. LOVE. Topic unknown

> Burning with passion,
> I shrink before the high dike
>   of other men's eyes.
> My heart is set on the stream,
> but how am I to reach it?

omoedomo / hitomezutsumi no / takakereba / kawa to
minagara / e koso watarane

* 145. LOVE. Topic unknown

> Yielding to the gale,
>   it has drifted to a place

I never dreamed of—
the smoke rising from salt fires
tended by Suma seafolk.

suma no ama no / shio yaku keburi / kaze o itami /
omowanu kata ni / tanabikinikeri

* 146. LOVE. Topic unknown

If this were a world
in which there were no such thing
as false promises,
how great would be my delight
as I listened to your words!

itsuwari no / naki yo nariseba / ika bakari / hito no koto
no ha / ureshikaramashi

* 147. LOVE. Topic unknown

In this world of ours,
what is it that resembles
the human heart?
Dyestuffs from the dayflower,[1]
all too quick to fade away.

yo no naka no / hito no kokoro wa / hanazome no / utsu-
roiyasuki / iro ni zo arikeru

1. The *hanazome*
(modern *tsuyukusa*),
a perennial of the
spiderwort family, was
used in dyeing fabric,
even though its color
was known for fading
quickly.

* 148. LOVE. Topic unknown

Though you made me think
your love inexhaustible
as sand on a beach,
the thing that proved limitless
was your power to forget.

arisoumi no / hama no masago to / tanomeshi wa /
wasururu koto no / kazu ni zo arikeru

* 149. MISCELLANEOUS. Topic unknown

> In this world of ours
>   what is there of constancy?
> Yesterday's deep pool
>   in the River of Tomorrow
>   today becomes a rapid.[2]

2. A pun involving the name of the Asuka (*asu* meaning "tomorrow") River, which often changed its course.

yo no naka wa / nani ka tsune naru / asukagawa / kinō no
fuchi zo / kyō wa se ni naru

* 150. ECCENTRIC POEMS. Topic unknown

> Beyond enduring,
>   this passion that attacks me
>   from pillow and foot:
> I get up and seat myself
>   in the middle of the bed.

makura yori / ato yori koi no / semekureba / semu kata
nami zo / tokonaka ni oru

* 151. ECCENTRIC POEMS. Topic unknown. [Spoken
by a young woman being pursued by suitors]

> Ah, what a trial!
> Even *you* make bold, it seems,
>   to chase after me—
> you scarecrow in a paddy
>   among the foot-wearying hills.

ashihiki no / yamada no sōzu / onore sae / ware o hoshi
chō / urewashiki koto

* 152. ECCENTRIC POEMS. Topic unknown

> As a mountain gorge
>   bids fair to vanish beneath
>   piles of cut timber,
> so I too may disappear
>   under my burden of sighs.

nageki o ba / kori nomi tsumite / ashihiki no / yama no
kai naku / narinubera nari

Sugawara no Michizane (845-903)

The scholar-poet Sugawara no Michizane spent most of his fifty-nine years
in the court hierarchy, beginning as a young man in various academic posts
that set the stage for a distinguished political career. The height of his glory
came in 899, when he was appointed to the high office of minister of the
Right. Ironically, his successes are now remembered only as a backdrop for
the unhappy fate that was to befall him when, in 901, the slanderous attacks
of a Fujiwara colleague led to his demotion to the position of governor-
general of Dazaifu in Kyūshū—in truth, a kind of banishment. He died
there in the spring of 903, of what the chroniclers call a broken heart.

Attacks on his rivals attributed to Michizane's vengeful spirit led to
posthumous honors and his enshrinement as a god several decades after his
death. But those honors were as nothing when compared to the renown he
gained in legend as an "ill-used" but always loyal minister. Legends aside,
his writings show that he was a fine scholar, as well as a poet in both Chi-
nese and Japanese. Understandably, his most famous work deals with the
most famous event of his life—his exile. But his earlier poems show rhe-
torical polish and a somewhat melancholy, brooding disposition that may
have developed within him long before it found any immediate cause.

153. *The Sound of Rapids*

To avoid noisy places is my nature,
yet I love the gurgling of a stream.
Like a hermit turning his pillow;

like an old zither being strummed.
One old pine—a silk umbrella on the bank;
scattering leaves—a boat moored in waves.
Tonight I have not a thing to do—
but read "Freewheeling" in my *Zhuangzi*![1]

1. "Freewheeling" is the first chapter in the great Taoist classic.

154. *Strolling Alone on a Spring Day*

Leaving my offices one day, I lament spring's
    passing;
at waterside, before blossoms, all alone I stand.
Time and again I gaze out toward the northeast[2]—
and my colleagues, they point at me and say
    I'm crazy.

2. The direction of the capital. Michizane was then serving as governor in Sanuki, on northern Shikoku.

155. *White Peony at Hokkeji*[3]

Your color is a straightforward white,
but still you are known as Peony.
You hate growing with common grasses;
you like to look like the Lotus of the Law.
In the earth—like light clouds shrinking;
out of season—like the cold of faint snow.
What do I hope to gain by walking around you?
Perhaps a measure of your pureness of heart.

3. A temple in Sanuki whose name contains the character for lotus.

156. *Idle Thoughts on a Winter Night*

Beneath eaves of white thatch, before the hearth—
the servant boy who was at my side leans against
    the wall, asleep.
My calendar says only a month of winter
    remains—
which means I have been magistrate here now for
    three years.[4]
By nature I don't like wine—but sorrow is hard to
    dispel;
with my heart set on poems, I cannot conduct
    government.

4. His appointment in Sanuki began in the spring of 886.

So with a thousand thoughts about my plight
   I sit—
while beyond the window the sky announces
   dawn's approach.

*157. PARTING/TRAVEL. Composed when he accompanied the Retired Emperor on an excursion to Miyanotaki[5]

> That fabric fashioned
>   by someone who weaves white threads
>   from water-soaked hemp—
> might I cut a piece of it
>   to wear over travel garb?

5. This excursion, by Retired Emperor Uda (867–931; r. 887–97), the poet's chief patron, took place in the Tenth Month of 898.

mizuhiki no / shiraito haete / oru hata wa / tabi no koromo ni / tachi ya kasanen

*158. MISCELLANEOUS: SPRING. Looking at plum blossoms in his garden after having been sentenced to exile

> If an east wind blows,
>   send me your fragrance by it,
>   blossoms of plum:
> do not forget the springtime
>   because your master is gone.

kochi fukaba / nioi okose yo / ume no hana / aruji nashi tote / haru o wasuru na

*159. SPRING. Tied to cherry blossoms in his garden when he was taking leave for a distant place[6]

> Blossoming cherry:
>   if you are one who does not
>   forget a master,
> you must send me messages
>   on breezes blowing my way.

6. Referring to his exile to northern Kyūshū.

sakurabana / nushi o wasurenu / mono naraba / fukikomu
kaze ni / kotozute wa se yo

* 160. MISCELLANEOUS. Composed on the way
to exile

>   Like the stars above,
>   I have a course to travel
>   and a place to stop:
>   why, then, should my disturbed thoughts
>   go drifting through the heavens?

amatsuhoshi / michi mo yadori mo / arinagara / sora ni
ukite mo / omōyuru kana

161. *To Console His Little Children*

Your elder sisters have stayed at home;
your elder brothers have been ordered away.[7]
So you, my little boy, my little girl—
we will go along together, chat together.
At midday you will eat before me;
at night we will rest in the same place.
Facing the dark, we shall have lamps and tapers;
struck by cold, we shall have tattered cotton.
In years gone by I saw poor children—
wandering in the capital, with no place to go.
Then there was that naked man, a gambler—
everyone calling him Namusuke.[8]
And the barefoot woman playing the harp—
the townsmen calling her Comptroller's Daughter.[9]
Their fathers were all of the nobility,
men who had their portion of wealth.
In the past, gold was to them like sand—
and now they haven't even enough to eat.
Compare your lot with theirs, my children—
and Heaven's treatment will seem most kind.

7. Only Michizane's two youngest children were allowed to accompany him into exile.

8. The son of a counselor who lost his court position and became a gambler.

9. Identity unknown.

162. *On a Winter Night, Thinking of His
Bamboos Back Home*

Since I was called so suddenly away,
you, sirs, have been far from me.[10]
With my post in the west,[11] my home in the east,
mountains and barriers have blocked all news.
And not only because of the distance between us,
but because of the cold assaults of Heaven.
Grieving in the quiet, I cannot sleep,
with flurry upon flurry of snow all night long.
Nearby I see white thatched-roofs buried;
afar I know your jade columns will be breaking.
With the house servant gone off early on,
who will bear the cold to brush the snow away?
Holding to straightness—you will bend low in
    confusion;
clinging to virtue—you will be broken in pieces.
Your long stalks would be good for fishing rods—
that now I regret not making long ago.
Your short stalks would be good for writing
    planks[12]—
that now I begrudge not binding into a book.
With my book in hand, my pole dangling out—
ah, such happiness would be beyond enduring.
But now a thousand words are of no use to me;
I can do no more than sigh and weep.
But even without me there for support,
your green shafts will be the last to wither away.

10. He is address-
ing his bamboo plants
here. Bamboo was re-
ferred to as *kimi*, or
"lord," because of its
upright nature.

11. His place of exile
in Kyūshū.

12. Used for poems
or sayings framed and
hung for display.

Ki no Tsurayuki (ca. 872-945)

Ki no Tsurayuki has the distinction of being at once the most praised and the most vilified poet in Japanese history—with both supporters and detractors regarding the same accomplishments, but from different points of view. Born into a once prominent family that had lost prestige under the domination of the Fujiwara family, he was a librarian in the Imperial Records Office for a time in his thirties, during which time he was very active in the poetic life of the court—meaning especially poem contests and the composition of poems for screens and public events. So fine a reputation did he make for himself in this milieu that, along with Ki no Tomonori (d. before 905?), Ōshikōchi no Mitsune (d. ca. 925?), and Mibu no Tadamine (b. ca. 850?), he was requested, sometime between 902 and 905, to compile the first imperially commissioned collection of Japanese poetry—*Kokinshū*. In addition, he was given the honor of penning the Japanese preface (there is also a Chinese preface) to that work, which became one of the most important critical documents in the history of Japanese poetry.

Later on, Tsurayuki was appointed to official posts in the administrations of Kaga (part of modern Ishikawa Prefecture), Mino (part of modern Gifu Prefecture), and Tosa (modern Kōchi Prefecture) provinces. He continued to be active in poetry, producing among other things *Tosa nikki* (Tosa Journal), the first great travel record of the classical tradition, in which he wrote about his return from Tosa to the capital in the mid 930's. But it is his role as compiler of *Kokinshū* and author of the famous preface that continues to be the focus of attention for both his allies and his enemies.

Those who condemn Tsurayuki complain that his approach had the effect of strangling the life out of poetry. And—though to blame him alone for the general trend of his time is of course unfair—there is some truth to these accusations. *Kokinshū*, which became a standard for all such collections to come, did in fact restrict poetry (which for Tsurayuki meant above all formal composition, referred to as *hare no uta*) to the fixed form of the uta and the fixed thematics of the seasons, love, felicitations, and several other topics. And it also strictly limited vocabulary and imagery

Ki no Tsurayuki

to what was considered proper and tasteful to the courtier's eye and ear. Finally, Tsurayuki's preface to the collection championed the lyrical expression of feeling, rather than any more intellectual or philosophical ideal, as the raison d'être of poetry.

This approach produced a tradition of highly refined and subtle expression that made the composition of passable verse possible to almost any well-educated courtier, while making truly exceptional poetry correspondingly more difficult. In other words, it made the composition of poetry one of the accouterments of anyone of high birth. Tsurayuki's comments on the work of Narihira, as stated in his preface, make the point clear. "Narihira," he says, "tries to express too much content in too few words." One senses that what disturbed Tsurayuki about Narihira was the latter's passion, his impatience with the restraints that to the compilers of *Kokinshū* were the basis of court civilization.

With all this as an introduction, it should surprise no one that Tsurayuki's own poetry shows both the strengths and the weaknesses of his approach. His command of technique is unsurpassed by any *uta* poet of any era save perhaps Fujiwara no Teika. In particular, his use of the preface (*jo*) (in poems 171–72) shows a complete control of resources; and the same is true of his careful employment of puns (169) and stock metaphors involving Six Dynasties "confusion of the senses" (164, 178). Moreover, he consistently manages to pack more into a short poem than one has a right to expect, as in his treatment of the New Year topos (163), in which he uses imagery that encompasses an entire year.

The drawback in all this is that, however skillfully he does it, Tsurayuki often seems to have little to say, making him seem more the virtuoso musician than the original composer. Yet some of his scenes (165, 168, 178, in particular) are so captivating, some of his evocation of moods (166, 173–76) so perfect, and some of his reworking of old themes (such as the "play" of perceptions in 170 and the dynamic relationship between dream and reality in 167) so effortless, that we forget his limitations and accept his offerings as we do Akahito's—as pure celebrations of beauty.

163. SPRING. Composed on the first day of spring

> Soaking my long sleeves,
> I took up in my cupped hands
>   waters that later froze.
> And today, as spring begins,
> will they be melting in the wind?

sode hichite / musubishi mizu no / kōreru o / haru tatsu
kyō no / kaze ya tokuramu

* 164. SPRING. On a snowfall

> When snow comes in spring—
>   fair season of layered haze
>   and burgeoning buds—
>   flowers fall in villages
>   where flowers have yet to bloom.

kasumi tachi / ko no me mo haru no / yuki fureba / hana
naki sato mo / hana zo chirikeru

*165. SPRING. Composed by command   *scene*

> Are they on their way
>   to pick young greens in the fields
>   at Kasugano—
>   those girls who call each other
>   with the sleeves of their white robes?

kasugano no / wakana tsumi ni ya / shirotae no / sode
furihaete / hito no yukuramu

* 166. SPRING. On seeing cherry blossoms for the
first time on a tree planted at someone's house

> Blossoming cherry
>   who have just this year begun   *mood*
>   to understand spring—
>   would that you might never learn
>   the meaning of scattering.

kotoshi yori / haru shirisomuru / sakurabana / chiru to iu
koto wa / narawazaranamu

167. SPRING. Composed when he was staying at a mountain temple

> On a spring hillside
>   I took lodging for the night;
> and as I slept
>   the blossoms kept on falling—
> even in the midst of my dreams.

yadori shite / haru no yamabe ni / netaru yo wa / yume no uchi ni mo / hana zo chirikeru

*168. SPRING. On kerria blooming near the Yoshino River

> Even their reflections
>   in the stream depths are scattered
>   by the blowing wind:
> kerria flowers on the bank
>   of the Yoshino river.

yoshinogawa / kishi no yamabuki / fuku kaze ni / soko no kage sae / utsuroinikeri

169. AUTUMN. Composed near Moruyama

> At Moru Mountain
>   white dewdrops and constant showers
> have trickled down so
>   that even the lowest leaves
> are dyed now in autumn hues.[1]

shiratsuyu mo / shigure mo itaku / moruyama wa / shitaba nokorazu / irozukinikeri

1. The name of the mountain involves a pun on the verb *moru*, "to drip."

*170. AUTUMN. Composed when he went to the northern hills to gather autumn leaves

> Unseen by men's eyes,
>   the colored leaves have scattered
>   deep in the mountains:

truly we may say brocade
   worn in the darkness of night!

miru hito mo / nakute chirinuru / okuyama no / momiji
wa yoru no / nishiki narikeri

*171. PARTING. Composed when he bid farewell
to someone with whom he had talked near a rocky
spring on the Shiga Mountain road

   As when a traveler
     seeks in vain to slake his thirst
   at a hillside spring
     soiled by drops from his cupped hands—
   so, unsatisfied, I part from you.

musubu te no / shizuku ni nigoru / yama no i no / akade
mo hito ni / wakarenuru kana

172. LOVE. Topic unknown

   Cresting over rocks,
   the flow of the Yoshino
     goes coursing by
   as swiftly as I've begun
     to fall in love with you.

yoshinogawa / iwanami takaku / yuku mizu no / hayaku
zo hito o / omoisometeshi

*173. LOVE. Topic unknown

   So it is like this
     between a man and a woman!
   I yearn for someone
     heard of as we hear the wind,
   and no easier to see.

mood

yo no naka wa / kaku koso arikere / fuku kaze no / me ni
minu hito mo / koishikarikeri

174. LOVE. Topic unknown

> Ah, the days, the months
> I have not touched the white wood
>   of my spindlewood bow—
> tensing up, easing down, each night,
> with never a moment of sleep.

te mo furede / tsukihi henikeru / shiramayumi / okifushi
yoru wa / i koso nerarene

mood

175. LAMENTS. Composed when Ki no Tomo-nori died[2]

2. Tsurayuki's cousin, one of the compilers of *Kokinshū*.

> I know that I too
> may never see tomorrow;
> but today at least,
> while my sun has not yet set,
> my grief is for another.

asu shiranu / waga mi to omoedo / kurenu ma no / kyō
wa hito koso / kanashikarikere

mood

*176. LAMENTS. On seeing plum blossoms at a house where the owner had died

> The hue is as rich
> and the perfume as fragrant
>   as in days gone by,
> but how I long for a glimpse
> of the one who planted the tree.

iro mo ka mo / mukashi no kosa ni / nioedomo / uekemu
hito no / kage zo koishiki

mood

177. AUTUMN. Written during the Engi era [901–23], when there was a request for autumn poems

> Ah, the autumn moon—
> shining forth with such brilliance

that I can make out
　the shapes of the crimson leaves
　　as they fall to earth.

aki no tsuki / hikari sayakemi / momijiba no / otsuru kage
sae / miewataru kana

* 178. SPRING. A poem from the Teiji-in Contest[3]

The wind that scatters
　cherry blossoms from their boughs
　　is not a cold wind—
and the sky has never known
　snow flurries like these.

sakura chiru / ko no shita kaze wa / samukarade / sora ni
shirarenu / yuki zo furikeru

179. WINTER. Topic unknown

Overcome by love,
I go out in pursuit of her—
　the river wind
　　so cold in the winter night
　　　that the plovers are crying.

omoikane / imogari yukeba / fuyu no yo no / kawakaze
samumi / chidori naku nari

3. Held by Retired
Emperor Uda (867–
931; r. 887–97) in 913.

scene

A Sequence from 'Kokinshū'

We know almost nothing about the process by which poems were put together to form *Man'yōshū*. In the case of *Kokinshū*, however, we know a great deal, both from the historical record and from the evidence of the text itself. As Ki no Tsurayuki's preface makes clear, the collection was compiled at court, by courtiers who were acting on imperial command to collect works of the past and present. Because of this charge, the anthology contains works attributed to approximately 130 different authors—as against *Man'yōshū*'s 530—including Hitomaro, Akahito, and others of ancient times, but concentrating chiefly on more recent poets, most notably Tsurayuki and the other compilers themselves. And in other ways, too, the collection created by Tsurayuki and his colleagues is different from its great forebear. First, it is much shorter and dominated by one genre—containing only just over 1,100 poems, virtually all of which are uta. Second, it is narrower in the range of subjects presented, restricting itself primarily to "public" poetry deemed suitable for formal presentation at court gatherings. Finally, it presents a new scheme of organization that reflected its authors' courtly preoccupations but also, almost paradoxically, a desire to transcend them.

Scholars term the editorial principles involved in the collection's organization *progression* (referring, for instance, to the chronological scheme of the four seasons and of images within each season, or to the course of a courtly romance followed in the five Love books) and *association* (referring to more delicate and smaller connections between conventional images and motifs). Yet no general terminology used to characterize the whole can adequately represent the effect of these principles on the parts, which is to create a tapestry best examined for detail, as the sequence below illustrates. Taken from the middle of the second (and last) book of Spring poems, it is unified by the dominance of one general subject—the falling of the cherry blossoms. But within the confines of that subject, it introduces a variety of techniques (conceits in poems 182–83; personification in 185, 193), subtopics and subthemes (chiefly reminiscence and transience, but also the fickleness of human affection, as in 186; travel in 189–90; and love

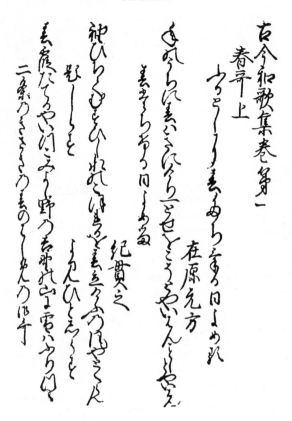

*The first page of '*Kokinshū*'*

in 194, 195, 198), and rhetorical approaches (fairly straightforward natural description in 197, 199; Six Dynasties–style reasoning and conjecture in 187–88, 192, 195–96) that combine to create a sense of subtle but complex change within a larger continuity. In addition, the compilers have introduced other spring images (haze, the warbler, and so on) to interrupt the flow of scenes, and created shorter sequences organized by author (189–90; 195–96) or idea (191–92). The result is a product that obscures the origins of the poems themselves, most of which were created in specific contexts. Poem 184, for example, was probably a bittersweet statement of affection for the old capital at Nara by Emperor Heizei (774–824; r. 806–9), who spent his last years there while out of favor with Emperor Saga (786–842; r. 809–23). And several of the poems were probably written as love poems (194–95, 198, in particular) or as descriptions of scenes painted on standing screens (183, 188, 196). One poem (192) has even been listed as anonymous in order to fit better with its predecessor, although records show that it was penned by Monk Sosei (late 9th century). Thus the whole work creates a rich fabric that is—as its fashioners intended—a showpiece for the courtly styles.

*180. SPRING. Ōshikōchi no Mitsune [d. ca. 925?]. On cherry blossoms scattering

> For cherry blossoms
>   to be descending like snow
>   is sorrow enough.
> How do the blowing breezes
>   propose that they should scatter?[1]

conceit

1. In other words, "It's bad enough that the blossoms must fall; why must the wind attack them so?"

yuki to nomi / furu dani aru o / sakurabana / ika ni chire to ka / kaze no fukuramu

*181. SPRING. Ki no Tsurayuki [ca. 872–945]. Composed on his return from an ascent of Mount Hiei

> No doubt the breezes
>   are wreaking their will with them—
> those cherry blossoms
>   I could but glimpse on high peaks
>   as I made my way toward home.

yama takami / mitsutsu wa ga koshi / sakurabana / kaze wa kokoro ni / makasubera nari

*182. SPRING. Ōtomo no Kuronushi [late 9th century].[2] Topic unknown

2. A contemporary of Tsurayuki.

technique : conceits

> Everyone feels grief
>   when cherry blossoms scatter.
> Might they then be tears—
>   those drops of moisture falling
>   in the gentle rains of spring?

harusame no / furu wa namida ka / sakurabana / chiru o
oshimanu / hito shi nakereba

*183. SPRING. Tsurayuki. A poem from the Teiji-in
Contest[3]

*(originally
(screen poem)*

3. Held by Retired
Emperor Uda in 913.

*technique:
conceits*

In the lingering wake
of the breeze that has scattered
the cherry tree's bloom,
petal wavelets ripple out
into the waterless sky.

sakurabana / chirinuru kaze no / nagori ni wa / mizu naki
sora ni / nami zo tachikeru

*184. SPRING. A poem by the Nara Emperor
[Heizei; 774–824; r. 806–9]

nostalgia

Even at Nara—
the ancient royal city
now a former home—
the flowers have come into bloom
in the colors of the past.

furusato to / narinishi nara no / miyako ni mo / iro wa
kawarazu / hana wa sakikeri

*185. SPRING. Yoshimine no Munesada [Arch-
bishop Henjō; 816–90]. Composed as a spring
poem

*technique:
personification
of breeze*

We cannot behold
the beauty of the blossoms
enshrouded in haze—
yet steal us their scent, at least,
spring breeze blowing from the hills.

hana no iro wa / kasumi ni komete / misezu tomo / ka o
dani nusume / haru no yamakaze

4. A son of Arch-
bishop Henjō and a
prominent poet.

5. A hundred-round
contest held in the early
890's.

and theme: fickleness

*186. SPRING. Monk Sosei [late 9th century].[4] A
poem from the Empress's Contest during the reign
of Emperor Uda[5]

> I shall dig no more
>   flowering trees to be planted,
> for when springtime comes
>   human affections copy
>   the blossoms' inconstancy.

hana no ki mo / ima wa horiueji / haru tateba / utsurou
iro ni / hito naraikeri

*187. SPRING. Anonymous. Topic unknown

*rhetoric:
reasoning &
conjecture*

> It is not as though
>   springtime came to some villages
>   and not to others.
> Why then may we see flowers
>   blooming and failing to bloom?

haru no iro no / itari itaranu / sato wa araji / sakeru saka-
zaru / hana no miyuramu

*188. SPRING. Tsurayuki. Composed as a spring
poem

*rhetoric:
reasoning and
conjecture*

*(originally
screen
poem)*

> Observe how the haze
>   of spring spreads its gauzy mantle
>   on Miwa Mountain:
> might flowers be blooming there
>   of which men have no knowledge?

miwayama o / shika mo kakusu ka / harugasumi / hito ni
shirarenu / hana ya sakuramu

i.e. "if a tree falls in a forest with no one there, does it make a sound?"

sub-theme *travel*

*189. SPRING. Sosei. Sent to the Urin-in Prince when the poet went to view flowers in the northern hills[6]

> Today I will press
>   deep into the hills of spring.
> If twilight descends,
>   can it be that I will find
>   no lodging under blossoms?

iza kyō wa / haru no yamabe ni / majirinamu / kurenaba
nage no / hana no kage ka wa

6. The Urin-in Prince, Tsuneyasu (d. 869), was a patron of both Sosei and his father, Archbishop Henjō.

author sequence

subtheme *travel*

*190. SPRING. Sosei. Composed as a spring poem

> How long might my heart
>   wander from this place to that
>   across the meadows?
> Forever and forever,
>   unless the blossoms scatter. →

itsu made ka / nobe ni kokoro no / akugaremu / hana shi
chirazu wa / chiyo mo henubeshi

end of "time" signaled by blossoms

*191. SPRING. Anonymous. Topic unknown

> There will always be flowers
>   bursting into glorious bloom
>   whenever spring comes,
> but whether I shall see them
>   rests with my allotted span.

haru goto ni / hana no sakari wa / arinamedo / aimimu
koto wa / inochi narikeri

"mortality" signaled by blossoms *idea author sequence*

*192. SPRING. Anonymous. Topic unknown

> If all in this world
>   resembled flowers in bloom,
>   then those bygone days

rhetoric: reasoning & conjecture *(actually by Sosei a Monk) made "anonymous" to fit above one better -*

[handwritten: nostalgia]

now forever in the past
would also come back again.

hana no goto / yo no tsune naraba / sugushiteshi / muka-
shi wa mata mo / kaerikinamashi

*193. SPRING. Anonymous. Topic unknown

[handwritten: resisting the passage of time]

Could I give commands
to such breezes as might blow,
I would say to them:
"There is here a single tree
from which you must stay away."

fuku kaze ni / atsuraetsukuru / mono naraba / kono hito-
moto wa / yoki yo to iwamashi

*194. SPRING. Anonymous. Topic unknown

[handwritten: subtheme: love]

7. The breaking of
the branch may be out
of spite toward the
warbler, whose song
reminds the lady that
her lover has not come,
or out of a resigned
determination to enjoy
the blossoms whether
the man comes or not.

Though he does not come—
the one whose call I await—
I have broken off
a branch of the flowering tree
the warbler begged me to spare.[7]

matsu hito mo / konu mono yue ni / uguisu no / nakitsuru
hana o / oritekeru kana

8. A contemporary of
Tsurayuki.

*195. SPRING. Fujiwara no Okikaze [early 10th
century].[8] A poem from the Empress's Contest dur-
ing the reign of Emperor Uda

[handwritten: subtheme: love]
[handwritten: rhetoric: reasoning and conjecture (intellectual)]

Of flowers that bloom
in endless variety,
all are inconstant—
yet which of us cherishes
grievances against springtime?

saku hana wa / chigusa nagara ni / ada naredo / tare ka
wa haru o / uramihatetaru

[handwritten: author sequence]

author sequence

(rhetoric: reasoning and conjecture originally screen poem)

*196. SPRING. Okikaze. Another poem from the Empress's Contest

> That the springtime haze
>   should have seemed many-colored
> was simply because
>   it reflected the blossoms
> on the mountains where it trailed.

harugasumi / iro no chikusa ni / mietsuru wa / tanabiku yama no / hana no kage ka mo

*197. SPRING. Ariwara no Motokata [early 10th century].[9] Another poem from the Empress's Contest

9. A grandson of Narihira.

rhetoric: natural description

> Distant though they be—
> those springtime mountains rising
>   where haze fills the sky—
> the fragrance of flowers in bloom
>   drifts in with the blowing breeze.

kasumi tatsu / haru no yamabe wa / tōkeredo / fukikuru kaze wa / hana no ka zo suru

*198. SPRING. Mitsune. On seeing scattering blossoms

subtheme: love

> The sight of the flowers
>   has worked a change in my heart,
> but I will take care
>   to show nothing in my face—
> lest someone should find it out.[10]

hana mireba / kokoro sae ni zo / utsurikeru / iro ni wa ideji / hito mo koso shire

10. The "someone" perhaps being a lover, who might mimic the blossoms' inconstancy.

thinks he mimics

*199. SPRING. Anonymous. Topic unknown

> Whenever the sound
>   of a warbler's plaintive call

rhetoric: natural description

> draws me to a field,
> I find the breezes blowing
> through blossoms of faded hue.

uguisu no / naku nobe goto ni / kite mireba / utsurou
hana ni / kaze zo fukikeru

Sone no Yoshitada (fl. ca. 980-1000)

Despite appearances to the contrary, the classical tradition did produce
some malcontents. One was Sone no Yoshitada, a low-ranking official about
whom we know little except that—according to old stories, at least[1]—he
had a difficult time getting along with his "betters" at court. There is evi-
dence of an impatient temperament in his poetry as well. For although
his abuses of decorum may seem minor to modern eyes, there is no doubt
that critics of his own day, schooled in Tsurayuki's orthodoxy, must have
been amazed by his colloquial style (poems 200–201), his penchant for dis-
tinctly uncourtly scenes (202), and what must at the time have seemed just
plain bad taste (205). And yet, when he wanted to, he could produce more
conventional work (203, 204) that later critics praised as early examples of
yūgen, or "mystery and depth."

1. The most famous story relates how he was thrown out of a poem contest spon-
sored by Retired Emperor En'yu (959–91; r. 969–84) when he showed up without being
invited.

200. AUTUMN. Topic unknown

Cry, then, cry out loud—
you cricket in your tangle
    of mugwort-timber![1]
The passing of autumn
    is indeed so sad a time.

1. *Yomogi ga soma*, a tangle of mugwort— a vine associated in the poetic imagination with deserted houses— so thick and high that it looks like a stand of timber.

nake ya nake / yomogi ga soma no / kirigirisu / sugiyuku
aki wa / ge ni zo kanashiki

201. LOVE. Topic unknown

What a waste, I thought.
Is anything more precious
    than your own life?
That's the way I once put down
a man in love—just like me.

ajikinashi / waga mi ni masaru / mono ya aru to / koi
seshi hito o / modokishi mono o

202. SUMMER. Topic unknown

A barge of timber
    floating down a logging stream
        makes a sad pillow—
but in summer it's a cool place
    to lie down for the night.

somagawa no / ikada no toko no / ukimakura / natsu wa
suzushiki / fushido narikeri

203. AUTUMN. Topic unknown

Over the paddies
    of Toba in Yamashiro
I look out and see
    where this morning, so faintly,
the autumn wind is blowing.

yamashiro no / tobada no omo o / miwataseba / honoka
ni kesa zo / akikaze wa fuku

204. AUTUMN. Topic unknown

> If not for the mist
>   blocking the way like a fence
>   through this mountain village,
> I could perhaps see the sleeves
>   of people passing far away.

yamazato ni / kiri no magaki no / hedatezu wa / ochikata-
bito no / sode no mitemashi

205. SUMMER. "The End of the Sixth Month"

> This woman of mine,
>   waking up with tangled hair
>   matted down with sweat—
> at noon on a summer day
>   can I think I don't love her?

wagimoko ga / ase ni sobotsuru / neyorigami / natsu no
hiruma wa / utoshi to ya omou

Izumi Shikibu (fl. ca. 970-1030)

Many of the great female poets of the Heian period served as ladies-in-waiting to members of the imperial family. The most famous of these salons was that of Empress Akiko, who included among her ladies Murasaki Shikibu, the author of *Genji monogatari*, as well as Ise no Tayū, Akazome Emon, and the woman known as Izumi Shikibu—perhaps the finest poet of the group. Notorious for her many love affairs even in her own lifetime, Lady Izumi is another in the long line of legendary lovers that began with Ono no Komachi, whose stylistic influence she reflects in poems that are at times passionate and intense, at times brooding and melancholy.

Lady Izumi was a woman of her own time, which often emphasized style over substance—or, more accurately, regarded style *as* substance. Thus she could produce fine descriptions of the seasons (poems 207, 220) and witty statements of aestheticism (218). But she also wrote one masterly poem on religious devotion (206); a touching lament that goes beyond her own personal grief to arrive at a more universal declaration (210); and several moving depictions of what may be termed the motif of the "lonely lady" (208, 216). Her finest work, while using the devices of the day, treats the various subtopics of love—yearning and waiting (212, 214, 219, 221), erotic excitement (213), dejection (217), the loneliness of one left behind (211)—with as much artistry and depth of feeling as any poet before or since.

206. BUDDHISM. A poem sent to His Holiness
Shōku

> From one darkness
>   into another darkness
>   I soon must go.[1]
> Light the long way before me,
> moon on the mountain rim!

1. In other words, "leaving the darkness of this life for the darkness of the next."

kuraki yori / kuraki michi ni zo / irinu beki / haruka ni
terase / yama no ha no tsuki

207. SPRING. Topic unknown

> "The spring haze is late
>   in spreading over the land"—
> that is what I hear
>   in the sound of the mountain stream
>   running beneath the stones.

harugasumi / tatsu ya osoki to / yamagawa no / iwama o
kuguru / oto kikoyu nari

208. SPRING. Topic unknown

> Of no use at all—
> these cherry blossoms blooming
>   around my house.
> For it is the tree's owner
>   people really come to see.

waga yado no / sakura wa kai mo / nakarikeri / aruji kara
koso / hito mo mi ni kure

209. AUTUMN. On "Morning Glories"

> For now, I am here,
> but can one trust the future?
> No, not in a world
>   that teaches us its ways
>   with the morning glory.

ari totemo / tanomu beki ka wa / yo no naka o / shirasuru
mono wa / asagao no hana

210. LAMENTS. Written after the death of her
daughter, Koshikibu no Naishi,[2] when she saw
the child the latter had left behind

2. Also a poet (poem
474); she died in child-
birth in 1025.

> After leaving us,
> she will be feeling sorry—
> but for which the more?
> No doubt for her own child,
> just as I for my child.

todomeokite / tare o aware to / omouran / ko wa masa-
ruran / ko wa masarikeri

211. LOVE. Written after the death of Prince Atsu-
michi[3]

3. One of her lovers,
who died suddenly
in 1007.

> Now that he's gone,
> how I wish I could recall
>   "That time, yes that time!"—
> some unhappy time with him
>   I might wish now to forget.

ima wa tada / so yo sono koto to / omoiidete / wasuru
bakari no / uki koto mogana

212. LOVE. Sent to a man who every night said
that he would come to her but never showed up

> If I live on
>   to wait tonight, then again
>   I will feel this way—
> which makes me wish my life might end
>   before the nightfall comes.

koyoi sae / araba kaku koso / omōeme / kyō kurenu ma
no / inochi to mogana

213. LOVE. Topic unknown

> With not a thought
>   for my black hair's disarray,
> I lay myself down—
>   soon longing for the one whose hands
>   have so often brushed it smooth.

kurokami no / midare mo shirazu / uchifuseba / mazu
kakiyarishi / hito zo koishiki

214. LOVE. Sent to a man who said he would come but then didn't, making her wait in vain all night

> I held off, hoping—
>   and did not even shut tight
>   my door of black pine.
>   Why then am I now seeing dawn
>   end only a winter night?

yasurai ni / maki no to koso wa / sasazarame / ika ni ake-
tsuru / fuyu no yo naran

215. MISCELLANEOUS. Written in Tango Province when she heard a deer cry at night, after learning that Lord Yasumasa would go out hunting the next morning[4]

4.   Fujiwara no Yasu-
masa (d. 1036) was her
husband at the time.

> It makes sense, of course—
>   for why should not the stag
>   be calling so,
>   when one thinks that this night
>   may be the last of its life?

kotowari ya / ikade ka shika no / nakazaran / koyoi bakari
no / inochi to omoeba

216. MISCELLANEOUS. Written when pondering
the uncertainty of the world

> Being a person
>   whom no one will mourn when gone,
> I should perhaps
>   say for myself while still here—
> "Ah, the pity, the pity."

shinobu beki / hito mo naki mi wa / aru ori ni / aware
aware to / ii ya okamashi

217. MISCELLANEOUS. Written upon seeing fireflies
near a purification stream, when she was on a pil-
grimage to Kibune Shrine, after being abandoned
by a man[5]

> So forlorn am I
>   that when I see a firefly
>   out on the marshes,
> it looks like my soul rising
>   from my body in longing.[6]

mono omoeba / sawa no hotaru o / waga mi yori / aku-
gareizuru / tama ka to zo miru

5. Purification
streams were small
streams where pil-
grims did ablutions
before entering a shrine.
Kibune Shrine is located
in the Kurama area of
Kyōto.

6. It was believed that
the soul (*tama*) could
leave the body in times
of stress.

218. WINTER. Topic unknown

> What am I to do
>   if the man I have waited for
>   should come to me now—
> not wanting footsteps to disturb
>   the snow of my garden court?

matsu hito no / ima mo kitaraba / ikaga semu / fumamaku
oshiki / niwa no yuki kana

219. LOVE. Written when she heard hail falling on
the bamboo leaves of her courtyard after waiting
for a visit from a man she expected any moment

> On the bamboo leaves
>   I can hear the hail falling—
> making it harder
>   for me to resign myself
>   to going to bed alone.

take no ha ni / arare furu nari / sarasara ni / hitori wa
nubeki / kokochi koso sene

220. AUTUMN. [Topic unknown]

> If someone would come,
>   I could show, and have him listen—
> evening light shining
>   on bush clover in full bloom
>   as crickets bring on the night.[7]

7. The word for
cricket (*higurashi*) is a
partial homophone of
hikureru, "nightfall."

hito mogana / mise mo kikase mo / hagi no hana / saku
yūkage no / higurashi no koe

221. LOVE. From a hundred-poem sequence

> In my idleness
>   I turn to look at the sky—
> though it's not as if
>   the man I am waiting for
>   will descend from the heavens.

tsurezure to / sora zo miraruru / omou hito / ama kudari-
komu / mono naranaku ni

From 'Songs in Japanese and Chinese'

The great flowering of native literature in the era of *Genji monogatari* and poets such as Izumi Shikibu can make one forget that Chinese poetry still had a place at court. One clear evidence that continental culture still loomed large in the sensibilities of the Japanese is *Wakan rōeishū* (Songs in Japanese and Chinese), an anthology compiled by Fujiwara no Kintō (966–1041) in 1018. Combining as it does lines from the work of famous Chinese poets, other Chinese lines written by such poets as Sugawara no Michizane and Minamoto no Shitagō (911–83), and uta by the major *Kokinshū* poets, all arranged by topics that likewise represent a blend of conventions, Kintō's work is unique, and, most would say, a bit confusing to read. Nevertheless, the anthology is a testament to the way Japanese poets adopted and adapted Chinese topics, imagery, and conceptions to their own practice, while at the same time revealing the snatches of Chinese poetry that those same poets (and later generations) probably knew best. The popularity of Bo Juyi (772–846), in particular, is evidenced by the dominance of his poems in the work and by the number of Japanese poets who seem to have been directly influenced by his conceptions.

SPRING NIGHT

222. Bo Juyi [722–846]

Turning the lamp to the wall, we lament together
    the moon's decline, late into the night;
walking on fallen blossoms, we grieve as one the
    end of spring and youth.

223. Ōshikōchi no Mitsune [d. ca. 925?]

Its effort is vain,
the darkness of this spring night:
true, we cannot see
    the color of the blossoms—
but how can it hide their scent?

haru no yo no / yami wa ayanashi / mume no hana / iro
koso miene / ka ya wa kakururu

THE END OF THE THIRD MONTH

224. Bo Juyi

I try to delay spring—but spring won't stay:
it departs, and men are left alone.
I detest the wind—but the wind won't be still:
it comes up, and the blossoms scatter.

225. Sugawara no Michizane [845–903]

1. This couplet and
the next form a single
poem in Michizane's
personal collection.

One needs no cart or boat to see spring on its way,
but has only to bid farewell to the warbler, to
    fallen flowers.[1]

226. Michizane

Ah, if only the glow of spring knew my thoughts—
tonight it would take lodging in this poet's house!

227. Mitsune

Even at a time
    when we were not lamenting
        its final day,
would it be easy to leave
    the shade of the blossoms?

kyō to nomi / haru o omowanu / toki dani mo / tatsu koto
yasuki / hana no kage ka wa

228. Ki no Tsurayuki [ca. 872–945]

> Now that the blossoms
>   have all fallen at my house
> I can only hope
>   that it will seem like home—
> a place to come to again.

hana mo mina / chirinuru yado wa / yuku haru no / furu-
sato to koso / narinubera nare

Summer Fan

229. Bo Juyi

At the height of summer—snow that never melts;
all year round—wind that never dies.
Autumn cool you can make with your hands;
a moon you can fold up and put in your breast
    pocket.

230. Sugawara no Funtoki [899–981][2]

Before I know it, night's first hour has passed—
while I enjoy the moon before autumn's first wind.

2. A grandson of Sug-
awara no Michizane.

Grasses

231. Yuan Zhen [779–831]

The beauty of Xi Shi's countenance—where is
    it now?

In the tips of the wild grasses, swaying in
    spring wind.[3]

3. Xi Shi was a
famous beauty of the
Spring and Autumn
period (722 B.C.–
481 B.C.) whose charms
so occupied the ruler of
Wu that he neglected
state affairs and lost his
throne.

232. Ōe no Asatsuna [886–957]

The hues of the grasses show forth all around, now
    that the snow has cleared;
the voices of the birds sound out everywhere, now
    that the dew is warm.

A House in the Mountains

4. A poem sent to a
friend in the capital
when Bo was in exile
near Lushan in Jiangxi
Province.

233. Bo Juyi[4]

In the Hall of State it is blossom time—where you
    sit beneath curtains of brocade.
But on Lu Shan it is raining tonight—where I sit
    inside a hut of grass.

234. Ki no Tadana [966–99]

On the mountain road, the sun sets: and what fills
    my ears?
—The woodcutter's song, the herdsman's flute.
At the valley door, birds return home: and what
    blocks my eyes?
—Smoke from bamboos, mist in the pines.

235. Anonymous

A mountain village—
    at times it seems a hard place
        to spend one's time.
But still life is better there
    than back in the vexing world.

yamazato wa / mono no sabishikaru / koto koso are / yo
no uki yori wa / sumiyokarikeri

LOOKING OUT ON A VISTA

236. Bo Juyi

Wind flutters white waves—thousands of flowers;
wild geese dot blue sky—one line of graphs.[5]

5. "Graphs" translates *zi*, "Chinese characters."

237. Minamoto no Shitagō [911–83]

Wild geese slanting away in one line, disappearing
    at a cloud's edge;
flowers remaining in the Second Lunar Month,
    flying over open fields.

238. Fujiwara no Atsushige [late 10th century][6]

Old eyes blur easily when looking into
    lingering rain;
regret for spring is hard to suppress when faced
    with sunset.

6. Scholar at the time of Emperor En'yū (959–91; r. 969–84).

239. Monk Sosei [late 9th century]

Looking far, I see
    willows and cherry blossoms
        mingling together—
making the capital
    into a brocade of spring.

miwataseba / yanagi sakura o / kokimazete / miyako zo
haru no / nishiki narikeri

Remembering Old Times

240. Bo Juyi

7. A metaphorical
term for the world of
the dead.

In the Yellow Earth,[7] who would know me?
And yet, now white-haired, I remember you.
I let the tears of my old age flow at will;
and one falls down on the letters you wrote.

8. Gold Vale was a
famous garden owned
by Shi Chong (A.D.
249–300), an official of
the Jin Dynasty. After
he was executed by im-
perial command, his
garden went to ruin,
becoming a symbol of
vain ambition. South
Tower was a famous
"moon-viewing tower"
in Wuchang during the
Six Dynasties period
(A.D. 222–589).

241. Funtoki

Gold Vale was a place where people got drunk on
    flowers:
now flowers bloom each year, but the host never
    returns.
South Tower was where people delighted in
    the moon:
now the moon comes with autumn—but where are
    the people?[8]

9. A version in *Shūi-
shū* (SIS 991) begins:
*inishie o / sara ni kakeji
to / omoedomo.*

242. Emperor Murakami [926–67; r. 946–67][9]

I vowed to myself
    to think no more of the past—
and yet here I am,
my eyes welling up
    with unexpected tears.

mukashi o ba / kakeji to omoedo / kaku bakari / ayashiku
me ni mo / mitsu namida kana

Love

243. Bo Juyi

In his temporary palace, he looks at the moon—
    pained at heart by its color;

Sugawara no Funtoki. Inscription: "Gold Vale was a place where people got drunk on flowers: / now flowers bloom each year, but the host never returns. / South Tower was where people delighted in the moon: / now the moon comes with autumn—but where are the people?

in night rain, he hears a gibbon—his bowels
  wrenched by its cry.[10]

10. Both this couplet and the next are from Bo's famous "Song of Ever-lasting Sorrow," a narrative poem retelling the grief of the Tang Emperor Xuan Zong after the death of his concubine, Yang Guifei.

244. Bo Juyi

As fireflies dart about in the hall at evening, he sits
  in silent sadness;
even burning to the end of the wick of his lonely
  lamp, he is still unable to sleep.

245. Mitsune

  This love I feel—
  I know not where it will take me,
    or its final end;
  but I know that to meet you
    is all I can think about.

waga koi wa / yukue mo shirazu / hate mo nashi / au o
kagiri to / omou bakari zo

246. Kakinomoto no Hitomaro [fl. ca. 680–700]

> So many nights now
>   have you failed to come to me,
>   despite my pleading,
>   that to give up all hope
>   might be better than waiting.

tanometsutsu / konu yo amata ni / narinureba / mataji to
omou zo / matsu ni masareru

Monk Nōin (988–1050?)

Although the most famous travelers of the Japanese literary tradition are
Saigyō (1118–90) and Bashō (1644–94), they were preceded by a num-
ber of men of similar bent. Chief among these is the man now known as
Nōin, a contemporary of Izumi Shikibu whose work, by contrast, seems
to come from a different world. Like Saigyō and Bashō, Nōin left lay life
at a relatively young age to give himself wholly to religion and travel; and
also like his more famous descendants, he studied poetry for a time under
a prominent poet in the capital—the first such "master-disciple" relation-
ship recorded in the canon, scholars tell us. Beyond this we know only that
he spent much of his life on the road, recording for posterity his impres-
sions of the places he passed, some of them of note as *utamakura*, or places
famous in poetry (as in poems 247, 249).

247. SPRING. A poem sent to someone in the First
Month of the year, when he was living in Tsu Prov-
ince

> Oh that I might share it
>   with a person of true feeling[1]—
> the spring vista
>   on the coast at Naniwa,
> in the land of Tsu.

kokoro aran / hito ni miseba ya / tsu no kuni no / naniwa
watari no / haru no keshiki o

1. By a person of
true feeling the poet
means someone with
a sensibility attuned—
in courtly terms, of
course—to the beauty
the scene affords.

248. WINTER. Written when he was spending the
night in a mountain village, during the Tenth
Month

> In the Godless Month[2]
>   I wake at night and listen
> to what gives voice
>   to a storm on this hillside—
> the sound of falling leaves.

kannazuki / nezame ni kikeba / yamazato no / arashi no
koe wa / ko no ha narikeri

2. Ancient name for
the Tenth Month of
the lunar calendar; de-
rived from an ancient
belief that the gods left
their normal shrines
during that period to
gather at Izumo, site
of an ancient shrine
dedicated to the deity
Ōkuninushi.

249. TRAVEL. Written at Shirakawa Barrier when
he was on a trip to Michinoku

> At the capital
>   it was with the spreading haze
>   that I took to the road.
> Now the autumn wind is blowing
>   at Shirakawa Barrier.

miyako o ba / kasumi to tomo ni / tachishikado / akikaze
zo fuku / shirakawa no seki

250. SPRING. Written when he was in a mountain village

> To a mountain village
> at nightfall on a spring day
> I came and saw this:
> blossoms scattering on echoes
> from the vespers bell.

yamazato no / haru no yūgure / kite mireba / iriai no kane ni / hana zo chirikeru

Minamoto no Toshiyori (1055-1129)

By the mid-eleventh century, poetry, once viewed as an elegant pastime among courtiers and their ladies, was fast becoming a more serious business—a semireligious vocation for a man like Monk Nōin, and a profession for families who owed their place in the scheme of things primarily to their work as critics, judges, and poets. Among these early professionals, Minamoto no Toshiyori (personal name also pronounced Shunrai) was one of the most diligent, and, to the minds of some, the most radical in his tastes. *Kin'yōshū* (Collection of Golden Leaves; 1126), the imperial anthology he compiled at the command of a more orthodox-minded emperor, was rejected in draft form several times; and throughout his life Toshiyori was embroiled in conflicts with critics and artists who were uncomfortable with his eccentricities. What put off poets of his own time, however, attracted poets of the late classical period, particularly Fujiwara no Shunzei (1114–1204) and his son Teika (1162–1241). For them, Toshiyori's imaginative handling of topics (all the poems save 256 below), his rustic imagery (252–53), and his ability to suggest depths of feeling beyond a quiet surface

(253 and 256) made his work a good model of what serious poetry should be about.

251. SUMMER. Written on "Wind on the Water in the Cool of Evening"

> When a breeze blows by,
>   drops of water come across
>   the lotus leaves,
>   cooling me down at evening
>   along with the crickets' cries.

kaze fukeba / hasu no ukiha ni / tama koete / suzushiku narinu / higurashi no koe

252. SUMMER. Written on "Grass on the Fields After Rain"

> In this village too
>   an evening shower must have passed:
>   in the cogon thickets [1]
>   there is not a blade of grass
>   unladen with drops of dew.

1. *Asaji*, a reedlike grass that grows in thickets on meadows and fields.

kono sato mo / yūdachi shikeri / asajifu ni / tsuyu no sugaranu / kusa no ha mo nashi

253. AUTUMN. Written when he received the topic "Miscanthus" [2] for a contest in "searching topics" held by Retired Emperor Horikawa

> Quails are crying out
>   on the banks of Mano Cove
>   as winds from the shore
>   raise waves in the miscanthus
>   on an evening in autumn.

2. Miscanthus translates *obana*, a plant resembling pampas grass, with long stalks topped with white plumes in autumn. In "searching topics" contests, poets chose topics at random and composed extemporaneously. Horikawa (1079–1107) reigned from 1086 till his death.

uzura naku / mano no irie no / hamakaze ni / obana nami yoru / aki no yūgure

254. MISCELLANEOUS. A lament from among the
poems of a hundred-poem sequence

> This world of ours—
>   it comes right along with me
>   just like a shadow:
>   I try to cast it from my thoughts
>   but it will not stay away.

yo no naka wa / ukimi ni soeru / kage nare ya / omoi
sutsuredo / hanarezarikeri

255. SUMMER. Topic unknown

> Ah, how it pains me
>   to see you burn so demurely,
>   you glowing fireflies!
>   It should make one sob out loud—
>   life in this world of ours.

aware ni mo / misao ni moyuru / hotaru kana / koe tatetsu
beki / kono yo to omou ni

3. *Kinuta,* a wooden
mallet and block used
to full cloth in the
autumn. In poetry, the
sound of fulling was
associated with the
loneliness of a woman
left waiting for a travel-
ing husband.

256. AUTUMN. ["Fulling Block"] [3]

> When the wind passes
>   in the pines, autumn already
>   seems lonely enough—
>   and then a fulling block echoes
>   through Tamakawa Village.

matsukaze no / oto dani aki wa / sabishiki ni / koromo
utsu nari / tamakawa no sato

From 'The Journal of Lady Ukyō Daibu'

For courtiers, poetry was as much a medium of self-expression as one of artistic expression. Nowhere is this more clear than in the genre of poetic diaries and memoirs, through which writers such as Murasaki Shikibu and Izumi Shikibu recorded bits and pieces of their lives, along with some of their finest poetry.

This is also true of a later and longer poetic memoir written by the woman known as Kenreimon-in Ukyō no Daibu—a lady-in-waiting to the Empress Tokuko (1157–1213), known later as Kenreimon-in.[1] One difference between Lady Daibu and earlier diarists, however, is that she lived not during the court's apex but during its decline—the Gempei Wars of 1180–85, immortalized in the classic *Heike monogatari* (The Tale of the Heike; early 13th century). Not surprisingly, these events form the background of her most moving scenes. The following passage, from the 1180's, is a case in point. In it, through prose that provides narrative continuity while also serving its chief function of preparing the reader for the poetry, she mourns the loss of her lover, the courtier-warrior Taira no Sukemori (1161?–1185),[2] who died in the Gempei Wars; gives an account of a visit to her former benefactor, Kenreimon-in; and records a short visit to Mount Hiei undertaken—unsuccessfully—to help her forget. The melancholy tone of the piece supports the work's main theme: the disappointment in the present that assaults a sensibility focused on the past—an appropriate theme with which to end the Classical Age.

1. A daughter of the great warrior Taira no Kiyomori (1118–81) who became consort to Emperor Takakura (1161–81; r. 1168–80) and mother of the boy emperor Antoku (1178–85; 1180–83). Antoku died in the sea at Dan no Ura during the last great battle between the Taira (Heike) and Minamoto (Genji) troops, carried into the waves by his grandmother. Kenreimon-in jumped into the sea too but was fished from the waves by a Minamoto warrior.

2. A grandson of Taira no Kiyomori.

257–70. From Part 4, poems 238–51

[1] Once as I was on my way somewhere else, I passed the site of his residence, which itself had gone to smoke long before.[1] Only the foundation stones remained, with grass growing thick around them and autumn flowers blooming here and there, dew dripping from their leaves; and the insect cries rising in confused chorus made me sad. Since I could not simply pass the place by, I stopped my carriage and took a moment to survey the scene, wondering when it would all end.

[257]   So now once again
            I look back with heavy heart
               on what was his home—
         knowing how senseless it is
               for my thoughts to linger here.

mata sara ni / uki furusato o / kaerimite / kokoro todo-
muru / koto mo hakanashi

These same thoughts quite occupied my mind, refusing to be cleared away—making me feel like a person who would like to die, but cannot. Un-happiness weighed me down with feelings beyond description.

[258]   Yes, I know we say
            the world is all uncertainty—
               but in the past
         no one ever knew despair
               so intense as mine.

sadamenaki / yo to wa iedomo / kaku bakari / uki tameshi
koso / mata nakarikere

* * *

[2] I had heard nothing of the Retired Empress ex-cept that she was residing in Ōhara, and I felt that I could not go see her without the intercession of

1. The reference is to Sukemori's house. Before abandoning the capital to Mina-moto troops, the Taira put the torch to their own homes.

a proper acquaintance.[2] But in the end I did go off for a visit, taking only my deep regard for her as go-between.

Well before my arrival, my tears began, called up by the scene along the mountain road as I approached. And then to see her hut,[3] her way of life there, everything around—it was more than I could look upon! Even one who had not known her former aspect could not have been pleased with such a picture; for one such as I it all seemed somewhere between dream and reality. The winds blowing from the late autumn hills down through the tops of the trees, the sound of water from a bamboo pipe, the call of a deer, the voices of insects—these are the same anywhere; but here they inspired a special sadness. In the past she had been surrounded by the "brocade of spring" in the capital,[4] with over sixty ladies attending upon her; now only three or four women were present, all of them looking so utterly changed in their ink-black attire that I could not even recognize them.[5] All we could find to say to each other was, "What must be, must be!," before the tears came, choking our voices so that we could say no more.

[259]   Is *now* the dream?
         Or was *long ago* the dream?
         I wander on, lost—
         unable to convince myself
              that this is reality.

ima ya yume / mukashi ya yume to / mayowarete / ika ni omoedo / utsutsu to zo naki

[260]   The moon in the clouds
             that I used to gaze up at
                 so long ago:
         how sad to see its light
             hidden in mountain shadows.

2. After the defeat of her family in 1185, Kenreimon-in had moved into a small house in the precincts of the Jakkō-in, in the Ōhara area, northeast of the capital. By a proper acquaintance, Lady Daibu may mean someone from the Minamoto forces then in control of the capital.

3. The word used is *iori*, generally translated "hut." *Heike monogatari* describes her dwelling as a small affair—a sleeping room and a chapel, although surely not so rustic as the word hut suggests.

4. An allusion to poem 239, by Monk Sosei.

5. The women in Kenreimon-in's small entourage had taken the tonsure along with their lady.

ōgimishi / mukashi no kumo no / ue no tsuki / kakaru
miyama no / kage zo kanashiki

Could this be the same person, I wondered,
whose visage once had not lost in comparison to
the glow of the blossoms or the light of the moon?
Gazing at her, I asked myself why I should return
to the capital, where I would surely make no good
memories. I was sick at heart.

[261]   You, my aching heart
               that I leave behind me now
                  in the deep mountains—
            become my guide to a place
               where I can live in peace.

yama fukaku / todomeokitsuru / waga kokoro / yagate
sumu beki / shirube to o nare

Suddenly everything around me made me think
of one thing only—to no longer be part of the
world.[6]

[262]   Overcome by grief,
            I go so far as to wish
               to be no longer—
            and surprise even myself
               with the degree of my grief.

nagekiwabi / waga nakaramashi to / omou made no / mi
zo warenagara / kanashikarikeru

* * *

[3] With nowhere to find comfort, I traveled to
a place that held no memories, and while there
thought of taking a long journey. But all this did
was to bring back thoughts of the past.[7]

[263]   It is in my power
               to let my heart guide the way
                  back along that road;

6. Probably meaning
to leave the lay world
and become a nun.

7. Probably a refer-
ence to the Taira's de-
parture from the capi-
tal in the fall of 1183.

but ah, how my sadness returns
    when I think of going away!

kaeru beki / michi wa kokoro ni / makasete mo / tabi-
datsu hodo wa / nao aware nari

[264]   "If I feel regret
      upon leaving the capital
        I have come to hate,"
    I reason, and realize—
    "How much more, then, must he . . ."[8]

8. That is, "How
much more sad Suke-
mori must have been
when he left the capi-
tal, never to return."

miyako o ba / itoite mo mata / nagori aru o / mashite to
mono o / omoiidetsuru

    My destination was near Sakamoto on Mount
Hiei. Cold clouds darkened the sky, and snow was
falling, making me feel far removed from the capi-
tal indeed. "What memories could such a place
hold?" I thought dejectedly. But as the hour grew
late, I heard calls from a flock of wild geese passing
overhead and, moved by that sound, found my eyes
welling up with tears.

[265]   Thinking my sadness
      to come from my surroundings,
        I fled to this place—
    to hear wild geese crying out,
    "All lodgings are the same."[9]

9. The poem involves
a pun on the word *kari*,
meaning both "wild
geese" and "tempo-
rary."

uki koto wa / tokorogara ka to / nogaruredo / izuku mo
kari no / yado to kikoyuru

    I had come past only one barrier-gate,[10] no dis-
tance at all. But the sound of the storm winds echo-
ing in the trees sounded somehow more fierce than
in the capital.

10. The Ōsaka Bar-
rier, which she would
have passed on her way
to Sakamoto.

[266]   There is just one gate
      between me and the capital—
        not great banks of clouds.

Yet it sounds different somehow—
that rush of mountain wind.

seki koete / iku kumoi made / hedatenedo / miyako ni wa
ninu / yamaoroshi kana

[4] I went about my devotions most earnestly,
praying only for the welfare in the next world of
the one I loved. But it was no good; I could do
nothing against my memories. So I got up and
looked outside, where I saw snow lying thick on
a wild orange tree, which made me think of the
time—I don't recall exactly when—that he had
come to me on a snowy morning at the palace,
his robes wrinkled after guard duty, offering me a
branch from a similar tree still covered with snow.
"Why," I asked, "did you take a sprig from *that*
tree?"[11] He responded by saying that he had devel-
oped an attachment for it because he so often stood
near it. Now it all came back to me, making me
more sad than I can say.

11.   As an officer in
the Imperial Body-
guards, Sukemori stood
guard near flowering
trees below the steps
into the Shishinden,
main building of the
emperor's residential
compound.

[267]   In the royal courts
              stands the wild orange tree
                    where he once stood.
              Does it yearn for him as do I—
              for one gone as melting snow?

tachinareshi / mikaki no uchi no / tachibana mo / yuki to
kienishi / hito ya kouramu

These were my first thoughts. The tree was all
leaves and no fruit, and of a lonely color.

[268]   You, orange tree—
              please answer me this question:
              the Fifth Month has passed,
              but might you still have the scent
              of the sleeves he wore long ago?[12]

12.   An allusion to
poem 138, anonymous.

koto towamu / satsuki narade mo / tachibana ni / mukashi
no sode no / ka wa nokoru ya to

The wind was blowing, making a bird-scarer
rattle with a sound that left me feeling forlorn.

[269]　Hearing the echo
　　　of a bird-scarer announcing
　　　　　"He is here no more," [13]
　　　I am saddened by the loss
　　　　　of the world that went before.

arishi yo ni / arazu naruko no / oto kikeba / suginishi
koto zo / itodo kanashiki

Gazing off into the distance toward the direc-
tion of the capital, I felt that life there was now far
away, as far as the clouds.

[270]　My heart drifting
　　　aimlessly, with unsure thoughts,
　　　　　I gaze at the sky—
　　　at clouds that give me no hint
　　　　　that there is an end in sight.

waga kokoro / ukitaru mama ni / nagamureba / izuku o
kumo no / hate to shi mo nashi

13.　The poem in-
volves a pun on *naru*,
"to sound" and "to
become."

The
Early Medieval Age

When Fujiwara dominance of court politics ended in the early 1100's, yielding to internecine strife among the warrior clans upon whom the aristocracy had long depended for military might, cultural changes were one inevitable result. Estates broke up under pressure from provincial warlords, staying the flow of income into noble coffers; the free flow of commerce was frequently interrupted; open violence occurred in the streets of the capital. No wonder that devout Buddhists saw in all of this a sign of the End of the Law, a period of protracted degeneracy predicted by the Buddhist sutras.

In fact, the Minamoto family, which took direct control of government through the shogunate after its triumph over the Taira in 1185, restored peace and stability to the land. But still the age seemed a dark one to the people of Kyōto. Court institutions lost power and importance; the old Buddhist establishments lost ground to popular sects; iconoclastic monks predicted dire trouble ahead. Finally, the Mongol invasions of the late thirteenth century threatened the state as never before.

In the midst of this, the court bided its time, hoping for the eventual restoration of its powers and concentrating its efforts and reduced *resources on the arts. The shogun, ruling from Kamakura through stewards and policemen placed on the land in all the provinces, encouraged this development, providing the old families with incomes adequate for their lifestyle yet not substantial enough to let them entertain thoughts of violence against the new order.*

Some courtiers were not satisfied with their new world; but most saw their situation as inescapable and approached the arts with a new sense of devotion inspired by the religious awakening of the day and the knowledge that they were the preservers of a glorious past. In so doing, they brought about a renaissance that fundamentally changed the poetic tradition they had inherited.

In a way, this is only to say that these courtiers of the Early Medieval Age (1185–1333) were more aware of the fragility of their traditions than their forebears had been. They approached their work in the spirit of a revival, albeit one that transcended the received wisdom of the past. Thus they too held poetry contests, but they took them more seriously—viewing them not just as elegant pastimes but as important events in a way of life that had become more precious because more threatened; they too compiled imperial anthologies—most prominently Shin kokinshū (New Kokinshū; 1205)—but with perhaps a greater sense of mission.

Often the prime movers in these activities were the emperors themselves, assisted by courtiers, many of them high-ranking, who became important patrons as well as artists. But once again it is poets of middling or lower rank—in this case particularly Fujiwara no Shunzei (1114–1204), Saigyō (1118–90), and Teika (1162–1241)—who deserve most credit for the developments of the day. They were the ones who treated their art with the highest seriousness; they were the ones who created a critical vocabulary to analyze the work both of past ages and of their own in an attempt to move beyond the limits of the Kokin age and create new approaches and new ideals for old forms. In the process, they also expanded the audience for poetry, adding some higher-ranking warriors and many priests of all persuasions to the body of their supporters and colleagues.

The chief medium of all these poets, regardless of their backgrounds, remained the uta, which was still memorialized in imperial anthologies. But they also wrote journals and travel records, kept personal anthologies, recorded poetry contests with judgments and words of criticism, penned critical treatises, and even came up with new subgenres such as the hundred-poem sequence (hyakushu uta). Finally, they began to realize the potential of linked verse (renga), a genre that had until that time been nothing more than a parlor game.

One inevitable by-product of their devotion as artists was factional strife, a feature that would continue to disrupt the poetic world until modern times. Sometimes the conflicts had their source in nothing more than petty jealousies and antagonisms; but more often they arose over genuine artistic issues ranging from acceptable diction to the limits of proper allusion. The squabbles themselves may seem of little consequence to later readers, but they are a testament to the seriousness these poets brought to their craft.

Fujiwara no Shunzei (1114-1204)

It is no more easy to decide who deserves attention as the first great poet of the Early Medieval Age than it is to say when that age actually began. But certainly Fujiwara no Shunzei, who in his ninety-one years did as much as any contemporary to rethink the purposes of poetry and remake its institutions, is one acceptable choice. Born into a minor branch of the Fujiwara family called the Mikohidari house, Shunzei (also read as Toshinari) led the typical courtier's life, serving in humble posts. Eventually, by his mid-thirties, he was named a provincial governor and achieved the third rank.

In 1176, stricken with a severe illness, he took the tonsure as a lay monk. But well before that time he had already dedicated himself to a way that he saw as entirely compatible with a religious temperament—the Way of Poetry. Studying under Fujiwara no Mototoshi (1060–1142), the conservative rival of Minamoto no Toshiyori (1055–1129), he developed a name for himself early on as both poet and critic. By the time of his death he enjoyed the patronage of the imperial family in a way never granted to one of his rank before, and was accepted as the doyen of a whole generation of younger poets—in this too setting a pattern for poets to come, who would see themselves not only as creative artists but as scholars and teachers. His artistic descendants came to venerate him as an almost religious figure, represented in one famous text as an old man in an old robe bent over his work late at night, reciting verses and experiencing to the utmost the emotional and spiritual depths of his vocation.[1]

Shunzei was as important a critic as he was a poet, serving as judge at numerous poetry contests and acting as compiler of *Senzaishū* (Collection of a Thousand Years; 1188), the seventh of the imperial anthologies. It was he, for instance, who did much toward furthering the critical reevaluation of *Kokinshū*, in which he saw virtues—namely intellectual brilliance and wittiness[2]—but also limitations as a model for a later and more sober age. In this he developed a credo of memorable succinctness: "Old words, with

1. The description is recorded by Shinkei (1406–75) in his *Sasamegoto* (Whisperings; 1463—NKBT, 66: 147).

2. He praises a number of *Kokinshū* poems, including KKS 2, by Tsurayuki (poem 163), for being *okashi*, "amusing or witty" (NKBZ, 50: 374).

new feeling." This was a basically conservative philosophy, but one that recognized the need to do more than simply mimic the past. Nor did his contributions stop there, for it was also he who enjoined the reading of *Genji monogatari* as a necessary part of any poet's training in the tradition of *aware*—the sort of sad, understated beauty that only an educated sensibility could detect. Finally, it was in Shunzei's critical writings—consisting of one major treatise, a few letters, and the judgments he wrote for poetry contests—that many of the ideals of medieval literary aesthetics were first articulated. This is true particularly for the word *yūgen*, which for him meant an aura of mystery, allusiveness, and depth of symbolic meaning of the sort seen earlier in some of Narihira's work[3] or in Shunzei's own famous poem on the quails crying at Fukakusa (see poem 273, below). Other ideals he contributed greatly to defining are *yojō* (overtones usually arising from allusions to works of the past or from connotations surrounding courtly words and images), *sabi* (an effect of loneliness that often goes hand in hand with *yūgen*, especially in monochromatic descriptions of nature), and *en* (rich, romantic beauty often associated with the atmosphere of the court and its traditions).

Even at his most forthcoming, however, Shunzei is a rather reticent critic—which makes one glad that he also left a corpus of poems, in which we see many of his ideals illustrated. A number of poems show that he is comfortable in all settings, public (see 276–77, 280, 287) or private (282, 288), and that he can use natural imagery for the most courtly of statements (286, in particular), themes (276), or devices (290)—or by contrast use it to produce more straightforward descriptions of profound beauty (278–79). Likewise we find in his work all tones, from the playful and witty (275, 284) to the wistful and somber (277, 287). And, although it would be a mistake to try to force any one of his poems into the definition of ideals he aimed for in a general way, some of his work goes remarkably far in presenting the effects of *yūgen* (279, 287, 289) and *sabi* (278, 282) in particular. Finally, some of his poems show his skillful use of *honkadori*, a technique in which the writer alludes to a famous poem from the past in order to add depth and overtones to his own creation (see 273, 277).

3. In addition to KKS 747, by Narihira (poem 115), he mentions KKS 404, by Tsurayuki (poem 171).

271. SPRING. [From a hundred-poem sequence composed in 1134]

The sound of the wind,
the sight of the rocky crags,

the incoming waves—
all are rough, like this ocean shore;
but what of you, cherry tree?

kaze no oto mo / iwa no keshiki mo / yoru nami mo /
araki isobe ni / ika ni sakura zo

272. LAMENTS. [From a hundred-poem sequence]

How is it that ducks
    are able to stay afloat
        out on the water,
    while I feel myself sinking
        even here on the land?

mizu no ue ni / ikade ka oshi no / ukaburan / kuga ni dani
koso / mi wa shizuminure

273. AUTUMN. Written as an autumn poem for a
hundred-poem sequence

Daylight fades away
    and the autumn wind on the fields
        pierces to the soul:
    a quail cries from the deep grass
        of Fukakusa Village.[1]

1. An allusion to
poems 120–21, by
Narihira.

yū sareba / nobe no akikaze / mi ni shimite / uzura naku
nari / fukakusa no sato

274. WINTER. Written as an autumn poem, when
he presented a hundred-poem sequence

Out on the ice pack
    that glitters with cold moonlight,
hail is falling,
    shattering my heart
        at Tamakawa Village.

tsuki sayuru / kōri no ue ni / arare furi / kokoro kuda-
kuru / tamakawa no sato

275. LOVE. A poem on "Love," written when there
was a contest at the home of the Regent-Minister
of the Right[2]

> Just to meet with her
>   I would exchange this body
>   for my next, I thought—
> but O how sad I would be
>   the time we were worlds apart![3]

au koto wa / mi o kaete to mo / matsu beki o / yoyo o
hedaten / hodo zo kanashiki

276. SPRING. Written for a five-poem sequence at
the house of the Regent-Chancellor[4]

> Will I see this again?
> A hunt for cherry blossoms
>   on Katano Moor—
> petals of snow scattering
>   in the first faint light of dawn.

mata ya mimu / katano no mino no / sakuragari / hana no
yuki chiru / haru no akebono

277. SUMMER. A poem on the topic "Cuckoo,"
written for a hundred-poem sequence requested by
the Lay Monk–Former Regent when he was Minis-
ter of the Right[5]

> Musing on the past,
> I sit in my hut of grass
>   amidst night showers.
> Must you add my tears to the rain,
> you cuckoo of the mountain?[6]

2. Fujiwara no [Kujō] Kanezane (1149–1207).

3. That is, "worlds apart" in the chain of rebirth.

4. Fujiwara no [Go-Kyōgoku] Yoshitsune (1169–1206).

5. Kanezane.

6. An allusion to a poem by Bo Juyi (772–846; poem 233).

mukashi omou / kusa no iori no / yoru no ame ni / namida
na soe so / yamahototogisu

278. AUTUMN. Written as part of a hundred-poem sequence

> From beneath the pines
> of the Fushimi Hills
> I look out afar—
> as dawn breaks over paddies
> where blows the autumn wind.

fushimiyama / matsu no kage yori / miwataseba / akuru ta
no mo ni / akikaze zo fuku

279. WINTER. Topic unknown

> Freezing in one place,
> breaking up in another,
> the mountain river
> is choked between great boulders—
> a voice in the light of dawn.

katsu kōri / katsu wa kudakuru / yamakawa no / iwama
ni musubu / akatsuki no koe

280. WINTER. Among poems presented to Cloistered Prince Shukaku as a fifty-poem sequence[7]

> After a snowfall,
> the *sakaki*[8] on the peak
> are covered over:
> and polished by the moonlight—
> Kagu's Heavenly Hill.

yuki fureba / mine no masakaki / uzumorete / tsuki ni
migakeru / ama no kaguyama

7. A son of Retired Emperor Go-Shirakawa (1127–92; r. 1155–58); d. 1202.

8. The *sakaki* is an evergreen used as a sacred emblem in Shinto rites.

281. WINTER. Written for *The Poem Contest in Fifteen-hundred Rounds*[9]

> Last day of the year:
>   as always, I think sadly—
>   the last one for me;
>   but then here I am this year
>   greeting the day once again.

kyō goto ni / kyō ya kagiri to / oshimedomo / mata mo
kotoshi ni / ainikeru ka na

9. A large contest sponsored by Retired Emperor Go-Toba (1180–1239; r. 1184–98) in 1201–2.

282. LAMENTS. Written in the autumn, after Teika's mother had passed on and he [Shunzei] went to visit her grave, staying that night in a nearby temple[10]

> I come so seldom,
>   and yet how sad in the night
>   sounds the wind in the pines.
>   And she, there beneath the moss—
>   does she too hear it, endlessly?

mare ni kuru / yowa mo kanashiki / matsukaze o / taezu
ya koke no / shita ni kikuramu

10. Teika's mother (Shunzei's wife) was Bifuku Mon-in no Kaga (d.1193).

283. LOVE. Sent to a woman on a rainy day

> Overcome by love,
> I gazed out upon the sky
>   above where you dwell—
> and saw the haze parted there
>   by a shower of spring rain.

omou amari / sonata no sora o / nagamureba / kasumi o
wakete / harusame zo furu

284. LOVE. Sent to a woman

> Enough: so be it!
> But at least promise to meet me
>   in the next world—

for your coldness hurts me so
        that I may not last too long.

yoshi saraba / nochi no yo to dani / tanomeoke / tsurasa
ni taenu / mi to mo koso nare

285. LOVE. From *The Poem Contest in Fifteen-hundred Rounds*

A pitiful state!
I napped, and met you in a dream
        a fleeting moment—
a memory that endures,
overpowering my mind.

aware nari / utatane ni nomi / mishi yume no / nagaki
omoi ni / musubōrenan

286. MISCELLANEOUS. Written for *The Hundred-poem Sequences of the Minister of the Right*[11]

The radiant moon
        circles on its course above,
beyond the clouds—
but here below it is blossoms
        that provide our world with light.

teru tsuki mo / kumo no yoso ni zo / yukimeguru / hana-
zoko no yo no / hikari narikeru

11. Kanezane.

287. MISCELLANEOUS. From *The Poem Contest in Fifteen-hundred Rounds*

The withered sight
        of my garden in autumn
            was forlorn enough—
but more so in this evening dew,
so ready to fade away.

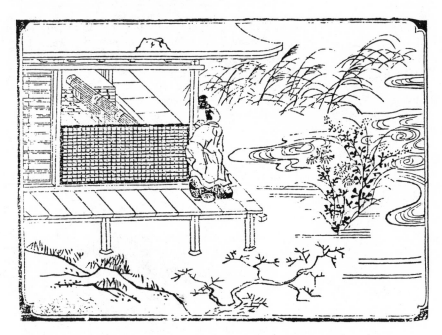

"The withered sight / of my garden in autumn / was forlorn enough— / but more so in this evening dew, / so ready to fade away." (SKKS 1561 *by Fujiwara no Shunzei*)

arewataru / aki no niwa koso / aware nare / mashite
kienan / tsuyu no yūgure

288. MISCELLANEOUS. Written when he was look-
ing at the poems of people long ago, choosing
poems for *Senzaishū*[12]

> Far in the future,
>   will someone remember me
>   with a tender heart—
>   sharing with me the habit
>   of musing on the past?

yukusue wa / ware o mo shinobu / hito ya aramu / muka-
shi o omou / kokoronarai ni

12. Collection of
a Thousand Years.
Seventh of the imperial
anthologies, compiled
by Shunzei in 1188.

289. MISCELLANEOUS. On the topic "Imperma-
nence" from a hundred-poem sequence presented
to Retired Emperor Sutoku [13]

My mind trailing on
    after thoughts of this world of ours,
I gazed out, and saw
    off in the empty sky—
a white cloud fading away.

yo no naka o / omoi tsuranete / nagamureba / munashiki
sora ni / kiyuru shirakumo

290. SPRING. Written on the topic "Going After
Blossoms in the Distance," when Retired Emperor
Sutoku was on a visit to the Konoe Mansion

How many times now
    have I crossed over hill crests
with the image
    of blossoms leading me on—
toward nothing but white clouds?

omokage ni / hana no sugata o / sakidatete / ikue
koekinu / mine no shirakumo

Monk Saigyō (1118-1190)

For most of his life Fujiwara no Shunzei shared his status as chief arbiter of poetic affairs with Saigyō, a monk who spent much of his time away from the society of the capital but still managed to maintain a place equal to that of his great friend among the elite literary circles of the age. On the surface, the two men could not have been more different. Shunzei came from a great court family, Saigyō from a low-ranking military clan. Shunzei was a man of the mind and intellect; though Saigyō was that too, he was also a man of physical prowess who learned swordsmanship and archery as a youth and maintained a strong physique through his many years on the road as a traveling ascetic. But in other important ways the two were very much alike, especially in their dedication to poetry as a way of religious devotion.

Saigyō made his feelings about Buddhism known early in life when, at age twenty-two, he took the tonsure as a priest of the Shingon sect. His precise motivations in this act are not known; whatever his reasons, he never abandoned them in a long life of activity as both a monk and a poet. At various times he lived on Mount Kōya, in the hills of Yoshino, and at other temples. And his many travels, whatever their contributions to his poetic opus, were generally undertaken as pilgrimages as well.

Scholars identify five major periods in Saigyō's life—the first covering the years before he took the tonsure in 1140; the second his life in the capital until 1147, when he took his first trip to the far north; the third from that date until he took up residence at Mount Kōya again in 1168 after a number of years on the road; and the fourth and fifth dividing up his final three decades, two of them spent at Mount Kōya and in travel and the final one in Ise and again on pilgrimage. Since the various periods, except for the first, of which we have little record, do not reflect great differences in his poetry or his lifestyle, however, they can actually work to confuse the picture of what was a relatively simple existence. Throughout his life, he maintained active contact with Shunzei and others in the capital. Despite his monkish attire, he seems to have been a personable man who had many friends, among both the humble and the mighty.

One effect of Saigyō's lifestyle was to create a monkish persona in his poetry that sometimes obscures his great skill and sophistication as an artist. Indeed, his consistent adoption of this guise of the "reluctant recluse" who has left the world but still finds himself drawn by it can be seen as one of Saigyō's major artistic accomplishments. For this carefree spirit, unfettered by the usual social obligations (poems 294, 309), given to the solitary life (318) yet still somehow yearning for the companionship of other men (303, 307), still somehow attached to the experience of beauty (296–97), is a wonderful tool with which to create irony, pathos, and sometimes humor, as well as a way to articulate the major religious themes that concerned him: a strong awareness of the frailty of human existence, of the constant change that is the way of the universe, and of man's paradoxical attraction to his own frail, changeable existence through his perception of natural beauty.

The pose, though, is still a pose; it cannot account for all of his work. For Saigyō uses other personae too, writing convincing love poetry (304–5, 319, 321) and descriptive nature poetry that show a thorough knowledge of the proper public styles (301, 313, 320). And his sometimes rustic manner notwithstanding, he knows the canon well enough to add depth to his scenes through the deft use of allusive variation (302, 321). Thus no one who knows his work well is surprised to learn that his own favorite among his poems (308) makes expert use of one of the most self-consciously artistic of devices—the *jo*, or preface. In this way, as in many others, Saigyō announces himself as a participant in the larger court tradition.

Shunzei saw these diverse features of Saigyō's work and gave him high praise for all of the poems he submitted for a mock poem contest in 1187.[1] Shunzei lauds one poem for its "elegant, lofty appearance" (*uruwashiku taketakaku miyu*; see poem 291), a pair for their "effect of refined beauty" (*sugata yū nari*; 292 and poem 500 in *One Hundred Poems by One Hundred Poets*), and several more for their "wit and charm" (*okashisa*; 293–94, 300). He also uses the terms *yūgen*, or "mystery and depth," several times (to describe the "feeling" of 297, and the "style" of 302) and *sabi*, or "loneliness" as well (to describe both the overall "effect" and the "feeling" of 299).

Perhaps once again because of his identity as a traveling monk, it is with this last ideal—the quality of "loneliness" that resonates through so many of his poems—that Saigyō is still most widely associated. But even here care needs to be taken not to trivialize his art. Realizing this, Shunzei, in his comment on Saigyō's famous poem stating his desire "to die in springtime,

---

1. The full text of the contest, titled *Mimosusogawa uta-awase* (The Mimosuso River Poem Contest), may be found in SKT 5.

beneath the blossoms" (311), went so far as to warn young poets away from the spare style of his colleague's mature work:

[This poem is] without the least outward beauty [*uruwashiki sugata ni wa arazu*], and yet for the style it represents, its parts match to great effect. Yet should one who has not gone far along the Way try to compose in this manner, he will not be up to it. This is something that can be achieved only after the poet has arrived [at the highest level].[2]

Since Saigyō wrote his death poem sometime before the age of fifty, it would appear that he "arrived" early. When he died—beneath the full moon and surrounded by blossoms in the spring of 1190, as his poem had requested—he left a legacy that has made him the most renowned of Japanese poets, rivaled in the minds of Japanese readers only by Bashō, who looked to him as a mentor in life and in art.

2. *Mimosusogawa uta-awase* 13.

291. SPRING. Written on "Blossoms"

> All around now
> the blossoms on the cherry trees
> are in their full bloom—
> each and every mountain ridge
> draped with clouds of white.

oshinabete / hana no sakari ni / narinikeri / yama no ha
goto ni / kakaru shirakumo

292. LOVE. Topic unknown

> I could not have known:
> that to the moonlight I saw
> far off in the clouds
> I would be giving my sleeves
> as lodging for the night.[1]

shirazariki / kumoi no yoso ni / mishi tsuki no / kage o
tamoto ni / yadosu beshi to wa

1. The moon was said to "take lodging" in dew, tears, and other things that reflect its light.

293. SPRING. Topic unknown

This morning, the ice
    that bound the rocks together
        will begin to melt—
water down beneath the moss
    seeking a pathway away.

iwama tojishi / kōri no kesa wa / tokesomete / koke no
shitamizu / michi motomuramu

294. SPRING. Written on "Blossoms"

The pathway I marked
    when last year I made my way
        into Yoshino—
I abandon now to visit
    blossoms I have not yet seen.

yoshinoyama / kozo no shiori no / michi kaete / mada
minu kata no / hana o tazunen

295. SPRING. Topic unknown

On a roadside
    next to a clear flowing stream
in a willow's shade
    I stopped—for a moment, I thought—
but ended up staying on[2]

michinobe ni / shimizu nagaruru / yanagikage / shibashi
tote koso / tachidomaritsure

296. AUTUMN. Topic unknown

It creates a heart
    even in those among us
who think of themselves
    as indifferent to all things[3]—
this first wind of autumn.

2. Some scholars suggest that this poem was written for the decoration of a standing screen.

3. Buddhist monks supposedly severed all connections to the world.

oshinabete / mono o omowanu / hito ni sae / kokoro o
tsukuru / aki no hatsukaze

297. AUTUMN. Topic unknown

> Even one who claims
>   to no longer have a heart[4]
>   feels this sad beauty:
>   snipes flying up from a marsh
>   on an evening in autumn.

kokoro naki / mi ni mo aware wa / shirarekeri / shigi
tatsu sawa no / aki no yūgure

4. *Kokoro naki mi*; a
monk who should no
longer feel any attach-
ment to the world.

298. AUTUMN. Topic unknown

> Near my little hut
>   out in the mountain paddies
>   a stag calls out,
>   startling me so that I jump—
>   and startle him in turn!

oyamada no / io chikaku naku / shika no ne ni / odoro-
kasarete / odorokasu kana

299. AUTUMN. Topic unknown

> Those crickets calling
>   in the chill air of deep night:
>   with autumn's advance
>   they must be failing—voices
>   sounding ever farther away.

kirigirisu / yosamu ni aki no / naru mama ni / yowaru ka
koe no / tōzakariyuku

300. WINTER. Topic unknown

> The clouds on the peak
>   that made me wait for the moon

have all cleared away.
It must have a kindly heart,
this first shower of winter!

tsuki o matsu / takane no kumo wa / harenikeri / kokoro
aru beki / hatsushigure kana

301. WINTER. Topic unknown

After the leaves fall
   in the village at the foot
      of Ogura Peak,
one can see through the branches
   the moon shining in the clear.

ogurayama / fumoto no sato ni / konoha chireba / kozue
ni haruru / tsuki o miru kana

302. WINTER. Topic unknown

That spring long ago
   at Naniwa in Tsu—
was it all a dream?
Now only dead leaves on the reeds
   rustle in the passing wind.[5]

5. An allusion to
poem 247, by Monk
Nōin.

tsu no kuni no / naniwa no haru wa / yume nare ya / ashi
no kareha ni / kaze wataru nari

303. WINTER. Topic unknown

Ah, such loneliness—
   if there were only someone
      to bear it with me.
Side by side we'd put our huts
   for winter in a mountain village.

sabishisa ni / taetaru hito no / mata mo are na / iori nara-
bemu / fuyu no yamazato

304. TRAVEL. Topic unknown

That one back home
  whom I promised to think about
    when I saw the moon:
on this night perhaps she too
  will be soaking her sleeves with tears.

tsuki miba to / chigiri okiteshi / furusato no / hito mo ya
koyoi / sode nurasuramu

305. LOVE. Topic unknown

Oh, to be hidden
  in a cleft between great rocks,
someplace far away,
  with no fear of being seen—
    there to bear my pains alone.

haruka naru / iwa no hazama ni / hitori ite / hitome
omowade mo / mono omowaba ya

306. MISCELLANEOUS. Topic unknown

While I sat thinking
  how my own shadow had waned,
the night too grew old—
  with the moon in the distance
    just about ready to set.

fukenikeru / waga mi no kage o / omou ma ni / haruka ni
tsuki no / katabukinikeru

307. MISCELLANEOUS. [Written in the Suzuka
Mountains, when he was on his way to Ise after he
had left the world to become a monk]

Suzuka Mountains—
  now that I have turned my back
    on the vexing world,

> what is to become of me
>   as the days go passing by?

suzukayama / ukiyo o yoso ni / furisutete / ika ni nari-
yuku / waga mi naruramu

308. MISCELLANEOUS. Written about Mount Fuji
when he was in the East Country doing religious
devotions

> As smoke that drifts
>   from the peak of Fuji,
> fading into sky
>   with no sure destination—
> so is the trend of my passion.

kaze ni nabiku / fuji no keburi no / sora ni kiete / yukue
mo shiranu / waga kokoro kana

309. MISCELLANEOUS. Topic unknown

> Here I am, thinking
>   I may never again leave
>   the Yoshino hills,
>   while they think as they wait,
>   "Surely once the blossoms fall . . ."[6]

6. The full thought is,
"Surely once the blos-
soms fall he will come
out of the hills."

yoshinoyama / yagate ideji to / omou mi o / hana chiri-
naba to / hito ya matsuramu

310. MISCELLANEOUS. Topic unknown

> A hard thing it is,
>   to be born in human form;[7]
> and every man
>   who floats lazily through life
>   must sink to the depths again.

7. By Buddhist doc-
trine, one had to pass
through the human
stage to attain enlight-
enment.

ukegataki / hito no sugata ni / ukabiidete / korizu ya tare
mo / mata shizumu beki

311. SPRING. From among poems on "Blossoms"

> This is what I want:
>   to die in the springtime,
>   beneath the blossoms—
> midway through the Second Month,[8]
>   when the moon is at the full.

negawaku wa / hana no shita nite / haru shinan / sono
kisaragi no / mochizuki no koro

8. March by the modern calendar, when the blossoms would have been in full bloom.

312. SPRING. Written when people were composing on the topic "Blossoms Falling in a Dream" at the home of the Kamo Virgin[9]

> In a dream I saw
>   the winds of spring scattering
>   the cherry blossoms—
> and after I woke, the sound
>   was still rustling in my breast.

harukaze no / hana o chirasu to / miru yume wa / samete
mo mune no / sawagu narikeri

9. At the beginning of each emperor's reign, young, unmarried women of high rank were called to serve as chief priestesses in the Shinto shrines at Ise and Kamo.

313. AUTUMN. From among his many poems on "The Moon"

> The sound of storm winds
>   clearing all the clouds away
>   is up in the pines—
> where even the moonlight now
>   seems of a deep green hue.

kumo haruru / arashi no oto wa / matsu ni are ya / tsuki
mo midori no / iro ni haetsutsu

314. WINTER. "Leaves Falling at Dawn"

> Raindrops, I first thought
>   as I lay awake in my bed—

but what I heard
    was the unbroken patter
        of leaves giving in to storm winds.

shigure ka to / nezame no toko ni / kikoyuru wa / arashi
ni taenu / konoha narikeri

315. MISCELLANEOUS. Topic unknown

One cannot rely
    on things to stay as they are—
for on the morrow
    this day we call today
        will be called yesterday.

areba tote / tanomarenu kana / asu wa mata / kino to kyō
o / iwaru bekereba

316. MISCELLANEOUS. On "Mutability"

I don't even know
    whose last remains they hold,
but how fearsome
    on the slopes of Toribe Hill
        are the graves in evening light!

naki ato o / tare to shiranedo / toribeyama / ono ono
sugoki / tsuka no yūgure

317. BUDDHISM. On his thoughts

Inferior even
    to a tree out in a field
without any limbs
    is a heart that knows nothing
        of the world yet to come.

no ni tateru / eda naki ki ni mo / otorikeri / nochi no yo
shiranu / hito no kokoro wa

318. MISCELLANEOUS. Topic unknown

> I have given up
>   all hope of having visitors
>   in my mountain home.
> If not for solitude,
>   how dismal my life would be!

tou hito mo / omoitaetaru / yamazato no / sabishisa naku
wa / sumiukaramashi

319. MISCELLANEOUS. "Love"

> What was I thinking—
>   to say I would gladly die?
> For I have heard
>   that in the next world too
>   we must suffer pains for love.

shinabaya to / nani omouran / nochi no yo mo / koi wa yo
ni uki / koto to koso kike

320. MISCELLANEOUS. A poem on "The Moon"

> Clear through the water
>   and down to the pond bottom
>   the moonlight shines—
> and ah, what a sheet of ice
>   it has spread upon the waves!

ikemizu ni / soko kiyoku sumu / tsukikage wa / nami ni
kōri o / shikiwatasu kana

321. MISCELLANEOUS. "Love"

> On that winter night
>   when plovers were crying out
>   in the river wind—
> the feeling he had back then
>   is the same one I had too.[10]

10. An allusion to
poem 179, by Tsura-
yuki.

kawakaze ni / chidori nakiken / fuyu no yo wa / waga
omoi nite / arikeru mono o

322. MISCELLANEOUS. Topic unknown

Out in the high waves
in the sea off Ashiya
a boat heads for shore:
oh that I too might make my way
so easily through the world!

nami takaki / ashiya no oki o / kaeru fune no / koto
nakute yo o / sugin to zo omou

Shunzei's Disciples

Shunzei attracted many students from the elite of court society, some num-
ber of whom became teachers in turn, thereby sustaining well into the next
century the greatest flowering of classical poetry since the time of *Kokin-
shū*. Perhaps foremost among these was Monk Jakuren (1139?–1202), a
son of Shunzei's elder brother who became the poet's ward at a young age
and in time attained a high reputation as a poet and critic himself. Like
Saigyō, he was a traveling monk, although he took the tonsure only in
his thirties, after beginning a career at court. And he too is a poet of *sabi*
(poems 323–24) and *yūgen* (325–26).

Archbishop Jien (1155–1225) was the brother of the Regent Fujiwara
no [Kujō] Kanezane (1149–1207), one of Shunzei's patrons. The author
of *Gukanshō* (Foolish Thoughts), one of Japan's first narrative histories,
he was a high-ranking cleric who served some years as chief priest of the

Tendai sect. As one would expect of a man from so noble a family, much of his work was composed for poem contests, employing allusion (327) or conceits (328) and in general showing a richness of conception that owes much to the high traditions of the court.

The Regent-Chancellor Fujiwara no [Go-Kyōgoku] Yoshitsune (1169–1206) was a nephew of Jien. Contemporaries praised him for his special mastery of the "lofty style" (see 331–32) as well as for his versatility. His treatment of the theme of impermanence in the form of the autumn wind blowing over the ruins of a gatehouse named "The Indestructible" (334) is one of the most famous poems of the canon.

Some poets, like Saigyō, mature early; others reach their full form only later. This was the case with Fujiwara no Ietaka (1158–1237), another master of the "lofty style" (335), who began to show his abundant talent only in his forties, but then went on to become one of the most important poets of the early thirteenth century. He was praised by later poets for his works in the style of *ushin*, or "intense feeling" (337–38), which became the highest ideal of the orthodox tradition throughout the rest of the medieval period.

Finally—although the list of Shunzei's students could go on much longer—comes one of Shunzei's own grandchildren, known to us only as Shunzei's Daughter. Born sometime around the year 1171, when Shunzei was already well on in years, she studied at his knee in her youth and married a prominent poet. She was a participant in the poem contests at court even after taking holy orders as a nun in 1213 and continued to be active until the death of her half-uncle Teika.

Monk Jakuren

323. SPRING. Presented as part of a fifty-poem sequence

> Toward what harbor
>   spring goes when it fades away
>   one cannot know—
> a barge of firewood falling
>   into River Uji's haze.

kurete yuku / haru no minato wa / shiranedomo / kasumi
ni otsuru / uji no shibabune

324. AUTUMN. Topic unknown

> Ah, solitude—
>   it is not the sort of thing
>   that has a color.
>   Mountains lined with black pine
>   on an evening in autumn.

sabishisa wa / sono iro to shi mo / nakarikeri / maki tatsu
yama no / aki no yūgure

325. MISCELLANEOUS. On "Seeing the First Bloom
of the Lotus"

1. The "spring" of
enlightenment, which
is often represented
in Buddhist texts by
the opening of a lotus
blossom.

> Here it is: this
>   must be that spring to come,[1]
> outside the vexing world:
> lotus blossoms opening
>   through my door, in the dawn sky.

kore ya kono / ukiyo no hoka no / haru naramu / hana no
toboso no / akebono no sora

326. [AUTUMN]. "Quail"

> Gone to ruin now
>   in a field rank with grasses
>   is the old house.
>   Dusk falls on the bamboo fence
>   where a quail is crying.

shigeki no to / arehatenikeru / yado nare ya / magaki no
kure ni / uzura naku nari

Archbishop Jien

327. SUMMER. Presented as part of a fifty-poem sequence

> With my cupped hands
>   I disturbed its reflection
>   in a mountain spring,
> and then found the moon had set—
> leaving me still wanting more.[2]

2. An allusive varia-
tion on poem 171, by
Tsurayuki.

musubu te ni / kage midareyuku / yama no i no / akademo
tsuki no / katabukinikeru

328. WINTER. On "Showers"

> Say, you winter showers—
> without these sleeves so drenched
>   by my troubled thoughts,
> what would you have left to dye
>   now that the leaves are red through?[3]

3. Comparing tears of
longing to red tears of
blood was a common
conceit.

yayo shigure / mono omou sode no / nakariseba / konoha
no nochi ni / nani o somemashi

329. WINTER. Topic unknown

> I left tracks behind
>   when I walked out on the snow
>   of my garden court—
> will people passing by now
>   think I have a visitor?

niwa no yuki ni / waga ato tsukete / idetsuru o / towareni-
keri to / hito ya miruramu

330. MISCELLANEOUS. From among the poems of
a fifty-poem sequence

"Why," I wonder,
    "is there no one who asks me
        why I sorrow so?"—
    till I gaze up at the sky
        and the bright gleam of the moon.

omou koto o / nado tou hito no / nakaruramu / aogeba
sora ni / tsuki zo sayakeki

Go-Kyōgoku Yoshitsune

331. SPRING. On the idea of the beginning of
spring

In fair Yoshino
    haze is trailing on the hills—
and in a village
    where white snow was just falling
        we know that spring has come.

miyoshino wa / yama mo kasumite / shirayuki no / furi-
nishi sato ni / haru wa kinikeri

332. SPRING. On the idea of the end of spring

At the old capital
    in the hills of Yoshino
        the blossoms are gone;
    it is through empty branches
        that spring breezes are blowing.

yoshinoyama / hana no furusato / ato taete / munashiki
eda ni / harukaze zo fuku

333. AUTUMN. On "Blossoms on the Grasses in the Moonlight," from a fifty-poem sequence

> Blossoms appeared
>> on the rough-stalked bush clover
>>> around my old home—
> and since then, night after night,
> the moon shimmers in my garden.

furusato no / motoara no kohagi / sakishi yori / yona yona
niwa no / tsuki zo utsurou

334. MISCELLANEOUS. On "Autumn Wind at a Barrier," from a poem contest held at the Poetry Bureau[4]

4. A government office charged with collecting poems for use in imperial anthologies.

> No one lives now
>> beneath the broken-down eaves
>>> of Fuwa Gatehouse;
> for years the only visitor
> has been the autumn wind.

hito sumanu / fuwa no sekiya no / itabisashi / arenishi
nochi wa / tada aki no kaze

Fujiwara no Ietaka

335. SPRING. "Spring Dawn"

> The haze is spreading
>> on Pine Mountain in Sue;
> and in dim dawn light,
> lifting up from off the waves—
> a cloudbank trailing in the sky.

kasumi tatsu / sue no matsuyama / honobono to / nami ni
hanaruru / yokogumo no sora

336. SUMMER. Topic unknown

Only this year
   has it begun to blossom.
How can it be, then,
   that the scent of the wild orange
     is one from so long ago?[5]

kotoshi yori / hana sakisomuru / tachibana no / ikade
mukashi no / ka ni niouramu

5. An allusion to
poem 138, anonymous.

337. WINTER. A winter poem, from a six-poem sequence presented to the Poetry Bureau

As I gaze out,
   how many times will its light
     be clouded on my sleeves—
the moon left in the dawn sky
     as night passes with rain showers?

nagametsutsu / ikutabi sode ni / kumoruramu / shigure ni
fukuru / ariake no tsuki

338. SUMMER. Topic unknown

In the evening light
   what will the sight of the sky
     do to my heart?
Just the sound of fall's first wind
     has made me sad this morning.

kureyukaba / sora no keshiki mo / ika naramu / kesa dani
kanashi / aki no hatsu kaze

Shunzei's Daughter

339. LOVE. On "Love/Clouds," from a fifty-poem sequence

> Burning in secret,
> my feelings will consume me.
> And how sad to think
>   that even the smoke of my fire
>   will end as an aimless cloud.

shitamoe ni / omoi kienamu / keburi dani / ato naki kumo no / hate zo kanashiki

340. LOVE. On "Love in Spring," from a fifteen-poem contest on love, held at Minase

> In hazy moonlight
>   the image of my lover
>   takes night lodging—
> here in teardrops on my sleeve,
> as in that springtime of old.[6]

6. An allusion to poem 115, by Narihira.

omokage no / kasumeru tsuki zo / yadorikeru / haru ya mukashi no / sode no namida ni

341. LOVE. [From a hundred-poem sequence]

> The door left ajar
>   when he so reluctantly
> arose to depart
>   I now leave open to the moon
> in the sky at break of day.

yasurai ni / idenishi mama no / ama no to o / oshi akegata no / tsuki ni makasete

342. AUTUMN. "The Moon"

Wait, you autumn moon!
Now I cannot be so sure
of seeing you travel
through the same old sky again
as I did so long ago.

mate shibashi / onaji sora yuku / aki no tsuki / mata
meguriau / mukashi naranu ni

Princess Shikishi (d. 1201)

Among the major poets of the late twelfth century, Princess Shikishi (also read Shokushi), a daughter of Retired Emperor Go-Shirakawa (1127–92; r.1155–58), is unusual in that she participated in none of the contests and other public activities that were such an important part of the milieu that produced *Shin kokinshū*. That forty-nine of her poems were chosen for that anthology (more than anyone else save for Saigyō, Jien, Yoshitsune, and Shunzei), however, shows the esteem in which she was held by her peers.

The first quality that strikes a reader of Princess Shikishi's work is her versatility. For although she is most often grouped with "passionate women" like Ono no Komachi and Izumi Shikibu, she writes fine seasonal poems that show great creativity in dealing with old topics—from the arrival of spring (see poem 343) or the scattering of cherry blossoms (344), to the search for coolness (353) in summer or the scent of the orange blossom (355). Likewise, she uses lines from old poems to create entirely new conceptions (see particularly 344, 356), some involving two references at once (350, 354). And her approach to the topic of love often shows originality in focusing directly on psychology without the mediation of natural images (345, 347)—an approach that presaged later years. What unites all her work is a combination of great imagination with Shunzei's ideals of *yūgen* and especially *en*—the romantic beauty associated with formal court composition.

343. SPRING. A spring poem, from a hundred-poem sequence

> Here deep in the hills,
> my pine door would never know
>   that springtime had come—
> but for a broken trickle
>   of jewels of melted snow.

yama fukami / haru to mo shiranu / matsu no to ni /
taedae kakaru / yuki no tamamizu

344. SPRING. From among the poems of a hundred-poem sequence

> With the blossoms gone,
> I look for no special color
>   as I gaze afar—
> and then from the empty sky
>   spring rain begins to fall.[1]

hana wa chiri / sono iro to naku / nagamureba / muna-
shiki sora ni / harusame zo furu

1. An allusion to Shokukks 270, by Narihira (s.n. 22).

345. LOVE. On "Secret Love," from a hundred-poem sequence

> Forgetting he can't know,
> I find myself at nightfall
>   lamenting my fate—
> yet aware that I alone
>   know our time is passing by.

wasurete wa / uchinagekaruru / yūbe kana / ware nomi
shirite / suguru tsukihi o

346. LOVE. Topic unknown

Here I am, waiting
    but trying to keep my heart
        from listening,
    while it ignores my efforts—
    that wind blowing over the reeds.

ima wa tada / kokoro no hoka ni / kiku mono o / shira-
zugao naru / ogi no uwakaze

347. LOVE. From a hundred-poem sequence

I cannot live on—
    not till tomorrow, though then
        he might be less cruel.
    Ah, but if only tonight
        he were to come—yes, come to me!

ikite yomo / asu made hito mo / tsurakaraji / kono yūgure
o / towaba toekashi

348. BUDDHISM. On "Entering into the State of
Repose Every Day," from a hundred-poem
sequence

In the stillness
    that comes with each new dawning,
    I look with sadness
        on those who are still dreaming
        in the darkness of deep night.[2]

shizuka naru / akatsuki goto ni / miwataseba / mada
fukaki yo no / yume zo kanashiki

349. SPRING. From a hundred-poem sequence

On the Sea of Grebes[3]
    a boat is making its way
        beyond the haze—

2. "The darkness of
deep night" refers to
living in this world
without the benefit of
Buddhist enlighten-
ment.

3. Niho no Umi, an
epithet for Lake Biwa.
The poem alludes to a
poem in *Genji mono-
gatari* about a boat
making its way across
Lake Biwa.

with its sail billowing forth
to make a vista of spring.

niho no umi ya / kasumi no ochi ni / kogu fune no / maho
ni mo haru no / keshiki naru kana

350. SPRING. Topic unknown

Even in my dreams
the breezes keep on blowing
through fading blossoms—
allowing no sense of calm
to my nap on a spring day.[4]

yume no uchi mo / utsurou hana ni / kaze fukeba / shizu-
gokoro naki / haru no utatane

4. An allusive varia-
tion on two poems:
poem 167, by Tsura-
yuki, and poem 447, by
Tomonori.

351. SPRING. From a hundred-poem sequence

Ah, how I have wished
for something besides blossoms
to give me comfort!
So scatter, then—be as aloof
as I will be watching you.

hana narade / mata nagusamuru / kata mogana / tsure-
naku chiru o / tsurenakute min

352. LOVE. A love poem

That from my first thought,
from my first gaze, I should feel
my breast burn with love
that today suddenly bursts forth—
how could I ever have known?

omou yori / mishi yori mune ni / taku koi o / kyō uchi-
tsuke ni / moyuru to ya shiru

353. AUTUMN. From a hundred-poem sequence presented to Retired Emperor Go-Toba in the second year of the Shōji era [1200]

> After its coolness,
> I follow on the tidings
>   of the passing wind—
> to where in the grassy fields
>   it sways leaves on the lilies.

suzushi ya to / kaze no tayori o / tazunureba / shigemi ni nabiku / nobe no sayuriba

354. LOVE. [From a hundred-poem sequence]

> Was it him I saw?
> On a night when I don't see him,
> a glimpse of the moon
>   brings with it a cold visage
>   that could just as well be his.[5]

mietsuru ka / minu yo no tsuki no / honomekite / tsurenakaru beki / omokage zo sou

355. SUMMER. [From a hundred-poem sequence composed in 1194]

> So rich in my hand
>   was the scent of the water,
> that I searched upstream—
> and found it flowing there
>   beneath a wild orange tree.

te ni kaoru / mizu no minakami / tazunureba / hana tachibana no / kage ni zo arikeru

5. An allusive variation on two poems: poem 131, by Komachi, and poem 444, by Mibu no Tadamine.

356. WINTER. [From a hundred-poem sequence composed in 1194]

> For a moment more
>> let me gaze on these maids
>>> in the clouds above—
> their shapes looking so serene
>> in the lamps of Abounding Light.[6]

kumo no ue no / otome no sugata / shibashi min / kage mo nodokeki / toyo no akari ni

6. An allusion to poem 426, by Archbishop Henjō. The Festival of Abounding Light (*toyo no akari no sechie*) was the final banquet of the Thanksgiving Services held during the Eleventh Month.

357. LOVE. [From a hundred-poem sequence composed in 1194]

> Here in the twilight
>> as the wind goes passing by
>>> in leaves on the reeds,
> I forget for the moment
>> that of late he's stopped coming.

tasokare no / ogi no hakaze ni / kono koro no / towanu narai o / uchiwasuretsutsu

358. MISCELLANEOUS. [From a hundred-poem sequence composed in 1194]

> The kind of place
>> where the way a traveler's tracks
> disappear in snow
>> is something you get used to—
> such a place is this world of ours.

tabibito no / ato dani mienu / yuki no naka ni / narureba naruru / yo ni koso arikere

Retired Emperor Go-Toba (1180-1239) and 'Shin Kokinshū'

As one of the courtly arts, poetry of course received the attention of the highest of courtly personages, the emperors. Indeed, the flowering of the uta in the early Heian period can largely be attributed to several emperors who encouraged the composition of poetry by sponsoring poem contests and, ultimately, the imperial collections that became repositories of the art. Retired Emperor Go-Toba, 82nd in the line of Japanese sovereigns, performed that function for the poets of his day. A vibrant, adept, and intelligent man, he showed an active interest not only in poetry but also in music, drama, dancing, and even sports such as kickball and archery. It was in the uta that he excelled above all else, devoting himself to it particularly for a decade or so after his retirement from the throne in 1198. It was during this time that he revived the Poetry Bureau, commissioned works from major poets, and eventually compiled *Shin kokinshū* (New *Kokinshū*), a title chosen to make his high ambitions clear.

Of course he was not alone in his task. Six men, including Monk Jakuren, Fujiwara no Teika, and Fujiwara no Ietaka, were assigned as compilers in 1201, working thereafter until the spring of 1205 on the project. But all through the process the Retired Emperor remained intimately involved, even to the point of frustrating some of his chosen compilers, in particular the young and equally obstinate Teika.

The design of the work follows *Kokinshū* and the other six imperial collections that had followed it. Seasonal books come first, all organized in a chronological fashion that represents the major images of the court traditions—plum blossoms, the warbler, and cherry blossoms for spring; dew, the moon, and falling leaves for autumn, and so on. Then come books on Felicitations, Laments, Parting, Travel, and Love, the last topic following a courtly love affair from beginning to end in five books that total over 400 poems. Last come poems on Miscellaneous topics and two new categories that show the importance of religion in the new age—Shinto and Buddhism. The only topics deleted from *Kokinshū* list are the Eccentric poems and Names of Things, both of which were considered too frivolous to poets who had come to see their genre as the most serious of art forms.

As in the case of the *Kokinshū*, most of the poems chosen for the work bespeak public, formal origins, meaning especially commissioned poem sequences and poem contests. As a result, the imagery of the work is generally elegant and refined, the diction courtly, and the topics conventional. And, not surprisingly, the work is a showcase particularly for the *taketa-kaki yō*, or "lofty style" favored by Go-Toba himself, as two examples from his corpus show (poems 359–60).

To his credit, however, Go-Toba did not allow his own tastes to dominate the work completely. Although critical of Teika's more experimental works, he included the best of them. And his hope for the collection as a whole was that it be accepted as a unified work of art above and beyond its parts. To this end, he included poems by 396 poets, ranging from Hitomaro to himself—although concentrating on his own salon and Shunzei and his students. Furthermore, the Retired Emperor organized the poems—within the basic structures described above—in new ways that made the text into a long string of "associated" themes, motifs, and images, as the sequence below makes clear. Taken from one of the Autumn books, it presents poems that share one basic theme—the withering and falling of autumn leaves. But within it one finds other progressions involving subthemes (love in 361, 364; famous places in 371–78), submotifs (crickets in 363, 364; rain showers in 371–74), and various rhetorical approaches (more objective in 374–78; more personal in 379–81)—all combining disparate poems composed on different occasions by different people into a series that becomes its own context.

Thus the Retired Emperor fashioned his masterpiece. Thereafter, he turned most of his attention to other things. Unfortunately for his own future, these included political intrigues, which in 1221 led to his exile to the Oki Islands in the rugged Japan Sea, where he died eighteen years later, an ironic fate for one so thoroughly dedicated to the high life of the capital that he had done so much to enrich.

Retired Emperor Go-Toba

359. SPRING. On the beginning of spring

> Dimly, only dimly—
> but, yes, spring has come at last
>   to the sky above:

in haze trailing on the slopes
of Kagu's Heavenly Hill.

honobono to / haru koso sora ni / kinikerashi / ama no
kaguyama / kasumi tanabiku

360. SPRING. Written on the topic "Spring View at
a Waterside Village"

Looking far, I see
the haze move low on the slopes
along Minase River—
and wonder how I ever thought
autumn the season for dusk.

miwataseba / yamamoto kasumu / minasegawa / yūbe wa
aki to / nani omoikemu

A Sequence from Book Five (Autumn) of *Shin kokinshū*

361. Shunzei's Daughter [b. ca. 1171]. From *The
Poem Contest in Fifteen-hundred Rounds*[1]

1. A large contest
sponsored by Retired
Emperor Go-Toba in
1201–2.

No visitor
accompanies the storm winds
that come with autumn—
covering with fallen leaves
the pathway to my home.[2]

2. An allusive varia-
tion on the anonymous
SIS 205 (s.n. 23).

tou hito mo / arashi fukisou / aki wa kite / konoha ni
uzumu / yado no michishiba

362. Shunzei's Daughter. [Another poem from *The
Poem Contest in Fifteen-hundred Rounds*]

Even the teardrops
that run aimlessly on my sleeves
have changed colors now—

while the withering goes on
in the autumn wind on the fields.

iro kawaru / tsuyu o ba sode ni / okimayoi / uragarete
yuku / nobe no akikaze

363. Retired Emperor Go-Toba. An autumn poem

Autumn progresses.
So cry out, then, you cricket
on this frosty night!
It shines a little colder now—
the moon in that mugwort patch.[3]

aki fukenu / nake ya shimoyo no / kirigirisu / yaya kage
samushi / yomogiu no tsuki

3. An allusive varia-
tion on poem 200, by
Sone no Yoshitada.

364. Fujiwara no Yoshitsune [1169–1206]. Pre-
sented as part of a hundred-poem sequence

A cricket cries out
near my straw mattress, in the cold
of a frosty night—
as I spread my single robe
to spend the night alone.[4]

kirigirisu / naku ya shimoyo no / samushiro ni / koromo
katashiki / hitori ka mo nemu

4. An allusive varia-
tion on poem 417, by
Hitomaro, and the
anonymous KKS 689
(s.n. 24).

365. Fujiwara no Kintsugu [d. 1227]. From *The
Poem Contest in Fifteen-hundred Rounds*

When I am awake
through a long Ninth Month night,
how cold is my bed!
The wind blowing this morning
will leave frost along its way.

nezame suru / nagatsuki no yo no / toko samumi / kesa
fuku kaze ni / shimo ya okuran

366. Archbishop Jien [1155–1225]. An autumn
poem, written as part of a six-poem sequence pre-
sented to the Poetry Bureau[5]

5.   A government
office charged with col-
lecting poems for use in
imperial anthologies.

> Deep into autumn
>   is the island of Awaji
>   in day's first light;
>   and there to see the dawn moon off—
>   the wind from off the bay.

aki fukaki / awaji no shima no / ariake ni / katabuku tsuki
o / okuru urakaze

367. Jien. On "Late Autumn"

> How many dawns now
>   have passed since the first night
>   of the long Ninth Month?
>   The moonlight in the grasses
>   seems more somber all the time.

nagatsuki mo / iku ariake ni / narinuran / asaji no tsuki
no / itodo sabiyuku

368. Monk Jakuren [1139?–1202]. Written for a
hundred-poem sequence requested by the Regent-
Chancellor when he was still a Guards' captain[6]

6.   Fujiwara no [Go-
Kyōgoku] Yoshitsune.

> To the bridge of clouds
>   over-spanned by magpie wings
>   comes autumn's close:
>   for at midnight the frost
>   spreads a chill throughout the sky.[7]

7.   An allusive varia-
tion on poem 420, by
Yakamochi.

kasasagi no / kumo no kakehashi / aki kurete / yowa ni
wa shimo ya / saewataruran

369. Prince Tomohira [964–1009]. Upon seeing the first crimson leaves on a cherry tree

> When did you have time
>   to send forth these crimson leaves,
> mountain cherry tree?
> Wasn't it just yesterday
>   that I grieved for your blossoms?

itsu no ma ni / momiji shinuramu / yamazakura / kinō ka
hana no / chiru o oshimishi

370. Retired Emperor Takakura [d. 1181].[8] On "Red Leaves Seen Through Mist"

> Beyond a fine mist
>   that dances on the mountainsides—
> leaves of crimson hue:
> although not too clearly,
>   that is what I think I saw.

usukiri no / tachimau yama no / momijiba wa / sayaka
naranedo / sore to miekeri

371. Lady Hachijō-in Takakura [early 13th century].[9] An autumn poem

> What will the branches
>   at Mimuro in Kannabi
>   be looking like now—
> when here on every mountain
>   the work of showers has begun?[10]

kannabi no / mimuro no kozue / ika naramu / nabete no
yama mo / shigure suru koro

8. Retired Emperor Go-Toba's father (1161–81; r. 1168–80).

9. A lady-in-waiting to Go-Toba's daughter Shōshi.

10. Showers were credited with "dyeing" the autumn leaves. An allusive variation on the anonymous KKS 284 (s.n. 25).

11. A temple Re-
tired Emperor Go-Toba
established in the East-
ern Hills of the capital.

372. Retired Emperor Go-Toba. For a sliding
panel depicting Suzuka River at Saishō Tennō
Cloister[11]

> For many days past
>   the flow of Suzuka
>   has been deep with leaves—
> but now on Yamada Moor
>   I hear only passing showers.

suzukagawa / fukaki konoha ni / hikazu hete / yamada no
hara no / shigure o zo kiku

12. Fujiwara no
[Kujō] Kanezane
(1149–1207).

373. Fujiwara no Shunzei [1114–1204]. On "Red
Leaves," written as a poem for a hundred-poem
sequence at the house of the Lay Monk and Former
Regent-Chancellor[12]

> Is it in the heart
>   of the leaves to change colors?
> Why else could it be
>   that the pines at Tatsuta
>   are never dyed by showers?

kokoro to ya / momiji wa suramu / tatsutayama / matsu
wa shigure ni / nurenu mono ka wa

13. A poet of the
mid-Heian period.

374. Fujiwara no Suketada [early 11th century].[13]
Upon seeing autumn leaves at the Ōi River

> My real desire
>   is to gaze without any fear
>   at the crimson leaves—
> but not here below a peak
>   known as Storm Mountain.

omou koto / nakute ya mimashi / momijiba o / arashi no
yama no / fumoto narazu wa

375. Sone no Yoshitada [fl. ca. 980–1000]. Topic unknown

> As the setting sun
>   shines on the groves of great oaks
>   on Sao Mountain,
> a cloudless sky is raining—
> as the leaves keep on falling.

irihi sasu / sao no yamabe no / hahasohara / kumoranu
ame to / konoha furitsutsu

376. Lady Kunaikyō [d. 1204?].[14] Presented as part of a hundred-poem sequence

> Are the storm winds
>   losing strength up on your peak,
> Mount Tatsuta?
> That never-crossed brocade bridge
>   seems to have drifted away.[15]

tatsuta yama / arashi ya mine ni / yowaruramu / wataranu
mizu mo / nishiki taekeri

14. A lady-in-waiting to Retired Emperor Go-Toba.

15. An allusive variation on the anonymous KKS 283 (s.n. 25).

377. Yoshitsune. Written on "Great Oaks" at a poem contest at his house when he was still a Guards' captain

> Among the great oaks,
>   even the dewdrops from the leaves
>   must have changed colors—
> for the grasses beneath the trees
>   show autumn's progress too.

hahaso hara / shizuku mo iro ya / kawaruramu / mori no
shitakusa / aki fukenikeri

378. Fujiwara no Teika [1162–1241]. Written on
"Great Oaks" at a poem contest at Yoshitsune's
house when Yoshitsune was still a Guards' captain

> The seasonless waves
> 　are displaying colors now
> 　　on Izumi River.
> Up in the Hahaso Groves
> 　storm winds must be blowing.[16]

16. An allusive varia-
tion on KKS 250, by
Fun'ya no Yasuhide
(s.n. 26).

toki wakanu / nami sae iro ni / izumikawa / hahaso no
mori ni / arashi fuku rashi

379. Minamoto no Toshiyori [1055–1129]. For a
sliding panel depicting autumn leaves scattered
around a broken-down house

> In my former home
> 　everything is buried now
> 　　by fallen red leaves;
> in memory fern by the eaves
> 　the autumn wind is blowing.[17]

17. The name *shino-
bugusa*, "memory
fern," was applied to
several ferns.

furusato wa / chiru momijiba ni / uzumorete / noki no
shinobu ni / akikaze zo fuku

380. Princess Shikishi [d. 1201]. An autumn poem,
composed for a hundred-poem sequence

> The paulownia leaves
> 　are hard to make a way through,
> 　　so thick have they fallen.
> Although it is not as if
> 　I'm expecting anyone.[18]

18. An allusive varia-
tion on KKS 770, by
Archbishop Henjō
(s.n. 27).

kiri no ha mo / fumiwakegataku / narinikeri / kanarazu
hito o / matsu to nakeredo

381. Yoshitada. Topic unknown

> No one ever comes;
>   and the leaves have all fallen,
>   scattered on the wind;
>   night after night, the voices
>   of the insects grow more weak.

hito wa kozu / kaze ni konoha wa / chirihatete / yona
yona mushi wa / koe yowaru nari

382. Fujiwara no Kintsugu. Written for a fifty-
poem sequence requested by Cloistered Prince
Shukaku[19]

> Even evergreens
>   are yielding now to the hues
>   of the crimson leaves—
>   changing colors in the wind
>   blowing over autumn hills.[20]

momijiba no / iro ni makasete / tokiwagi mo / kaze ni
utsurou / aki no yama kana

383. Fujiwara no Ietaka [1158–1237]. From *The
Poem Contest in Fifteen-hundred Rounds*

> You lowermost leaves
>   dyed red by dew and showers
>   in Moru's shadow:
>   I'll drench myself for a branch—
>   a remembrance of autumn.[21]

tsuyushigure / moruyama kage no / shitamomiji / nuru
tomo oramu / aki no katami ni

384. Monk Saigyō [1118–90]. Topic unknown

> With leaves on the vines
>   entwining the pine branches

19. A son of Re-
tired Emperor Go-
Shirakawa (1127–92;
r. 1155–58).

20. An allusive varia-
tion on KKS 362, by
Sakanoue Korenori
(early 10th century;
s.n. 28).

21. An allusive varia-
tion on poem 169, by
Tsurayuki.

                    now scattered and gone,
                 autumn down in the foothills
22. An allusive varia-   will be sending forth harsh winds.[22]
tion on a sacred song,
KKS 1077 (s.n. 29).   matsu ni hau / masaki no kazura / chirinikeri / toyama no
                       aki wa / kaze susaburan

                       385. Former Consultant Fujiwara no Chikataka
                       [d. 1165]. Written for a poem contest held at the
                       house of the Hosshōji Lay Monk and Former
23. Fujiwara no   Regent-Chancellor[23]
Tadamichi (1097–
1164).   On Katano Moor
                           of the ever-crying quail
                         it strikes the wax trees
                           as if to take all their red leaves—
                         this autumn wind blowing by.

                       uzura naku / katano ni tateru / hajimomiji / chirinu bakari
                       ni / akikaze zo fuku

Fujiwara no Teika (1162-1241)

Raised the heir of Shunzei, Fujiwara no Teika (or Sadaie) came in time to occupy a place much like his father's in the literary world, but for him the honors came only after long years of frustration. Since most of Teika's troubles came about because of his tempestuous relationship with Retired Emperor Go-Toba, it would be easy to blame Go-Toba for everything that happened. But all the sources, including especially Teika's own diary, make it clear that much of the fault rested with that irritable and short-tempered perfectionist himself.

As a young man, Teika was an innovator who wrote poems that offended the tastes of Go-Toba and others for their over-creative treatment of standard topics (see poems 390, 393, 398), abuse of normal sense and syntax (391–93, 398), and general impatience with existing patterns of expression (387). And even after age mellowed him somewhat, he remained committed to the proposition of "making it new." In doing so, he expanded the use of existing techniques such as *honkadori*, or allusive variation (employed in half of the twenty-five poems below) and further refined such existing ideals as *sabi* (see 397, 399–400). Furthermore, he created new poetic ideals, the chief one described by the word *yōen*, a variation on Shunzei's *yūgen* that added to "mystery and depth" a romantic, dreamy atmosphere (see particularly 393, 395, 398, 401, 403) achieved by rich imagery and complex syntactical patterns that immediately drew attention to themselves. This in itself was an offense to those who were accustomed to more straightforwardly referential poetry.

Thus in his youth Teika was in some ways like Narihira; but in the latter half of his life he came to resemble even more Ki no Tsurayuki as an arbiter of taste whose standards would influence many generations. After succeeding to the headship of the Mikohidari house upon Shunzei's death in 1204, he lived an active life as contest judge and teacher, and continued to write poetry, eventually developing a new ideal that he called *ushin*, or "sincerity of feeling." At first he seems to have meant by this only a strongly subjective tone employed in poems that still employed many rhetorical devices such as prefaces, pivot-words, and conceits (see particularly 401, 403, 407), but later on he favored a plain style that conveyed great emotional power in simple, mellifluous language (408–10)—an ideal that would become a standard for conservative poets for centuries to come.

To make the picture of Teika's last years complete, however, one must add that during the last quarter century of his life he seems to have composed relatively little in the uta form. Since he had severed most of his contacts with Go-Toba not long after Shunzei's death, he was unaffected by the Retired Emperor's rebellion against the warrior government. Indeed, as time went on, Teika gathered more honors, receiving promotions in rank and office that brought him to the office of middle counselor in 1232. And that same year he was asked to act as sole compiler of the ninth imperial collection, which came to be titled *Shin chokusenshū* (The New Imperial Anthology). He used the opportunity to give his ideal of *ushin* more concrete definition.

It was also during his last several decades that Teika collected and collated many ancient texts, including the great collections of poetry, *Genji monogatari*, and other romances, diaries, and essays—in this way establishing himself as a figure that later ages would revere as a literatus par excellence. And perhaps more for amusement than anything else, he also spent a good deal of time in those years composing linked verse (renga), a relatively new genre that became the arena for whatever spirit of play he had left. Only a handful of his links remain (see 411–14), and they show a consciousness still dominated by the conventional topics and conventions of the uta poet. But scholars point out, with justice, that the fledgling genre gained greatly from his interest, which served at least to legitimize it in the eyes of later poets, who would bring it to its full artistic potential.

386. AUTUMN. "The Moon," composed for a poem contest at the Kamo Shrine during the Ninth Month of the first year of the Genryaku era [1184]

"Think of the past!"—
so the moonlight seems to say,
itself a remnant
    of autumns long since gone,
    that I could never know.

shinobe to ya / shiranu mukashi no / aki o hete / onaji katami ni / nokoru tsukikage

387. TRANSIENCE

An apparition!
Don't even call it a dream.
In this world of ours,
    what we hear about, what we see
        as transience—this is it!

maboroshi yo / yume to mo iwaji / yo no naka wa / kakute kikimiru / hakanasa zo kore

388. LOVE. "Unfulfilled Love"

You've forgotten, you say?
All right, then, I too will forget—
that when we parted

I said I would convince myself
it was nothing but a dream.

wasurenu ya / sa wa wasurekeri / waga kokoro / yume ni
nase to zo / iite wakareshi

389. MISCELLANEOUS. Topic unknown

> At a pondside
>   where a heron is standing,
> the pines have grown old—
> and I feel I am somewhere else
>   than in the capital.

sagi no iru / ike no migiwa ni / matsu furite / miyako no
hoka no / kokochi koso sure

390. SPRING. "Spring Daybreak"

> Only the haze?
> No, by blossoms and warblers
>   it is held fast—
> as I too am bound by spring
>   in my house, at break of day[1]

kasumi ka wa / hana uguisu ni / tojirarete / haru ni komo-
reru / yado no akebono

1. The "it" of line 3
is evidently the poet's
house; and the first
line too is elliptical,
seemingly asking the
rhetorical question, "Is
my house bound by
haze alone?"

391. WINTER. "Winter Morning"

> After a full year
>   of gazing out, one morning
>   I open my door—
> to a thin snowfall, frozen—
>   the far edge of loneliness.

hitotose o / nagametsukuseru / asatoide ni / usuyuki
kōru / sabishisa no hate

392. LOVE. "Love with the Moon as an Image"

> He seemed reluctant
>   to take his leave of me then,
> in the same moonlight
>   that shines in tears on these sleeves,
> still awaiting his return.

yasurai ni / idenishi mama no / tsuki no kage / waga
namida nomi / sode ni matedomo

393. SPRING. Among the poems composed for a
fifty-poem sequence requested by Cloistered Prince
Shukaku[2]

2.   A son of Re-
tired Emperor Go-
Shirakawa; d. 1202.

> On this spring night
>   my floating bridge of dreams
>   has broken away:
>   and lifting off a far peak—
> a cloudbank trailing in the sky.[3]

3.   An allusion to
the final chapter of
Genji monogatari,
"The Floating Bridge
of Dreams."

haru no yo no / yume no ukihashi / todaeshite / mine ni
wakaruru / yokogumo no sora

394. SPRING. From a fifty-poem sequence
requested by Cloistered Prince Shukaku

> Through the wide heavens
>   the scent of plum blossoms moves
>   like a spreading haze;
>   but still not clouded over
> is the moon of this spring night.[4]

4.   An allusive varia-
tion on SKKS 55, by Ōe
no Chisato (fl. ca. 890;
s.n. 30).

ōzora wa / mume no nioi ni / kasumitsutsu / kumori mo
hatenu / haru no yo no tsuki

395. SPRING. From a hundred-poem sequence

> Blossoms of plum
>   perfume my sleeves with their scent,

vying there for space
   with shafts of sparkling moonlight
      spilling down through the eaves.[5]

mume no hana / nioi o utsusu / sode no ue ni / noki moru tsuki no / kage zo arasou

5. An allusion to poem 115, by Narihira.

396. SPRING. From a fifty-poem sequence requested by Cloistered Prince Shukaku

Weary wild geese who came
   through skies once chilled by frost
      now head back north—
and on their departing wings
   fall the soft rains of spring.[6]

shimo mayou / sora ni shioreshi / karigane no / kaeru tsubasa ni / harusame zo furu

6. Wild geese winter in Japan and return to Siberia in the spring.

397. AUTUMN. Among the poems of a hundred-poem sequence requested by Monk Saigyō

Looking far, I see
   no sign of cherry blossoms
      or crimson leaves.
A reed-thatched hut on a bay
   on an evening in autumn.[7]

miwataseba / hana mo momiji mo / nakarikeri / ura no tomaya no / aki no yūgure

7. An allusion to scenery along the Akashi coast as described in the "Akashi" chapter of *Genji monogatari*.

398. AUTUMN. Written for a fifty-poem sequence on the moon, at the home of the Regent-Chancellor[8]

On her mat of straw,
   she waits as the autumn wind
      deepens the night,
spreading moonlight for her robe—
   the Maiden of Uji River.[9]

8. Fujiwara no [Go-Kyōgoku] Yoshitsune (1169–1206).

9. An allusive variation on the anonymous KKS 689 (s.n. 24).

samushiro ya / matsu yo no aki no / kaze fukete / tsuki o
katashiku / uji no hashihime

399. WINTER. From a hundred-poem sequence

> No shelter in sight
>   to give my pony a rest
>   and brush off my sleeves—
> in the fields around Sano Ford
>   on a snowy evening.[10]

10. An allusive variation on MYS 265, by Naga Okimaro (7th century; s.n. 31).

koma tomete / sode uchiharau / kage mo nashi / sano no
watari no / yuki no yūgure

400. TRAVEL. A travel poem

> With the autumn wind
>   turning back the flowing sleeves
>   of a traveler,
> how lonely in evening light
>   is the bridge above the gorge!

tabibito no / sode fukikaesu / akikaze ni / yūbe sabishiki /
yama no kakehashi

401. LOVE. A love poem

> The years have gone by,
>   with my prayers still unanswered—
>   as Hase's bell
>   signals evening from its peak,
> sounding somehow far away.[11]

11. An allusive variation on poem 488, by Minamoto no Toshiyori.

toshi mo henu / inoru chigiri wa / hatsuseyama / onoe no
kane no / yoso no yūgure

402. LOVE. [Written as a love poem]

> After his tryst,
>   he too may be looking up

"After his tryst, / he too may be looking up / on his way back home—/ while for me a night of waiting / ends with the dawn moon."
(SKKS 1206 *by Fujiwara no Teika*)

on his way back home—
while for me a night of waiting
ends with the dawn moon.

kaerusa no / mono to ya hito no / nagamuran / matsu yo
nagara no / ariake no tsuki

403. LOVE. From *The Minase Fifteen-poem Contest*[12]

When we parted,
dewdrops fell down on my sleeves
of pure white hemp—
your coldness harsh as the hue
of the piercing autumn wind.[13]

12. A contest held by Retired Emperor Go-Toba at his Minase villa in the Ninth Month of 1202.

13. An allusive variation on the anonymous MYS 3182 (s.n. 32).

shirotae no / sode no wakare ni / tsuyu ochite / mi ni
shimu iro no / akikaze zo fuku

404. LOVE. Topic unknown

Those long black tresses
    that I roughly pushed aside:
now strand upon strand
    they rise in my mind's eye
        each night as I lie down.[14]

14. An allusive varia-
tion on poem 213, by
Izumi Shikibu.

kakiyarishi / sono kurokami no / suji goto ni / uchifusu
hodo wa / omokage zo tatsu

405. AUTUMN. An autumn poem, written for a hundred-poem sequence during the Yōwa era [1181]

If you think on it,
    you can see no change in color
        on Heaven's High Plain:
autumn is not in the sky
    but in the light of the moon.

ama no hara / omoeba kawaru / iro mo nashi / aki koso
tsuki no / hikari narikere

406. LOVE. Written on the idea of "Old Love," during the Fourth Month of the fifth year of the Kempō era [1217]

With me unresolved
    to die of the love I feel,
        the years have gone by—
my heart strengthened by the thought
    that, living, I may see him again.[15]

15. An allusive varia-
tion on the anonymous
SIS 646 (s.n. 33).

koishinanu / mi no okotari zo / toshi henuru / araba au yo
no / kokorozuyosa ni

407. LOVE. On the topic "Famous Place / Love,"
from a hundred-poem sequence composed at the
house of the Palace Minister in the second year of
the Kempō Era [1214][16]

16. Fujiwara [no
Kujō] Michiie (1193–
1252).

> Age after age
>   the sea breeze on the beach
> at Windblown Strand
>   has dashed sand against the shore
>   to be shattered—like my heart.

yo to tomo ni / fukiage no hama no / shiokaze ni / nabiku
masago no / kudakete zo omou

408. LOVE. On the idea of "Falling in Love" [1215]

> Yesterday, today,
> I have spent gazing afar
>   at banners of cloud;
> but how can one I've never met
>   know I was thinking of her?[17]

17. An allusive varia-
tion on the anonymous
KKS 484 (s.n. 34).

kinō kyō / kumo no hatate ni / nagamu tote / mi mo senu
hito no / omoi ya wa shiru

409. AUTUMN. "Miscanthus in a Quiet Garden"
[1225]

> Wave though they may,
> those sleeve-like plumes of grass
>   can do no good—
> at a house no one visits,
> by an old bamboo fence.[18]

18. An allusive varia-
tion on KKS 243, by
Ariwara no Mune-
yana (d. 898), a son
of Narihira (s.n. 35).
On miscanthus, see the
note to poem 253.

maneku tote / kusa no tamoto no / kai mo araji / towa-
renu sato no / furuki magaki wa

410. SPRING. "Blossoms in a Quiet Time" [1229]

> While I gazed out,
> barely conscious that I too

was growing old,
how many times have blossoms
scattered on the spring wind? [19]

19.   An allusive varia-
tion on poem 423, by
Komachi.

waga mi yo ni / furu to mo nashi no / nagame shite / iku
harukaze ni / hana no chiruran

411. SPRING. Written in the fifth year of the Kempō
era [1217], for a session at the residence of the Re-
tired Emperor [20]

20.   Retired Emperor
Go-Toba.

So, this is what
I have heard about—the peak
of Ikoma Mountain.

What had looked to me like snow—
it was a grove of blossoms!

kikiokishi / kore ya ikoma no / mine naran; yuki to
mietaru / hana no hayashi wa

412. WINTER

Near the bamboo fence,
white winter chrysanthemums.

Season's first showers
clear—though by then the sunshine
has faded away.

hosanu magaki no / fuyu no shiragiku; hatsushigure /
haruru hikage mo / kurehatete

413. SHINTO

This morning again they emerge—
the mountain folk of Ono.

21.   One of the pre-
liminary events in the
Aoi Festival held at the
Kamo Shrine in north-
ern Kyōto early each
summer.

From mighty Kamo,
the Miare Procession
going down the road. [21]

kesa mo izuru / ono no yamabito; chihayaburu / kamo no
miare no / michinobe ni

414. LOVE

>If only for this one night,
>let us share a pillow.

>Till now I relied
>   on the straight path of my dreams
>   as reality.

koyoi bakari ya / makura sadamenu; tanomekoshi / yume
no tadachi wa / utsutsu nite

'One Hundred Poems by One Hundred Poets'

As the headnotes of many poems in *Shin kokinshū* make clear, by the early 1200's the *hyakushu uta*, or "hundred-poem sequence," had become a major poetic genre. In the beginning such sequences were usually commissioned in preparation for the compilation of imperial anthologies—a function they continued to serve throughout the rest of court history. But in the hands of some poets these small anthologies gained an artistic integrity of their own. This was particularly true of Fujiwara no Teika, whose *Complete Works*, compiled by the poet himself in 1216 and added to later on, contains over twenty hundred-poem sequences, the first composed in 1181 and the last in 1224. In addition to these sequences of his own poems, he compiled several collections of famous poems from his and earlier ages, the most well known of which is titled *Ogura hyakunin isshu* (The Ogura

Sequence of One Hundred Poems by One Hundred Poets). Although the precise date of the work is not clear, it most likely was put together in the mid-1230's, when Teika was spending most of his time at his estate just to the west of the capital in a place called Ogura.

As the title of the work indicates, it presents a series of one hundred poems by some of the most famous poets of the tradition, beginning with Emperor Tenji and ending with Retired Emperor Go-Toba and his son, Emperor Juntoku (1197–1242; r.1210–21). Perhaps because it offered such an excellent overview of the uta in all ages, it became a popular tool for instructing novices in the art, eventually even becoming the basis of a card game that is still played in Japan at New Year's celebrations.

But the popularity of the work should not be allowed to detract from its status as a work of art. For it is apparent that Teika put great care into its creation, choosing both poets and poems with definite ends in mind. First of all, he has included in his list a number of poets that others of his age probably would not have—among them Sone no Yoshitada, Minamoto no Toshiyori, and Toshiyori's father, Tsunenobu. And he has omitted such poets as Ōtomo no Kuronushi, Minamoto no Shitagō, and Fujiwara no Motozane, for whom even Shunzei had high regard. In this way, the sequence becomes very much Teika's own version of poetic history. There are other strong biases in the work as well, the most significant being one against the age of *Shin kokinshū*—which he makes evident by failing to include a number of important poets of Go-Toba's salon and by using poems from other anthologies to represent himself, Ietaka, Jien, and even Go-Toba himself. At the same time, he shows favor for earlier anthologies, particularly *Kokinshū*, *Shūishū*, *Goshūishū*, and *Senzaishū*.

In these respects, it may be said that the work represents the Teika of old age and not youth, a conclusion that is supported by his choice of poems in the *ushin* style, many of which employ the rhetorical techniques associated with the classical period, especially the preface, the conceit, the apostrophe and other kinds of personification, and too many pivot-words to count.[1] Surprisingly, however, the dominant topic of the work, which is arranged chronologically by poet, is one we associate with youth—love. Forty-four of the poems fall directly into that category, with a number more treating love as a subtheme (419, 444, 455, 476, 492, 498, 505, 508). Indeed, the work reads like a primer for those who want to understand poetic love in all its variations, from statements of secret passion and frustrated ardor,

---

1. Prefaces, poems 417, 428, 432, 460, 462–63, 491, 502; conceits, 439, 441, 446, 451, 481, 483, 486, 489–90, 494, 496, 503–4; apostrophe, 425–26, 438, 480, 487–88, 503; other personification, 430, 444, 447–48, 461, 469, 471, 485–86, 499–500, 510; a few of the pivot-words, 423, 430, 439, 441, 476, 510–11.

to fulfillment, dedication, confusion and uncertainty, and rejection and complaint.[2] Also presented are a few examples of the witty repartee (476, 481, 486) that was so much a part of court life in both fiction and reality, and two sarcastic statements (452, 467) that reveal—albeit playfully—the sadness of the waiting woman's plight.

For those who care to look for them, Teika has created other patterns as well, including two poems that originally formed one round in a poem contest that the judge could not decide (454–55), a pair that represent old age and youth (see 463–64), another pair by the wives of regents complaining about their fate (467–68), and a series of seven by ladies (470–76) who were all in the salons of the consorts of Emperor Ichijō (980–1011; r. 986–1011). Moreover, he has done much to make the sequence a family affair, with poems by fathers and sons (Emperor Yōzei and Prince Motoyoshi, Fun'ya no Yasuhide and his son Asayasu, Fujiwara no Akisuke and his son Kiyosuke, and so on through a list that numbers more than twenty such pairs), mothers and daughters (Izumi Shikibu and her daughter Koshikibu, Murasaki Shikibu and her daughter Daini no Sammi), and in several cases three generations (Minamoto no Tsunenobu, his son Toshiyori, and his grandson Shun'e; Kiyowara no Fukayabu, his son Motosuke, and his granddaughter Sei Shōnagon; Fujiwara no Tadamichi, his son Archbishop Jien, and his grandson Yoshitsune). In the same way, he has taken care to use poems that present many of the most famous place-names associated with the poetic tradition, from Fuji in the East Country to Suma on the coast to the west, with the most prominent places—Tatsuta, Yoshino, Naniwa, and a few more—appearing twice. It may be that, beyond the sequence's purely artistic features, what attracted the attention of courtiers in the first place was the fact that it could be read as a primer on poetic convention, history, and geography.

Finally, it should be noted that Teika used his sequence as a last refutation of Go-Toba by using one of the latter's poems that—although written before his exile—has none of the color of the Retired Emperor's days at court. In this way, too, Teika declares the priority of *ushin* as the unifying ideal of the court tradition, or at least of that tradition as he chose to perceive it.

In the translation, the information on the topical books in which the poems first appeared and the original headnotes have been relegated to the footnotes in an effort to retain the impression conveyed by Teika's text. The note numbers coincide exactly with the poems' location in the sequence

2. Secret passion, poems 453–54, 503, 506; frustrated ardor, 433, 435, 473; fulfillment, 464; dedication, 427, 434, 470, 472; confusion and uncertainty, 428, 457, 460, 463, 479, 494, 502, 511; rejection and complaint, 444, 456, 458, 462, 477, 488, 499–500, 504.

(e.g., poem 450 is no. 36 of 100), eliminating the need for the identifying marginal numbers used elsewhere in the book.

1. AUTUMN. Com-   415. Emperor Tenji [626–71; r. 688–71][1]
pare poem 7.

Out in autumn fields
    stands my makeshift hut of grass—
its thatch so rough
    that the long sleeves of my robe
    are always wet with dew.

aki no ta no / kariho no io no / toma o arami / waga koro-
mode wa / tsuyu ni nuretsutsu

2. SUMMER.   416. Empress Jitō [645–702; r. 690–97][2]

Spring has gone away
    and summer come, it would seem—
from those white hemp robes
    laid to dry in the sunlight
    on Kagu's Heavenly Hill.

haru sugite / natsu kinikerashi / shirotae no / koromo
hosu chō / ama no kaguyama

3. LOVE.   417. Kakinomoto no Hitomaro [fl. ca. 680–700][3]

Long as the long tail
    of pheasants of the mountains,
foot-wearying hills:
    so long is the night before me
    when I must spend it alone.

ashibiki no / yamadori no o no / shidario no / naganaga-
shi yo o / hitori ka mo nen

418. Yamabe no Akahito [early 8th century] [4]

> At Tago Bay
>   I came out, and looked afar—
> to see the hemp-white
>   of Mount Fuji's lofty peak
>   under a flurry of snow.

tago no ura ni / uchiidete mireba / shirotae no / fuji no
takane ni / yuki wa furitsutsu

4. WINTER. Compare poem 37.

419. Sarumaru Tayū [late 9th century?] [5]

> Deep back in the hills
>   a stag walks through red leaves,
> calling for his mate—
> and ah, when I hear his voice,
> how forlorn the autumn seems.

okuyama ni / momiji fumiwake / naku shika no / koe kiku
toki zo / aki wa kanashiki

5. AUTUMN.

420. Middle Counselor [Ōtomo no] Yakamochi
[718?–85] [6]

> When I see the white
>   of frost covering the bridge
> made by magpie wings
>   to traverse the high heavens—
> then I know the night is late.

kasasagi no / wataseru hashi ni / oku shimo no / shiroki o
mireba / yo zo fukenikeru

6. WINTER. "Bridge made by magpie wings" is a conventional metaphor for the Milky Way.

421. Abe no Nakamaro [701–70] [7]

> Raising my eyes
>   to the broad plain of heaven,
> I see the same moon
>   that shone at Mount Mikasa
>   in Kasuga, far away.

7. TRAVEL. Composed in China in 753, at a farewell party before leaving for Japan after more than thirty years.

ama no hara / furisake mireba / kasuga naru / mikasa no
yama ni / ideshi tsuki ka mo

8. An obscure figure
whom Tsurayuki
counted among the Six
Geniuses (*rokkasen*)
of Japanese poetry.
MISCELLANEOUS.
The place-name Uji
is homophonous with
uji, meaning bitter or
painful.

422. Monk Kisen [early 9th century][8]

> In my little hut
>   southeast of the capital,
> I live as I wish—
> and yet I hear this place called
>   Ujiyama, Bitter Hills.

waga io wa / miyako no tatsumi / shika zo sumu / yo o
ujiyama to / hito wa iu nari

9. SPRING.

423. Ono no Komachi [fl. ca. 850][9]

> Behold my flower:
> its beauty wasted away
>   on idle concerns
> that have kept me gazing out
>   as time coursed by with the rains.

hana no iro wa / utsurinikeri na / itazura ni / waga mi yo
ni furu / nagame seshi ma ni

10. Semimaru was
a recluse who sup-
posedly lived near
Ausaka, "Meeting
Hill." MISCELLA-
NEOUS.

424. Semimaru [10th century?][10]

> Here it is: the gate
>   where people coming and going
>   must part company,
> where both friends and strangers meet—
> on the slopes of Meeting Hill.

kore ya kono / yuku mo kaeru mo / wakarete wa / shiru
mo shiranu mo / ōsaka no seki

11. TRAVEL. Sent
to his family when
he was heading into
exile on the island of
Oki. "Eighty Isles"
(*yasoshima*) is a meta-
phor for the Japanese
islands.

425. Consultant [Ono no] Takamura [d. 852][11]

> You on your fishing boats—
> please tell this to my loved ones:

that my boat has passed
safely through the Eighty Isles
on the broad plain of the sea.

wata no hara / yasoshima kakete / kogiidenu to / hito ni
wa tsuge yo / ama no tsuribune

426. Archbishop Henjō [816–90] [12]

O winds from on high—
blow shut that path through the clouds
and make these maids stay.
I would gaze a moment more
on their heavenly shapes.

amatsukaze / kumo no kayoiji / fukitoji yo / otome no
sugata / shibashi todomemu

12. MISCELLA-
NEOUS. Composed
at court when he was
watching a perfor-
mance of Gosechi
Dancers—daughters
of court officers who
provided entertainment
during the Thanks-
giving Services of the
Eleventh Month.

427. Retired Emperor Yōzei [868–84; r. 877–84] [13]

From Tsukuba Peak
water falls down to become
Mina River's flow—
just as my small love has grown
into a deepening pool.

tsukubane no / mine yori otsuru / mina no kawa / koi zo
tsumorite / fuchi to narinuru

13. LOVE. Sent to an
imperial princess.

428. The Kawara Minister of the Left [Minamoto
no Tōru; 822–95] [14]

As wholly confused
as cloth dyed in moss-fern design
from Michinoku—
so distraught is my heart now,
and for no one else but you.

michinoku no / shinobu mojizuri / tare yue ni / midareso-
menishi / ware naranaku ni

14. LOVE. *Shinobu
mojizuri* refers to an
ancient dyeing pro-
cess in which *shinobu*,
a kind of fern, was
rubbed into cloth, cre-
ating a "confused"
pattern.

15. SPRING. Sent to
someone with a gift of
wakana, young edible
sprouts gathered in the
fields each spring.

429. Emperor Kōkō [830–87; r. 884–87][15]

It was just for you
    that I went to the spring fields
        to pick these young greens—
    and all the while on my sleeves
        the snow kept on falling.

kimi ga tame / haru no no ni idete / wakana tsumu / waga
koromode ni / yuki wa furitsutsu

16. Yukihira was
Narihira's brother.
PARTING. Written
when he was appointed
to serve as governor of
Inaba Province.

430. Middle Counselor Ariwara no Yukihira [818–
93][16]

I must depart now
    for the pines that await me
        at Mount Inaba—
    but should I hear that you too pine,
    I will hurry back to you.

tachiwakare / inaba no yama no / mine ni ouru / matsu to
shi kikaba / ima kaerikon

17. AUTUMN. Com-
posed for a screen
painting represent-
ing autumn leaves on
the Tatsuta River. In
tie-dyeing, the cloth
is twisted in order to
make bands of differing
shades of color.

431. Ariwara no Narihira [825–80][17]

Not even in the age
    of the mighty gods of old
        was such a thing known:
    Tatsuta's waters tie-dyed
        with leaf-bands of Chinese red.

chihayaburu / kamiyo mo kikazu / tatsutagawa / kara-
kurenai ni / mizu kukuru to wa

*pillow word
(makurakotoba)*

18. LOVE. Written
for a poem contest.

432. Fujiwara no Toshiyuki [d. 901][18]

At Suminoe
    waves come to shore day and night;
    but you come neither—
    afraid that even on dream-paths
        you might possibly be seen?

suminoe no / kishi ni yoru nami / yoru sae ya / yume no kayoiji / hitome yokuramu

433. Lady Ise [fl. 930][19]

> What are you saying?
> That I cannot meet you—
> not even for a time
>   brief as the space between joints
>   on the reeds at Naniwa?

naniwagata / mijikaki ashi no / fushi no ma mo / awade kono yo o / sugushiteyo to ya

19. A lady-in-waiting to the consort of Emperor Uda (867–931; r. 887–97); she later became his mistress. LOVE.

434. Prince Motoyoshi [890–943][20]

> Like a channel buoy
>   bobbing off Naniwa strand,
> my name is tossed about.
> But still I will come to you—
>   though it be death to proceed.

wabinureba / ima hata onaji / naniwa naru / mi o tsuku-shite mo / awamu to zo omou

20. Son of Emperor Yōzei (poem 427). LOVE. Sent to a lady after their secret relationship had become known.

435. Monk Sosei [late 9th century][21]

> Because you promised
>   you would be coming at once,
> I waited all night—
>   even then greeting only
>   the moon of a Ninth Month dawn.

ima komu to / iishi bakari ni / nagatsuki no / ariake no tsuki o / machiidetsuru kana

21. LOVE. The Ninth Month was the "long month," according to custom.

436. Fun'ya no Yasuhide [late 9th century][22]

> As soon as it blows,
>   the autumn trees and grasses

22. A contemporary of Ono no Komachi; one of Tsurayuki's Six Poetic Geniuses. AUTUMN. Written for a poem contest. The word *arashi*, "storm wind," is homophonous with the stem of the verb *aru*, "to be withered" or "to be rough."

> begin to wither:
> not for nothing do they name it
> Witherer—this mountain wind!

fuku kara ni / aki no kusaki no / shiorureba / mube yama-
kaze o / arashi to iuran

23. A major court
poet during the reign
of Emperor Uda.
AUTUMN. Written for
a poem contest.

437. Ōe no Chisato [late 9th century][23]

Looking at the moon,
I feel the sadness in things
    everywhere around—
even knowing that autumn
    does not come for me alone.

tsuki mireba / chiji ni mono koso / kanashikere / waga mi
hitotsu no / aki ni wa aranedo

24. TRAVEL. Com-
posed at Tamukeyama,
Offering Hill, when
he accompanied Re-
tired Emperor Uda on
a journey to Nara.

438. Sugawara no Michizane [845–903][24]

Before this journey
    I had no time for prayer strips:
so Gods, accept instead
    that brocade of autumn leaves
        on the slopes of Offering Hill.

kono tabi wa / nusa mo toriaezu / tamukeyama / momiji
no nishiki / kami no ma ni ma ni

439. The Sanjō Minister of the Right [Fujiwara no
Sadakata; 873–932][25]

25. LOVE. Sent to a
woman. "Secret vines"
(sanekazura) is em-
ployed here for the
metaphorical possibili-
ties of its name.

If true to their name,
    these "secret vines" I send you
        from Meeting Hill
may wind me a way to you
    unseen by the eyes of men.

na ni shi owaba / ausakayama no / sanekazura / hito ni
shirarede / kuru yoshi mogana

Sugawara no Michizane. Inscription: "Before this journey / I had no time for prayer strips: / so Gods, accept instead / that brocade of autumn leaves / on the slopes of Offering Hill." (KKS 420)

26. AUTUMN. Com-
posed at the request of
Retired Emperor Uda
as an invitation to his
son, Emperor Daigo
(885–930; r. 897–930),
to join him on a visit to
the Ōi River.

440. Lord Teishin [Fujiwara no Tadahira; 880–
949][26]

You autumn leaves
    on the slopes at Ogura—
if you have a heart,
    put off your falling this once:
    till the Emperor's visit.

ogura yama / mine no momijiba / kokoro araba / ima
hitotabi no / miyuki matanan

27. LOVE. The name
of the river, Izumi-
gawa, acts as a pun
in this poem—*itsu*,
"when," and *mi*, "see."

441. Middle Counselor Fujiwara no Kanesuke
[877–933][27]

From the Mika Moor
    waters gush forth to become
    When-See River.
But just *when* did I *see* you,
    that I should be so in love?

mika no hara / wakite nagaruru / izumigawa / itsu miki
tote ka / koishikaruran

28. Grandson of Em-
peror Kōkō (poem
429). WINTER.

442. Minamoto no Muneyuki [d. 939][28]

In a mountain home
    the loneliness increases
    in the winter time—
when one knows that people too
    will vanish with the grasses.

yamazato wa / fuyu zo sabishisa / masarikeru / hitome mo
kusa mo / karenu to omoeba

29. AUTUMN.
Topic: "White Chry-
santhemums."

443. Ōshikōchi no Mitsune [d. ca. 925?][29]

What else can I do
    but make a guess, and pick one?
Beneath the first frost,

one cannot be sure just which
are the white chrysanthemums.

kokoro ate ni / oraba ya oran / hatsu shimo no / oki-
madowaseru / shiragiku no hana

444. Mibu no Tadamine [b. ca. 850]³⁰

Since that parting
  when I saw that distant look
    in the late moon's glare,
nothing seems more cruel to me
  than the hours before dawn.

ariake no / tsurenaku mieshi / wakare yori / akatsuki
bakari / uki mono wa nashi

445. Sakanoue no Korenori [early 10th century]³¹

In the early light
  one could almost mistake it
    for moonrays at dawn—
white snow falling down
  at Yoshino Village.

asaborake / ariake no tsuki to / miru made ni / yoshino no
sato ni / fureru shirayuki

446. Harumichi no Tsuraki [d. 920]³²

In this mountain stream
  the winds have constructed
    a fishing weir—
halting the flow downstream
  of the autumn leaves.

yamakawa ni / kaze no kaketaru / shigarami wa / nagare
mo aenu / momiji narikeri

30. One of the com-
pilers of *Kokinshū*.
LOVE.

31. WINTER. Head-
note: "Written when
he saw snow falling
on a trip to Yamato
Province."

32. AUTUMN. Head-
note: "Written at Shiga
Pass." On fishing weirs,
see the note to poem 33.

33. Tsurayuki's
cousin; one of the com-
pilers of *Kokinshū*.
SPRING. Headnote:
"Written when he saw
cherry blossoms fall-
ing."

447. Ki no Tomonori [d. before 905?] [33]

> On a peaceful day
>   so warm in the tranquil light
>   of the springtime sun,
>   how is it that the blossoms fall
>   with so little sense of calm?

hisakata no / hikari nodokeki / haru no hi ni / shizu-
kokoro naku / hana no chiruran

34. MISCELLA-
NEOUS.

448. Fujiwara no Okikaze [early 10th century] [34]

> Who is there left now
>   that can claim to know me well?
>   Takasago's pines
>   are venerable, of course—
>   but they are hardly old friends.

tare o ka mo / shiru hito ni sen / takasago no / matsu mo
mukashi no / tomo naranaku ni

35. SPRING. Written
when, after not visit-
ing for a long time,
he stopped at an inn
in Hase where he had
always stayed when
on pilgrimage to the
temple. When the pro-
prietor said that the inn
was there as always for
him, Tsurayuki broke
off a branch from a
plum tree standing
nearby and composed
this poem.

449. Ki no Tsurayuki [ca. 872–945] [35]

> About the people
>   living on in this old place
>   I cannot be sure—
>   but the plum blossoms at least
>   have the scent of long ago.

hito wa isa / kokoro mo shirazu / furusato wa / hana zo
mukashi no / ka ni nioikeru

36. SUMMER. Head-
note: "Written toward
dawn when the moon
was particularly capti-
vating."

450. Kiyowara no Fukayabu [early 10th century] [36]

> On this summer eve
>   a new dawn seems to begin
>   before night is done:
>   but in which of those clouds
>   has the moon found a lodging?

natsu no yo wa / mada yoi nagara / akenuru o / kumo no
izuku ni / tsuki yadoruramu

451. Fun'ya no Asayasu [late 9th century] [37]

    Pure white drops of dew
       blown across the autumn moor
    by a steady wind
       are scattered everywhere—
    jewels without a string.

shiratsuyu ni / kaze no fukishiku / aki no no wa / tsura-
nuki tomenu / tama zo chirikeru

37. Son of Yasu-
hide (poem 436).
AUTUMN. Headnote:
"Topic unknown."

452. Lady Ukon [mid-10th century] [38]

    I am forsaken—
    but about myself I don't care.
    Instead I must fear
       for the life you swore away
         when we made our vows of love.

wasuraruru / mi o ba omowazu / chikaiteshi / hito no ino-
chi no / oshiku mo aru kana

38. A lady-in-waiting
to the consort of Em-
peror Daigo. LOVE.
Headnote: "Topic un-
known."

453. Consultant Minamoto no Hitoshi [880–951] [39]

    Like yearning bamboo
       hidden in the grassy fields,
    I longed in secret.
    Why now has my love for you
       become more than I can hide?

asajifu no / ono no shinohara / shinoburedo / amarite
nado ka / hito no koishiki

39. LOVE. Head-
note: "Sent to some-
one." *Shino* is a slender
bamboo plant whose
name is a partial homo-
phone of the verb *shi-
nobu*, "to yearn in
secret."

40. LOVE. Written
for a poem contest.

454. Taira no Kanemori [d. 990][40]

I yearn in secret
    but the truth of my passion
        must show in my face—
so much so that someone asks
    if there's something on my mind.

shinoburedo / iro ni idenikeri / waga koi wa / mono ya
omou to / hito no tou made

41. Son of Tadamine
(poem 444). LOVE.
Written for a poem
contest.

455. Mibu no Tadami [mid-10th century][41]

A man in love,
    that is what people call me
        already, it seems—
and I just beginning to have
    feelings I have told no one.

koi su chō / waga na wa madaki / tachinikeri / hito
shirezu koso / omoisomeshi ka

42. Father of Sei Shō-
nagon (poem 476);
one of the compilers of
Gosenshū (Later Col-
lection; 951). LOVE.
Headnote: "Written by
proxy for a man whose
lover had turned cold
toward him."

456. Kiyowara no Motosuke [908–90][42]

Have you forgotten
    wringing tears from our sleeves—
vowing that our love
    would stand high above the waves
        like Pine Mountain in Sue?

chigiriki na / katami ni sode o / shiboritsutsu / sue no
matsuyama / nami kosaji to wa

43. LOVE. Head-
note: "Topic
unknown."

457. Middle Counselor Fujiwara no Atsutada
[906–43][43]

Compared with the way
    my heart longs for you now
        after we have met,
those yearnings I had before
    seem like nothing at all.

aimite no / nochi no kokoro ni / kurabureba / mukashi wa
mono o / omowazarikeri

458. Middle Counselor Fujiwara no Asatada [910–66][44]

Ah, if our meetings
    were altogether to cease,
then my resentment
    toward you—and toward myself—
might come to an end as well.

au koto no / taete shinaku wa / nakanaka ni / hito o mo
mi o mo / uramizaramashi

44. Son of Sadakata (poem 439). LOVE. Written for a poem contest.

459. Lord Kentoku [Fujiwara no Koretada; 924–72][45]

I can't even think
    of a soul who might tell me,
"How I pity you"—
and so I go on living,
but wasting my life away.

aware to mo / iu beki hito wa / omōede / mi no itazura
ni / narinu beki kana

45. LOVE. Sent to a woman who had turned cold toward him.

460. Sone no Yoshitada [fl. ca. 980–1000][46]

Over Yura bar
    go fishermen in their boats,
oarless, just drifting
    with no more sense of direction
      than have I on my path of love.

yura no to o / wataru funabito / kaji o tae / yukue mo
shiranu / koi no michi kana

46. LOVE. Headnote: "Topic unknown."

47. AUTUMN. Composed on the topic "Autumn Visiting a Run-down House," at the Kawara Estate. The once grand estate, built by Minamoto Tōru (poem 428), was by then a ruin choked by vines and thickets.

461. Monk Egyō [late 10th century][47]

Here I sit alone
   in a house quite overgrown
with *mugura* vines
   where no one pays me a visit—
only the autumn has come.

yaemugura / shigereru yado no / sabishiki ni / hito koso miene / aki wa kinikeri

48. LOVE. Written for a hundred-poem sequence.

462. Minamoto no Shigeyuki [d. 1000?][48]

Like waves in the wind
   that throws them against the rocks,
so my rejection
   leaves my own heart shattered
whenever I long for you.

kaze o itami / iwa utsu nami no / onore nomi / kudakete mono o / omou koro kana

49. One of the compilers of *Gosenshū*. LOVE. Headnote: "Topic unknown." Guards kept watchfires burning outside the outer enclosure of the palace all night.

463. Ōnakatomi no Yoshinobu [921–91][49]

As watchmen's fires
   that blaze around the palace
in the dark of night
   but nearly perish in the day—
so burns the fire of my passion.

mikakimori / eji no takuhi no / yoru wa moe / hiru wa kietsutsu / mono o koso omoe

50. Son of Koretada (poem 459). LOVE. Headnote: "Sent to a woman after returning from her chambers."

464. Fujiwara no Yoshitaka [954–74][50]

The life that before
   I would gladly have given
just to be with you—
   now I find myself wanting it
only to go on and on.

kimi ga tame / oshikarazarishi / inochi sae / nagaku
mogana to / omoikeru kana

465. Fujiwara no Sanekata [d. 998] [51]

    So do I love you—
    but how can I find the words
        to tell you I yearn
            like Ibuki's moxa weeds,
    consuming me from within?

kaku to dani / e ya wa ibuki no / sashimogusa / sa shi mo
shiraji na / moyuru omoi o

466. Fujiwara no Michinobu [972–94] [52]

    That every new dawn
        leads to another nightfall—
    yes, this I know.
    Yet still how much I resent
        the first faint light of day!

akenureba / kururu mono to wa / shirinagara / nao ura-
meshiki / asaborake kana

467. The Mother of Captain of the Right Michi-
tsuna [936?–95] [53]

    When one lies alone
        lamenting the whole night through
            until break of day,
    how slowly the time goes by—
    ah, but yes—you wouldn't know.

nagekitsutsu / hitori nuru yo no / akuru ma wa / ika ni
hisashiki / mono to ka wa shiru

51. Great-grandson of
Tadahira (poem 440).
LOVE. Headnote:
"Sent to a woman for
the first time." *Mogusa*
was burned on the skin
to treat various ills.

52. LOVE. Head-
note: "Sent to a woman
after returning from
her chambers on a
snowy day."

53. Author of *Kagerō
nikki* (The Gossamer
Journal; late 10th cen-
tury). LOVE. Sent
to her husband, the
Regent Fujiwara no
Kaneie (929–90), when
he complained about
being kept waiting
outside her gate after
coming late one night.

"When one lies alone / lamenting the whole night through / until break of
day, / how slowly the time goes by— / ah, but yes—you wouldn't know."
(SIS 912 by The Mother of Captain of the Right Michitsune)

468. The Mother of Provisional Minister Gidō [d. 996][54]

> To never forsake
> is a vow so hard to keep—
> and so long a time!
> Almost you make me wish
> today the last of my life.

wasureji no / yukusue made wa / katakereba / kyō o
kagiri no / inochi to mogana

54. LOVE. Sent after the first visit of her new husband.

469. Major Counselor Fujiwara no Kintō [966–1041][55]

> The waterfall's sound
> faded into nothingness
> a long time ago—
> but its name has come down
> still to be heard today.

taki no oto wa / taete hisashiku / narinuredo / na koso
nagarete / nao kikoekere

55. Compiler of *Shūishū* and *Wakan rōeishū*. MISCELLANEOUS. Written when a group of courtiers visited an old waterfall. The first line of the *Shūishū* version reads *taki no ito wa* ("The waterfall's thread").

470. Izumi Shikibu [fl. ca. 970–1030][56]

> In last remembrance
> of the world I soon must leave
> to return no more,
> this is what I most desire:
> one final meeting with you.

arazaran / kono yo no hoka no / omoide ni / ima hitotabi
no / au koto mogana

56. LOVE. Headnote: "Sent to someone when she was gravely ill."

471. Murasaki Shikibu [fl. 996–1010][57]

> Quite by chance we met,
> and then before I was sure
> who it really was,

57. A lady-in-waiting to Shōshi, consort of Emperor Ichijō (980–1011; r. 986–1011); author of *Genji monogatari*. MISCELLANEOUS. Written after a brief reunion with a childhood friend.

the moonlight had disappeared,
hidden behind midnight clouds.

meguriaite / mishi ya sore to mo / wakanu ma ni /
kumogakurenishi / yowa no tsukikage

472. Daini no Sammi [early 11th century][58]

Near Arima Hill
the wind through Ina's bamboos
blows constantly—
and just as constant am I
in my resolve not to forget.

arimayama / ina no sasahara / kaze fukeba / ide soyo hito
o / wasure ya wa suru

473. Akazome Emon [early 11th century][59]

I could just as well
have slept instead of waiting
late into the night;
but here I am, up to see
the setting of the moon.

yasurawade / nenamashi mono o / sayo fukete / katabuku
made no / tsuki o mishi kana

474. Koshikibu no Naishi [d. 1025][60]

Mother is away
past Ōe and Ikuno,
near Heaven's *Ladder*,
whence would come her *letter*—
but neither have I yet seen.

ōeyama / ikuno no michi no / tōkereba / mada fumi mo
mizu / ama no hashidate

475. Ise no Tayū [fl. 1008–60]⁶¹

> Anciently they bloomed
> in the Nara capital—
> these eightfold cherries
> now displaying their colors
> in the ninefold palace courts.

inishie no / nara no miyako no / yaezakura / kyō kokonoe
ni / nioinuru kana

476. Sei Shōnagon [d. 1027?]⁶²

> Try if you wish
> to fool others with rooster calls
> in the depths of night—
> but still closed to your passage
> will be the gate at Meeting Hill.

yo o komete / tori no sorane wa / hakaru tomo / yo ni
ausaka no / seki wa yurusaji

477. Fujiwara no Michimasa, Master of the Left
Capital [992–1054]⁶³

> Now, yes even now,
> I would like to have a way
> to say at least this:
> —and not by a messenger—
> that I have now given up.

ima wa tada / omoitaenan / to bakari o / hitozute narade /
iu yoshi mogana

478. Middle Counselor Fujiwara no Sadayori
[995–1045]⁶⁴

> In morning's first light
> the mists on Uji River
> are all breaks and gaps—

61. Granddaughter of Ōnakatomi no Yoshinobu (poem 463); a lady-in-waiting to Empress Shōshi. SPRING. Written when someone presented eightfold cherries from Nara as a gift. *Yaezakura* is a variety of wild cherry with eight-petaled blossoms. "Ninefold palace courts" (*kokonoe*) refers to the imperial palace compound.

62. A lady-in-waiting to Teishi, consort of Emperor Ichijō; Kiyowara Motosuke's daughter (poem 456) and Kiyowara no Fukayabu's great-granddaughter (poem 450). MISCELLANEOUS. The poem alludes to an ancient Chinese story. See s.n. 36.

63. LOVE. Composed when it became impossible to see a woman he had been visiting in secret.

64. WINTER. On weirs, see the note to poem 33. Headnote: "Written when he traveled to Uji."

*"Try if you wish / to fool others with your rooster calls / in the depths
of night— / but still closed to your passage / will be the gate at Meeting Hill."*
(GSIS 939 by Sei Shōnagon)

and appearing everywhere,
bamboo stakes of fishing weirs.

asaborake / uji no kawagiri / taedae ni / arawarewataru /
seze no ajirogi

479. Lady Sagami [fl. 1035–61][65]

    Anger and sorrow
        have made my never-dry sleeves
            a complete ruin—
    but still more hateful to me
        is love's ruin of my good name.

urami wabi / hosanu sode dani / aru mono o / koi ni
kuchinan / na koso oshikere

65. A lady-in-waiting to a princess. LOVE. Written for a poem contest.

480. Major Archbishop Gyōson [1055–1135][66]

    Can't we both agree
        to care for one another,
    mountain cherry tree?
    For outside of your blossoms
        no one knows me here at all.

morotomo ni / aware to omoe / yamazakura / hana yori
hoka ni / shiru hito mo nashi

66. MISCELLANEOUS. Headnote: "Written at Ōmine, when he saw a cherry tree in bloom where he didn't expect one."

481. Suo no Naishi [late 11th century][67]

    True, this arm of yours
        could pillow me for a dream
            on this spring night—
    but I fear that afterward
        it might toss my name about.

haru no yo no / yume bakari naru / tamakura ni / kainaku
tatan / na koso oshikere

67. A lady-in-waiting in the courts of Emperors Shirakawa (1053–1129; r. 1069–86) and Horikawa (1079–1107; r. 1086–1107). MISCELLANEOUS. Composed on a moonlit night when Fujiwara no Tadaie (1033–91; Shunzei's grandfather), overhearing her whisper to a lady nearby that she would like to have a pillow, playfully offered his arm as a substitute.

68. MISCELLA-
NEOUS. Headnote:
"Written when he
saw the moon shining
brightly around the
time when he decided
to retire as emperor
because of illness."

482. Retired Emperor Sanjō [976–1017; r.1011–16][68]

If—against my will—
I should live on to look back
  on this vexing world,
I shall remember fondly
  this moon shining in the night.

kokoro ni mo / arade ukiyo ni / nagaraeba / koishikaru-
beki / yowa no tsuki kana

69. AUTUMN. Writ-
ten for a poem contest.
An allusive variation
on KKS 283 and 284
(s.n. 25).

483. Monk Nōin [988–1050?][69]

The winds of a storm
  blowing on Mount Mimuro
have brought autumn leaves
  down to Tatsuta River—
and made it a rich brocade.

arashi fuku / mimuro no yama no / momijiba wa / tatsuta
no kawa no / nishiki narikeri

70. AUTUMN.
Headnote: "Topic un-
known."

484. Monk Ryōzen [mid-11th century][70]

Out of loneliness
  I got up and left my hut
    just to look around:
but outside it was the same—
autumn evening everywhere.

sabishisa ni / yado o tachiidete / nagamureba / izuku mo
onaji / aki no yūgure

71. Father of Toshi-
yori (poem 488).
AUTUMN. Headnote:
"Written on 'Autumn
Wind at a House in the
Paddies' when people
gathered at the moun-
tain village of Mina-
moto no Morokata
[d. 1081] in Umezu."

485. Major Counselor Minamoto no Tsunenobu
[1016–97][71]

When evening falls,
the rice plants out near my gate
  make a rustling sound—

then through my reed-thatched hut
    comes a gust of autumn wind.

yū sareba / kadota no inaba / otozurete / ashi no maroya
ni / akikaze zo fuku

486. Lady Kii [fl. 1061–1113] [72]

   Those frivolous waves
     for which the Takashi strand
       is so justly famous—
   I dare not go too near them,
   for fear of drenching my sleeves.

oto ni kiku / takashi no hama no / adanami wa / kakeji ya
sode no / nure mo koso sure

487. Provisional Middle Counselor Ōe no Masa-
fusa [1041–1111] [73]

   At Takasago
     the cherry trees on the peak
       are all in bloom now—
   O haze out on the foothills,
   please don't stand in their way!

takasago no / onoe no sakura / sakinikeri / toyama no
kasumi / tatazu mo aranamu

488. Minamoto no Toshiyori [1055–1129] [74]

   You mountain wind-blasts
     blowing from Hase Temple:
   in my prayer I asked
     for you to sway her my way—
   not to make her rebuffs more harsh.

ukarikeru / hito o hatsuse no / yamaoroshi yo / hageshi-
kare to wa / inoranu mono o

72. LOVE. A reply
in a contest to a poem
written by Teika's
grandfather Toshitada
(1071–1123) where
he says he would like
to come to his love
"like waves brought
by the wind against a
rough shore."

73. Confucian
scholar; Akazome
Emon's great-grandson
(poem 473). SPRING.
Topic: "Looking at
Cherry Blossoms on
the Hills in the Dis-
tance."

74. LOVE. Topic:
"Praying in Vain to
Meet One's Love."

75. Poet, contest
judge, and scholar.
MISCELLANEOUS.
Sent to Chancellor
Tadamichi (see next
poem) after a request
for his son to be ap-
pointed to a priestly
office had been ignored.
See s.n. 37.

489. Fujiwara no Mototoshi [1060–1142][75]

> Your promise to me
>   was the very dew of life
>   to a struggling plant—
> but, alas, now this year too
>   autumn draws near its end.

chigiri okishi / sasemo ga tsuyu o / inochi nite / aware
kotoshi no / aki mo inumeri

76. MISCELLA-
NEOUS. Topic: "A
Distant View Over
the Sea."

490. The Hosshōji Lay Monk and Former Chan-
cellor [Fujiwara no Tadamichi; 1097–1164][76]

> Out on the broad sea
>   I gaze into the distance
> at what looks like clouds
>   off in the far heavens—
> so high are the white-capped waves.

wata no hara / kogiidete mireba / hisakata no / kumoi ni
mayou / okitsu shiranami

77. LOVE. Head-
note: "Topic
unknown."

491. Retired Emperor Sutoku [1119–64; r.1123–
41][77]

> In a swift current
>   a boulder may block the rush
> of falling water
>   and split streams that in the end
> will join together again.

se o hayami / iwa ni sekaruru / takikawa no / warete mo
sue ni / awamu to zo omou

78. WINTER. Head-
note: "On 'Plovers
at a Barrier Gate.'"
The poem alludes to
descriptions of the
scenery in the "Suma"
chapter of *Genji mono-
gatari*.

492. Minamoto no Kanemasa [early 12th cen-
tury][78]

> Those plovers crying
>   between Awaji Isle and land—

how many long nights
    do they keep the guards from sleep
        at their posts on Suma's shore.

awajishima / kayou chidori no / naku koe ni / ikuyo neza-
menu / suma no sekimori

493. Fujiwara no Akisuke, Master of the Left
Capital [1090–1155]⁷⁹

79. AUTUMN. Writ-
ten for a hundred-poem
sequence.

From behind a rift
    torn in the high trailing clouds
by the autumn wind
    breaks forth the shining moon—
and ah, the clear gleam of its rays!

akikaze ni / tanabiku kumo no / taema yori / moreizuru
tsuki no / kage no sayakesa

494. Taiken Mon-in no Horikawa [mid-12th cen-
tury]⁸⁰

80. LOVE. Written
for a hundred-poem
sequence.

How can I be sure
    that your heart will never change—
with my own feelings
    as tangled this next morning
        as my black hair after sleep?

nagakaran / kokoro mo shirazu / kurokami no / midarete
kesa wa / mono o koso omoe

495. The Gotokudaiji Minister of the Left [Fuji-
wara no Sanesada; 1139–91]⁸¹

81. Nephew of Shun-
zei (poem 497). SUM-
MER. Topic: "Hear-
ing a Cuckoo Calling
at Dawn."

When I turned to look
    off toward the direction
        of the cuckoo's call,
the only thing left to me
    was the moon in the dawn sky.

hototogisu / nakitsuru kata o / nagamureba / tada ariake
no / tsuki zo nokoreru

496. Monk Dōin [Fujiwara no Atsuyori; b. 1090][82]

Though deep in despair,
I have not yet felt my life
    drained away by love;
but less resistant to pain
    are my ever-flowing tears.

omoiwabi / sate mo inochi wa / aru mono o / uki ni taenu
wa / namida narikeri

497. Fujiwara no Shunzei, Master of the Grand
Empress's Household Office [1114–1204][83]

From this world of ours
    there is simply no escape:
even in deep hills
    where I go to flee my cares
    I hear the call of a stag.

yo no naka yo / michi koso nakere / omoiiru / yama no
oku ni mo / shika zo naku naru

498. Fujiwara no Kiyosuke [1104–77][84]

If I should live on,
I may yet recall this time
    with tender feelings—
for those times I once thought hard
    seem now like fond memories.

nagaraeba / mata konogoro ya / shinobaren / ushi to
mishi yo zo / ima wa koishiki

499. Monk Shun'e [1113–91?]⁸⁵

On those long nights
    when I am up lamenting,
all seems cruel to me—
    even the stubborn darkness
        seen through the crack in my door.

yomosugara / mono omou koro wa / akeyaranu / neya no
hima sae / tsurenakarikeri

500. Monk Saigyō [1118–90]⁸⁶

As if to tell me,
    "Grieve on!" the moonlight shines down—
but that cannot be.
    Yet still that is where my tears
        seem to want to look for blame.

nageke tote / tsuki ya wa mono o / omowasuru / kako-
chigao naru / waga namida kana

501. Monk Jakuren [1139?–1202]⁸⁷

Needles on the black pines
    are not yet dry of raindrops
from a passing shower
    when already mist is rising
on an evening in autumn.

murasame no / tsuyu mo mada hinu / maki no ha ni / kiri
tachinoboru / aki no yūgure

502. Kōka Mon-in no Bettō [late 12th century]⁸⁸

Because of one night—
    brief as the space between joints
        on Naniwa's reeds—
    am I to be a buoy,
        tossed by waves of love?

85. Son of Toshiyori (poem 488). LOVE. Headnote: "A love poem."

86. LOVE. Topic: "Love Before the Moon."

87. AUTUMN. From a fifty-poem sequence.

88. A lady-in-waiting to the consort of Retired Emperor Sutoku (poem 491). LOVE. Written for a poem contest. Topic: "Lovers Meeting at a Traveler's Inn."

Monk Jakuren. Inscription: "Needles on the black pines / are not yet dry of raindrops / from a passing shower / when already mist is rising / on an evening in autumn." (SKKS 491)

naniwae no / ashi no karine no / hitoyo yue / mi o tsuku-
shite ya / koi wataru beki

503. Princess Shikishi [d. 1201][89]

    Like a string of jewels,
    break now—shatter, my life!
    For if I live on
        I must surely lose the strength
        to conceal my secret love.

tama no o yo / taenaba taene / nagaraeba / shinobu koto
no / yowari mo zo suru

504. Inbu Mon-in no Tayū [mid-12th century][90]

    Look here, look at these!
    Would even a fisher's sleeves
        at Ojima Isle,
    drenched, drenched, over and again,
    change so in color as mine?

miseba ya na / ojima no ama no / sode dani mo / nure ni
zo nureshi / iro wa kawarazu

505. The Go-Kyōgoku Regent and Former Chan-
cellor Fujiwara no Yoshitsune [1169–1206][91]

    A cricket cries out
        near my straw mattress, in the cold
        of a frosty night—
    as I spread my single robe
        to spend the night alone.

kirigirisu / naku ya shimoyo no / samushiro ni / koromo
katashiki / hitori ka mo nen

89. LOVE. Head-
note: "On 'Secret
Love,' written for
a hundred-poem
sequence."

90. LOVE. Head-
note: "A love poem,
written for a poem
contest." An allusive
variation on GSIS 827,
by Minamoto no Shige-
yuki (late 10th cen-
tury). See s.n. 38.

91. AUTUMN. Writ-
ten for a hundred-poem
sequence.

92. A lady-in-waiting to Go-Toba's consort, Ninshi. LOVE. Headnote: "On 'Love/Rock.'"

506. Nijō-in no Sanuki [1141?–1217?][92]

My sleeves are like
   rocks hidden in the offing
      even at ebb tide—
for no one knows they are here,
and never are they dry.

waga sode wa / shiohi ni mienu / oki no ishi no / hito koso shirane / kawaku ma mo nashi

93. A son of Minamoto no Yoritomo (1147–99) and third of the Kamakura shoguns. TRAVEL. Headnote: "Topic unknown."

507. The Kamakura Minister of the Right [Minamoto no Sanetomo; 1192–1219][93]

Ah, this world of ours—
always it should be like this:
a fishing skiff off shore
   pulled along by men with ropes—
a sight that pierces the heart!

yo no naka wa / tsune ni mo gamona / nagisa kogu / ama no obune no / tsunade kanashi mo

94. AUTUMN. Headnote: "On 'Fulling Block.'" An allusive variation on poem 445, by Sakanoue no Korenori.

508. Consultant Asukai Masatsune [1170–1221][94]

In fair Yoshino
   autumn winds blow from the mountains,
late into the night;
and cold in the old capital—
the sound of mallet on block.

miyoshino no / yama no akikaze / sayo fukete / furusato samuku / koromo utsu nari

95. MISCELLANEOUS. Headnote: "Topic unknown." "Ink-black sleeves" refers to the robes of a cleric. At the time, Jien was Tendai Abbot, one of the highest of all ecclesiastical callings.

509. Archbishop Jien [1155–1225][95]

Although unworthy,
I now must guide the people
   of the vexing world—
living in the high timbers,
wearing my new ink-black sleeves.

ōkenaku / ukiyo no tami ni / ōu kana / waga tatsu soma
ni / sumizome no sode

510. The Lay Monk and Former Chancellor [Fuji-
wara no (Saionji) Kintsune; 1171–1244] [96]

> My courtyard is strewn
>   with storm-beckoned blossoms,
> and not with snow—
> the only thing descending here
> is my body as it grows old.

hana sasou / arashi no niwa no / yuki narade / furiyuku
mono wa / waga mi narikeri

96. MISCELLA-
NEOUS. Headnote:
"Written when he saw
blossoms falling."

511. Provisional Middle Counselor Fujiwara no
Teika [1162–1241] [97]

> On Matsuo Beach
>   I wait in the pines at dusk
>   for one who won't come—
> and like the blazing salt mounds,
> I too am consumed by fire.

konu hito o / matsuo no ura no / yūnagi ni / yaku ya
moshio no / mi mo kogaretsutsu

97. LOVE. Written
for a poem contest. An
allusive variation on
MYS 935, by Kasa no
Kanamura (s.n. 39).
Seaweed was burned to
extract its salt.

512. Fujiwara no Ietaka of Junior Second Rank
[1158–1237] [98]

> As day nears its end
>   with a breeze rustling in the oaks
>   along Nara Stream,
> the people doing ablutions
> are the sole sign of summer.

kaze soyogu / nara no ogawa no / yūgure wa / misogi zo
natsu no / shirushi narikeru

98. SUMMER. Writ-
ten for a screen paint-
ing. An allusive varia-
tion on GSIS 231, by
Minamoto no Yori-
tsuna (d. 1097) and
the anonymous SKKS
1375 (s.n. 40). Ritual
washings (*misogi*) were
undertaken on the
last day of the Sixth
Month, symbolizing
purification from sins.

513. Retired Emperor Go-Toba [1180–1239;
r.1184–98][99]

99.   MISCELLA-
NEOUS. Headnote:
"Topic unknown."

> People can seem kind,
>   and people can seem cruel—
>   when quite foolishly
>   I wear myself out worrying
>   over the world and its ways.

hito mo oshi / hito mo urameshi / ajikinaku / yo o omou
yue ni / mono omou mi wa

514. Retired Emperor Juntoku [1197–1242;
r.1210–21][100]

100.   Go-Toba's son.
MISCELLANEOUS.
Headnote: "Topic un-
known." *Shinobugusa*
is a fern whose name
is a partial homophone
with the verb *shinobu*,
"to think fondly of
the past."

> In the stone-built palace
>   the old eaves are overgrown
>   with Memory Fern—
>   but ah, what a past is here
>   still left to be remembered!

momoshiki ya / furuki nokiba no / shinobu ni mo / nao
amari aru / mukashi narikeri

Minamoto no Sanetomo (1192-1219)

Judging from his title "Barbarian-subduing Chieftain," or shogun, one
would not guess that Minamoto no Sanetomo, third of the military poten-
tates of the Kamakura period, was also a fine poet. But in fact this third

son of the great warrior Yoritomo (1147–99) was a courtier in his own right who not only composed poetry but also rose as high as minister of the Right in the court hierarchy. His poetic education began when he was young and continued until his premature death at the age of twenty-eight, victim of an assassin's blade. Among his teachers was Teika himself, who carried on an active correspondence with the young man from 1206 on, providing criticism as requested and even writing a short treatise that has become a classic of its kind (*Kindai shūka*; Superior Poems of Our Time).

One of the elements of Sanetomo's work that Teika expressed misgivings about was his preference for a deliberately archaic style that seems to have found its inspiration in *Man'yōshū*. And, although many of his poems are undistinguishable from others of his own time, the ones that have made him famous are those that do indeed reveal a remarkable directness of expression. One thing this means for the student of his poetry is that the critical terminology of Shunzei and Teika—except perhaps for the word "loftiness" (*take*)—does not suit his work. Instead, one must use words like "directness" and "realism," terms that are far from *yūgen* and *yōen* but have a freshness all their own.

515. WINTER. Written on the first day of the Tenth Month

> Autumn's gone away.
> The wind has blown from the trees
> every single leaf;
> and the mountains are forlorn
> now that winter has come.

aki wa inu / kaze ni konoha no / chirihatete / yama sabishikaru / fuyu wa kinikeri

516. WINTER. "Hail"

> A fighting man
> straightens arrows in his quiver
>   with one backstretched hand—
> hail glancing from his wristguard
> onto Nasu's grassy moor.[1]

mononofu no / yanami tsukurou / kote no ue ni / arare tabashiru / nasu no shinohara

1. The *kote*, a leather guard, was worn to protect the wrist from the bowstring's recoil.

517. WINTER. On the topic "White"

> On a white sandspit
>   where seagulls have come to earth
>   snow has been falling—
> and in the clearing sky above,
> the clear gleam of the moon.

kamome iru / oki no shirasu ni / furu yuki no / hareyuku
sora no / tsuki no sayakesa

518. MISCELLANEOUS. Written down when look-
ing out on the sea so engulfed in haze that it looked
to be one with the sky

> The sky and the sea,
> or the sea and then the sky—
> one can't tell them apart,
> with both the haze and the waves
>   now cresting so high.

sora ya umi / umi ya sora tomo / miewakanu / kasumi mo
nami mo / tachimichinitsutsu

519. TRAVEL. When he crossed over the pass at
Hakone, he saw a little island where waves were
breaking. "Do you know the name of this sea?"
he asked those with him, and composed this when
they replied that it was the Izu Sea:

> Just over the peak
>   of Hakone's high pass—
> there is Izu Sea,
> where I behold waves breaking
>   on the shores of a little isle.

hakoneji o / waga koekureba / izu no umi ya / oki no
kojima ni / nami no yoru miyu

520. TRAVEL. Written when the rain was falling
hard as he made his way back from a pilgrimage to
the two shrines[2]

> By now the spring rain
>   must have drenched him to the skin
> as he walks that path
>   through the foot-wearying hills.
> Who is he, though, that mountain man?

harusame ni / uchi sohochitsutsu / ashihiki no / yamaji
yukuramu / yamabito ya tare

2. Izu and Hakone,
both dedicated to the
patron deities of the
shogunal house.

521. BUDDHISM. A poem on "On the Middle Way
of the Greater Vehicle"[3]

> Our life in this world
>   is like the image one sees
>   inside a mirror—
> something that's not really there,
> but then not really not there.

yo no naka wa / kagami ni utsuru / kage ni are ya / aru ni
mo arazu / naki ni mo arazu

3. The Mahayana
tradition, which holds
there are three Ways
to enlightenment: the
Way of Emptiness, the
Way of Temporality,
and the Middle Way,
which promises a unity
of consciousness.

522. MISCELLANEOUS. Written upon seeing waves
breaking against a rocky shore

> From the broad sea,
> waves roar in with a crashing
>   hard against the shore—
> breaking, then shattering,
> bursting, and scattering!

ōumi no / iso mo todoro ni / yosuru nami / warete kuda-
kete / sakete chiru ka mo

523. MISCELLANEOUS. "Black"

> In midnight gloom
>   as black as leopard-flower seeds,
> off beyond the clouds,
>   hidden behind layers of cloud—
> I hear wild geese calling.

ubatama ya / yami no kuraki ni / amagumo no / yaegumo-
gakure / kari zo naku naru

524. MISCELLANEOUS. "Plovers"

> In dawn's first dim light
>   no trace of the boat marks the waves
> where plovers cry out
>   loudly, as if in complaint.
> But alas, how long will they last?

asaborake / ato naki nami ni / naku chidori / ana koto-
gotoshi / aware itsu made

525. MISCELLANEOUS. "Cherry Tree"

> With each passing spring
>   this old, rotting cherry tree
> must think fondly
>   of what it was in the past—
> and yet it does no good.

inishie no / kuchiki no sakura / haru goto ni / aware
mukashi to / omou kai nashi

Kyōgoku Tamekane (1254-1332)
and His Faction

Despite his relative inactivity as a poet in the last decade or so of his life, Teika still occupied a place similar to his father's in literary circles. And after his death, his reputation grew, until he became the model for medieval poets of all persuasions. Within several decades, however, his descendants began to argue over just what the precise dimensions of Teika's model should be. Some saw the Teika of youth as most worthy of emulation; others opted for the Teika of old age. When disputes over estate rights were added to the conflict, the foundation was set for an argument that would last two hundred years.

It was the more conservative side—the senior Nijō line descending from Teika's formal heir—that won out in practical terms, dominating poetic circles much of the time and supervising the compilation of ten of the remaining twelve imperial anthologies. But scholars are virtually unanimous in proclaiming the artistic superiority of the poetry of the other school—referred to as the Kyōgoku/Reizei faction because it represented those two branches of the Mikohidari family.

The most powerful poet of the school was Kyōgoku Tamekane, a grandson of Teika's who was in many ways as impetuous and irascible as his ancestor. He began studying the family traditions in his youth and soon developed a distinct style, producing descriptive poems that attempted to let the images of the natural world stand on their own, without overt intervention on the part of the poet himself. For this approach he was upbraided by the Nijō poets, who complained that there was little in his poems to distinguish them from prose—and clumsy prose at that. But there is a remarkable freshness in his work all the same. Often he focuses on a moment of subtle change in the landscape or in the human heart with sensitive descriptions that anticipate the haiku of Bashō.

By himself, though, and in an environment that was in general opposed to his project, Tamekane could never have accomplished what he did. Fortunately for him, he had the support of two powerful patrons, Emperor Fushimi (1265–1317; r. 1287–98), and his Empress, Eifuku Mon-in (1271–1342), who agreed with his poetic approach. Their salon became the fortress of the Kyōgoku style, which was eventually represented by two imperial anthologies.

Always a volatile personality, Tamekane suffered many political reverses during the reigns of emperors opposed to his views. He was exiled in 1298, but was allowed to return to the capital in 1303. Then, in 1316, he was exiled again, this time never to return. His poems, however, continued to have influence throughout the rest of the tradition, providing an alternative to the plain style of the Nijō school that was to influence not only uta but also linked verse during the chaotic days of the Late Medieval Age.

Kyōgoku Tamekane

526. SPRING. On "Spring Rain," composed when he held a poem contest at his home

> On an evening
>   set aglow with the crimson
>   of plum blossoms,
> the willow boughs sway softly;
> and the spring rain falls.[1]

1. An allusive variation on poem 95, by Yakamochi.

ume no hana / kurenai niou / yūgure ni / yanagi nabikite / harusame zo furu

527. SUMMER. From among his summer poems

> Sifting through branches,
> the rays of the morning sun
>   are still very few—
> and how deep is the coolness
>   back among the bamboos!

eda ni moru / asahi no kage no / sukunasa ni / suzushisa fukaki / take no oku kana

528. TRAVEL. On "Travel at Night," from a
hundred-poem sequence

> He passes the inn
>   where he was to spend the night—
> drawn on by the moon.
> Already on tomorrow's path
>   is the midnight traveler.

tomaru beki / yado o ba tsuki ni / akugarete / asu no
michi yuku / yowa no tabibito

529. LOVE. From a fifty-poem sequence on the
topic "Love Left Unexpressed"

> With him bound by fear
>   and I too much reserved
>   to ask him to come,
> this night we should be sharing
>   simply wastes itself away.

hito mo tsutsumi / ware mo kasanete / toigatami / tanome-
shi yowa wa / tada fuke zo yuku

530. LOVE. On "Waiting, in Love"

> I keep on waiting,
> with my heart encouraging
>   the sun on its way:
> "Will the day never end?"
> "It is taking far too long!"

matsu koto no / kokoro ni susumu / kyō no hi wa / kureji
to sure ya / amari hisashiki

531. LOVE. Topic unknown

> How many times
>   have we met only to fear
>   it was the last time?

Now the sadness we felt then
no one else can know.

oriori no / kore ya kagiri mo / iku omoi / sono aware o
ba / shiru hito mo nashi

532. MISCELLANEOUS. "Distant View of the Sea"

Out on the waves
the last rays of the evening sun
shimmer for a moment,
but that far little island
is already in darkness.

nami no ue ni / utsuru yūhi no / kage wa aredo / tōtsu
kojima wa / iro kurenikeri

533. SPRING. Topic unknown

The sun is almost down
when on the horizon's edge
something new appears—
deep back in the hazy hills,
a still more distant peak.

shizumihatsuru / irihi no kiwa ni / arawarenu / kasumeru
yama no / nao oku no mine

534. WINTER. Topic unknown

Starting, then stopping,
the hail moves through my garden
all at a slant;
shining banks of cloud
darken in the sky above.

furiharuru / niwa no arare wa / katayorite / iro naru kumo
ni / sora zo kureyuku

535. MISCELLANEOUS. From among his miscella-
neous poems

> The sky's expanse
>   is covered over everywhere
>   · with clouds of concern—
> blessing our nation, our soil,
> with rain sent from above.

ōzora ni / amaneku ōu / kumo no kokoro / kuni tsuchi
uruu / ame kudasu nari

Retired Emperor Fushimi

536. MISCELLANEOUS. On "Wind in the Pines"

> To avoid getting wet
>   I took cover a moment
>   in the shade of pines—
> where the rain made me listen
>   to the sound of the wind.

nururu ka to / tachiyasuraeba / matsukage ya / kaze no
kikaseru / ame ni zo arikeru

537. MISCELLANEOUS. On "Wind," from among
his miscellaneous poems

> Echoing high
>   in the tops of the pine trees,
> it comes tumbling down
>   until in the grass its voice dies—
> the wind below the mountain slope.

hibikikuru / matsu no ure yori / fukiochite / kusa ni koe
yamu / yama no shita kaze

538. SUMMER. From among his summer poems

> The moon emerges,
>   and the light of the stars
>   undergoes a change;
>   a cool wind is blowing
>   through the dark of the night sky.

tsuki ya izuru / hoshi no hikari no / kawaru kana / suzu-
shiki kaze no / yūyami no sora

539. LOVE. From among his many love poems

> In the midst of love
>   I see one thing in everything
>   within my gaze—
>   not a tree, not a blade of grass
>   but is a vision of you.

koishisa ni / naritatsu naka no / nagame ni wa / omokage
naranu / kusa mo ki mo nashi

Eifuku Mon-in

540. WINTER. Topic unknown

> The river plovers—
>   is the chill of the moonlight
>   keeping them awake?
>   Every time I start from sleep
>   I hear their voices calling.[2]

kawa chidori / tsukiyo o samumi / inezu are ya / neza-
muru goto ni / koe no kikoyuru

541. LOVE. A love poem

> He made no promise—
>   so I try to tell myself

2. An echo of poem
179, by Tsurayuki.

not to be bitter,
until this long night too
ends with a lonely dawn.

tanomeneba / hito ya wa uki to / omoinasedo / koyoi mo
tsui ni / mata akenikeri

542. SPRING. "Blossoms at Evening"

On cherry petals
the rays of the setting sun
flutter a moment—
and then, before one knows it,
the light has faded away.

hana no ue ni / shibashi utsurou / yūzukuhi / iru to mo
nashi ni / kage kienikeri

The
Late Medieval Age

The shogunal government established in Kamakura by the Minamoto clan in 1185 was able to suppress the violence that had ushered in the medieval age for a time. But the forces that violence represented—the dissatisfaction of rural warlords with their political place, the weakening of traditional loyalties at all levels of society, the rise of volatile new religious movements, and the growth of an entrepreneurial class ready to take advantage of any opportunity for gain—could not be stayed forever. The Kamakura government gradually lost control of the country in the late thirteenth century and fell in the 1330's to one of its own captains, who set up another shogunal dynasty, the Ashikaga. A century and a half later, after failing to maintain a strong central government, that dynasty—also known as the Muromachi Shogunate—collapsed in its turn, leaving the country in a fragmented state that would continue until 1600.

During most of this time the traditions of the court managed to survive. Court poets continued to produce poetry in the old settings, and also continued to argue with one another, producing two traditions—generally referred to as the "liberal" and the "conservative"—that together produced the last flowering of the uta. Personal anthologies *were compiled; hundred-poem sequences were commissioned; mem-oirs and travel accounts were written; poetry contests continued to be held in the mansions of the nobility. More imperial anthologies were produced as well, the last—twenty-first in the line that had begun more than five hundred years before with* Kokinshū—*appearing in 1439.*

On the surface, then, traditional standards were staunchly main-tained. But even in Kyōto, the last bastion of court culture, major changes were taking place. First, the old genres continued to find new practitioners and new audiences outside the halls of the traditional aris-tocracy. Now not only men of the shogunal families, but also provincial warriors became active participants in literary life, inviting poets to their city homes, where they held contests and collected books for their libraries. In the end, the Ashikaga shoguns and their generals even dis-placed the noble families as the prime stimulus behind the compiling of new imperial anthologies—an expensive venture that the traditional aristocracy could no longer support alone. And, although these new members of the literary class by and large accepted courtly standards of taste in the arts, their participation nonetheless broadened the horizons of the *uta*, allowing more "realistic" description and more "vulgar" vocabulary into the canon. In this setting, Chinese poetry, now com-posed by Zen monks whose monasteries were important centers of intellectual life, became popular again—and among poets who often showed more allegiance to their own sources of power and religious ideas than to the courtly past.

More important than any of this, however, was the gradual upsurge among all classes of interest in linked verse—a courtly form, but one without the *uta's* illustrious history. Teika and his associates had toyed with the form as an amusement some years before; but by the late four-teenth century *renga* was equal in popularity to the *uta* even among many court poets. Here, too, the aesthetic standards of the past con-tinued to hold sway. But no one could pretend that the composition of linked verse required the knowledge of the classical canon demanded by the more prestigious *uta* form. For this reason, many of the most famous *renga* poets, whose knowledge of court literature came through years of hard dedication, lamented the increasing popularity of their own genre. Desiring to identify themselves with the court tradition, they compiled imperial anthologies of linked verse and wrote treatises in support of its claims as a courtly form.

But the forces for social change could not be denied. Throughout the 1400's, the country was in a period of turmoil and change. While Kyōto itself became a battlefield for opposing warlords, castle towns appeared all over the landscape. Trade with China stimulated economic activity and gave rise to a money economy, a trend that was further stimulated by the fragmentation of estates and increasing specialization in commerce and light industry. In a word, the country was changing fast, leaving those tied to the old ways behind. Although the court classes, supported by friends among the warrior elite, managed to hang on for a while, they would never again be at the center of cultural life.

Their place as patrons was taken by wealthy warriors and merchants who invited new poets to their Kyōto homes and to their provincial towns. Most of these new poets were men of humble background, eager professionals who purveyed culture as they taught poetry—both uta and renga—for favors and fees. Inevitably, their participation in poetic affairs introduced a plebeian element into the literary mix of the day, eventually creating a subgenre of renga known as haikai—a lighter, more energetic genre that would propel poetry into the modern age.

Monk Tonna (1289-1372)

All poets of the late medieval age looked to Teika as the founder of their tradition; but some looked to other and earlier poets as well. For the monk Tonna, this second mentor was Saigyō. Like his poetic forebear, Tonna came from a military family and took the tonsure at around age twenty, undergoing religious training on Mount Hiei. Then he traveled in Saigyō's footsteps and even stayed in a hut where Saigyō had lived in the Eastern Hills of the capital at Kyōto. In other ways, however, he could not follow Saigyō's example. In the twelfth century, the poetic world had been more open; in Tonna's time, it was clearly divided into two camps, the conservative Nijō faction and the more liberal Kyōgoku-Reizei faction.

Tonna opted for the conservative approach, the prudent course at the time. Thus his poetry, in both the uta and linked verse, is chiefly in the plain style encouraged by the Nijō family. *Ushin* was his guiding ideal, and one that he realized as well as anyone of his period (see poems 543, 546, 552). For, while lacking the energy of Tamekane, his poems have quiet virtues— a fine mastery of the descriptive style of *sabi*, or "loneliness" (see 543, 549, and 553, in particular), and an "educated" imagination that make him as good a poet in linked verse (550–53) as in the uta.

543. SUMMER. On "Summer Flowers Before the Wind," written for a poem contest between young and old at the home of the Minister of Popular Affairs[1]

1. Probably a reference to Nijō Tamefuji (1275–1324).

> In summer grasses
> the leaves on the reeds disappear
> in the rank growth,
> but revealing them in passing
> is the dusk wind on the fields.[2]

2. An allusive variation on SIS 139, by Tsurayuki (s.n. 41).

natsukusa no / shigemi ni mienu / ogi no ha o / shirasete suguru / nobe no yūkaze

544. SUMMER. "Fireflies in the Fields"

> On Miyagi Moor,
>   in the gloom beneath the trees,
> fireflies dart about—
> more numerous than dewdrops
>   in their tangle of light.[3]

3. An allusive varia-
tion on KKS 1091
(s.n. 42).

miyagino no / ko no shita yami ni / tobu hotaru / tsuyu ni
masarite / kage zo midaruru

545. SUMMER. On "Summer Cool," from three
poems composed at the house of the Tōji-in Minis-
ter of the Left, Posthumous

> Crying cicadas
>   are in one voice with the sound
> that reverberates
> —cool, in the shade of the pines—
> from a mountain cascade.

naku semi no / koe mo hitotsu ni / hibikikite / matsu kage
suzushi / yama no takitsuse

546. LOVE. On "Thoughts," from ten poems writ-
ten at the home of the Mikohidari Major Coun-
selor[4]

4. Nijō Tameyo
(1250–1338).

> What am I to do?
> For if there is one place
>   you can't trust your thoughts
>   as a guide along the way—
> it is on the path of love.

ika ni sen / omoi nomi koso / shirube to mo / tanomi-
gataki wa / koiji narikere

547. LOVE. On "Waiting for Love," from a fifty-
poem sequence presented to Shōgō-in[5]

> I told him myself
>   that I would not expect him
>   to come this evening;
>   yet I can't give up fretting,
>   waiting for I don't know what.

tanomaji to / hito ni wa iishi / yūgure o / omoi mo sutezu /
nan to matsuran

5. A cloister located
just northeast of Kyōto.
The abbot of the time
was Prince Kakujo
(1250–1336).

548. BUDDHISM. From among poems presented
to Hie Shrine by the Captain of the Left Guards
on "Color is no different from the sky; the sky is
no different from color," from *The Heart of the
Prajna Sutra*[6]

> Clouds disappear
>   and the sky clears to deep blue,
>   but as I gaze up,
>   that color, too, in a while
>   has faded into emptiness.

kumo kiete / midori ni haruru / sora mireba / iro koso
yagate / munashikarikere

6. A shorter ver-
sion of *Prajnapara-
mita Sutra*.

549. AUTUMN. On "A Snipe Before the Moon,"
written at the house of the Regent on the night of
the thirteenth day of the Ninth Month

> Up from the paddies
>   where the moon has stayed the night,
>   a snipe leaves its roost—
>   rising up from the icepack
>   into the dawning sky.[7]

tsuki yadoru / sawada no tsura ni / fusu shigi no / kōri
yori tatsu / akegata no sora

7. An allusive varia-
tion on poem 297, by
Saigyō.

550. AUTUMN

Amongst the sorrows
there is also happiness—
all mixed together.

Waiting for the moon to come out
on an evening in autumn.

uki koto ni / ureshiki koto ya / majiruran; tsuki machi-
izuru / aki no yūgure

551. AUTUMN

Didn't someone once weave letters
over a rich brocade?[8]

Along the ridge
autumn geese make their way
above crimson leaves.[9]

nishiki no ue ni / moji ya oruran; yama no ha no / momiji
o wataru / aki no kari

8. An allusion to an old Chinese story in which a lady sent her husband a message embroidered in cloth.

9. Link: the pattern of the geese above the leaves suggests letters woven over brocade.

552. MISCELLANEOUS

If you cast it all away
the load will get much lighter.

Don't brush it off
and it will break in the snow—
bamboo by the window.

furisutenureba / yo koso karokere; harawazuba / yuki ni
ya oremu / mado no take

553. AUTUMN

> After the village
>   has grown old, still there's someone
>   left living there.
>
> With the wind in the reeds
>   comes the sound of a fulling block.[10]

10. On fulling blocks,
see the note to poem
256.

furusato to / naru made hito no / nao sumite; ogi fuku
kaze ni / koromo utsu nari

A Sequence from 'Fūgashū'

In all, court civilization produced twenty-one imperial anthologies of uta.
But most critics agree that after the eighth, *Shin kokinshū*, only several re-
ward study. Most prominent among these are *Gyokuyōshū* and *Fūgashū*—
both compiled by advocates of the Kyōgoku-Reizei school.

In the case of *Gyokuyōshū* (Collection of Jeweled Leaves; 1313), it was
Emperor Fushimi, no doubt conscious of the model of Retired Emperor
Go-Toba, who sponsored the activities that led to the work's compila-
tion. Even with his help, however, the project was accomplished only with
great difficulty. And when Emperor Fushimi died in 1317, just eight months
after the compiler, Kyōgoku Tamekane, had been sent into exile on Sado,
it appeared that the last great generation of court poets had come to a
dismal end.

But Fushimi's Empress, Eifuku Mon-in, survived; one of the dead sover-
eign's sons, Hanazono (1297–1348; r. 1308–18), proved to have his father's
talents, as well as his patience. Together the two resolved that the unortho-
dox tradition should not die, sponsoring contests, issuing requests, and in

general moving toward one last statement, which would in time become the collection known as *Fūgashū* (Collection of Elegance; 1347).

As it turned out, the Former Empress died before seeing the command for the work issued. But she was clearly a force behind it—as Emperor Hanazono, himself a retired sovereign for nearly twenty years before the opportunity for a new anthology appeared, must have wanted to indicate when he included sixty-eight of her poems in the final product, more than anyone save Emperor Fushimi himself.

In design, the collection is like its predecessors, with books on the seasons, love, and other topics, all organized according to the ideal of associational progression that had first been implemented fully in *Shin kokinshū* a century and a half before. But in one way the seventeenth collection is distinctive: unlike the other imperial collections, it is a somber work, characterized more by a sense of foreboding and loss than such representations of "court culture" were generally allowed to be. That Emperor Hanazono, wistful over the recent past when his father had sponsored a lively and forward-looking court, was the chief compiler of the work is probably the chief reason for its dark tones. But in the 1340's, when the country was in the middle of a long period of civil war, the somberness can only have seemed entirely natural.

The following sequence of twenty poems, taken from the fourth of five Love books, is an appropriately melancholy example. To show the unity of mind within the tradition, Hanazono has chosen poems from early writers—Ki no Tsurayuki, Izumi Shikibu, some anonymous poets from *Man'yōshū*, and Ono no Komachi—as well as works of his own day. But he has also organized his series to show the contrasts between earlier conventions and those of his own time. Tsurayuki's poem (554) leads off, relying on natural imagery to convey mood; six poems later, with Eifuku Mon-in's "Love" poem (560), we enter the world of intense emotion more directly expressed. In order to not appear too obvious, however, Hanazono then presents five poems that in one way or another use the sky in their metaphorical designs (561–65), returning thereafter to psychological description at the end. The sequence thus presents a masterly treatment of its topic—the anguish of those rejected in love—while including some of the finest poets of the unorthodox school, most notably Tamekane, Retired Emperor Fushimi, Eifuku Mon-in, Retired Emperor Hanazono, and his heir, Retired Emperor Kōgon (1313–64; r. 1331–33).

554. Ki no Tsurayuki [ca. 812–945]. Topic un-
known

> You returning geese,
> please pass this message along—
> how in my travels,
> here on my pillow of grass,
> I long so for my woman!

kaeru kari / waga koto tsute yo / kusamakura / tabi wa
imo koso / koishikarikere

555. Izumi Shikibu [fl. ca. 970–1030]. Written the
morning after a man she had been expecting had
not come

> Even at the sound
>   of a water rail knocking
> I might have gone out
>   and opened my door of black pine—
> just to give myself some hope.[1]

1. The call of the rail,
kuina, was conven-
tionally described as
"knocking."

kuina dani / tataku oto seba / maki no to o / kokoroyari
ni mo / akete mitemashi

556. Anonymous. Topic unknown

> Just what must I do
>   in order to forget her?
> My love for the woman
>   is only getting stronger,
> impossible to forget.

ika ni shite / wasururu mono zo / wagimoko ni / koi wa
masaredo / wasurarenaku ni

557. Anonymous. Topic unknown

> Leaving my woman
>   back in my old home village
>   in Ōhara,

I can't get to sleep at night—
seeing her in my dreams.

ōhara no / furinishi sato ni / imo o okite / ware ineka-
netsu / yume ni mietsutsu

558. Anonymous. Topic unknown

> With no way now
>   for me to meet my woman,
> must I burn within
>   like the high peak of Fuji
>   in the land of Suruga?

wagimoko ni / au yoshi mo nami / suruga naru / fuji no
takane no / moetsutsu ka aran

559. Ono no Komachi [fl. ca. 850]. Topic unknown

> Let the world go on,
> changeable as the waters
>   of Tomorrow River—
> so long as no rift opens
>   to separate you and me.

yo no naka wa / asukagawa ni mo / naraba nare / kimi to
ware to ga / naka shi taezu wa

560. Eifuku Mon-in [1271–1342]. On "Love"

> Perhaps on this day
>   he is remembering me
>   with special fondness—
> for I too more than usual
>   find myself yearning for him.

kyō wa moshi / hito mo ware o / omoiizuru / ware mo
tsune yori / hito no koishiki

561. Princess Shinshi [mid-14th century].² "Stak-
ing One's Life on Love"

The sky's color,
   even the sight of the trees—
all seem sad to me
   when life itself seems to hang
      in the balance of my thoughts.

sora no iro / kusaki o miru mo / mina kanashi / inochi ni
kakuru / mono o omoeba

562. Former Major Counselor Kyōgoku Tamekane
[1254–1332]. On "Love/Clouds"

Tinted with the dye
   that has sunk into my heart
      with thoughts of love,
even the clouds I see now
   make me think only of you.

mono omou / kokoro no iro ni / somerarete / me ni miru
kumo mo / hito ya koishiki

563. Retired Emperor Hanazono [1297–1348;
r. 1308–18]. On "Love/Clouds"

That I gaze out so
   —my thoughts overflowing with love—
she of course can't know.
I am the one who has dyed
   those clouds in the evening sky.

koi amaru / nagame o hito wa / shiri mo seji / ware to
somenasu / kumo no yūgure

564. Eifuku Mon-in. On "Love/Clouds"

At this very moment
   there is little chance he too

is gazing at it—
yet I hate to see disappear
that one cluster of clouds.

ima shimo are / hito no nagame mo / kakaraji o / kiyuru
mo oshiki / kumo no hitomura

565. Retired Emperor Fushimi [1265–1317;
r. 1287–98]. From among his love poems

I would not yet
be stirred from these thoughts of love—
not while my feelings
still seemed to be encouraged
by the shades of the evening sky.

sore o dani / omoisamasaji / koishiki no / susumu mama
naru / yūgure no sora

566. Shinsaishō of Retired Emperor Fushimi's en-
tourage [early 14th century].[3] From among her
love poems

Unable to sleep,
I lose myself so wholly
in thoughts of love
that my heart becomes one
with the color of my lamp.

nerareneba / tada tsukuzuku to / mono o omou / kokoro
ni kawaru / tomoshibi no iro

567. Former Sovereign Kōgon [1313–64; r. 1331–
33]. From among his love poems

Of so little worth
have been the days and the months
I wasted waiting,
that if I were to die now
it would be no great loss.

3. A sister of Yama-
momo Kaneyuki (b.
1254) who served as a
lady-in-waiting to Re-
tired Emperor Fushimi.

machisugusu / tsukihi no hodo o / ajiki nami / taenan
totemo / takekaraji mi o

4. Her father was
Nijō Noriyoshi (late
13th century).

568. Noriyoshi's Daughter.[4] From among her love
poems

> Now I have felt it:
> that extreme of love's anguish
>   I once disbelieved—
> so that now I wish only
> I'd never known him at all.

kaku ya wa to / oboeshi kiwa mo / oboekeri / subete hito
ni wa / narede zo aramashi

569. Yamamomo Toshikane, former senior assis-
tant governor-general at Dazaifu. From among his
love poems

> "It's over," I thought,
> and decided to regard him
>   as cruel at heart.
> But what pain it causes me
> when he asks, "How have you been?"

ima wa tote / tsuraki ni nashite / miru hito no / sate mo
ika ni to / iu shi mo zo uki

5. Tamekane's
(older?) sister.

570. Tameko of the Second Rank [1252?–1316?].[5]
From among her love poems

> Ah, to know nothing
> of love or the cruelty
>   he has caused me—
> to be the person I was
> now such a long time ago.

koishisa mo / hito no tsurasa mo / shirazarishi / mukashi
nagara no / waga mi to mogana

571. Retired Emperor Hanazono. On "Love That Increases as the Days Go By"

> A pitiful state:
> to again today hear harsh words
>   that I must bear
> before I have awakened
>   from the pain of yesterday's.

kikisouru / kinō ni kyō no / ukifushi ni / samenu aware mo / ayaniku ni shite

572. Major Counselor Ōgimachi Kinkage [1297–1360].[6] Topic unknown

> To show resentment
>   would no doubt make him conclude
>   "Let her be, then"—
> and so for the time being
>   I must hold my pain within.

uramitaraba / sa koso arame to / omou kata ni / omoi-musebite / suguru koro kana

6. A major Kyō-goku poet who assisted Hanazono in compiling *Fūgashū*.

573. Retired Emperor Fushimi. Topic unknown

> No, to think that way
>   would leave me nothing at all
>   as a hope to cling to–
> so not yet will I decide
>   that this means she must hate me.

itodo koso / tanomidokoro mo / naku narame / uki ni wa shibashi / omoisadameji

Poems by Zen Monks I

During the late Heian and Kamakura periods, direct commerce between China and Japan came to an almost total halt—unless of course one counts the attempted invasions of Japan by the Mongol Yuan dynasty in the late 1200's, which were themselves a chief source of the rift between the two countries. But even during those years, interest in Chinese literature and philosophy continued, especially among Buddhist monks, whose primary texts were in Chinese. This was particularly true in the monasteries of the thriving Zen sect, whose offices, under the sponsorship of the Ashikaga shoguns, were instrumental in establishing more open contact between the two traditions in the mid-1300's. Often this meant travel to the great temples of the continent for Japanese monks seeking to gain a proper Zen education; but even for those who did not go to China, the influence of Chinese intellectual life was substantial. And many who encountered that tradition in any way came away with an attachment to what detractors called the "wild words and fancy speech" of poetry as well. In this way began the tradition of Gozan poetry—the poetry of the Five Mountains of Zen.[1]

Despite the seeming uniformity imposed by their priestly robes, these men had disparate backgrounds. All were alike, however, in being Zen priests by profession: all entered the priesthood as children or young men and spent their lives in various official capacities within temples and monasteries. Strictly speaking, poetry was thus a pastime for them, and one that their own teachings often condemned as frivolous. But to fly in the face of convention was a Zen precept, after all; and the Gozan poets seem to have been very attached to their games, however often they debunked them.

Of the thirteen poets here chosen to represent the Gozan tradition of this period, six—Tetsuan Dōshō, Musō Soseki, Kokan Shiren, Mugan So'o, Ryūshū Shūtaku, Gidō Shūshin—never went to China; all the others did.

---

1. "Five Mountains" originally referred to the five chief temples of the Zen sect. Later the term came to refer to Zen establishments in general.

Monk in a flatboat

One, Sesson Yūbai, stayed there for over twenty years, some of which time was spent in jail or exile. Likewise, some of these poets, notably Musō Soseki, Kokan Shiren, Gidō Shūshin, and Zekkai Chūshin, became the abbots of great temples; most of the others chose ascetic life in the provinces or ended up fleeing to escape factional strife or political intrigue. What all of them share is a dedication to Zen and to Zen poetry—most of it in Chinese, but some in their native language—in which they often choose to hide behind the monkish personas of the vagabond, the hermit, the fool, and above all the carefree spirit who indulges himself in the beauties of the natural world.

Dōgen Kigen (1200–1253)

1. A phrase describing the Zen tradition, which was based not on the sutras but on direct experience.

574. "Depending on Neither Words nor Letters"[1]

What is no part
    of the words we toss aside
        so casually,
leaves not a trace of itself
    in the marks of the brush.

iisuteshi / sono koto no ha no / hoka nareba / fude ni mo
ato o / todomezarikeri

575. [From a group of impromptu poems about his grass hut]

Long as the long tail
    of pheasants of the mountains,
the foot-wearying hills:
    so long is the night before me—
    and yet it too ends with dawn.[2]

2. An allusive variation on poem 417, by Hitomaro.

ashibiki no / yamadori no o no / shidario no / naganaga-
shi yo o / aketekeru kana

576. [From a group of impromptu poems about his grass hut]

Should someone ask me
    "Just what sort of thing is it—
what you call Buddha?"
I say, "Icicles hanging
    from a mosquito net!"

ika naru ka / hotoke to iite / hito towaba / kaiya ga moto
ni / tsurara inikeri

577. "Worship Service"

> In a snowfall
> that obscures the winter grasses,
> a white heron—
> using his own form
> to hide himself away.

fuyukusa mo / mienu yukino no / shirasagi wa / ono ga
sugata ni / mi o kakushikeri

Tetsuan Dōshō (1260–1331)

578. *Spring*

Each spring it's my heart that stirs first of all;
I revise my poems, chanting them endlessly.
Rain on peach blossoms by the creek—a
   thousand tears;
smoke in the willows on the bank—a mound of
   sorrows.

Musō Soseki (1275–1351)

579. BUDDHISM. "On All Steps as Steps on the
Way"

> When there is nowhere
> that you have determined
> to call your own,
> then no matter where you go
> you are always going home.

furusato to / sadamuru kata no / naki toki wa / izuku ni
yuku mo / ieji narikeri

580. BUDDHISM. Topic unknown

> Don't think of the moon
>   as something that emerges
>   and then sinks away,
>   and there will be no mountain rim
>   to trouble your mind.[3]

3. In other words, "Don't trust in appearances and you will not be deceived."

izuru to mo / iru to mo tsuki o / omowaneba / kokoro ni kakaru / yama no ha mo nashi

Kokan Shiren (1278–1346)

581. *Winter Moon*

In the mountain groves, tree after tree, all without
    leaves;
in the vault of heaven, not a single cloud, and
    little wind.
Dawn glows forth, bringing frost that shines with
    chilly light;
put a sign up on the universe: The Palace of
    Boundless Cold.[4]

4. That is, the imagined Palace on the Moon.

Sesson Yūbai (1290–1346)

582. *Random Feelings*

I don't care for the praise of men, nor do I fear
    men's slander.
So far am I estranged from the world, that my
    mind is as indifferent as water.
The ropes that bound me in prison I outlasted, and
    now for three years I am in the capital.[5]
I chant poems, composing them as I see fit—
    forthright words needing no decoration.

5. The poet was jailed briefly by the Mongol government in 1314 and thereafter lived three years in Chang'an.

Betsugen Enshi (1294–1364)

583. *Extemporaneous*

The courtyard is so lonely in autumn rain
that I open the window and gaze all day at
   the peak.
From the beginning of the world my two eyes
have been fixed to those mile-high pines on top.

Chūgan Engetsu (1300–1375)

584. *Imitating the Old Style*

Strong, strong is the wind of the Last Days;[6]
from the earth dust rises, swirl upon swirl.
In the heavens, the sun shines faintly;
in the world of men, both good and evil flourish.
Mole crickets and ants go after stench and filth;
but the phoenix perches on the parasol tree.[7]
Here there is one man far from worldly concerns:
he moves freely among the white clouds.

6. The last of the Buddhist kalpas, or cycles, in which all things are destroyed. Chūgan is referring to the period of civil war between the Northern and Southern courts.

7. The phoenix was said to perch only on top of a parasol tree (J. *aogiri; Firmiana platanifolia*), and then only when a saint was about to appear in the world.

Mugan So'o (d. 1374)

585. *Thinking of Old Times*

Bird chatter makes the world seem far away;
floating clouds make me miss distant friends.
One monk is standing by the temple gate;
the setting sun lights half of the mountain.

Ryūshū Shūtaku (1308–88)

586. Men: The Best Thing for All Things Is to Give Up!

The best way for men to solve their problems is to
    give up—
scurrying about, east and west, gets you only
    gray hair.
Hidden away here, I sit and doze off, facing the
    mountains—
and soon all sorrow, all happiness just seem to
    fade away.

587. Watching the Moon on a Lake at Night

At night I go in a fine boat, playing with
    blue waves;
water and sky are clear—except for Lady
    Chang E![8]
I tap a tune on my gunwales, but no one gets my
    message;
only the autumn wind joins in my boatsong.

8. An epithet for the moon.

Gidō Shūshin (1325–88)

588. Sparrow in the Bamboos

He doesn't go for the grain in the storehouse,
nor does he peck holes in the landlord's place.
In the mountain groves he can make his living,
perching for the night atop a tall bamboo.

589. Painting of an Orchid

Here I live in a temple in the city;
but it's like being in a house in the forest.

Before my eyes I see nothing of the vulgar world:
fine grasses and two or three flowers.

590. *Diversions*

Half my life was hardship, and now I must worry
  about old age;
my heart is like dying embers that will never be
  red again.
Peach and plum trees take pleasure in spring
  wind—but I can't;
it's the fine grasses around the pond back home
  that occupy my dreams.
Swallows come to the south country for
  festival day;[9]
wild geese put the sun at their backs and head into
  cold sky.
From sleep I rise and go to the west window,
  touching my writing desk:
men and their gains, their losses—let the cock and
  worm have them.[10]

9. Harvest festivals were held in most villages around the time of the spring and autumn equinoxes.

10. In a famous poem, Du Fu (712–70) described the futility of a fight between a cock and a worm.

Chūjo Joshin (14th century)

591. *Thoughts in Autumn*

It's not the cold of autumn that keeps me from
  dreams,
but what I feel before the grasses and trees in my
  courtyard.
My plaintain has lost its leaves; my parasol tree
  is old;
and night after night—the sound of wind, the
  sound of rain.

592. *Recovering from Illness*

Since late spring illness has held me, and now it's
    autumn;
while I lay on my bed, the days flowed by
    like water.
Willow catkins and peach blossoms are now
    dreams in the past;
leaves falling from the parasol and calling crickets
    make me worry.
Illness comes in many varieties, after all—but still
    from one's nature;
and even if you live to a hundred, your body must
    rest in the end.
Day and night, a cool wind blows from the sky's
    far edge;
thin and weak, I still want to climb once to the
    tower by myself.[11]

11. Wang Can (A.D.
177–217), also known
as Zhongxuan, wrote
a famous prose-poem
titled "Climbing to
the Tower."

Zekkai Chūshin (1336–1405)

593. *Climbing to the Tower After a Rain*

In the sky a rain shower passes, washing autumn's
    newness clean;
with my friend I climb the tower that overlooks
    the river.
How I wish I could write a lament as lasting as
    Zhongxuan's![12]
But even the broken fog and sparse trees are more
    than I can bear.

12. See preceding
note.

Ichū Tsūjo (d. 1429)

594. *Hermit in the City*

If all your life you have declined rank and fame,
then even amidst the world's dust your dreams are
    serene.
Ten thousand ages, in mountain forests and in
    cities,
the pine-wind has spoken always with one voice.

595. *Falling Leaves*

Autumn leaves go on the wind, slanting down one
    by one:
in a single night the mountain cottage is engulfed
    by them.
Without a thought, the Poet-Monk sweeps them
    into the creek:
not at all like the way he treats falling blossoms in
    spring.

Monk Zenna (late 13th-early 14th centuries) and Monk Gusai (d. 1376)

Throughout the Late Medieval Age, the uta continued to be the most pres-
tigious form of poetry; but it was not the most popular. That distinction

went to renga, or linked verse, a genre that in its communal approach—
one poet composing a verse to be "linked" to by another poet extempora-
neously, with as many as a score of poets participating—admirably suited
the age. At first, most renga poets were amateurs, many of them aristocrats
or priests for whom linked verse was a kind of elegant game played with
uta vocabulary and aesthetics as its pieces. In time, however, true experts
in the art of linking emerged and began to behave like professionals, what-
ever their formal status. Called *rengashi*, or masters of linked verse, they
would play a crucial role in the poetic world for the next three centuries.

One of the first of these semiprofessional masters was a monk named
Zenna. Among his accomplishments was the consolidation of the rules of
the genre in a short list that showed a deepening awareness of the aesthetic
potential of the form. And Zenna's actual compositions, too, reveal his
skill in the art of linking, as is evident in the following example:

> In a test of endurance
> I would prove the weaker.

> Sooner to fall
> than the cherry blossoms
> will be my tears.

> kokoro kurabe ni / yowari koso seme; hana yori mo /
> saki ni otsuru zo / namida naru

If constant change is the guiding ideal of the genre, this link has realized
it completely, changing what appears in the first verse (written by an un-
identified companion) to be a rejected lover's statement of defeatism into a
cry of regret from a man who knows that soon the cherry blossoms must
be taken on the wind. Such deft changes in context are at the heart of
linked verse.

Yet some of the links attributed to Zenna show that in his day the genre
had not yet developed some of the qualities that would mark it in its fullest
articulation:

> In no time at all
> the eaves out by the garden
> went to pieces, and

> The old bamboo water pipe
> no longer carries water.

> hodo mo naku / niwa no nokiba no / yaburureba; furuki
> kakehi wa / mizu no tsutawazu

Here we have two verses that form a complete scene—too complete, in fact, for the tastes of later renga masters, who insisted that each verse in a sequence be independent, both conceptually and grammatically. To them the link above read too much like an uta that had simply been divided into two parts.

Only a few decades later, however, renga poets had moved beyond such halting attempts, as is apparent in the work of Monk Gusai. A student of both Zenna and an uta poet of the Reizei family, Gusai was from the beginning a thorough professional, despite his priestly status. And he was fortunate to find an avid student at court in the high-ranking courtier Nijō Yoshimoto (1320–88). Together, these two men established the foundation of "serious" linked verse—*ushin renga*, borrowing a term from Teika—in the form of a new rulebook, several treatises, and the first of two imperially recognized anthologies of the genre, entitled *Tsukubashū* (The Tsukuba Collection, 1356). The anthology set a pattern for the future by including only *hokku* ("first verses," referring to the inaugural verse of a full sequence) and two-verse "links" (*tsukeku*) naming only the author of the second verse. For ever after the emphasis in linked verse was less on long sequences for their own sake than on the art of "linking" itself.

It is Yoshimoto who has received credit for the rulebook, the treatises, and the anthology; but as his teacher, Gusai was also involved in those enterprises. And he is clearly the superior poet. Above all, he has abundant imagination, which produces ingenious or arresting links (see 602, 604, 605, and 599, 600 respectively), a beautiful but subtle style (598, 604, 607–9), and a thorough knowledge of the canon that makes for poems of allusive power (601, 603, 606). Virtually all of his work evokes the later Teika's tone of "deep feeling" (see 604, 606 in particular).

Monk Zenna

596. SPRING

In a test of endurance
I would prove the weaker.

Sooner to fall
than the cherry blossoms
will be my tears.

kokoro kurabe ni / yowari koso seme; hana yori mo / saki
ni otsuru zo / namida naru

597. MISCELLANEOUS

In no time at all
    the eaves out by the garden
        went to pieces, and

The old bamboo water pipe
    no longer carries water.

hodo mo naku / niwa no nokiba no / yaburureba; furuki
kakehi wa / mizu no tsutawazu

Monk Gusai

598. SPRING

At an unexpected place
    I ask lodging for the night.

Going toward blossoms,
I let my heart take its course—
    forgetting myself.

omowanu kata ni / yado o koso toe; hana ni yuku /
kokoro ya ware o / wasururan

599. AUTUMN

1. *Yakata*, a war-
rior stronghold within
the city.

At an old city stronghold,[1]
    autumn is no longer known.

With no master now,
a skiff lies abandoned on shore—
    moon for a rider.

furinuru yakata ni / aki mo shirarezu; nushi mo naki / ura
no sutebune / tsuki nosete

600. WINTER

Let the price of my offense
be whatever it must be!

The moon's still above
the snow on the hunting grounds
in dim dawn light.[2]

tsumi no mukui wa / sa mo araba are; tsuki nokoru /
kariba no yuki no / asaborake

2. Link: the shedding of blood was a sin according to Buddhist doctrine—one that the exhilaration of the moment makes the speaker willing to pay for.

601. BUDDHISM. From a thousand-verse sequence composed at the house of the Regent[3]

Ah, such a cold moon—
it makes me wish for a friend
to come and visit!

From a temple on the plain,
a far bell in the autumn night.[4]

tsuki samushi / toburaikimasu / tomo mogana; nodera no
kane no / tōki aki no yo

3. Nijō Yoshimoto (1320–88).

4. An echo of a Chinese poem from *Wakan rōeishū*, by Bao Rong (fl. 820; s.n. 43).

602. LOVE

In the pond, a rock
where waterfall becomes spray.

The tears I shed
come down in a cascade
on my inkstone.[5]

ike ni ishi aru / takitsu shiranami; naku namida / suzuri
no ue ni / ochisoite

5. Link: in the second verse, the "pond" becomes the well of an inkstone.

603. MISCELLANEOUS

The light of the moon:
is it truly there, or not?

A monkey cries out
    from a pool back in the rocks
        of a mountain gorge.[6]

6. Link: according to
an old Zen cautionary
tale, five hundred mon-
keys drowned trying
to grasp the moon re-
flected in water.

makoto ni tsuki no / kage wa aru ka wa; saru sakebu /
iwaogakure no / tani no mizu

604. LAMENTATION

The moon is scarcely known here,
so far back in the mountains.

Leave the world behind
    and you have only your shadow
        as a companion.

tsuki o shiranu ya / miyama naruran; sutsuru mi ni /
waga kage bakari / tomonaite

605. MISCELLANEOUS

Spring and summer have passed
    and now autumn is upon us.

When the snow comes—
    what will they look like then?
    Pines up on the peak.[7]

7. Link: the first verse
having gone through
spring, summer and
autumn, the second
goes on to winter, but
with the timeless image
of the pine.

haru natsu sugite / aki ni koso nare; yuki no koro / mata
ika naran / mine no matsu

606. TRAVEL

> Mountains lined with black pine
> on a chilly evening.
>
> On I go, and on,
> but at the head of the stream—
> no houses in sight.[8]

maki tatsu yama no / samuki yūgure; yuki yukite / kono
kawakami wa / sato mo nashi

8. An allusive variation on poem 324, by Monk Jakuren.

607. SPRING. Written for a sequence composed
beneath the cherry blossoms

> It bids them to come,
> but has no real love for blossoms—
> this blustery wind.

sasoite mo / hana o omowanu / arashi kana

608. SUMMER. Written at Saihōji[9]

> An echo, perhaps?
> From the valley, then the peak—
> a cuckoo's call.

amabiko ka / tani to mine to no / hototogisu

9. A temple located in the western outskirts of the capital.

609. AUTUMN. Written in the second year of Bunna
[1353] for a sequence composed at a farewell party
for Dōyo,[10] who was departing for Harima

> The clouds have left;
> and the wind has settled down—
> for the autumn rain.

kumo kaeri / kaze shizumarinu / aki no ame

10. Sasaki Dōyo (1306–73), a warrior-poet.

Secretary Shōtetsu (1381-1459)

By the beginning of the fifteenth century, the uta was an old genre whose glories seemed all to be in the past. To be sure, the two factions that constituted Teika's heritage argued on, but both approaches were by then bound by traditions that did little to encourage excellence. In the midst of this mediocrity, one poet stood out—Secretary Shōtetsu (so named after one of his priestly offices), who is recognized as the last great poet of the classical uta form. Nominally affiliated with the Kyōgoku-Reizei line, he could not escape some involvement in the factional disputes of his time; but his avowed allegiance was to Teika himself, not to his quibbling descendants. This dedication led him to produce poems whose complex syntax, ethereal beauty, and symbolic depth make him the heir of Teika indeed.

Shōtetsu's legacy to later generations was substantial: a personal anthology of over ten thousand poems, a major treatise-memoir, and a number of students who became the great renga poets of the next generation, although he himself composed little linked verse. His finest poems attain the intensity (see 610–11) and rhetorical complexity (613, 616, 619) of Teika, and aspire to the styles of *yūgen* (613, 615, 616, in particular) and *ushin* (610, 612, 614).

610. WINTER. "Wind of an Evening Shower."
Written at his monthly poetry meeting, on the twenty-fifth day of the month

> Up above the winds
> of the passing evening shower
> that roars through the fields
> withering all in its way—
> You clouds! You driven leaves!

fukishiori / nowaki o narasu / yūdachi no / kaze no ue
naru / kumo yo konoha yo

611. SPRING. "Spring Wind"

> Blow with color, please—
> you first wind striking the flowers
>   in the hearts of men
> before the grasses and trees
>   even know that spring has come.

iro ni fuke / kusaki mo haru o / shiranu ma no / hito no
kokoro no / hana no hatsukaze

612. SPRING. "Bell at Spring's End"

> This evening
>   the vespers bell rings dully
>   off through the haze.
> There where its echo doesn't sound,
> might spring be going away?

kono yūbe / iriai no kane no / kasumu kana / oto senu
kata ni / haru ya ikuramu

613. SPRING. "Falling Blossoms"

> Blossoms opened, to fall
>   in the space of just one night,
> as if in a dream—
> no more to be mistaken
>   for those white clouds on the peak.[1]

sakeba chiru / yo no ma no hana no / yume no uchi ni /
yagate magirenu / mine no shirakumo

1. An echo of a scene in the "Lavender" chapter of *Genji monogatari*, in which Genji, disappointed in love, wishes to "disappear, mistaken for one in a dream."

614. AUTUMN. "Morning Glories"

> Not at all like me—
> how with each passing day
>   while the autumn sun
> wanes, the blossoms wax stronger
>   on the morning glories.

mi zo aranu / aki no hikage no / hi ni soete / yowareba
tsuyoki / asagao no hana

615. WINTER. "Snow on the Mountain at Dusk"

> Still hanging back,
> the clouds too seem hesitant
>   to cross at evening
> over the untrodden snow
>   of the plank bridge on the peak.

watarikane / kumo mo yūbe o / nao tadoru / ato naki yuki
no / mine no kakehashi

616. LOVE. "Love in Spring"

> Toward dusk last night
>   I thought I saw the dim form
>   of the one I love—
> now brought to my mind again
>   by haze around the dawn moon.

yūmagure / sore ka to mieshi / omokage mo / kasumu zo
katami / ariake no tsuki

617. SPRING. "Spring Moon in Lingering Cold"

> In the chill of night,
> the melting snow makes a sound
>   as it hits the stones—
> dripping from the icicles
>   with the falling moonbeams.

sayuru yo no / yuki no shizuku wa / oto tatete / noki no
taruhi ni / otsuru tsukikage

618. MISCELLANEOUS. "Distant View at Evening"

> The sea, the mountains—
> now they are only images
>   that I saw before
> the progress of nightfall
>   hid them from my sight.

umi yama wa / tada omokage zo / mishi kata no /
kureyuku mama ni / meji wa tayuredo

619. LOVE. "Frustrated Love, in Winter"

> Too tense to sleep,
> I hear a bell in the frosty night—
> "Waking whom," I muse,
> "for a tryst that will strengthen
>   the bond of lover's vows?"[2]

2. An allusion to a
scene in the "Morn-
ing Glories" chapter
of *Genji monogatari*,
in which Genji, after
dreaming of the now-
deceased Fujitsubo,
laments his wakeful-
ness.

tokete nenu / shimoyo no kane wa / ta ga naka ni / fukuru
chigiri o / odorokasuran

Takayama Sōzei (d. 1455)

After the death of Nijō Yoshimoto in 1388, linked verse went through a
period of artistic decline that came to an end only half a century later with
the advent of a completely new generation of poets led by Takayama Sōzei,
a military man who eventually became the Renga Steward of the Ashikaga
shogunate.

Sōzei studied under a number of masters, among them Shōtetsu, whose careful instruction in the ideals of court civilization is credited with giving polish and depth to the works of Sōzei and a number of his contemporaries. But Sōzei remained a renga poet, and it was the special demands of that genre on which he concentrated. In particular, he became known for his ability at the demanding art of linking, as this example shows:

> I look out, and snow is falling,
> with the moon still in the sky.
>
> A new day begins.
> And of my dream of yesterday
> not a trace remains.
>
> mireba yuki furi / tsuki zo nokoreru; akenikeri / kinō no
> yume wa / ato mo nashi

Here Sōzei's response does what a link must always do—namely, create a new or expanded context for its predecessor. The beauty of his verse, however, is that it accomplishes this so completely, linking "a new day begins" to "the moon still in the sky," "I look out" to "my dream," and "trace" to "snow." Thus each image in the first verse is answered with a complement in the second, creating the elegant scene of a man waking at dawn, his dream melting away as surely as must a fine snowfall. So perfect is the fit between the verses, in fact, that readers must remind themselves that they are reading not one poem but *two* separate verses in a state of dynamic tension.

A classical critic would no doubt classify the effect of Sōzei's verse as *ushin*, and correctly so. But the dynamic of linking that is at the heart of the verse is something more than that. And it is his creative skill in this last regard that earned Sōzei his reputation as a renga poet. His poems exhibit most of the courtly charms, from wit (622, 625–26) to *sabi* (620). In addition, however, a close examination of his links reveals the imagination of a man used to the *za*, or linking session, the man who can find a concrete image to fill out an abstract idea (621), discover the irony in what seems a straightforward request (622), and see the potential for one image in another—see the rain in a dewdrop (623).

620. AUTUMN

> In a country village
> how lonely is autumn dusk!
>
> Wave though they may,
> who will come to visit
> plumes of pampas grass? [1]

nozato no aki no / kure zo sabishiki; maneku to mo /
susuki ga moto wa / tare ka kon

1. An allusive varia-
tion on poem 409,
by Teika.

621. AUTUMN

> Autumn seems more chilly
> with harsh winds blustering by.
>
> Guarding the late crop
> at the foot of distant hills—
> a hut of grass. [2]

aki samuge naru / kogarashi zo fuku; oshine moru / tōya-
mamoto no / kusa no io

2. Paddy guards were
stationed to guard
crops against deer and
other animals.

622. LOVE

> Around my love, at least,
> don't block the way—you spreading haze!
>
> Moonlight is a worry
> as I make my way in secret
> beneath the night sky. [3]

kimi ga atari wa / kasumazu mogana; tsuki mo ushi /
shinobigayoi no / yowa no sora

3. Link: wanting to
remain concealed, the
speaker is happy for
the heavy mist, but still
wants it to lift around
the place where his love
dwells.

623. TRAVEL

Have just a dewdrop of care:
we're in this world together.

Taking night shelter
    from people you've never seen—
in the rain, at dusk.

tsuyu no nasake mo / are na onaji yo; mizu shiranu / hito
ni yado karu / ame no kure

624. MISCELLANEOUS

I look out, and snow is falling,
with the moon still in the sky.

A new day begins.
And of my dream of yesterday
    not a trace remains.

mireba yuki furi / tsuki zo nokoreru; akenikeri / kinō no
yume wa / ato mo nashi

625. MISCELLANEOUS

Ah, a female's jealous heart
    can make her seem a demon.

Guarding her nest
    beneath the eaves of a tile roof—
a barn swallow.

netamu kokoro ya / oni to naruran; su o kakuru / kawara
no noki no / tsubakurame

626. AUTUMN

Returning in kind
    the patter of the showers—
falling autumn leaves.

chiru oto o / shigure ni kaesu / momiji kana

Bishop Shinkei (1406-1475)

Like Sōzei, Bishop Shinkei of the Jūshin-in came from the provinces, in his case Kii, where his family seems to have been associated with the Hatake-yama, one of the most important military clans of the Ashikaga shogunate. Unlike his older contemporary, however, he became a professional cleric at a young age and eventually achieved high rank in the Buddhist hierarchy. His long life of religious training is apparent in many of his poems (see 633, 641–42) and treatises. But equally obvious is his tutelage under Shōtetsu, with whom he studied for thirty years. Indeed, Shinkei was in many ways a frustrated uta poet, who turned to renga largely because his low social standing made acceptance in aristocratic circles difficult. Even in later life, when linked verse was clearly his chief occupation, he urged renga poets to embrace the ideals of the courtly uta tradition as their own, openly criti-cizing those, including Sōzei, who in his opinion did not adequately live up to those aesthetic standards.

Thus it comes as no surprise to find in his work examples of *yūgen* (par-ticularly in 634) and *ushin* (629–30, 635, 646), an expert use of allusive variation (630, 632, 637, 639), and scenes that he would describe as em-bodiments of *hie sabi*, or "chilly loneliness" (see especially 627, 636, 648)—his extension of the *sabi* of Saigyō and others. Yet in his work he also shows a fine comprehension of some of the special demands and resources of linked verse. In particular, he is a master of what he called "distant link-ing" (*soku*, as opposed to *shinku*, or "close linking"), in which a verse is joined to its predecessor less through word associations and reasoning than through mood and suggestion (see 634–35, 638, 641). It is this emphasis on subtlety and aesthetic resonance, learned largely from Shōtetsu, that gives Shinkei's work a depth that is often lacking in poets of less complete classical training.

Yet there were other reasons for the melancholy hues of Shinkei's poems, the chief one being the violence of his age, which is best symbolized by the Ōnin War of 1467–77. Fought in the streets of Kyōto, that conflict reduced much of the capital to ashes, sending its displaced residents to Nara and elsewhere for safety. For Shinkei, this meant moving to the East Country,

where he had powerful patrons. It was there that he wrote several of his
most important essays and composed much of his finest poetry, acting the
part of the teacher to students from the great military families of the area.
He probably felt his stay would be a short one; but as the war in Kyōto
dragged on, it became apparent that he might never see the halls of the
capital again. Retiring to a hermitage on the coast just southwest of mod-
ern Tōkyō, he settled into the reclusive life in 1471 and died there four
years later as a somewhat unwilling *rengashi*, or master of linked verse.

627. WINTER

A pitiful sight—
that smoke rising at evening
from a brushwood fire.

His charcoal sold at market,
a man heads back into the hills.

aware ni mo / mashiba oritaku / yūkeburi; sumi uru ichi
no / kaerusa no yama

628. WINTER

Each person I meet
I ask the way to an inn—
but no one replies.

Hats against driven snow
go down the path at a slant.

au hito mo / yado wa to toeba / mono iwade; fubuki ni
kasa o / katabukuru michi

629. LOVE

Not a trace of pity toward me—
he goes on, endlessly cruel.

I've had enough
of this world, I told him—
but still he won't come.

aware mo kakezu / nao zo tsurenaki; kono yo ni wa /
araji to iu o / toimosede

630. TRAVEL

One cannot be sure of living
even until the evening.

In the dim dawn light
I watch the waves in the wake
of a departing boat.[1]

1. An echo of poem
57, by Sami Mansei.

kururu made ni wa / mi o tanomazu; asaborake / fune
yuku ato no / nami o mite

631. MISCELLANEOUS

The moon I had awaited
is on the mountain rim.

In a test of wills
with the cuckoo, I stayed up—
and now day is breaking.

machitsuru tsuki no / kakaru yama no ha; hototogisu /
kokoro kurabe ni / yo wa akete

632. MISCELLANEOUS

Now I realize the truth
of what my father told me.

Because of a dream,
I can forget the vexation
I felt at Suma Bay.[2]

2. An allusion to the
"Suma" and "Akashi"
chapters of *Genji
monogatari*, in which
the spirit of the exiled
Genji's father comes
to him in a dream and
counsels him on how to
deal with his predica-
ment.

oya no oshie no / makoto o zo shiru; yume yue ya / suma
no urami o / wasururan

633. SPRING

Never again
would I be born to suffer
in a body like this.

Just take joy in the moon,
spend your time among flowers.

futatabi wa / hito to naraji to / omou mi ni; tada tsuki ni
mede / hana ni kurasamu

634. SPRING

At dawn, one cannot tell
what is dream, what reality.

Blossoms scattering
in the light of the moon
are not of this world.

yume utsutsu to mo / wakanu akebono; tsuki ni chiru /
hana wa kono yo no / mono narade

635. SPRING

Well one may wish—
but will those who have parted
return once again?

Late into the evening,
mountains where blossoms fall.

omou to mo / wakareshi hito wa / kaerame ya; yūgure
fukashi / sakura chiru yama

636. AUTUMN

With whom can I share
the feelings wrought in my heart
by the autumn sky?

In the reeds, the evening wind;
in the clouds, wild geese calling.

waga kokoro / tare ni kataran / aki no sora; ogi ni
yūkaze / kumo ni karigane

637. LOVE

I am used to rising at dawn—
from doing it night after night.

How cruel of the moon
to remain always in the sky
while I must go home.[3]

akatsuki oki ni / naruru yona yona; tsuki zo uki / iku
kaerusa ni / nokoruran

3. An allusive varia-
tion on poem 444, by
Tadamine.

638. LOVE

No one in the garden now—
except the wind in the pines.

After he has gone,
I stand alone in the night—
lost in forlorn thoughts.

hito naki niwa wa / tada matsu no kaze; kaeru yo ni /
kokorobosoku mo / tatazumite

4. An allusion to a scene in the "Evening Faces" chapter of *Genji monogatari*, where a pigeon calling out from the bamboo at Genji's home reminds him of the call he heard just after Yūgao's death in a run-down retreat a few nights before.

639. MISCELLANEOUS

It seems to portend rain—
the voice of the passing wind.

From bamboos swaying
    in a grove near the paddies,
a pigeon calling.[4]

ame ni ya naran / fuku kaze no koe; sue nabiku / tanaka no take ni / hato nakite

640. MISCELLANEOUS

To find the resolve
    to leave the world behind
    is no easy thing.

Thinking of his noble house,
a warrior steadies his heart.

mi o sutsuru / kokoro wa yasuku / naki mono o; ie o omoeba / isamu mononofu

5. An allusion to the Tendai doctrine of the three Ways: the Way of Emptiness, the Way of Temporality, and the Middle Way. The wind and the echo are both transient forms.

641. MISCELLANEOUS

The wind can no more be seen
    than an echo in the mountains.

In every thing
    we judge what is, what is not,
only by outer form.[5]

kaze mo me ni minu / yama no amabiko; monogoto ni / tada ari nashi o / katachi nite

642. BUDDHISM

> Now the Buddha himself
>   has become my parent.
>
> It reproaches men
>   for napping, when it rings out—
> the temple bell.

hotoke zo hito no / oya to narinuru; utatane o / isamuru
tera no / kane narite

643. LAMENTATION

> How cruel it seems
>   for sleeves to be parted so—
> not a word spoken.
>
> Parent leaving the world behind,
> little one that won't let go.

amari uki / sode no wakare wa / mono iwade; sutenuru
oya ni / sugaru midorigo

644. AUTUMN

> The one looking—
>   he also lends some color
>   to the moonlight.

miru hito o / iro naru tsuki no / hikari kana

645. WINTER

> Clear skies over snow—
>   not a single mountainside
>   that's not a mirror.

yuki harete / kagami o kakenu / yama mo nashi

646. AUTUMN. Composed in the East Country dur-
ing the Ōnin era [1467–69], when the world was in
turmoil

> Rainclouds gather—
> but with more calm than the storms
>   raging in the world.[6]

6. See Sōgi's compan-
ion verse (poem 661),
also written in the East
Country around the
same time.

kumo wa nao / sadame aru yo no / shigure kana

647. AUTUMN

> Listening to it,
> you forget about the moon—
> in passing rain.

kiku hodo wa / tsuki o wasururu / shigure kana

648. WINTER

> Red leaves rotting,
> morning frost glistening white
>   at waterside.

momiji kuchi / asashimo shiroki / migiwa kana

649. SPRING

> Hide yourself in haze
>   from people who come in droves—
> mountain cherries!

murete tou / hito ni wa kasume / yamazakura

Monk Sōgi (1421-1502)

Monk Sōgi, the best known of all renga masters, was a student of both Sōzei and Shinkei who managed, in the course of a long career, to realize in his own poetry the strengths of both his teachers. Born in obscurity outside the capital, he began his life as a Zen priest and wore monkish robes all of his life. But it was in linked verse that Sōgi made his reputation, serving as tutor and critic first to men of artistic interests in the provinces and later even to the nobility in the capital. During his last several decades, he lived in a home in the northern section of Kyōto, where he gave lectures, wrote commentaries, taught students the niceties of his art, and compiled anthologies of his own work and of his teachers'. Eventually he received the command to put together the second imperially recognized collection of the genre—entitled *Shinsen Tsukubashū* (The New *Tsukuba* Collection; 1495).

In order to understand Sōgi fully, one must keep in mind that even during his long period of residence in the capital he was often away on journeys, maintaining contact with his patrons in the East Country and elsewhere. In this sense he was one of the first of the great traveling artists, whose work in bringing "higher" culture to the countryside is a major feature of Japanese history throughout the fifteenth and sixteenth centuries.

Although nominally aligned with the conservative Nijō faction, Sōgi transcended petty divisions in his actual work. Thus we find *ushin* as a consistent feature of his poems, but also witty conceptions that could have come from *Kokinshū* (see poems 658, 662, 664), lofty scenes in the manner of Yoshitsune and Emperor Go-Toba (665), and descriptive poems reminiscent of Tamekane (650, 660). From Sōzei he learned the art of careful linking (650, 655, 657, 660), and from Shinkei the art of "distant" linking (658–59) and the importance of overtones (652–53, 657, 659).

In one way he exceeded both his teachers: namely, in his mastery of the complete one-hundred verse sequence as an artistic whole. Among other things, this meant a willingness to produce what the sequence needed at the moment—a close link or a distant one, a striking verse or a plain one, a transition to a new thematic topic or a continuation of the current one, and so on. That the two most famous of all full sequences—*Minase sangin hyakuin* (Three Poets at Minase; 1488) and *Yuyama sangin hyakuin* (Three Poets at Yuyama; 1491)—were both produced with his participation and under his direction shows that he had this rare quality of restraint in abundance.

One might say, indeed, that what the hundred-verse sequence demanded was a group of poets willing to restrain their individual artistic egos. This was something Sōgi, perhaps because of a supreme inner confidence, found easy to do, as the following verses make clear. For even taken from their context in a full sequence, Sōgi's work above all shows an ability to treat all the topics of classical poetry, and to do so in conceptions that in turn reveal the variety of the tradition he so fully articulated.

650. SUMMER

Just a hint of thunder clouds
    in the evening sky.

On summer mountains,
    the faint disk of the moon—
    night just beginning.

keshiki bakari no / yūdachi no sora; natsuyama no /
tsukishiro usuki / yoi no ma ni

651. AUTUMN. Written when a number of people had tried to create a link for [the first verse]

They come about on their own—
    the principles of all things.

Water need not think
    to offer itself as lodging
    for clear moonlight.

onozukara naru / kotowari o miyo; yadosu to mo / mizu
wa omowanu / tsuki sumite

652. WINTER

> Not a cloud around the moon
>   in the sky at break of day.
>
> Over my pillow,
>   it was rain showers and wind
>   that ended my dream.

kumo naki tsuki no / akatsuki no sora; sayo makura /
shigure mo kaze mo / yume samete

653. MISCELLANEOUS

> Off where there's no sign of smoke
>   everything is at peace.
>
> For people who dwell
>   in the mountains, it is haze
>   that sustains life.[1]

taku hi mo mienu / kata ya nodokeki; yama ni sumu /
hito wa kasumi o / inochi nite

1. An allusion to a
Chinese poem by Qin
Xi (709–93; s.n. 44).

654. MISCELLANEOUS

> A thing of uncertainty—
>   the way of the warrior.
>
> For whose glory
>   does a man care less for life
>   than for honor?

hakanaki mono wa / mononofu no michi; ta ga tame no /
na nareba mi yori / oshimuran

2. An example of
wakan renku, or
"linked verse in Japa-
nese and Chinese,"
which was very popu-
lar in Zen monas-
teries. The first verse,
although romanized
here in Japanese, is
Chinese in the original.

655. MISCELLANEOUS

A spring's voice? Rain at the window.[2]

The clouds are right at the eaves,
passing a mountain village.

izumi no koe / mado wa mata ame; kumo wa nokiba o /
suguru yamazato

656. BUDDHISM

Over rocks, a path toward
a temple on a lone hill.

Leaning on his staff,
a pilgrim at his devotions
is now old in years.

michi wa iwa fumu / katayama no tera; tsue ni yoru /
okonaibito no / toshi furite

3. By itself the first
verse is spoken by
someone whose secret
love has been revealed.
Sōgi's link changes it
into another kind of
complaint: it is use-
less to keep feelings
secret if by so doing
you destroy all chances
of meeting the one
you love.

657. LOVE

My care to remain secret
has all been to no purpose.

If I can't see her,
what good can it do me
to keep my good name?[3]

shinobu kai naku / mi ya suginamashi; awade na no /
tatanu bakari wa / ikaga sen

4. An allusion to the
famous anecdote about
Zhuangzi, in which he
dreams he is a butterfly,
then wakes to find him-
self a man, and is never
sure again in which
world he resides.

658. SPRING

That man's life is but a dream—
is what we now come to know.

Its house abandoned,
the garden has become home
to butterflies.[4]

hito o yume to ya / omoishiruran; sumisuteshi / sono wa
kochō no / yadori nite

659. SPRING

> On which mountain
>   of these covered with blossoms
>   shall I seek lodging?
>
> For a bird kept in a cage—
>   ah, the heartbreak of spring!

hana zo saku / izure no yama ka / yadoruran; ko ni iru
tori no / haru no awaresa

660. AUTUMN

> Bushes bending toward earth
>   before a snowy daybreak.
>
> A storm passes
>   and in the garden, moonlight—
>   night growing cold.

kusaki orifushi / yuki no akebono; nowaki seshi / niwa
no tsukikage / yoru saete

661. WINTER. On the topic "Storm," written in Shinano when the world was in turmoil

> To age is enough—
>   now I must watch the world's storms
>   from a makeshift hut.[5]

yo ni furu mo / sara ni shigure no / yadori kana

5. A companion to
Shinkei's verse on the
same topic (poem 646).

662. SUMMER. A verse on "Cooling Down," written for a thousand-verse sequence at the house of the Governor of Ise[6]

> Oh, for some blossoms—
> to bid storm winds to visit
> this summer garden!

hana mogana / arashi ya towan / natsu no niwa

663. SPRING

> Wait to scatter,
> blossoms: for now there's no wind
> I can complain to.

machite chire / hana ni kakotan / kaze mo nashi

664. SUMMER. Written at the artificial hill of Ōuchi Masahiro's garden, when the latter asked him to compose a first verse describing the place[7]

> The pond—a sea;
> the branches—thick groves far back
> in summer hills.

ike wa umi / kozue wa natsu no / miyama kana

665. AUTUMN. Written at the Enmyōji Temple in the Echigo provincial seat

> Ah, for coolness
> it rivals the water's depths—
> this autumn sky.

suzushisa wa / mizu yori fukashi / aki no sora

6. Kitabatake Noritomo (d. 1471).

7. Ōuchi Masahiro (d. 1495) was a prominent warlord.

'Three Poets at Minase'

One of the ironies of medieval literary history is that the great antholo-gies of linked verse compiled by Nijō Yoshimoto, Sōgi, and others contain only bits and pieces of the works they represent and no full *hyakuin*, or hundred-verse sequences. Partly this is because the single link was in fact the major unit of composition for renga poets; but still it can be argued that to appreciate the true artistry of renga poets one must see them at work in the fullest form of their art.

Of the many sequences that suggest themselves for such a purpose, the most appropriate is *Minase sangin hyakuin*. This work, traditionally considered the best of its kind—a sort of primer for aspiring poets—was composed by Sōgi and two disciples, Shōhaku (1443–1527) and Sōchō (1448–1532), in 1488 and presented as a votive offering to a shrine at Minase dedicated to the memory of Emperor Go-Toba. Yet, significantly, one need know almost nothing more than its status as a votive offering (and not even that much, for ninety-eight of the verses) to understand the Minase sequence. For linked verse, as mentioned in the Introduction, is a conventional art form; there is no demand for the individualistic expression that is at the heart of lyric poetry in the West. In this sense, then, *Minase sangin hyakuin* is an example of perfection achieved through well-known conventions rather than a work of more singular excellence.

The conventions for *hyakuin* were known by poets as rules, the most basic of which may be simply stated. First is the rule that each verse in the sequence must stand on its own, semantically and grammatically. Second is that each verse must combine with its predecessor to form a complete poetic statement. Then comes a host of prescriptions that in sum demand variety and constant change in the sequence—one set limiting the num-ber of poems running in series in the primary categories (verses in the categories of Autumn and Spring restricted to at the most five verses in series, those in Winter, Summer, Travel, Shinto, Buddhism, Lamentation, Mountains, Waters, and Dwellings to three); another limiting repetition (azalea once, wild geese twice, "the world" five times, and so on); and still

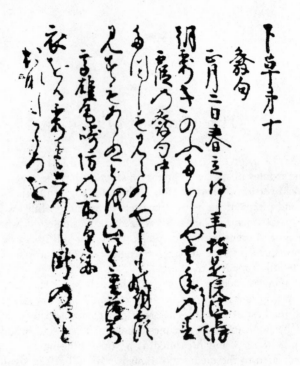

A leaf from one of Sōgi's personal anthologies

another limiting the recurrence of thematic and lexical categories, words,
and images (instances of the category Love to be separated by at least five
verses, instances of "pine" to be separated by at least seven, and so on).
In a word, the rules demand that every full sequence represent the entire
court tradition—all of the categories of the imperial *uta* anthologies and
other revered works—but in a way that allows no one topic, theme, or
idea to dominate the whole. Even the images that are virtually required by
tradition to appear in every sequence—the moon and cherry blossoms—
are restricted to eight and four appearances, respectively, making it certain
that neither will preponderate.

Yet this does not mean that a renga sequence is simply a series of short
uta, since in linked verse the artistic energy is focused less on individual
verses than on the links between them. Sometimes the link does little more
than fill out the scene presented by its predecessor, as in this example from
the Minase sequence:

726. Shōhaku

> In morning calm
> the sky retains not a trace
> of last night's clouds.

asanagi no / sora ni ato naki / yoru no kumo

727. Sōchō

> In snow, how bright is the gleam
> of far mountains all around!

yuki ni sayakeki / yomo no tōyama

Here Sōchō expands on Shōhaku's scene, adding snow—which brings with it the season of Winter—as a shining reminder of a stormy night. Such expansion or elaboration is central to the nature of every *hyakuin*.

Not all links are so straightforward. Again, a link from the Minase sequence can be used to illustrate.

685. Shōhaku

> Must it interrupt my dreams—
> this hateful wind in the reeds?

yume ni uramuru / ogi no uwakaze

686. Sōchō

> All there was to see
> were sad remnants of my old home,
> people I once knew.

mishi wa mina / furusatobito no / ato mo ushi

Since the word "dream" generally indicates the category of Love in linked verse, the speaker of Shōhaku's verse—as a single statement—can be taken to be a frustrated lover, unable to meet his companion even in his dreams; but in his link Sōchō changes the site of the dream to another speaker's run-down home. A lover's complaint thus becomes a Lament over lost time, shifting the theme in a way that opens up new possibilities of development.

The essence of a linked-verse sequence, then, is a dialectical movement that produces now a prosaic scene, now a more striking one, here a simple extension, there a complete change in interpretation, setting off exclamations against sighs and speaking for a host of people including travelers, lovers, old men, recluses, peasants, and emperors—all in a symphonic structure that contains the poems within a formal whole while resisting comprehensive interpretations.

fluid ✱

Finally, it is important to note that all linked-verse sequences are highly allusive: in the general sense, because the vocabulary of the genre is mostly borrowed from the uta tradition, and more specifically, because poets constantly draw on the resources of famous poems of the past. This is particularly so in *Minase sangin hyakuin*, which, as noted above, was composed in memory of Emperor Go-Toba, on the anniversary of his death-date and near a shrine dedicated to his name. That Sōgi and his disciples were very much aware of the circumstances surrounding their composition is evident in the first verse of the sequence, in which Sōgi alludes very directly to Go-Toba's famous *Shin kokinshū* poem describing spring dusk along the Minase River (see poem 360) and also in the last, in which Sōchō alludes to another of the former sovereign's poems (SKKS 1635; s.n. 45). Beyond these two references, there is no overt indication of the circumstances surrounding the sequence's creation (the headnote simply reads, "A hundred-verse renga sequence composed by Sōgi, Shōhaku, and Sōchō on the twenty-second day of the First Lunar Month of the second year of the Chōkyō era [1488]"); and elsewhere the poets allude to *Kokinshū*, *Genji monogatari*, and a number of other classical sources. Rather than being dedicated to one man specifically, then, *Minase sangin hyakuin* as a whole conjures up the courtly past (along with a number of more plebeian scenes) as that past is inscribed in the poetic themes and images of the tradition of which Go-Toba was a part. The vision thus is a fragmented one, in a way an objective correlative for the Buddhist law that underlies all the rules of linked verse and much of the aesthetic consciousness in Muromachi Japan—namely, the law of impermanence.

In the translation, the topical category to which each verse would belong according to the renga rulebooks is included in a headnote, with brief comments on links between verses and other background information given in marginal notes. It should be understood that these aids to interpretation represent an attempt to "read" the text within the tradition of classical poetics and are not part of the work itself.

666. Sōgi. [SPRING]

[1]   Some snow still remains
      as haze moves low on the slopes
      toward evening.[1]

yukinagara / yamamoto kasumu / yūbe kana

1. An allusion to
poem 360, by Retired
Emperor Go-Toba.

667. Shōhaku. [SPRING]

[2]   Flowing water, far away—
      and a plum-scented village.

yuku mizu tōku / ume niou sato

668. Sōchō. [SPRING]

[3]   Wind off the river
      blows through a clump of willows—
      and spring appears.[2]

kawakaze ni / hitomura yanagi / haru miete

2. Link: spring "ap-
pears" in swaying
willows.

669. Sōgi. [MISCELLANEOUS]

[4]   A boat being poled along,
      sounding clear at break of day.[3]

fune sasu oto mo / shiruki akegata

3. Link: swaying wil-
lows become visible at
break of day.

670. Shōhaku. [AUTUMN]

[5]   Still there, somewhere:
      the moon off behind the mist
      traversing the night.[4]

tsuki ya nao / kiri wataru yo ni / nokoruran

4. Link: heavy mist
makes the sky still
seem dark at daybreak.

671. Sōchō. [AUTUMN]

Out on frost-laden fields
    autumn has come to its end.[5]

shimo oku nohara / aki wa kurekeri

672. Sōgi. [AUTUMN]

[7]   With no care at all
        for the insects crying out,
        grasses wither away.

naku mushi no / kokoro to mo naku / kusa karete

673. Shōhaku. [MISCELLANEOUS]

[8]   Pay a visit, and by the fence—
        a path standing in the open.[6]

kakine o toeba / arawa naru michi

674. Sōchō. [MISCELLANEOUS]

[9]   So deep in the hills,
        the village spends all its time
            amidst rough winds.[7]

yama fukaki / sato ya arashi ni / okururan

675. Sōgi. [MISCELLANEOUS]

[10]   If you're not used to the life,
        the solitude is hard to bear.[8]

narenu sumai zo / sabishisa mo uki

676. Shōhaku. [LAMENT]

[11] No more of that, now:
this is no time to lament
that you are alone.[9]

imasara ni / hitori aru mi o / omou na yo

9. Link: words of self-encouragement, counseling resignation.

677. Sōchō. [LAMENT]

[12] Have you not learned before this
that all things must always change?[10]

utsurowan to wa / kanete shirazu ya

10. An echo of poem 129, by Komachi.

678. Sōgi. [SPRING]

[13] Dew trying in vain
to form on cherry blossoms—
a pitiful sight.[11]

okiwaburu / tsuyu koso hana ni / aware nare

11. Link: a concrete example of the abstract principle stated in poem 677.

679. Shōhaku. [SPRING]

[14] Still some sunlight remains—
faint rays shining through the haze.[12]

mada nokoru hi no / uchi kasumu kage

12. Link: the failure of the dew is credited to the faint rays of the evening sun.

680. Sōchō. [SPRING]

[15] "Has nightfall come?"—
birds cry out above, making
their way toward home.[13]

kurenu to ya / nakitsutsu tori no / kaeruran

13. Link: the birds are fooled by the faint sun into thinking night has fallen.

681. Sōgi. [TRAVEL]

14. Link: the traveler under the forest canopy relies on the birds to tell him night is coming.

[16]   So far into the hills,
        there's no sky to show the way.[14]

miyama o yukeba / waku sora mo nashi

682. Shōhaku. [WINTER TRAVEL]

15. The "showers" are the traveler's tears.

[17]   A break in the storm—
        but still showers on the sleeves
        of a travel robe.[15]

haruru ma mo / sode wa shigure no / tabigoromo

683. Sōchō. [AUTUMN TRAVEL]

16. Link: moonlight is "wasted" in the teardrops of a common traveler.

[18]   Here on a pillow of grass
        the moonlight seems like a waste.[16]

waga kusamakura / tsuki ya yatsusan

684. Sōgi. [AUTUMN LOVE]

17. Link: time passes in vain for one unable to meet his lover.

[19]   For too many nights
        the time has gone by in vain—
        autumn deepening.[17]

itazura ni / akasu yo ōku / aki fukete

685. Shōhaku. [AUTUMN LOVE]

18. Link: wind in the reeds keeps the speaker from dreams of his lover.

[20]   Must it interrupt my dreams—
        this hateful wind in the reeds?[18]

yume ni uramuru / ogi no uwakaze

686. Sōchō. [LAMENT]

[21]   All there was to see
      were sad remnants of my old home,
      people I once knew.[19]

mishi wa mina / furusatobito no / ato mo ushi

19. Link: the "remnants" are now those of a dream of home.

687. Sōgi. [LAMENT]

[22]   Up ahead, in my old age,
      what will I rely on then?[20]

oi no yukue yo / nani ni kakaran

20. Link: from the past, the speaker turns to the future.

688. Shōhaku. [LAMENT]

[23]   So without color
      are these verses of mine—
      yet some solace, still.[21]

iro mo naki / koto no ha o dani / aware shire

21. Link: a reply to the query of poem 687.

689. Sōgi. [MISCELLANEOUS]

[24]   This too can serve as a friend—
      the sky as dusk descends.

sore mo tomo naru / yūgure no sora

690. Sōchō. [SPRING]

[25]   Today, clouds replace
      the blossoms that scattered—
      crossing a peak.[22]

kumo ni kyō / hana chirihatsuru / mine koete

22. Link: with the blossoms gone, the clouds must serve as companions. An echo of poem 290, by Shunzei.

23. "The time has come" for the wild geese to depart for the continent, as they do each spring. An allusion to SZS 36, by Minamoto no Toshiyori (s.n. 46).

24. *Oboroge* means both "hazy" and "uninteresting." Link: the speaker asks the geese to stay and enjoy the moon. An allusion to SKKS 182, by Princess Shikishi (s.n. 47).

25. Link: the speaker asks his companion to stop and enjoy the moon before parting. An allusion to SKKS 58, by Monk Jakuren (s.n. 48).

26. Link: the wind carries the sound of a fulling block (see the note to poem 256) from the village at the far edge of the field.

691. Shōhaku. [SPRING]

[26] "The time has come!" I hear—
the call of wild geese in spring.[23]

kikeba ima wa no / haru no karigane

692. Sōgi. [SPRING]

[27] A dim moon, yes,
but obscure in its beauty?
Wait a moment—see.[24]

oboroge no / tsuki ka wa hito mo / mate shibashi

693. Sōchō. [AUTUMN TRAVEL]

[28] A brief sleep, vagrant as dew—
then faint light of autumn dawn.[25]

karine no tsuyu no / aki no akebono

694. Shōhaku. [AUTUMN]

[29] At the field's far edge
stands a village, distantly,
where mist is rising.

sueno naru / sato wa haruka ni / kiri tachite

695. Sōgi. [AUTUMN]

[30] Carried by on passing wind—
the sound of mallet on cloth.[26]

fukikuru kaze wa / koromo utsu koe

696. Sōchō. [WINTER]

[31] Even on cold days
    I have only these thin sleeves,
    every nightfall.[27]

sayuru hi mo / mi wa sode usuki / kuregoto ni

27. Link: the sound
of the fulling block
makes the speaker
lament his poverty.

697. Shōhaku. [LAMENT]

[32] An uncertain livelihood—
    in the hills, gathering wood.

tanomu mo hakana / tsumagi toru yama

698. Sōgi. [LAMENT]

[33] I had not lost hope—
    but now my way through the world
    has come to nothing.[28]

saritomo no / kono yo no michi wa / tsukihatete

28. Link: a man
down on his luck lives
a hard life in the hills.
An allusion to GSS
1083, by Narihira
(s.n. 49).

699. Sōchō. [LAMENT]

[34] What a wretched situation!
    Is there nowhere left to go?

kokorobososhi ya / izuchi yukamashi

700. Shōhaku. [LOVE]

[35] The end of my life—
    that is all I can wait for,
    the morning after.[29]

inochi nomi / matsu koto ni suru / kinuginu ni

29. Link: life is
wretched for the per-
son who can have only
one night with his love.

701. Sōgi. [LOVE]

[36]   What could be the cause of it—
         that I should feel such love again? [30]

nao nani nare ya / hito no koishiki

30. Link: after one
night, the speaker is
resigned to forget—
until he begins to feel
love again.

702. Sōchō. [LOVE]

[37]   While I still have you,
         why think of anyone else?
         Why this discontent? [31]

kimi o okite / akazu mo tare o / omouran

31. Link: in love with
one person, the speaker
wonders why he should
be attracted to another.

703. Shōhaku. [LOVE]

[38]   No resemblance do I see
         to that other countenance.

sono omokage ni / nitaru dani nashi

704. Sōgi. [LAMENT]

[39]   The shrubs, the grasses—
         even these long bitterly
               for the old capital. [32]

kusaki sae / furuki miyako no / urami nite

32. Link: "that other
countenance" now is
the former state of the
old capital.

705. Sōchō. [LAMENT]

[40]   Even here in my house of pain,
         I still have some attachments. [33]

mi no uki yado mo / nagori koso are

33. Link: bitterness
inspired by nostalgia is
itself a kind of attach-
ment.

706. Shōhaku. [LAMENT]

[41] Before time passes,
remember your parent fondly—
and take comfort now.[34]

tarachine no / tōkaranu ato ni / nagusameyo

34. Link: a new context for the "pain" is found in the grief of one who has lost a parent.

707. Sōgi. [LAMENT]

[42] Days, months move toward their ends,
rolling on as in a dream.[35]

tsukihi no sue ya / yume ni meguramu

35. Link: the speaker warns us to find comfort in memories while they are still vivid.

708. Sōchō. [TRAVEL]

[43] Leaving this shore,
a boat stops for its last stop
before far Cathay.[36]

kono kishi o / morokoshibune no / kagiri nite

36. Link: a boat leaving for the continent may seem to have a long journey ahead— but the return trip will soon come.

709. Shōhaku. [BUDDHISM]

[44] Ah, to hear of a Law
that could free one from rebirth![37]

mata umarekonu / nori o kikabaya

37. Link: "this shore" refers to this life, which the speaker is leaving for the "far shore" of enlightenment.

710. Sōgi. [AUTUMN LOVE]

[45] "Till we meet again"—
like dew my feelings languish
only to return.[38]

au made to / omoi no tsuyu no / kiekaeri

38. Link: even after meeting the Good Law, the speaker finds his dedication fragile as dew.

711. Sōchō. [AUTUMN LOVE]

39. Link: sometimes
one's resolve weakens,
like dew scattered on
autumn wind; but it
always comes back.

[46]   Though wearied by autumn wind
         I go on with the deception.[39]

mi o akikaze mo / hitodanome nari

712. Shōhaku. [AUTUMN LOVE]

40. Link: an allusion
to the plight of the Saf-
flower Lady in *Genji
monogatari*, who de-
spairs while Genji is
away in exile.

[47]   Of no use at all,
            the call of the pine cricket
                from wormwood tangles.[40]

matsumushi no / naku ne kai naki / yomogiu ni

713. Sōgi. [AUTUMN]

41. Link: the speaker
laments his lack of
resolve to leave the
world behind. Based
partly on an allusion to
SKKS 1560, by Shunzei
(s.n. 50).

[48]   Rope-cordons mark the mountain—
            where only the moon resides.[41]

shimeyū yama wa / tsuki nomi zo sumu

714. Sōchō. [LAMENT]

42. Link: the bell
sounds to wake the
speaker, but still he
procrastinates, reluc-
tant to leave the world.

[49]   A bell sounds, and I
            see what's there ahead of me—
         unable to sleep.[42]

kane ni waga / tada aramashi no / nezame shite

715. Shōhaku. [WINTER LAMENT]

43. Link: despite
advancing age—sym-
bolized by white hair—
the speaker cannot
bring himself to leave
the world.

[50]   How thick it lies on the head—
            this frost, night after night.[43]

itadakikeri na / yona yona no shimo

716. Sōgi. [WINTER]

[51] In winter's blight
      stands a somber crane, in reeds
      by a little cove.⁴⁴

fuyugare no / ashitazu wabite / tateru e ni

44. Link: now the frost accumulates on a crane's head.

717. Shōhaku. [MISCELLANEOUS]

[52] In the tide-wind at nightfall—
      boatmen out in the offing.

yūshiokaze no / okitsu funabito

718. Sōchō. [SPRING]

[53] Drifting aimlessly,
      the haze spreads out and away—
      but toward what end?⁴⁵

yukue naki / kasumi ya izuku / hate naran

45. Link: based partly on an allusion to poem 460, by Yoshitada.

719. Sōgi. [SPRING]

[54] You can't see where it came from—
      spring in a mountain village.⁴⁶

kuru kata mienu / yamazato no haru

46. Link: spring came from a place unknown, and departs the same way.

720. Shōhaku. [SPRING]

[55] Among green branches—
      a trickle of late blossoms
      falling to earth.⁴⁷

shigemi yori / taedae nokoru / hana ochite

47. Link: late cherry blossoms fall amid green branches, signaling that spring will soon depart.

721. Sōchō. [AUTUMN]

[56]   Parting the way beneath trees—
        a pathway heavy with dew.

ko no moto wakuru / michi no tsuyukesa

722. Sōgi. [AUTUMN]

[57]   It's autumn, true—
        but how can my dry rock house
        admit rain showers?[48]

48. Link: the showers
are the hermit's tears.

aki wa nado / moranu iwa ya mo / shigururan

723. Shōhaku. [AUTUMN BUDDHISM]

[58]   Here I am, in sleeves of moss—
        yet still the moon seems at ease.[49]

49. Link: the moon-
light is reflected in rain-
drops on the monk's
sleeves.

koke no tamoto mo / tsuki wa narekeri

724. Sōchō. [AUTUMN BUDDHISM]

[59]   Now we discover
            how devoted is the heart
            of the recluse.[50]

50. Link: the ability
to appreciate such
beauty is evidence of a
fine sensibility.

kokoro aru / kagiri zo shiruki / yosutebito

725. Sōgi. [TRAVEL]

51. Link: an allusion
to the story of a Chi-
nese official who left
the capital to become
a farmer-hermit. See
s.n. 51.

[60]   Over waves now at peace—
        a boat seen rowing away.[51]

osamaru nami ni / fune izuru miyu

726. Shōhaku. [MISCELLANEOUS]

[61]   In morning calm
           the sky retains not a trace
           of last night's clouds.

asanagi no / sora ni ato naki / yoru no kumo

727. Sōchō. [WINTER]

[62]   In snow, how bright is the gleam
           of far mountains all around!⁵²

yuki ni sayakeki / yomo no tōyama

52. Link: a clear morning sky makes the last night's snowfall shine brightly on the mountains.

728. Sōgi. [WINTER]

[63]   Never do I tire
           of life in my mountaintop hut—
           even after the leaves.

mine no io / konoha no nochi mo / sumiakade

729. Shōhaku. [MISCELLANEOUS]

[64]   One learns to bear solitude
           from the sound of the pine-wind.⁵³

sabishisa narau / matsukaze no koe

53. Link: based on an allusion to SKKS 565, by Hōribe no Nari-mochi (d. 1159; s.n. 52), in which pines inspire feelings of solitude after the leaves have fallen.

730. Sōchō. [BUDDHISM]

[65]   Who besides myself
           might be arising at dawn
           time upon time?⁵⁴

tare ka kono / akatsukioki o / kasanemashi

54. Link: a monk comforts himself by thinking that others too must be awaking early to begin devotions.

731. Sōgi. [AUTUMN TRAVEL]

55. Link: the query
of poem 730 is now
rhetorical—a lament
over the loneliness of
the road.

[66]   Only the moon could know this—
        how sad one is on a journey.[55]

tsuki wa shiru ya no / tabi zo kanashiki

732. Shōhaku. [AUTUMN]

56. Link: frost sets
the season as late
autumn.

[67]   Already dew-laden,
        and now frost too withers them—
        my autumn sleeves.[56]

tsuyu fukami / shimo sae shioru / aki no sode

733. Sōchō. [AUTUMN]

57. Link: the beauti-
ful plumes of flowering
miscanthus (see the
note to poem 253) fall
in late autumn.

[68]   Plumes on flowering miscanthus—
        what a shame that they must fall![57]

usu hanasusuki / chiramaku mo oshi

734. Sōgi. [AUTUMN]

58. Allusions to
poems 273, by Shunzei,
and 253, by Toshiyori.

[69]   A quail cries out
            where dusk falls beyond a cliff—
        on a cold day.[58]

uzura naku / katayama kurete / samuki hi ni

735. Shōhaku. [LAMENT]

59. Link: further
development of the
allusion to poem 273,
with an added allusion
to poems 120–21, by
Narihira.

[70]   Once a village, now a field—
        but the lonely life goes on.[59]

no to naru sato mo / wabitsutsu zo sumu

736. Sōchō. [LOVE]

[71]   If he should return,
        he will see how patiently
        I have waited.[60]

kaerikoba / machishi omoi o / hito ya min

60. Link: a woman
waits at a run-down
house for her man to
return.

737. Sōgi. [LOVE]

[72]   Whose heart could it possibly be—
        to feel itself so aloof?[61]

utoki mo tare ga / kokoro naru beki

61. Link: so long has
she waited that the
woman begins to resent
her man.

738. Shōhaku. [LOVE]

[73]   Since the beginning
        it has been untrustworthy—
        the way of love.[62]

mukashi yori / tada ayaniku no / koi no michi

62. Link: a change in
perspective in which
the speaker of poem
737 becomes a man
complaining of his
lover's coldness, and
poem 738 a sarcas-
tic reply.

739. Sōchō. [LOVE]

[74]   That it will not stay forgotten
        makes you hate the world the more.[63]

wasuraregataki / yo sae urameshi

63. Link: despite the
pain, love refuses to be
forgotten.

740. Sōgi. [MISCELLANEOUS]

[75]   Living in the hills,
        what knowledge should one have
        of springs and autumns?[64]

yamagatsu ni / nado haruaki no / shiraruran

64. Link: now the
speaker is a man who
has fled to the hills
but cannot escape his
memories.

741. Shōhaku. [SUMMER]

65. Link: even the
grasses show time's
passage.

[76]   Grasses that no one planted,
         rank around a brushwood door.[65]

uenu kusaba no / shigeki shiba no to

742. Sōchō. [SPRING]

66. Link: a lazy
farmer leaves his pad-
dies half-plowed, just
as he lets the grasses
grow around his hut.

[77]   Alongside a fence—
         fallow paddies left behind,
         only half-plowed.[66]

katawara ni / kakio no arada / kaeshisute

743. Sōgi. [SPRING]

67. Link: the man
leaves his paddies
to find shelter from
the rain.

[78]   A man goes walking away,
         hazy in the evening rain.[67]

yuku hito kasumu / ame no kuregata

744. Sōchō. [SPRING]

68. Link: based on
an allusion to SKKS
82, by Ietaka (s.n. 53),
in which the speaker
asks a bush warbler
for lodging. In poem
744, the man walks off
when the warbler will
not sing.

[79]   The place where I stop
              for shelter, the bush warbler
                   no longer likes.[68]

yadori sen / no o uguisu ya / itouran

745. Shōhaku. [SPRING]

69. Link: the warbler
will not sing because
he does not want to
disturb the stillness
beneath the blossoms.

[80]   Ah, the stillness of the night,
         beneath cherry trees in bloom.[69]

sayo mo shizuka ni / sakura saku kage

746. Sōgi. [SPRING]

[81]   Lamp turned aside,
    I look to blossoms for my light—
    day about to break.[70]

toboshibi o / somukuru hana ni / akesomete

70. An allusion to
poem 222, by Bo Juyi.

747. Sōchō. [LOVE]

[82]   Who will it be, dreaming now—
    that fine arm for a pillow?[71]

ta ga tamakura ni / yume wa mieken

71. Link: awake in
the night, the speaker
wonders if blossoms
might be appearing in
someone else's dream.

748. Shōhaku. [LOVE]

[83]   I gave up all thought
    of seeing that pledge fulfilled—
    as the years went by.[72]

chigiri haya / omoitaetsutsu / toshi mo henu

72. Link: the rejected
speaker wonders if
someone else might
be enjoying his lover's
charms.

749. Sōgi. [LAMENT]

[84]   At such an age, who can hope
    for a visit to the hills?[73]

ima wa no yowai / yama mo tazuneji

73. Link: now facing
death, the speaker
laments not having
left the world behind
long ago.

750. Sōchō. [LAMENT]

[85]   So thoroughly
    have I hid myself away—
    they'll think I'm dead.[74]

kakusu mi o / hito wa naki ni mo / nashitsuran

74. Link: after so
many years in the hills,
a hermit loses hope for
a visit from friends.

751. Shōhaku. [LAMENT]

75. Link: still the re-
cluse lives on, despite
his desire for final re-
lease.

[86] Still it hangs on in the world—
this jewel string that is my life.[75]

sate mo ukiyo ni / kakaru tama no o

752. Sōgi. [MISCELLANEOUS]

76. Link: the speaker
continues to hang on to
life, reduced to burning
pine needles for fuel.

[87] Needles from the pines—
every morning, every evening
going up in smoke.[76]

matsu no ha o / tada asayū no / keburi nite

753. Sōchō. [MISCELLANEOUS]

77. Link: a question
for which the preced-
ing 752 is an answer.

[88] People living at seaside—
what do they do to survive?[77]

uraba no sato yo / ika ni sumuran

754. Shōhaku. [AUTUMN TRAVEL]

78. Link: a traveler
unable to sleep in harsh
weather wonders how
local people survive
under such conditions.

[89] With the autumn wind
and a rough beach for a pillow—
I despair of sleep.[78]

akikaze no / araisomakura / fushiwabinu

755. Sōgi. [AUTUMN]

79. Link: awake in
the night, a man hears
wild geese calling.

[90] Wild geese cry from the mountains,
the moon sinking in the sky.[79]

kari naku yama no / tsuki fukuru sora

756. Sōchō. [AUTUMN]

[91]   Tomorrow I'll watch
         as the dewdrops disappear
         from bush clover.[80]

kohagihara / utsurou tsuyu mo / asu ya min

80.   Link: based on an allusion to the anonymous KKS 221 (s.n. 54), which describes dew on bush clover as the tears of wild geese passing overhead.

757. Shōhaku. [LOVE]

[92]   Like the fields of Ada Moor—
         so is the heart of that man.[81]

ada no ōno o / kokoro naru hito

81.   Link: the speaker laments the fickleness of a lover whose feelings are as changeable as the dews on Ada Moor—"Moor of Transience."

758. Sōgi. [LOVE]

[93]   You must not forget—
         that we promised to the end,
         dream or reality.[82]

wasuru na yo / kagiri ya kawaru / yume utsutsu

82.   Link: the speaker chastises his lover for not honoring a pledge to remain faithful.

759. Sōchō. [LAMENT]

[94]   I think, but no longer know
         what I mean by "long ago."[83]

omoeba itsu o / inishie ni sen

83.   Link: the lover replies, "But when was it that we made the pledge?"

760. Shōhaku. [BUDDHISM]

[95]   One Buddha leaves us
         for another to appear—
         in this world of ours.[84]

hotoketachi / kakurete wa mata / izuru yo ni

84.   Link: the Buddha has no end, appearing in one incarnation and then another.

85. Link: just as the
breezes bring life to
the bare trees of win-
ter, so does the Buddha
appear constantly in
the world.

761. Sōgi. [SPRING]

[96]   A grove of withered trees—
          yet even here spring winds blow.[85]

kareshi hayashi mo / harukaze zo fuku

762. Sōchō. [SPRING]

86. Link: "peace-
ful" (*nodoka*) is a
term traditionally ap-
plied to spring land-
scapes alone.

[97]   Mountains at morning—
          but how many frosty nights
          preceded the haze?[86]

yama wa kesa / iku shimoyo ni ka / kasumuran

763. Shōhaku. [SPRING]

87. Link: haze is a
harbinger of spring.

[98]   Smoke makes for a peaceful scene
          around a makeshift hut.[87]

keburi nodoka ni / miyuru kariio

764. Sōgi. [MISCELLANEOUS]

[99]   Among the lowborn too
          must be some who spend their time
          in tranquility.

iyashiki mo / mi o osamuru wa / aritsubeshi

765. Sōchō. [MISCELLANEOUS]

88. Link: based on an
allusion to SKKS 1635
(s.n. 45), by Retired
Emperor Go-Toba.

[100]   For all men everywhere
          the Way lies straight ahead.[88]

hito ni oshinabe / michi zo tadashiki

Poems by Zen Monks II

The Gozan poets of the fifteenth and early sixteenth centuries followed the pattern of their predecessors. They too lived their lives as monks, studying sutras and histories and treatises in Chinese and writing most of their poetry in that language as well. Many were active in the high culture of the capital; others lived the reclusive life. All appear to have concealed their own personalities behind the personas of the Zen tradition.

All, that is, except the monk Ikkyū (1394–1481), whose iconoclastic words and acts make him worthy of separate attention. Born the illegitimate son of Emperor Go-Komatsu (1377–1433), he seems always to have had supreme confidence in himself, which he later exhibited in behavior that shocked the staid—and generally corrupt—world of the great Zen monasteries in Kyōto. Seeking to "do as the ancients did" rather than to follow the orthodoxy of his time, he engaged in antics that angered his teachers. His connections with the court made him a man of influence nonetheless; but he preferred to stay on the fringes of the established hierarchy most of his life. In his last years, he even lived openly with a blind minstrel woman known in his poems as Mori. All of this made his chosen sobriquet, Crazy Cloud (Kyōun), seem entirely appropriate and endeared him to later generations. To many, he is the quintessential Zen monk.

Shinden Seihan (d. 1447)

766. *Spending a Night at Chōraku Temple*[1]

Last night I spent amidst Ten Thousand Pines;
at dawn I heard the bell of Eternal Peace.
Mountain beauty comes in through the gate;
jade sky deepens the color of my robes.

1. Temple of Eternal Peace, located in Ise Province; also called the Mountain of Ten Thousand Pines.

Monk on the road

2. A reference to Ishō Tokugan, master of the temple. The dragon was often used as a symbol of high spiritual attainment.

I am a wandering traveler—a tired old bird;
but the Old Master is a true recluse—a flying
    dragon.[2]
Wind has blown mist to the neighboring village:
so tonight again I will follow you home.

Ikkyū Sōjun (1394–1481)

767. *Raincloak, Rainhat*

For woodcutters and fishermen, learning and
    practice are complete:

what use to them are the curved chairs and wood
    floors of Zen?
In straw sandals, with bamboo staff—through
    three thousand worlds;
resting in water, eating the wind—for the space of
    twenty years.

768.

> Like dew that vanishes,
> like a phantom that disappears,
> or the light cast
>   by a flash of lightning—
> so should one think of one's self.

tsuyu to kie / maboroshi to kie / inazuma no / kage no
gotoku ni / mi wa omou beshi

769. *Sunset in a Fishing Village*

On my raincape—ice; all over my body—frost;
at a fisher's shack on a mossy bank, wealth and
    rank have no end.
White haired, I sing vainly, poems broad as rivers
    and seas;
my tall fishing rod takes the light of the
    setting sun.

770. *A Pledge to Lady Mori, in Recognition of
My Debt*

The leaves on the tree had fallen, but spring
    came again,
making green growth, producing flowers, renewing
    old ties.
Ah, my Mori, if ever I forget your kindness
    toward me,
may I be reborn a beast for a million generations
    to come.

3. Chinese founder of
the Linji (J. Rinzai) sect
of Zen.

771. *Praising Master Linji*[3]

Whack! Whack! Whack! Whack! Whack!
With each opportunity, he slays or saves.
Devils and demons show in his eyes:
bright, bright—like the sun and the moon.

Keijō Shūrin (1440–1518)

772. *Enjoying Blossoms at a Mountain Temple*

Going into green hills, I'd like to be like a crow at
    evening;
under the white cherry tree is the House of the
    King of Karma;[4]
the monk there does not think to regret the passing
    of spring:
time and again he strikes the bell, shocking the
    blossoms as they fall.

4. The Buddha, lord
of past, present, and
future.

773. *Windows Torn, and No Paper*

I would patch them, but my bag has not a
    half-sheet of paper;
ah, well—at least torn windows don't have to be
    pushed open.
Wind blowing from the corner of my bed puts out
    my lamp;
rain falling from my eaves drips down to wet my
    inkstone.

Gesshū Jukei (1470–1533)

774. *Lampstand*

No snow, no fireflies, the night not even cool yet,
but here I am, already close to the small light in
    my study.
For ten years I have read beneath this two-foot
    lampstand—
this lamp that sends light ten thousand
    meters high.

775. *Drinking on a Peaceful Evening in Spring*

Drinking wine before the blossoms, I sit in the
    spring wind;
in the late night air it's quiet, but inside the
    banqueting goes on.
I sip up the drop of moonlight in my wine cup in
    one gulp;
my breast is now like the sky: The Palace of
    Boundless Cold.[5]

5. The imagined
Palace on the Moon.

Comic Linked Verse

Journals and diaries of the Late Medieval Age make it clear that even the
most serious renga parties involved a good deal of "unorthodox" play,

most of it occurring among serious poets who saw no purpose in recording for posterity what they deemed lapses in decorum. Humorous poetry was nothing new, of course; even *Kokinshū* had contained unorthodox poems. But by the days of Sōgi and Sōchō, this alternative style was rapidly developing a tradition of its own, referred to as *haikai renga*, or unorthodox linked verse. By the early sixteenth century, that tradition even had several anthologies to its credit, the most prominent being *Chikuba kyōginshū* (Crazy Verses on Bamboo Stilts) and *Inu Tsukubashū* (A Dog's *Tsukuba* Collection).

Exactly who put these collections together is unknown, although the renga master Yamazaki Sōkan (d. 1534?) is credited as the compiler of the *Dog's Collection*. And since all of the poems in both are anonymous, all we know about their authors is that some "serious" poets must have been among them. Happily, though, the poems stand well on their own. Some of these unorthodox links seem to be humorous responses to serious verses (poems 777, 781, 786); others seem to go the other way (787, 789, 791). In any case, wordplay (783), outlandish metaphor (776, 785), riddles (779, 784, 788), and irreverent (790) or ribald humor (785, 787, 789, 791) are the stock devices of this alternative tradition that would eventually produce Bashō, Buson, and Issa.

From *Chikuba kyōginshū*

776. AUTUMN. "Bug"

> Suu-suu goes the sound
>   of wind blowing in the reeds.

> That bug calling
>   seems to have lost a front tooth—
> giving in to old age.

suisui kaze no / ogi ni fuku koe; naku mushi mo / mukaba
ya nukete / yowaruran

777. LOVE. "Wife"

> If I'm going to leave the world,
> now is the time to decide.
>
> Ugly to look at
> and no kids from this wife—
> and still she complains!

yo o saran to wa / ima zo anzuru; mimewaroku / ko
umanu sai ni / shikararete

778. MISCELLANEOUS

> At a gap in the fence
> someone whispers, "Hush!"
>
> The cat from next door
> is getting ready to pounce
> on a mouse!

kaki no kiwa nite / shitsu to koso iu; konezumi o / tonari
no neko ya / tsukamuran

779. MISCELLANEOUS

> Next to one who's left the world—
> a woman lying asleep.
>
> From Bishop Henjō
> Komachi will keep concealed
> her pillow-words.[1]

shukke no soba ni / netaru nyōbo; henjō ni / kakusu
komachi ga / makura kotoba

1. Link: an allusion
to a famous exchange
of poems between the
two poets recorded in
GSS 1195–96 (s.n. 55).

780. MISCELLANEOUS

Every morning, every evening
I hear nothing but howling.

There on the corner
they won't give their skinny mutt
anything to eat![2]

2. Link: the crying
of a baby becomes
the howling of an
abused dog.

ashita yūbe ni / hoyuru o zo kiku; waga kado ni / mono
mo kuwasenu / sekareinu

From *Inu Tsukubashū*

781. SPRING

Even while he's dreaming
he seems to suffer pain.

On a flower, asleep—
a butterfly is pommeled
by drops of rain.[3]

3. Link: an allu-
sion to Zhuangzi's
dream; see the note to
poem 658.

yume no naka ni mo / itaku arurashi; hana ni nuru /
kochō wa ame ni / tatarete

782. SPRING

4. *Yukihotoke*, a
snowman, was conven-
tionally used to sym-
bolize the transience of
all worldly things.

He's melted away,
so true is he to his name—
this snow buddha![4]

kienikeri / kore zo makoto no / yukihotoke

783. SPRING

Break a branch off here,
and you'll get bit on the shin—
by a dog-cherry.

oru hito no / sune ni kamitsuku / inuzakura

784. SUMMER

> What an unlikely place
> to be lighting a lamp!
>
> Just how is it
> that a firefly's behind
> can be made to glow?

aranu tokoro ni / hi o tomoshikeri; ika ni shite / hotaru
no shiri wa / hikaruran

785. AUTUMN. A first verse written at the request of someone in Sakamoto

> A monkey's behind—
> like a leaf that never loses
> its autumn red.[5]

saru no shiri / kogarashi shiranu / momiji kana

5. A note appended to the text says, "If there are young boys present," [the first line can be read] "a monkey's face." The "young boys" would be young male homosexuals.

786. WINTER

> Beneath the moon and the sun—
> that's where I've been sleeping.
>
> From a calendar
> he's taken paper to patch
> holes in his bedclothes.

tsukihi no shita ni / ware wa nenikeri; koyomi nite /
yabure o tsuzuru / furufusuma

787. MISCELLANEOUS

Is there any hair, or not?
He feels around, to make sure.

With no disciple,
the monk has shaved his head
all by himself.

ke no aru naki wa / sagurite zo shiru; deshi motanu /
bōzu wa kami o / jizori shite

788. MISCELLANEOUS

A time when you want to cut
and yet don't want to cut.

kiritaku mo ari / kiritaku mo nashi;

Link One

He catches the thief—
but when he takes a good look,
it's his own son!

nusubito o / toraete mireba / waga ko nari

Link Two

The brilliant moon
is hidden behind a branch
of cherry blossoms.

sayaka naru / tsuki o kakuseru / hana no eda

789. MISCELLANEOUS

> He wets his head thoroughly,
> then slides himself smoothly in.
>
> Without a rainhat
>   a man in a straw raincloak
>   takes shelter from the rain.

atama nurashite / tsutsu to irikeri; mino o kite / kasa kinu
hito no / amayadori

790. MISCELLANEOUS

> Ah, to savor the good taste
>   of Hitomaro's poems!
>
> A mountain pheasant
>   from the foot-wearying hills—
>   makes a good soup!⁶

hitomaro no uta no / aji no mumasa yo; ashibiki no /
yamadori no shiru / tare mo kue

6. Link: an allusion to poem 417, by Hitomaro.

791. MISCELLANEOUS

> The other one got drenched—
>   and I got wet through too.
>
> In falling rain
>   two umbrellas show respect
>   by exchanging bows.

hito o mo nureshi / ware mo nurekeri; ame furi ni / tagai
no rei ni / kasa nugite

Early Haikai

The century and a half that separates *Shinsen Tsukubashū* and its mongrel cousin from Matsuo Bashō (1644–94) was a turbulent time for Japanese society—too turbulent, perhaps, for the literary arts, which produced little worthy of note during those years. Yet Bashō did have more immediate forebears than the ones (like Sōgi) that he claimed openly. Three of these—Arakida Moritake (1473–1549), Matsunaga Teitoku (1571–1653), and Nishiyama Sōin (1605–82)—deserve special attention.

Of the three, Moritake and Teitoku share the trait of considering themselves serious masters of linked verse. Moritake had studied with Sōgi himself, and Teitoku with the master Satomura Jōha (1524–1602). For them, haikai seems still to have been a light amusement of sorts, and not the sort of thing on which to build a reputation. That it is their less orthodox efforts that are remembered now is a testament to the sterility of the old ways and the vitality of the new.

It is above all this energy that characterizes Nishiyama Sōin, an older contemporary of Bashō who, in his later years at least, made no pretense to being a master of the serious genre. With him haikai returned at times to the "poor taste" and frivolity of the anonymous poets of *Inu Tsukubashū*. Bashō reacted against this inanity, as he did also against Teitoku's prettiness; but both men contributed to Bashō's eventual mastery of the poetry of common life.

Arakida no Moritake

Arakida Moritake

792. [MISCELLANEOUS]

> A nobleman
>   pursues his writing practice—
> by light from fine snow.
>
> The bamboo is bent over now.
> But soon it will come up right![1]

tenarai o / mesaruru hito no / awayuki ni; take nabiku
nari / itsu ka agaran

1. Link: the last line refers to the young man's calligraphy as well as the bamboo.

793. [SUMMER]

> In the mountain stream
>   what is reflected back is—
> the head of a bonze.
>
> Ah, what a cool place this is
>   to give a bald pate a rest![2]

2. Link: out in the natural world the monk does not have to worry about anyone ridiculing him for cooling his bald pate.

yamamizu ni / utsuroinuru wa / bōzu nite; ika ni suzu-
shiki / hage ga yasurai

794. [LOVE]

> To the blind minstrel
>   from a blind accompanist—
> comes a letter.
>
> Welling up from the eyes,
> the tears come tumbling down.

zatō e to / goze no moto yori / fumi no kite; horori to me
yori / namida ochikeri

3. An old warrior
who dyed his hair to
disguise his age before
going into battle dur-
ing the Gempei War.
An ancient farm rite
for chasing away in-
sects from the fields
bore his name because
he was cut down in a
rice paddy, supposedly
turning into an insect
at the point of death.

4. An allusion to KKS
832, by Kamutsuke
no Mineo (d. 901?;
s.n. 56).

795. [SPRING]

> Ah, it's Sanemori[3]—
> at the village of Deep Grass.
>
> His sidelocks and beard
>   are dyed black as charcoal—
> cherry blossoms.[4]

sanemori nare ya / fukakusa no sato; binbige no / iro wa
sumizome / sakura nite

796. [SPRING]

> A fallen blossom
>   returning to the bough, I thought—
> but no, a butterfly.

rakka eda ni / kaeru to mireba / kochō kana

797. [SUMMER]

> The summer night
> is opening to a new dawn—
> but not so my eyes!

natsu no yo wa / akuredo akanu / mabuta kana

Matsunaga Teitoku

798. [MISCELLANEOUS]

> As if I'd met up
> with a sudden rain shower—
> dewdrops on my sleeves.
>
> At the same time, we looked back
> on our path beneath black pines.

murasame ni / auta yō naru / sode no tsuyu; tomo ni
mimodosu / maki no shitamichi

799. [AUTUMN]

> Even at midday,
> who says you may pilfer fruit
> from a stranger's tree?
>
> Ah, but for a chained monkey
> the discipline is severe.

hirunaka ni / yoso no ko no mi o / katsu mono ka; tsuna-
geru saru ni / shitsuke susamaji

800. [SPRING]

Even the haze
has arrayed itself in stripes
for the year of the tiger.[5]

kasumi sae / madara ni tatsu ya / tora no toshi

5. Each year in the
Chinese zodiac's
twelve-year cycle is
named after an animal.

801. [AUTUMN]

It is the cause
for all these people napping—
the autumn moon.

minahito no / hirune no tane ya / aki no tsuki

802. [AUTUMN]

Showers of *sake*:
drinking *this* rain, not a soul
but turns red as leaves![6]

sake ya shigure / nomeba momijinu / hito mo nashi

6. Rain showers were
credited with "dyeing"
the leaves in autumn.

Nishiyama Sōin

803–10. Eight verses from a hundred-poem solo
sequence on love

[803] Now more than ever before
I would settle this affair.

namanaka shinde / rachi aken naka

[804]   These days, all the time
        I'm completely tired out—
        sick with thoughts of love.[7]

7. Link: the affair
now is a love affair.

itsumo tada / yami hōketaru / mono omoi

[805]   Getting up, then lying down,
        gazing out into the sky.[8]

8. An allusion to
poem 112, by Narihira.

okitari netari / sora nagametari

[806]   Long, long ago
            there was a certain fellow
        with a fickle heart.[9]

9. Another refer-
ence to Narihira, who
was known for his
fickle heart.

mukashi mukashi / otoko arikeri / adagokoro

[807]   Surely she looked younger
            when I first went calling![10]

10. Link: a fickle man
has second thoughts
about his new wife.

komusume ka tote / yobishi kuyashisa

[808]   Just a peek I got—
        underneath the umbrella
            when it turned round.

mikaeshi no / kasa no uchi o mo / chira to mite

[809]   "Hail to the Buddha Amida!"
        Love is something you can't trust.[11]

11. Link: partly based
on reference to an
Amida rainhat, so
named because it was
worn pushed back on
the head, resembling
a halo.

namu amida butsu / koi wa kusemono

[810]   In the moonlight
            he runs through his troubles
        faster than his beads.[12]

12. Link: a "worldly"
monk cannot put the
world behind him.

tsuki ni kuru / jūzu no tsubutsubu / uki omoi

811. SPRING

> Looking at blossoms
>   one cannot help feeling pain—
> in the back of your neck!

nagamu tote / hana ni mo itashi / kubi no hone

812. AUTUMN

> Here I am, tramping
>   on fallen leaves where he bore well
>   his loneliness.[13]

13. An allusion to poem 303, by Saigyō.

sabishisa ni / taeshi ato fumu / ochiba kana

The
Early Modern Age

Oda Nobunaga (1534–82), Toyotomi Hideyoshi (1536–98), and Toku-
gawa Ieyasu (1542–1616), the three great unifiers who brought an end
to medieval Japan in the late sixteenth century, were also amateur poets
who particularly enjoyed linked verse. Their world, on the other hand—
an urban world dominated less by hereditary lords than by samurai,
merchants, tradesmen, and upstarts of all sorts—soon came to think of
even that genre as old and outdated.

This new world was of course not all of a piece. Noble families still
remained; and farmers still made up the largest part of the population.
But in the Early Modern Age (1600–1868), it was cities—Edo, Kyōto,
and Ōsaka, first of all, and then the numerous castle towns of the prov-
inces—that were at the center of literary and artistic life. And what
city-dwellers wanted was what was new and lively, whether in clothing,
language, hobbies, or poetry. The puppet drama of Chikamatsu (1653–
1724), the fictions of Saikaku (1642–93), the woodblock prints of
Moronobu (1618–94), Utamaro (1753–1806), Hokusai (1760–1849),
and Hiroshige (1797–1858)—all answered a clearly articulated con-
sumer demand.

It was no accident, then, that the carefree spirit of haikai came to dominate Edo poetry. In the beginning, this meant a conscious harking back to the haikai of the late Muromachi period. Later, under the influence of Matsuo Bashō (1644–94) and Yosa Buson (1716–83), an attempt was made to revive the high ideals of Saigyō and Sōgi. But even Bashō and Buson stopped short of going back to the standards of classical linked verse. What they wanted was a contemporary form that could contain a broad range of themes, both classical and modern.

By Bashō's time, however, it was becoming difficult to make any generalizations about poetry at all. No longer was interest in poetry of any type limited to any class. Professionals of all sorts, from samurai bureaucrats to doctors, took poetry as their hobby; merchants, craftsmen, scholars, and clerics thought of it as their avocation. And ready to serve them were scores of professional teachers in a whole variety of genres—including haikai most prominently, but also traditional forms, humorous uta, and finally that curious hybrid, senryū, or humorous haikai.

Another feature of the era was that for the first time it made classics of the past available to a broad section of the literate population through printed books. As a result, the ancient past was rediscovered, creating a boom in National Studies that now could look beyond the imperial anthologies to Man'yōshū for inspiration. This in turn led to revivals of all sorts, eventually even in the uta.

So the Edo period was as diverse as the city after which it was named—a world populated by a diverse citizenry who were avid consumers of entertainments of all sorts and participants in the competing intellectual traditions of Zen, Confucianism, Buddhism, and the new Nationalism. Understandably, these currents produced a muddy river: a jumble of currents and crosscurrents that seldom left viewers bored as it coursed by.

Matsuo Bashō (1644-1694)

Matsuo Munefusa, the most famous of all Japanese poets, was born into a low-ranking samurai household in Ueno, a castle town in the ancient province of Iga. There as a young man he studied poetry and the classics with the young lord of the fief, no doubt also holding some menial post in the clan hierarchy. After the sudden death of his friend and patron in 1666, he seems to have gone on the road for a time—studying in Kyōto, some records say, although he no doubt still lived much of the time in his hometown. Eventually, however, he turned his back on the past and moved to Edo, where he became a master of his art of *haikai renku*, or unorthodox linked verse.[1] It was there, in 1680, that he moved into a house in the Fukagawa district; several months later it was adorned by a grateful student with a plantain tree, or *bashō*, the name that became his favorite sobriquet.

Bashō was a professional with no other source of income but his art. As such, he taught students in Edo and acted as judge at contests. He took frequently to the road as well—an activity that also brought poetic rewards for a man who wanted earnestly to follow in the footsteps of past travelers like Saigyō and Sōgi. He approached his journeys with a sense of religious devotion, and even wore the robes of the Zen sect, whose doctrines and practices he studied under a master for a time. But for him, as for his mentors, poetry was itself a kind of religious pursuit. His travel records—the most famous of which is *Oku no hosomichi* (The Narrow Road of the Interior; 1702)—recount visits to temples, but places of poetic interest were equally central to his concerns.

Scholars identify at least three periods in Bashō's career. The first takes in his work as a young man, until around the time he moved into his Fukagawa house in 1680—a period of learning and practice. Thereafter, his work took a turn away from the triviality and vulgarity of the day and toward more serious and subtle concerns in a process of mellowing that is apparent in his poem on a crow coming to roost in a bare tree in autumn dusk (see poem 815). For this period, the phrase "new words, old heart"—

1. See the next section for more details on this genre.

芭蕉之像

Matsuo Bashō

a reversal of Shunzei's dictum—can serve as a guide. Like poets of earlier ages, he used terms such as *sabi* ("loneliness") in attempts to describe his ideals, yet insisted that those ideals must be revealed in the common words and images of the here and now (see 820, 829, 839, 844).

[handwritten note: opening verse of linked verse "here & now"]

It was this approach that produced much of Bashō's greatest poetry, but in his last four or five years he attempted to go beyond the old ideals to something new and fresh—what he called *karumi*, or "lightness." The term remains somewhat obscure even today; and it appears that he had not fully formulated his new project when death took him at the age of fifty-one. But some of his last haiku (see 846, 860, 863, 873–74) and last sequences (864–72) do show a light touch that seems like a self-conscious return to the carefree spirit of youth, albeit a youth tempered with the darker wisdom of age (862, 877).

The following selections of haikai, excerpts from renku sequences, and haibun (hokku—"first verses"—introduced by a prose preface) are arranged chronologically.

813. WINTER. [1677]

Robes of frost he dons,
and for bedclothes spreads the wind—
castaway child.

shimo o kite / kaze o shikine no / sutego kana

814. AUTUMN. [1679]

Looking far, I see,
I gaze out at, I behold—
autumn in Suma.

miwataseba / nagamureba mireba / suma no aki

815. AUTUMN. [1680]

[handwritten note: see Keene WWW p. 78]

On a bare branch
a crow has settled down to roost.
In autumn dusk.

kareeda ni / karasu no tomarikeri / aki no kure

816. SUMMER. [1681]

Evening faces—showing
    white when at night I go to the backhouse,[1]
taper in hand.

yūgao no / shiroku yoru no kōka ni / shisoku torite

817. AUTUMN. Responding to Kikaku's verse about "a firefly eating thorns."[2] [1682]

A man that eats
    his meal amidst morning glories—
that's what I am!

asagao ni / ware wa meshi kuu / otoko kana

818. WINTER. "Under a Raincloak."[3] [1682]

I was living a forlorn life behind the door of my grass hut, feeling more and more lonely with every gust of autumn wind; so I borrowed Myōkan's blade, took up the skill of the Bamboo-cutter, and hacked at bamboo, bent bamboo—declaring myself "the old man who makes his own raincloak."[4] I was so clumsy at my work that even after a full day the thing wasn't done, which made me ill at ease; and as the days went by I got sick of it. Each morning I would paste paper on, each evening adding more after the first had dried. I added color, using persimmon juice, and then had to harden it all with lacquer. Finally, after about twenty days, the thing was done. The fringes were either rolled inward or rolled outward, at a slant, making it look like a half-opened lotus leaf. A most unusual shape, it was—far from the ordinary: like Saigyō's "wretched" cloak, perhaps; or the cloak Su Dongpo wore under snowy skies.[5] "Should I go see the dew of Miyagino or take my walking stick through the snows of Wu?" I mused[6]—rushing through hail, waiting for showers to pass. Thus my thoughts ran

1. *Kōka*, a euphemism for the toilet.

2. "A firefly eating thorns" is a poetic expression for choosing the hard way, thriving on adversity.

3. A body-length raincloak made of straw or bamboo.

4. Myōkan was a famous sculptor of the Nara period; the other reference is to the old man in the ancient tale *Taketori monogatari* (The Tale of the Bamboo-cutter).

5. Bashō here refers to Saigyō's life on the road. Paintings of the Chinese poet Su Dongbo(1036–1101) often depict him dressed in a raincloak, making his way on horseback through the snow.

6. The first allusion is to KKS 1091, an Eastern Song (s.n. 42). The second is to a line in a Chinese poem, "My raincloak is heavy with the snows of Wu."

on, so pleased was I, so excited by my creation. At such times one sometimes feels things. I thought again of Sōgi drenched in showers,[7] and took up my brush, writing this down inside my cloak:

> To age is enough—
> and then to have to watch showers
> from Sōgi's hut!

yo ni furu mo / sara ni sōgi no / yadori kana

7. An allusion to poem 661, by Sōgi.

819. AUTUMN. "Strike the Fulling Block!" [1684]

Alone, I took lodging in the recesses of Yoshino, far back in the mountains where white clouds piled on the peaks,[8] where mist and rain buried the valleys,[9] with the sound of wood being cut on the west[10] and the sound of bells from temples on the east—all striking deep into my heart when once I spent the night in the priests' dormitory of a certain temple.

> Strike the fulling block,
> let me hear that forlorn sound—
> temple wife![11]

kinuta uchite / ware ni kikaseyo ya / bō ga tsuma

8. An allusion to poem 290, by Shunzei.

9. An allusion to a line from the Chinese poet Du Mu (803–53): "In the southern dynasties, four hundred eighty temples; how many towers there in the smoky rain?"

10. An allusion to a poem by the Chinese poet Du Fu (712–70): "In spring mountains, I search on alone, with no companion; I hear axes cutting wood, and the mountains seem only more quiet."

11. An allusion to poem 508, by Masatsune. On fulling blocks, see the note to poem 256.

820. WINTER. Sundown on the seashore. [1684]

> The sea grows more dark,
> with the ducks' voices sounding faintly white.

umi kurete / kamo no koe honoka ni shiroshi

Verses 1–6 from the Sequence *Charcoal Vendor*. [Winter 1684]

821. Jūgo [d. 1717; WINTER]

[1]   You, charcoal vendor—
       that woman you call your own:
       Bet she's a black one! [12]

12. An allusive varia-
tion on poem 76,
anonymous.

sumiuri no / ono ga tsuma koso / kurokarame

822. Yamamoto Kakei [d. 1716; WINTER]

[2]   He works to make others pretty—
       mirror-shiner, in the cold. [13]

13. Link: one winter
occupation suggests
another.

hito no yosoi o / kagamitogi samu

823. Tsuboi Tokoku [d. 1690; WINTER]

[3]   White briar-rose:
       frost on a horse's bones,
       in second bloom. [14]

14. Link: an image by
the roadside.

hana mubara / bakotsu no shimo ni / sakikaeri

824. Okada Yasui [1648–1743; AUTUMN]

[4]   I saw a crane from that window—
       and now that faint dawn moon. [15]

15. Link: a house by
the roadside.

tsuru miru mado no / tsuki kasuka nari

825. Bashō. [AUTUMN]

[5]   A day with no
          autumn wind—a day with no
          sake in my pot! [16]

16. Link: a recluse
discovers there is noth-
ing in the pot to keep
him warm.

kaze fukanu / aki no hi kame ni / sake naki hi

826. Takahashi Uritsu [d. 1726; AUTUMN]

[6]   Into the streets to display
      an umbrella made of reeds.[17]

ogi oru kasa o / ichi ni furasuru

17. Link: off to the
city a man goes, to earn
some drinking money.

827. SPRING. Sitting at a travel lodge for a rest at
midday. [1685]

    Azaleas all arranged;
    and in their shadow—
    a woman cutting up codfish.

tsutsuji ikete / sono kage ni / hidara saku onna

828. AUTUMN. With Saigyō's poem in mind. [1685]

    Clouds, now and again—
    giving us a moment's rest
      from moon-viewing.[18]

kumo ori ori / hito o yasumuru / tsukimi kana

18. An allusion to
SANKS 370, by Saigyō
(s.n. 57).

829. SPRING. [1686] *The ancient pond*

    At an old pond, *jumps in*
    a frog takes a sudden plunge.
    The sound of water.

furuike ya / kawazu tobikomu / mizu no oto

see p. 399 # 994
See Keene WWW p. 88

830. AUTUMN. Moon-viewing at his hut. [1686]

    Moon at the full—
    round and round the pond I walk,
    the whole night through.

meigetsu ya / ike o megurite / yomosugara

831. WINTER. "First Snow." [1686]

Wanting to be back at my own grass hut to see the
year's first snow even if I was visiting elsewhere, I
had returned home in haste any number of times—
whenever I saw the sky cloud up. Then, on the
eighteenth day of the Twelfth Month, I was over-
joyed to see the snow coming down:

> First snow of the year—
> what good luck that I was home
> in my own hut.

hatsuyuki ya / saiwai an ni / makariaru

832. WINTER. "A Ball of Snow." [1686]

19. Dates 1649–1710.
One of Bashō's dis-
ciples.

A certain Sora has taken temporary lodging in
a place nearby,[19] and we visit each other all the
time, morning or night. When I'm getting a meal
together, he helps by breaking up firewood; when
I'm boiling tea, he comes over and breaks ice for
water. He's a man who enjoys the solitary life; our
friendship's strong as iron. One night, he came
visiting after a snowfall:

> You stoke up the fire,
> and I'll show you something fine:
> a big ball of snow!

kimi hi o take / yoki mono mise / yuki maruge

833. SUMMER. [1687]

> I'll get drunk, then sleep—
> among the wild pinks blossoming
> on top of a rock.

yōte nemu / nadeshiko sakeru / ishi no ue

834. SUMMER. Written when visiting the weed-
tangled yard of a man who had gone off to live
somewhere else. [1687]

> You, who raised melons—
> if only you were here too,
> taking the night air.

uri tsukuru / kimi ga are na to / yūsuzumi

835. SUMMER. "Village People." [1687]

We call the lotus Lord of Flowers.[20] And one hears
that among flowers the peony is the Rich Man. But
rice seedlings come forth from the mud and are
more pure than the lotus; and in the autumn, when
those fragrant plants ripen, they are richer than the
peony. Thus this one plant is as good as two—truly
pure and rich.

20. So nicknamed be-
cause of its prominence
in Buddhist allegory.

> Village people
>   making poems in the paddies—
> their own capital!

*noblemen of
the rice paddies*

satobito wa / ine ni uta yomu / miyako kana

836. SUMMER. At the mountain in Gifu. [1687]

> At the castle ruins
>   it's cool water from the old well
> I'll want first of all.

shiro ato ya / furui no shimizu / mazu towamu

837. AUTUMN. At Zenkōji

> Here in the moonlight,
>   the Four Gates, the Four Sects—
> they're all one.[21]

21. Referring to the
various Ways to en-
lightenment and the
four major Buddhist
sects: Tendai, Shingon,
Zen, and Ritsu.

tsukikage ya / shimon shishū mo / tada hitotsu

838. WINTER. On a cold night. [Between 1680 and 1688]

> My water jar cracks—
> broken by ice in the night
> as I lie awake.

kame waruru / yoru no kōri no / nezame kana

839. SUMMER. At Takadachi, in the far north. [1689]

22. Written at Hira-izumi, site of an ancient fortress that had been obliterated centuries before.

Yoshi-tsune

> Summer grasses—
> all that is left to us now
> of warriors' dreams.[22]

*The summer grasses
for many brave
warriors
the aftermath of
dreams*

natsukusa ya / tsuwamonodomo ga / yume no ato

840. SUMMER. [At Ryūshakuji;[23] 1689]

23. A small hilltop temple located in what is now Yamagata City.

Keene p. 89

> Ah, such stillness:
> that the very rocks are pierced
> by cicadas' drone!

*How still it is
Stinging into the
stones
the locust's trill.*

shizukasa ya / iwa ni shimiiru / semi no koe

841. SUMMER. [1689]

> It takes the hot sun
> and pushes it into the sea—
> Mogami River.

atsuki hi o / umi ni iretari / mogamigawa

24. The western Milky Way.

842. AUTUMN. "Silver Stream."[24] [1689]

While on a walking tour along the Northern Road I stopped at a place called Izumo Point in Echigo. And there was Sado Isle, eighteen *li* off over the

blue waves, lying sideways, thirty-five *li* from east
to west.[25] I felt I could reach out and touch it,
so clear was my view of the place, even down to
the crevasses and steep cliffs of the peaks and the
deepest corners of its valleys. I was thinking how
unfortunate it is that now, instead of as a place
to admire, a real treasure from which much gold
had come long ago, the island is known only as a
frightening land to which many criminals and ene-
mies of the court have been sent into exile. Then,
lost in my revery, I opened the shutters, hoping for
some relief from the melancholy of travel on the
road. The sun had already sunk into the sea and
the moon was a dim blur, but the Silver Stream
was there, suspended in the heavens, its stars twin-
kling in the cold as I listened to the sound of waves
carried from the offing, my soul as if torn from
its body, my bowels wrenched, my heart suddenly
so full of sadness that I could not think of sleep,
but stood there, weeping so hard that I could have
wrung the tears from my ink-black sleeves.

25. One *li* = 0.5 km
(about a third of a
mile).

> Across rough seas,
> it arches toward Sado Isle—
> The River of Heaven.[26]

26. Another name for
the Milky Way.

araumi ya / sado ni yokotau / ama no kawa

843. AUTUMN. At Iro Beach in Echizen. [1689]

> Such loneliness!
> It triumphs even over Suma,[27]
> this autumn strand.

27. An allusion to
the harsh landscape of
Suma as described in
the "Suma" chapter of
Genji monogatari.

sabishisa ya / suma ni kachitaru / aki no kaze

844. AUTUMN. At a place called Nakamura in
Ise. [1689]

> The autumn wind—
>   and a field of graves at Ise
>   adding to the chill.

aki no kaze / ise no hakahara / nao sugoshi

845. WINTER. [1689]

> First winter shower—
>   even a monkey is wanting
>   a straw raincoat.[28]

28. *Komino*, a small
raincoat that makes the
monkey look like a tiny
version of his master.

hatsushigure / saru mo komino o / hoshige nari

846. SPRING. [1690]

> Beneath cherry trees
>   everything from soup to fish
>   is gone to blossoms.[29]

29. Fish translates
namasu, a dish con-
sisting of raw fish and
vegetables soaked in
vinegar.

ko no moto ni / shiru mo namasu mo / sakura kana

847. SUMMER. [1690]

> He'll be dying soon,
>   but there's not a hint of it
>   in the cicada's voice.

yagate shinu / keshiki wa miezu / semi no koe

848. SUMMER. [1690]

playing with convention

> In the capital
>   still I think of the capital—   _long for, miss_
>   when a cuckoo calls.[30]

30. The cuckoo's call
brought the capital to
the mind of travelers.

kyō nite mo / kyō natsukashi ya / hototogisu

Taking the night air along the Kamo River in Kyōto

849. SUMMER. "Taking the Night Air at Fourth
Avenue, Riverside."[31] [1690]

They call it "taking the night air at Fourth Ave-
nue, Riverside": people lining up their stands in
the riverbed from moonrise early in the Sixth
Month, on until the dawn moon of mid-month—
drinking *sake* the night long, eating, and partying.
The women bind themselves with the showiest
sashes; the men deck themselves out in long jack-
ets. And there in the throng are priests and old
people too—and even apprentices to coopers and
smiths, all looking smug and at ease, singing and
reveling. Now, that's life in the capital!

> Ah, the river wind—
> in robes of persimmon color,
> taking the night air.

kawakaze ya / usugaki kitaru / yūsuzumi

31. The east end
of Fourth Avenue,
on the banks of the
Kamo River.

850. AUTUMN. [1690]

The moon at the full—
and not a single handsome
face in the room.

meigetsu ya / za ni utsukushiki / kao mo nashi

851. AUTUMN. [1690]

A tall paulownia,
and a quail calling out
behind a high fence.

kiri no ki ni / uzura naku naru / hei no uchi

Verses 23–30 from *Even the Kite's Feathers*. [Winter 1690]

852. Nakamura Fumikuni [late 17th century; MIS-CELLANEOUS]

[23]   Still skin and bones—
with not the strength as yet
to get out of bed.

yasebone no / mada okinaoru / chikara naki

853. Nozawa Bonchō [d. 1714; MISCELLANEOUS]

[24]   In borrowed space next door
a carriage is pulled in.[32]

32. Link: a visitor
comes to comfort a
sick friend.

tonari o karite / kuruma hikikomu

854. Bashō. [LOVE]

[25] Ah, the wretched man!
It's a thorny way I'll send him,
through my prickly hedge.[33]

ukihito o / kikokugaki yori / kugurasen

33. Link: a lady is upset with a man too late in coming to visit.

855. Mukai Kyorai [1651–1704; MISCELLANEOUS]

[26] When suddenly he must leave,
she reaches out with his sword.[34]

ima ya wakare no / katana sashidasu

34. Link: to avoid prying eyes, a lady sends her man home the back way.

856. Bonchō. [MISCELLANEOUS]

[27] No sign of patience
in the hand that runs quickly
through tousled hair.[35]

sewashige ni / kushi de kashira o / kakichirashi

35. Link: a hurried farewell.

857. Fumikuni. [MISCELLANEOUS]

[28] Look at his resolution,
crazy with the thought of death.[36]

omoikittaru / shinigurui miyo

36. Link: a warrior hastily trims his hair before donning a helmet for battle.

858. Kyorai. [AUTUMN]

[29] In the wide blue sky
the moon still remains shining
at break of day.[37]

seiten ni / ariakezuki no / asaborake

37. Link: early morning is a good time to prepare to die.

859. Bashō. [AUTUMN]

To Lake Biwa comes autumn,
with Mount Hira's first frost.[38]

38. Link: moonlight
is reflected in frost.

kosui no aki no / hira no hatsushimo

860. WINTER. [1690]

As a rule, I hate
      crows—but, ah, not on such a
snowy morning!

higoro nikuki / karasu mo yuki no / ashita kana

861. WINTER. "Snow-capped, Withered Miscan-
thus." [39] [1691]

39. On miscan-
thus, see the note to
poem 253.

With no sure place of my own in the world, I spent
the last six or seven years on the road, sleeping
the sleep of the traveler; but I could not forget the
friends and students I have grown close to these
many years, and so I bore up against my many
bodily ills and returned once again to the Musa-
shi Moors—receiving callers at the door of my hut
daily, to whom I offer this in reply:

Yes, somehow I have
      made it back—a snow-capped,
withered miscanthus.

to mo kaku mo / narade ya yuki no / kareobana

862. SPRING. First day of the year. [1693]

Year in, year out,
      the monkey wears the mask
of a monkey's face.[40]

40. Written at the end
of the year. The impli-
cation is that the new
year will be no differ-
ent from the last.

toshidoshi ya / saru ni kisetaru / saru no men

863. SPRING. [1693]

Spring rain falling—
and following the wasp nest down,
a leak from the roof.

harusame ya / hachi no su tsutau / yane no mori

Verses 28–36 from *Summer Night*. [Summer 1694]

864. Gakō [late 17th century; MISCELLANEOUS]

[28]   Even a change of clothes
        he brings along to the boat.

kigae no bun o / fune e azukuru

865. Bashō. [AUTUMN]

[29]   With seal attached
        comes a box with a letter—
        on a moonlit eve.[41]

fū tsukeshi / fumibako kitaru / tsuki no kure

41. Link: an important communication comes to a man about to board a boat.

866. Kagami Shikō [1665–1731; AUTUMN]

[30]   How leisurely is their walk—
        high ladies at Obon time.[42]

soro soro ariku / bon no jōroshu

42. Link: fine ladies are not bothered by a messenger's arrival. At Obon, the Festival of Lights, held in early autumn, the spirits of departed souls are remembered by lantern processions.

867. Hirose Izen [1646–1711; AUTUMN]

43. Link: in early
autumn, people put
crickets, fireflies, and
other bugs in boxes to
watch for amusement.

[31]   Bugs in boxes,
        swinging at the corner of
            Fourth and Riverside.⁴³

mushiko tsuru / shijō no kado no / kawaramachi

868. Suganuma Kyokusui [d. 1717; MISCELLA-NEOUS]

44. Link: workers do
not have the leisure to
think about bugs.

[32]   Hefted up from a flat boat—
        one bale of mat facing.⁴⁴

takase o aguru / omote hitokori

869. Gakō. [MISCELLANEOUS]

45. Link: the river
is a busy place, with
cargoes being handled
and even a troop of sol-
diers marching by in
formation.

[33]   For just a moment
            the spears go out of sight
                above the bridge.⁴⁵

ima no ma ni / yari o mikakusu / hashi no ue

870. Izen. [MISCELLANEOUS]

46. Link: the revery
of a man staring at
passing lances is bro-
ken by the sound of a
temple bell.

[34]   From a great bell comes
            the sound of a dull bong.⁴⁶

ōki na kane no / don ni kikoyuru

871. Shikō. [SPRING]

47. Link: even the
bell does not bring out
a recluse who refuses
to enjoy the blossoms.

[35]   Flowers all around
            at the height of bloom, but still
                he keeps his door shut.⁴⁷

sakari naru / hana ni mo tobira / oshiyosete

872. Gakō. [SPRING]

[36] Benches all pushed aside—
under a wisteria arbor.[48]

koshikake tsumishi / fujidana no shita

48. Link: while the cherry blossoms are in full bloom, a man can take his leisure beneath a wisteria arbor.

873. SUMMER. [1694]

In morning dew,
dirty but oh so very cool—
mud on the melon.

asatsuyu ni / yogorete suzushi / uri no doro

874. SUMMER. When he was visiting at the house of Mokusetsu in Ōtsu.[49] [1694]

Ah, cool at last!
My feet flat on the wall
for a midday nap.

hiya hiya to / kabe o fumaete / hirune kana

49. Mokusetsu Mochizuki (dates unknown); one of Bashō's disciples.

875. AUTUMN. [1694]

A lightning flash—
and into the gloom it goes:
a heron's cry.

inazuma ya / yami no kata yuku / goi no koe

876. AUTUMN. "My Words to Live By: never speak of others' shortcomings; never boast of your own strengths." [Date unknown]

Say just a word,
and your lips have gone cold—
in autumn wind.

mono ieba / kuchibiru samushi / aki no kaze

50. Written just a few   877. WINTER. Written while he was ill.[50] [1694]
days before his death.

Ill on a journey,
I run about in my dreams
over withered fields.

tabi ni yande / yume wa kareno o / kakemeguru

'Out in the Streets'

By Bashō's day, orthodox linked verse of the kind composed by Sōgi had been overtaken by *haikai renku*, a less tradition-bound genre that retained the central formal features of renga but allowed itself greater variety in theme and imagery. It was this genre that provided Bashō his vocation. Although the basic structural principles of *haikai renku* were identical to those of orthodox linked verse, the typical sequence was shorter—thirty-six verses in most cases. Likewise, the rules were somewhat different, albeit still involving proscriptions on seriation, repetition, and intermission. In all, however, poets of the newer genre allowed themselves more freedom than their forebears when it came to composing by the book. Just as they used more "common" imagery, they felt little hesitation in dispensing with a rule that got in the way of an artistic goal.

Bashō was involved in literally hundreds of *kasen*, or thirty-six-verse sequences. *Ichinaka wa* (Out in the Streets), the one translated below, was composed near Kyōto in the summer of 1690 with his students Mukai Kyorai (1651–1704) and Nozawa Bonchō (d. 1714), and represents the three poets at their best in a sequence that, like *Minase sangin hyakuin*, has long been considered a model of its kind.

Techniques of linking had of course changed somewhat since the Muromachi period. In general, the trend—which reached its fullest expression with Bashō—was away from obvious, "close" links and toward connections that involved more subtlety and imagination. This feature of the work of Bashō and his disciples is described as *nioi*, or "scent," a term intended to express the way one verse carries on the mood or tone of its predecessor like a flower's scent carried on the wind. An example from *Ichinaka wa* serves to illustrate.

Bonchō

> A priest there, in growing cold:
> going back to his temple?

Bashō

> With his monkey,
> a monkey-master roams the world
> with the autumn moon.

sō yaya samuku / tera ni kaeru ka; saruhiki no / saru to
yo o heru / aki no tsuki

Were this traditional linked verse, the reader would be tempted to make these two scenes into one involving both the priest and the monkey-master walking the same road—something that the later tradition can of course not prohibit. But the point of the link for Bashō and his disciples is the "scent" of loneliness carried from one verse to the next. No "dramatic" link is necessary to produce the obvious aesthetic effect of juxtaposing the monk and the worldly monkey-master.

Other terms were applied to such techniques. In *Ichinaka wa*, for instance, poets of Bashō's time used the term *kuraizuke*, or "linking by providing rank or station," to the eleventh verse (888); the term *suiryōzuke*, or "linking by surmise," to the twenty-sixth (903); and the term *omokagezuke*, or "linking by suggested allusion," to the thirtieth (907). More important than such terms, however, is an understanding of the artistic ideals of the genre, which demand from the reader close attention to the subtle scents, varied in texture and value, that float through the entire sequence.

In the translation, some aids to interpretation have been included—the category to which each verse would belong in the headnotes and a few comments on "links" between verses in the marginal notes. As in the earlier case of *Minase sangin hyakuin*, these comments represent an attempt to "read" the text in terms of its own tradition and are not part of the text itself.

878. Nozawa Bonchō [d. 1714; SUMMER]

[1]   Out in the streets
            are smells of every sort—
        and the summer moon.

ichinaka wa / mono no nioi ya / natsu no tsuki

879. Bashō [1644–94; SUMMER]

[2]   "It's hot! Oh, but it's hot!"
            voices say, at every gate.

atsushi atsushi to / kadokado no koe

880. Mukai Kyorai [1651–1704; SUMMER]

[3]   Second weeding
            not done yet, and already—
        ears on the rice.[1]

1. Link: the scene shifts from town to countryside.

nibankusa / tori mo hatasazu / ho ni idete

881. Bonchō. [MISCELLANEOUS]

[4]   He taps off the ashes—
            to get at one dried sardine.[2]

2. Link: a farmer takes a brief moment for lunch.

hai uchitataku / urume ichimai

882. Bashō. [MISCELLANEOUS]

[5] Seems in these parts
       no one's seen a coin before.
       What a nuisance!³

kono suji wa / kane mo mishirazu / fujiyusa yo

3. Link: the farm
is given a definite
location, deep in the
countryside.

883. Kyorai. [MISCELLANEOUS]

[6] So long it's ridiculous—
       that sword stuck in his belt.⁴

tada tohyōshi ni / nagaki wakizashi

4. Link: a swagger-
ing traveler trying to
look important ends up
looking silly.

884. Bonchō. [SPRING]

[7] From a clump of grass
       jumps a frog, and gives a fright—
       at nightfall.⁵

kusamura ni / kawazu kowagaru / yūmagure

5. Link: for all his
swagger, the man with
the sword is easily
frightened.

885. Bashō. [SPRING]

[8] While out picking butterburs,
       she swings the lamp—till it's out!

fuki no me tori ni / ando yurikesu

886. Kyorai. [SPRING]

[9] She got religion
       back when the cherry blossoms
       were only buds.⁶

dōshin no / okori wa hana no / tsubomu toki

6. Link: the extin-
guished lamp calls
to mind Buddhist
awakening.

887. Bonchō. [WINTER]

7. Link: a Buddhist
devotee looks back on
hard years.

[10]   At Nanao in Noto
         life's hard in the winter.[7]

noto no nanao no / fuyu wa sumiuki

888. Bashō. [MISCELLANEOUS]

8. Link: food is hard
to come by in winter.

[11]   Look at me, so old
         I'm down to sucking the juice
             from fishbones.[8]

uo no hone / shiwaburu made no / oi o mite

889. Kyorai. [MISCELLANEOUS LOVE]

9. Link: an echo of
a scene from "The
Safflower" chapter
of *Genji monogatari*
involving an old gate-
keeper.

[12]   He admits the one she awaits—
         with the key to the side gate.[9]

machibito ireshi / komikado no kagi

890. Bonchō. [MISCELLANEOUS]

10. Link: servant
women, leaning to get
a peek at a visitor, push
over a screen.

[13]   Leaning too close,
         they topple the standing screen—
             those serving women![10]

tachikakari / byōbu o taosu / onagodomo

891. Bashō. [MISCELLANEOUS]

11. Link: now the
screen surrounds a
bathing area in a coun-
try inn.

[14]   A sorry bathroom, this—
         bamboo grating for a floor.[11]

yudono wa take no / sunoko wabishiki

892. Kyorai. [AUTUMN]

[15]   Fennel berries
          are blown down to the ground—
          by an evening gale.[12]

uikyō no / mi o fukiotosu / yūarashi

12. Link: the cold
bath grating is matched
by an evening storm.

893. Bonchō. [AUTUMN]

[16]   A priest there, in growing cold:
          going back to his temple?

sō yaya samuku / tera ni kaeru ka

894. Bashō. [AUTUMN]

[17]   With his monkey,
          a monkey-master roams the world
          with the autumn moon.

saruhiki no / saru to yo o furu / aki no tsuki

895. Kyorai. [MISCELLANEOUS]

[18]   Once a year, he pays up—
          his one lone bale of tax.[13]

nen ni itto no / jishi hakaru nari

13. Link: the monkey-
master is off to account
for his income, how-
ever small.

896. Bonchō. [MISCELLANEOUS]

[19]   Five or six logs
          of fresh timber, thrown across
               mud puddles.[14]

goroppon / namiki tsuketaru / mizutamari

14. Link: a poor
farmer's balancing
act, both literally and
figuratively.

897. Bashō. [MISCELLANEOUS]

[20]   A slip—and he's soiled his fine socks
        in the black earth of the road.[15]

15. Link: fine socks belong to someone of high status.

tabi fumiyogosu / kuroboko no michi

898. Kyorai. [MISCELLANEOUS]

[21]   Hurrying along
            behind his master's horse—
        a sword-bearer.[16]

16. Link: the man in the socks is now a warrior's sword-bearer.

oitatete / hayaki ouma no / katanamochi

899. Bonchō. [MISCELLANEOUS]

17. Link: two men bearing different burdens and of different rank share a similar fate.

[22]   The errand boy has spilled
            the water he's carrying.[17]

detsuchi ga ninau / mizu koboshitari

900. Bashō. [MISCELLANEOUS]

[23]   Straw mats protect
            the doors and sliding screens—
        a house for sale.[18]

18. Link: the well of an abandoned mansion has the best water around.

toshōji mo / mushirogakoi no / uriyashiki

901. Kyorai. [AUTUMN]

[24]   The peppers—those "ceiling-guards"—
        turned red as the time went by.[19]

19. Link: guards watch over an empty house.

tenjōmamori / itsu ka irozuku

902. Bonchō. [AUTUMN]

[25] Without a sound,
hands make straw into sandals
in the moonlight.[20]

koso koso to / waraji o tsukuru / tsukiyo sashi

20. Link: peppers
need only time to pro-
duce; men must labor.

903. Bashō. [AUTUMN]

[26] To shake out fleas, she leaves
her bed—in early autumn.[21]

nomi o furui ni / okishi hatsuaki

21. Link: while
her child sleeps, the
mother works late into
the night.

904. Kyorai. [MISCELLANEOUS]

[27] Nothing caught,
it's rolled onto its side—
empty mousetrap.[22]

sono mama ni / korobiochitaru / masuotoshi

22. Link: strange
what catches the eye in
the middle of the night.

905. Bonchō. [MISCELLANEOUS]

[28] So warped it no longer fits—
the lid of the old wood chest.[23]

yugamite futa no / awanu hanbitsu

23. Link: next to the
empty mousetrap sits
an old wooden chest.

906. Bashō. [MISCELLANEOUS]

[29] In a grass hut
for just a little while,
and then off again.[24]

sōan ni / shibaraku ite wa / uchiyaburi

24. Link: the man
does not fit in any-
where, as warped as his
old chest.

25. Link: the image of an old traveling monk brings to mind the distant past, when to have a poem chosen for one of the imperial anthologies was a lifetime wish.

907. Kyorai. [MISCELLANEOUS]

[30] What a joy to be alive
        when poems are being chosen![25]

inochi ureshiki / senjū no sata

908. Bonchō. [MISCELLANEOUS LOVE]

[31] In countless ways
        I have known the vagaries
            of being in love.[26]

26. Link: an old poet looks back on a long life.

samazama ni / shina kawaritaru / koi o shite

909. Bashō. [MISCELLANEOUS]

[32] In this floating world of ours
        all must meet Komachi's end.[27]

27. Link: after a lifetime of love, all end as the Komachi of legend did—wizened, ugly, and alone.

ukiyo no hate wa / mina komachi nari

910. Kyorai. [MISCELLANEOUS]

[33] What can it be—
        to bring the tears on so,
            just sipping gruel?[28]

28. Link: someone consoles an aging friend with gruel and sympathy.

nani yue zo / kayu susuru ni mo / namidagumi

911. Bonchō. [MISCELLANEOUS]

[34] When the master is away—
        how broad seems the kitchen floor.[29]

29. Link: a servant finds himself depressed when the master is away.

orusu to nareba / hiroki itajiki

912. Bashō. [SPRING]

[35]   On his open palm
          he lets a flea crawl about
             in blossoms' shade.[30]

tenohira ni / shirami hawasuru / hana no kage

30. Link: the broad
floor becomes the
broad palm of a man
taking his ease.

913. Kyorai. [SPRING]

[36]   With haze not moving at all—
          ah, what a sleepy noon.[31]

kasumi ugokanu / hiru no nemutasa

31. Link: nothing
moves on a sleepy
noon, except the flea.

Bashō's Disciples

By the time of his death in 1694, Bashō had attracted several thousand students in places all over Japan. Among these, around fifty could be called disciples in the strict sense, of which eight are chosen here to represent the character of Bashō's school in the decades after his death.

To readers of the Genroku era (1688–1704), Takarai Kikaku (1661–1707) was clearly Bashō's chief disciple. Born in Edo to a physician-samurai, Kikaku studied medicine and Chinese poetry from a young age. But in his early teens he already showed a talent for haikai that sent him seeking instruction from Bashō. More urbane and sharp-edged than his teacher, he nonetheless gained the older man's respect, which he enjoyed even after he voiced disagreements over the direction of the master's work just before the latter's death.

Less independent and more personally bound to Bashō were three men with whom he composed much of his famous work in the renku form. First among these was Mukai Kyorai (1651–1704), Nagasaki-born son of a physician who first entered Bashō's gate in the mid-1680's and remained a faithful servant even after the master's death, when he produced a short treatise, titled *Kyoraishō* (Kyorai's Notes; 1702–4) that is one of our chief sources on Bashō's ideas and ideals, as well as a rich font of anecdote. Likewise dedicated was Naitō Jōsō (1662–1704), a samurai from Owari. Poor health turned him from active military service to the literary life and eventually to Bashō, whom he mourned for a full three years; he continued as a devout disciple until his own death a decade after the master's. And then there was Nozawa Bonchō (d. 1714), not just the son of a physician but a physician in fact, who became a disciple around 1690, helped Kyorai with the compilation of the haikai collection *Sarumino* (Monkey's Rain-cloak; 1691), and continued to be an advocate of the Bashō style for the remainder of his life.

An even earlier and perhaps more devoted disciple, although a lesser poet, was Hattori Ransetsu (1654–1707), an Edo samurai who seems to have begun his studies with Bashō in the mid-1670's. Devoted to Zen as well as poetry, Ransetsu was a thorough eccentric, albeit one who attracted many students of his own and did much to carry on the Bashō style.

Sugiyama Sampū (1647–1732) and Kawai Chigetsu (1634?–after 1708) were not only devoted students, but patrons as well. The former, from a merchant family, in fact gave Bashō the famous Bashō Hut in Edo; and the latter, a woman who had at one time served in a Kyōto palace and later married a rich warehouseman, lost her husband, and became a nun, also used her wealth to support the Bashō school on into the next century. Finally, there is Morikawa Kyoriku (1656–1715), a latecomer to the Bashō school who taught Bashō painting in return for instruction in haikai.

Takarai Kikaku

914. [MISCELLANEOUS]

Stories about ancestors
spoken on a frosty night.

In fading lamplight
dead spirits are beckoned back
into the world.

senso o mishiru / shimo no yogatari; tomoshibi o / kuraku
yūrei o / yo ni kaesu ya

915. [AUTUMN]

> Eyes staring, body turning—
> sleepless night, up with the moon.

> Husband soon to come,[1]
> a new bride hears a mallet strike[2]—
> first of the season.

hochi hochi to shite / nenu yo nenu tsuki; mukoiri no /
chikazuku mama ni / hatsuginuta

1. The man is being
adopted into the family
as heir.

2. *Kinuta*; see the
note to poem 256.

916. [MISCELLANEOUS]

> Lonely night ahead—
> feet weary from the long trek
> to Mount Lu Shan.[3]

> A thousand voices intoning
> the holy name of Kannon.[4]

ashibiki no / rozan ni tomaru / sabishisa yo; chigoe
tonauru / kannon no mina

3. An allusion to
poem 233, by Bo Juyi.

4. The Buddhist god-
dess of mercy.

917. SPRING. Visiting Daionji[5]

> Ah, the scent of plum—
> with it even a beggar's house
> deserves a peek.

ume ga ka ya / kojiki no ie mo / nozokaruru

5. A temple in back
of Edo's notorious
Yoshiwara pleasure dis-
trict. Beggars lived in
makeshift huts nearby.

918. SUMMER

> Evening shower—
> and gazing out into it,
> a woman alone.

yūdachi ni / hitori soto miru / onna kana

919. SUMMER. [Written upon the request of the disciples of a physician who had recently died]

> Six-footers all,
>   but the strength's gone out of them
>   in Fifth Month Rains.

rokushaku mo / chikara otoshi ya / satsukiame

920. SUMMER

> Resting uneasily
>   on a pillar of mosquitoes—
>   a bridge of dreams.[6]

6. An allusion to poem 393, by Teika.

kabashira ni / yume no ukihashi / kakaru nari

921. SUMMER. After having a bad dream on the sixteenth of the Sixth Month of the third year of Genroku [1690]

> That dream I had
>   of being stabbed—was for real!
>   Bitten by a flea.

kiraretaru / yume wa makoto ka / nomi no ato

922. AUTUMN

> Ah, the full moon—
>   casting on the straw floor mats
>   a pine's shadow.

meigetsu ya / tatami no ue ni / matsu no kage

923. AUTUMN. After rain

> A rain fog
>   rides it out on a plantain, *banana palm*
> swaying in the wind.

amagaeru / bashō ni norite / soyogikeri

924. WINTER

> "It's mine," I think—
> and the snow seems lighter
>   on my straw hat.

waga yuki to / omoeba karoshi / kasa no ue

Mukai Kyorai

925. [MISCELLANEOUS]

> Snow-portending cold blows in
>   on an island under north wind.

> To light the lamp
>   he climbs, as nightfall begins
>   on a hilltop temple.[7]

yukike ni samuki / shima no kitakaze; hi tomoshi ni /
kurereba noboru / mine no tera

7. A lamp was kept burning all night at Buddhist temples as a symbol of the constancy of the Law.

926. [MISCELLANEOUS]

> All worldly cares
>   can be forgotten for a while
>   on a holiday.

> In haste comes a messenger
>   with a letter from his lord.[8]

8. Link: a message interrupts a samurai's holiday.

mono omoi / kyō wa wasurete / yasumu hi ni; mukae
sewashiki / tono yori no fumi

927. SPRING

Blossom guards—
poking white heads together
for a little chat.

hanamori ya / shiroki kashira o / tsukiawase

928. SPRING

Just two days ago
I crossed that mountain back there—
cherries in full bloom.

ototoi wa / ano yama koetsu / hanazakari

929. SUMMER

Ah, the cool sound
of fields and mountains replete—
with Hail Amidas!

suzushiku mo / noyama ni mitsuru / nebutsu kana

930. SUMMER. Written upon the death of his
younger sister, Chine

Here in my hand
it faded away, sadly—
the firefly's light.

te no ue ni / kanashiku kiyuru / hotaru kana

931. SUMMER

> Even stones and trees
>> shine back into your eyes—
>> so hot it is!

ishi mo ki mo / manako ni hikaru / atsusa kana

932. AUTUMN

> More than the blind,
>> it's those who can't speak I pity[9]
>> —gazing at the moon.

mekura yori / oshi no kawayuki / tsukimi kana

9. That is, those who are unable to utter words of praise.

933. WINTER

> "All right, all right!"
>> I say, but still he keeps banging
>> on my gate, in snow.

ō ō to / iedo tataku ya / yuki no kado

934. WINTER. Passing over Hori Canal[10]

> Can't bear to turn
>> and look up at the dawn moon—
>> so cold it is!

ariake ni / furimukigataki / samusa kana

10. A canal running north and south between Tōin and Ōmiya streets in Kyōto.

Naitō Jōsō

935. SUMMER

An evening shower
sends ants scurrying down
a bamboo stalk.

yūdachi ni / hashirikudaru ya / take no ari

936. AUTUMN

A lightning bolt
splits in two and strikes
the mountaintop.

inazuma no / warete otsuru ya / yama no ue

937. WINTER. At the bedside of old Bashō when
he was ill

Hunching down
beneath the medicine pot—
ah, but it's cold!

uzukumaru / yakan no moto no / samusa kana

Nozawa Bonchō

938. [AUTUMN]

11. *Kintsuba* (lit.,
"sword-guard of gold"),
here referring to a
samurai who has been
shown his lord's favor
by the gift of a gold
sword-guard.

"Guard of Pure Gold" [11]—
things are easy for a man
with a name like that!

Ah, but he likes his hot bath—
night after night, beneath the moon.

kintsuba to / hito ni yobaruru / mi no yasusa; atsuburo-
zuki no / yoiyoi no tsuki

939. [MISCELLANEOUS]

Asleep at midday,
the pale blue heron standing tall
seems so serene.

How softly the rushes sway,
rustling in shallow waters.

hiru neburu / aosagi no mi no / tōtosa yo; shoro shoro
mizu ni / i no soyoguran

940. SPRING

Out go the ashes,
clouding blossoms of white plum
along the fence.

hai sutete / hakubai urumu / kakine kana

941. SPRING

A warbler calls—
and my clogs' teeth stick in the mud
of the paddy path.[12]

uguisu ya / geta no ha ni tsuku / oda no tsuchi

12. The speaker's
wooden clogs get stuck
in the mud when he
stops for a moment
to enjoy the war-
bler's song.

942. SPRING

A row of storehouses—
with a pathway behind them,
traveled by swallows.

kura narabu / ura wa tsubame no / kayoimichi

13. A line from "Bell on the Mountain," by the Chinese poet Wang Anshi (1021–86).

943. AUTUMN. "Not a single bird call—making the mountain more still" [13]

Something makes a sound.
Fallen there all by himself—
a scarecrow.

mono no oto / hitori taoruru / kakashi kana

944. WINTER

I called to him—
but no fishmonger appears
out there in the hail.

yobikaesu / funauri mienu / arare kana

945. WINTER

Far, far it stretches,
a river tracing one line
on the snowy moor.

naganaga to / kawa hitosuji ya / yuki no hara

Hattori Ransetsu

946. AUTUMN

The moon shining full—
and smoke crawling away,
over the water.

meigetsu ya / keburi haiyuku / mizu no ue

Hattori Ransetsu. Inscription: "Looking like someone / curled up under his quilts— / the Eastern Hills." (NKBT, 92, no. 366)

947. WINTER

Looking like someone
    curled up under his quilts—
the Eastern Hills.[14]

14. Higashiyama,
the hills on the eastern
border of Kyōto.

futon kite / netaru sugata ya / higashiyama

948. WINTER

Plum blossom—just one;
    and just one plum blossom's worth
        of welcome warmth.[15]

15. The plum blos-
som is a harbinger of
the warmth of spring.

ume ichirin / ichirin hodo no / atatakasa kana

Sugiyama Sanpū

949. [MISCELLANEOUS]

This morning again
    he makes do with altar rice
        offered yesterday.

Always he seems to lose out,
despite that intelligent face.[16]

16. Rice offered on
the altar the day before
makes the man's only
meal. Link: the man
looks smart but cannot
hold a job.

mata kesa mo / hotoke no meshi de / rachi o ake; son
bakari shite / kashikogao nari

950. [WINTER]

Got water from my neighbor,
but it's no good for making tea.

With the bamboos gone,
    the ground is all uneven
        under hard frost.[17]

17. Good tea de-
mands something
better than the hard
water begged next
door. Link: the best
water comes from a
well back on rough
ground where bamboo
used to grow.

Sugiyama Sanpū

moraiyoseshi mo / cha ni awanu mizu; yabu kowasu / ato
wa ukitatsu / shimogashira

951. SPRING

> Up goes the mattock,
>   glittering in the sunlight
>   on spring fields.

furiagaru / kuwa no hikari ya / haru no nora

952. AUTUMN

> No warning, and then
>   "Ah!" I've lost my first tooth—
>   in autumn wind.

gakkuri to / nukesomuru ha ya / aki no kaze

(handwritten annotation above line: red leaves/tooth autumn)

953. WINTER

Down into my collar
I pull my head, looking up
at the winter moon.

erimaki ni / kubi hikiirete / fuyu no tsuki

Kawai Chigetsu

954. SUMMER

A cuckoo calls me—
to give my hands a moment's rest
by the water spout.

uguisu ni / temoto yasumemu / nagashimoto

955. SUMMER

18. Chigetsu, widowed just a year before, imagines the male mosquito to be searching for his mate.

Alone in my bed—
with a male mosquito passing,
voice full of sorrow.[18]

hitorine ya / yowataru oka no / koe wabishi

956. WINTER

Waiting for spring—
this ice showing still its mix
of dust and chaff.

matsu haru ya / kōri ni majiru / chiri akuta

Morikawa Kyoriku

957. SPRING

Among rice seedlings—
water strewn with blossoms
from the cherry trees.

nawashiro no / mizu ni chiriuku / sakura kana

958. SPRING

Term of duty done,[19]
he stops, umbrella in hand—
gazing at dusk rain.

dekawari ya / karakasa sagete / yūnagame

19. The prescribed
term of duty for a
servant in a samurai
household in the capi-
tal was six months.
Here a man stops
to reminisce before
leaving for home.

959. WINTER

The razor flies
over his full-bearded face—
so cold it is!

ōhige ni / kamisori no tobu / samusa kana

Yosa Buson (1716-1783)

For some decades after the death of Bashō and his chief disciples, the world of haikai—now a complete industry, with its own teachers, students, salons, publishers, and readers—was dominated by poets who imitated their forebears with little imagination or insight. But by midcentury a revival of the Bashō styles was beginning; and by the 1770's the revival had produced the poet-painter Yosa Buson.

Born in Settsu Province (modern Osaka), Buson spent only a few years in Edo as a student in his early twenties; thereafter he spent most of his life in the Kyōto area—one reason, perhaps, why he felt more of an affinity for Bashō than for urbanites like Kikaku who dominated haikai circles in the Tokugawa capital. But he differed greatly from Bashō in one important respect: he took a far more casual attitude toward his art—an attitude typical of the *bunjin*, or literati, of the day. These men lived artistic lives, dabbling in painting, the tea ceremony, and all varieties of poetry, but always with the easy manner of the dilettante scholar. For this reason, Buson disavowed any ambition of becoming a poet of high seriousness, instead using the persona of the bystander who records his experience with consummate taste but little philosophical intention or deep feeling.

In some ways, this was nothing but a pose that Buson knew would be vitiated by his poems. Yet it is true that he seems more detached than Bashō; above all he strives to describe what he sees, emphasizing, on the surface, at least, the concrete detail of perception over the ideas and ideals of conception. His delight in bright, finely drawn pictures of the same natural world that he depicted in his paintings is an undeniable feature of his poetry (see poems 965–66, 970, 975, 980, 985, 995) at all stages of his career.

Beneath the surface, however, Buson's poems often provide a tension that makes them much more than paintings in words. The tension is sometimes provided by actual movements (as in 960, 970, 980, 987) that as a painter he could only suggest, sometimes by contrasting images or ideas (see 965, 968, 975, 978, 985, 989, 995), and sometimes by drama hinted at (963–64, 977) but never played out. In some of his best work, the tension

Haikai master correcting his students' work

is provided by underlying feelings—sometimes even romantic feelings (as in 964, 986), rarely found in Bashō—that provide the spark for his best portraits (see 961, 966, 969, 977, 984, in particular). Finally, to give him credit where it is due, it must be said that he creates images in his poetry that the medium of painting would find impossible to do—suggesting cold in a rat's gingerly footsteps (992), the inner loneliness of a monk snowed in for winter (993), and a small cascade of day-old water colored by a camellia's bloom (987).

Poems of Known Dates (arranged chronologically)

960. SUMMER. [Before 1757]

 Ah, what a pleasure
  to cross a stream in summer—
 sandals in hand.

natsukawa o / kosu ureshisa yo / te ni zōri

961. SUMMER. [1758]

They've separated,
but she tramples her pride
at rice planting time.[1]

1. In a small village,
everyone works at
planting time—even a
wife who is separated
from her husband.

sararetaru / mi o fumikonde / taue kana

962. SPRING. "In Memoriam, Sōoku."[2] [1767]

2. A haikai poet who
died in 1766.

Old Sōoku hung my painting "Sitting Beneath a
Pine" on his wall and loved it dearly. Thus our
acquaintance became more than casual over the
years, and since I was away on an errand when he
breathed his last, that spring came to an especially
forlorn end. Now the first anniversary of his death
is here, and I stand before his grave. Please, old
friend, don't look at me with harsh eyes, as one of
the vulgar world.

From my incense stick
ashes are spilling over—
flowers of the pine.

senkō no / hai ya koborete / matsu no hana

963. WINTER. [1768]

"Please, give me a room!"—
he tosses his swords aside
in windblown snow.

yado kase to / katana nagedasu / fubuki kana

964. SUMMER. [Before 1771]

A bat flits by—
and the wife from across the street
takes a look my way.

kawahori ya / mukai no nyōbō / kochi o miru

965. SUMMER. [Before 1771]

> Fuji all alone—
> the one thing left unburied
> by new green leaves.

fuji hitotsu / uzuminokoshite / wakaba kana

966. WINTER. [Before 1771]

> Withering wind!
> Reading words on a stone shaft,
> one priest, alone.

kogarashi ya / ishibumi o yomu / sō hitori

967. SPRING. [1771]

> A bird, far away—
> into the sun, high into the sun
> over a spring stream.

> People and violets,
> all along a slender path.[3]

tori tōku / hi ni hi ni takashi / haru no mizu; hito ya
sumire no / hito suji no michi

3. Link: a path lined with violets runs beside the stream, stretching far into the distance.

968. SUMMER. [Before 1772]

> A stonecutter
>   stops to cool his chisels
>   in clear water.

ishikiri no / nomi hiyashitaru / shimizu kana

969. [MISCELLANEOUS; 1772]

"Pardon, but somewhere near here
    there's supposed to be a shortcut."

All by himself,
a man who's become a monk
    is planting his rice.[4]

4. Link: a recluse is
working alone in his
fields when a lost man
comes asking direc-
tions.

moshi kono hen ni / chikamichi ya aru; tada hitori / hōshi
naru mi no / ta o uete

970. [MISCELLANEOUS; 1772]

A boat left abandoned,
    tied up by the back gate.

Standing on one foot,
a crane is falling asleep when comes
    a gust of wind.[5]

5. Link: the crane,
unable to sleep, is in
poor form—just like an
abandoned skiff.

issō tsunagi / suteshi urakado; kataashi de / nekakaru
tsuru ni / yamaoroshi

6. An allusion to The
Ten Foot–Square Hut
of Kamo no Chōmei
(1155–1216), in which
the author describes his
life of religious devo-
tion in a small hut,
from which he looks
out on pines and wis-
teria to the west—the
direction of the Para-
dise of Amida.

971. [MISCELLANEOUS; 1773]

By the pine boughs,
the purple of wisteria
    still in blossom.

Saying his Hail Amidas,
he moves only toward death.[6]

matsugae wa / fuji no murasaki / sakinokori; nembutsu
mōshite / shinu bakari nari

972. SPRING. Written on the tenth day of the
Fourth Month, at Hajin's Midnight Cottage.[7]
[1776]

> After they've fallen,
> their image remains in the mind—
> those peonies.

chirite nochi / omokage ni tatsu / botan kana

7. Hayano Hajin
(1677–1742) was a hai-
kai poet and major
leader in the revival
movement under whom
Buson studied in Edo.

973. SUMMER. [1777]

> In his hut of grass
>   he's got a fine mosquito net—
> that monk of the Law!

kusa no to ni / yoki kaya taruru / hōshi kana

974. SUMMER. [1777]

> Rains of the Fifth Month—
> they're happy to have a moat
>   round the encampment![8]

samidare no / hori tanomoshiki / toride kana

8. The full moat
makes a small castle
look more imposing.

975. SUMMER. [1777]

> Rains of the Fifth Month:
> before a swollen river
>   stand houses—just two.

samidare ya / taiga o mae ni / ie niken

976. SUMMER. [1777]

Ah, what coolness—
echoing out from the bell,
the sound of the bell!

suzushisa ya / kane o hanaruru / kane no oto

977. AUTUMN. [1777]

Ah, it cuts deep—
to step on my dead wife's comb,
here where we slept.

mi ni shimu ya / naki tsuma no kushi o / neya ni fumu

978. SPRING. [After 1777]

Spring rain falling—
and talking as they walk along,
a raincloak, an umbrella.

harusame ya / monogatari yuku / mino to kasa

979. WINTER. [After 1777]

So cold a moon!
Feeling small stones bite into
the soles of my shoes.

kangetsu ya / koishi no sawaru / kutsu no soko

980. SPRING. [After 1777]

There's no loincloth
on that butt blown into view—
in the spring breeze.

fudoshi senu / shiri fukareyuku ya / haru no kaze

981. [WINTER; 1780]

> At the house next door,
> he's still talking away—
> an oil seller.

> Three feet now on the ground
> in the snowy twilight.[9]

tonari nite / mada koe no suru / abura uri; sanshaku
tsumoru / yuki no tasogare

9. Link: an oil seller
is not easily deterred
from his rounds.

982. [MISCELLANEOUS; 1780]

> On a night lit by the moon,
> a distant flash of lightning.

> She looks out and sees
> that there's no one in the cart—
> a chilling sight.[10]

tsuki no yogoro no / tōki inazuma; aogimite / hito naki
kuruma / susamajiki

10. An allusion to Sei
Shōnagon's reference
in her *Pillow Book*
to an empty cart as a
"chilling sight."

Poems of Unknown Date

983. SPRING

> Days getting longer
> and memories building, going
> far into the past.

osoki hi no / tsumorite tōki / mukashi kana

984. SPRING

> Elbow showing white,
> a monk takes a moment to nap—
> in twilit spring.

hiji shiroki / sō no karine ya / yoi no haru

SPRING

> On a temple bell
>   it has stopped, and gone to sleep—
> a butterfly.

tsurigane ni / tomarite nemuru / kochō kana

986. SPRING

> Among pear blossoms,
>   reading a letter by moonlight
>   there—a woman.

nashi no hana / tsuki ni fumi yomu / onna ari

987. SPRING

> A camellia falls,
>   spilling out rain water
>   from yesterday.

tsubaki ochite / kinō no ame o / koboshikeri

11. So short is the
night that going down
the Yodo River one
sees the doors along
the banks closed up,
with occupants asleep,
at Fushimi, but open
and showing the morn-
ing's bustle at Yodo, a
few miles on.

988. SUMMER

> On a short night:
> doors pulled shut at Fushimi,
> windows open at Yodo.[11]

mijikayo ya / fushimi no toboso / yodo no mado

989. SUMMER

> With not a leaf left
>   moving, what an awesome place
>   is this summer grove!

ugoku ha mo / nakute osoroshi / natsu kodachi

990. AUTUMN

From the second floor
   comes a monk staying the night—
in an autumn gale.[12]

kyakusō no / nikai orikuru / nowaki kana

12. Even a monk
seeks human compan-
ionship on a stormy
night.

991. AUTUMN

Here are Saigyō's
   bedclothes laid out for the night—
crimson leaves.

saigyō no / yagu mo dete aru / momiji kana

992. WINTER

Over the dishes
   go the sound of rat footsteps—
ah, how cold it is!

sara o fumu / nezumi no oto no / samusa kana

993. WINTER

Locked in for winter,
my heart feels so far away—
even from Buddha.

fuyugomori / hotoke ni utoki / kokoro kana

994. WINTER

At that old pond
   the frog is growing old now—
among fallen leaves.[13]

furuike no / kawazu oiyuku / ochiba kana

13. An allusion to
Bashō's most famous
poem (poem 829).

995. WINTER. From a dream

> Two villages,
> with one pawnshop between them—
> in a winter grove.

futatsumura ni / shichiya ikken / fuyukodachi

996. SPRING. "Year's End"

Running through the streets of fame and profit,
drowning in the ocean of desire, I've tormented
myself, wearing my life away. And it goes with-
out saying that especially hard is the way of things
on the last day of the year, with people bustling
around, knocking on doors, babbling on about it
all, feet trotting along as if floating on air—in all,
a disgusting business. But how can one as worth-
less as I escape the world's dusty ways? In a corner
I sit, mumbling to myself "As the year ends, I put
on my travel hat, strap on my straw sandals,"[14]
my heart clear, but wishing it could only be so
for me—to make those words my own motto for
meditation. But, since old Bashō left us, there's
been no old Bashō. Once more a year ends; once
more a year must begin.

> Bashō left us,
> and since then never has the year
> come to such an end.

bashō sarite / sono nochi imada / toshi kurezu

14. A *hokku* ("first verse") by Bashō.

Buson's Contemporaries

Standard literary histories generally organize their treatments of Edo haikai around the "big three"—Bashō, Buson, and Issa. In fact, however, neither of the last two was as dominant in his age as Bashō, making it more proper to speak of Buson's contemporaries than his disciples. A case in point is Tan Taigi (1709–71), a poet who set up house in the Shimabara pleasure district of Kyōto in 1748 and spent the rest of his life there pursuing the art with Buson as a chief ally. Equally famous as Buson at the time, Taigi gained a fine reputation for his versatility and the "human touch" that is evident in poems like poem 1001, in which he depicts the end of autumn via the gentle image of a man hugging his knees to his chest against the growing cold.

Also prominent at the time were Ōshima Ryōta (1718–87) and Kaya Shirao (1738–91), both professional poets working primarily in Edo. Though both maintained their independence from Buson and Taigi, they were very different in every other way—the former known for his wit and urbanity, the latter for his insistence on the natural world as the only proper material for haikai.

Even more independent courses were taken by Yokoi Yayū (1702–83), a high-ranking samurai who toiled with his brush in Owari, and the woman known as Chiyojo (1703–75), the daughter of a craftsman of Kaga Province. Perhaps because of his high station, Yayū—his formal name was Tokitsura—never attached himself to a specific teacher, instead working on his own to produce both poetry and haibun (hokku—"first verses"—with a prose introduction) that made him famous. Chiyojo too, although dismissed by modern critics as trite and conventional, was highly esteemed in her time for verses such as poem 1010, which is one of the most well known of all hokku.

Thus the eighteenth century produced a number of masters unaffiliated with Buson. Nevertheless, Buson did have some true disciples. Chief among these was Takai Kitō (1741–89), who was to Buson what Kyorai was to Bashō. His father too had been a haikai master; and he carried on the tradition, becoming the recognized successor of Buson in terms of both artistic genealogy and style.

Finally, another disciple should be mentioned—but one who studied under Buson as a painter more than a poet. Named Matsumura Gekkei (1752–1811), this student took his lessons from Buson in Kyōto, then moved to Ōsaka and became the founder of a school of painting there after Buson's death. It is to him that we offer thanks for the preservation of many of his master's paintings, and for the illustrations to the haibun piece *Shin hanatsumi* (Picking New Blossoms; 1777).

Tan Taigi

997. SPRING

> Kerria in bloom:
> a leaf, a flower, a leaf,
> a flower, a leaf.

yamabuki ya / ha ni hana ni ha ni / hana ni ha ni

playfull, visual

998. SUMMER

> Passed to a new hand,
> the firefly shines its light—
> between her fingers.[1]

utsusu te ni / hikaru hotaru ya / yubi no mata

1.   One summer amusement was catching fireflies, which would be placed in baskets or in the sleeves of a girl's kimono. Here one girl is passing a firefly from her own hand to a friend's.

999. AUTUMN

> Ah, first time in love:
> in light from paper lanterns,
> a face, another face.

hatsukoi ya / tōrō ni yosuru / kao to kao

1000. AUTUMN

> Blown to the ground,
> lifted up, blown down again:
>   is a scarecrow.

fukitaosu / okosu fukaruru / kakashi kana

1001. AUTUMN

> Autumn's moving off:
> my knees pulled up against me
>   seem to belong there.

yuku aki ya / idakeba mi ni sou / hizagashira

1002. WINTER

> I swept at them,
> but in the end gave up sweeping
>   the fallen leaves.

hakikeru ga / tsui ni wa hakazu / ochiba kana

Ōshima Ryōta

1003. SPRING

> Ah, this world of ours:
> just three days I don't look out—
>   and cherry blossoms!

yo no naka wa / mikka minu ma ni / sakura kana

1004. WINTER

In the flame of my lamp
I see just a hint of wind
on a night of snow.

tomoshibi o / mireba kaze ari / yoru no yuki

Kaya Shirao

1005. AUTUMN

The mist rises—
and on the grassy moor a spider's
web, showing white.

kusa no hara / kiri harete kumo no / i shiroshi

1006. WINTER

By my coal fire
I interrupt my night studies
to warm my palms.

uzumibi ya / yagaku ni aburu / tanagokoro

Yokoi Yayū

1007. SPRING

In darkness, I break
a scented branch and see the white—
yes, of plum blossoms!²

2. An allusion to
poem 223, by Mitsune.

yami no ka o / taoreba shiroshi / ume no hana

reference to convention of dew. 405

 1008. SUMMER

Blossoms of noonflower:
not timed right to take the dew
at either end!³

hirugao ya / dochira no tsuyu mo / ma ni awazu

3. The ephemeral
asagao ("morning
glory") and *yugao*
("moonflower") are
associated with equally
ephemeral dew. But
the *hirugao*, or "noon-
flower," comes out
at the wrong time of
day to be associated
with dew of any kind,
morning or evening.

Chiyojo

1009. SPRING

Spring rain falls—
and grins of earth break out
all over the fields.

harusame ya / tsuchi no warai mo / no ni amari

1010. AUTUMN

With the well bucket
    taken over by morning glories—
I go begging water.

asagao ni / tsurube torarete / moraimizu

1011. WINTER. Written when she became a nun

No more need now
    to use my hands on my hair—
by the coal brazier.⁴

kami o yū / te no hima akite / kotatsu kana

4. With her hair cut,
she can now put her
hands near the bra-
zier for warmth in-
stead of using them to
straighten her coiffure.

Takai Kitō

1012. SPRING. In the city

> In printmakers' shops
> 　weights hold down the papers—
> in the spring breeze.

ezōshi ni / shizu oku mise ya / haru no kaze

1013. AUTUMN

> With what utter calm
> 　he makes his way through sumo fans—
> this winning wrestler!

yawaraka ni / hito wakeyuku ya / kachizumō

5. The beautiful woman is simply a metaphor for the fireworks—a "beautiful thing" that disappears, perhaps jumping into the river, perhaps into the man's cup.

1014. AUTUMN

> With the fireworks done,
> that beautiful woman has jumped
> 　into my *sake* cup.[5]

hanabi tsukite / bijin wa sake ni mi o / nagekekemu

Matsumura Gekkei

1015. SPRING

> At Fukakusa,
> plum blossoms on a moonlit night—
> against dark bamboos.

fukakusa no / ume no tsukiyo ya / take no yami

1016. Autumn

Two or three feet
of autumn echo resounding—
at paddy draining.

nisan shaku / aki no hibiki ya / otoshimizu

Comic Poetry

By the 1700's Edo was one of the world's liveliest cities, with a large and boisterous population that demanded amusements and entertainments of all sorts. Chief among these were *kabuki* drama and erotic or comic fictions; but poetry too had its place in urban life—and not only haikai, which by then had developed into a serious art form, but also comic poetry that took on the task of mocking traditional forms.

One of these comic forms was *zappai*, or "miscellaneous haikai," a genre that traced its roots to Bashō's "light" style, although the master would doubtless have disavowed the association. Some poets wrote their works in the form of renku links (1017–19), with the initiating verses eventually reduced to formulaic topics (as in 1022–33), others simply used the first five-syllable part of a verse as a straight line for parody (1020–21). In time, the genre's practitioners abandoned linking altogether in favor of individual parodies of orthodox hokku (1034–37). Many collections of these verses appeared in the Edo period, the most famous one, titled *Yanagidaru* (Willow Keg), being compiled by Karai Senryū (1718–90), a "judge" (*tenja*) of the time, whose name was eventually taken by the form as its own. Thus began the tradition of *senryū*.

At the same time, comic uta—called *kyōka*, or "madcap uta"—was also making a name for itself in the capital. Here the authors were usually of higher social status, with Chinese learning and a good knowledge of the old Japanese poems they enjoyed parodying. Another difference was that kyōka poets signed their names to their work—something creators of senryū did not do. The three *kyōkashi*, or masters of comic uta, represented here all had long careers and some social status, despite their tendency to debunk their own work as mere diversion from more serious poetry.

Whereas orthodox haikai generally looked for inspiration to the natural world, senryū found its material in the human comedy of ordinary life (see especially 1019–20, 1023, 1031–32, 1034) and wry observation (1033, 1036). Kyōka poets, on the other hand, tended to emphasize wordplay so complicated that it can only be suggested in translation (see 1038–39). Beyond that, the comic genres shared a penchant for the risqué or vulgar (1021–23, 1037, 1041) and for parody of "serious" themes and sentiments (1017, 1020–21, 1034, 1038, 1042–44).

Senryū (arranged chronologically)

 1017. [1692]

> Bored with the whole affair,
> he has to stifle his yawns.
>
> No poem from him,
> looking up at Suma's moon:
> he's blind to beauty!

sozoro akubi o / nomikominikeru; uta nakute / suma no tsuki miru / akimekura

1018. [1693]

> Fool around with cinnabar
> and you'll end up getting red.
>
> Packing tobacco
> with her little finger like that—
> who's been teaching her?[1]

1. A girl in the pleasure quarter has picked up the fashionable way to pack tobacco in a pipe at a young age.

shu ni majiwareba / akaku narikeri; tabako tsugu / koyubi no soru wa / ta ga shinan

1019. [1693]

> With a face that shows nothing,
> he just sits there quietly.
>
> Died of an overdose—
> but now the doctor explains
>   he was beyond help.

nukaranu tsura o / shite itarikeru; morikorosu / isha
gōbyō to / na o tsukete

 1020. [1702]

> With spring over now:
>
>   mosquito net comes back home,
>   quilts go to be pawned.

haru sugite / kaya ga modoreba / yagi ga rusu

1021. [1702]

> When a new day dawns:
>
>   suddenly he awakes, to find
>   the woman's ugly!

akenureba / akujo ni koi no / niwakazame

1022. [1736]

> Ah, there's plenty of space here,
> there's plenty of space here:
>
> Upstream just a bit,
> I take a pee, while someone else
>   is doing ablutions!

hiroi koto kana / hiroi koto kana; kawakami de / shoben
sureba / kori o toru

1023. [1755]

What a lively bunch they are,
what a lively bunch they are:

Every visitor
   has a joke for the new bride
      the morning after.

nigiyaka na koto / nigiyaka na koto; kuru hodo no / kazu
wa odokeru / yome no asu

1024–30. Seven verses in sequence from the first
Yanagidaru collection [1765]

[1024] Ah, but it's dark in there,
         ah, but it's dark in there:

         I went to look,
         and came out feeling sticky—
         warehouse sale.

kurai koto kana / kurai koto kana; mi ni itte / shippoku
izuru / haraikura

[1025] Ah, well then, very well then,
         well then, very well then:

         The soot sweeper
            washes his face, revealing—
         someone I know!

kore wa kore wa to / kore wa kore wa to; susuhaki no /
kao o araeba / shitta hito

[1026] Ah, well then, very well then,
         well then, very well then:

         Borrowed a hot twig,
         and blew on it, blew on it—
         bumping into someone![2]

2. Intent on keep-
ing a borrowed flame
alive until he can light
his own fire, a man
bumps into someone in
the alley.

kore wa kore wa to / kore wa kore wa to; himorai no /
fukifuki hito ni / tsukiatari

[1027] Ah, but it's been a long time,
but it's been a long time:

Back from a journey,
he picks up his child, then goes off
to visit next door.

hisashiburi nari / hisashiburi nari; tabimodori / ko o
sashiagete / tonari made

[1028] Ah, but it's been a long time,
but it's been a long time:

The horse of Sano
ends up eating the best beans—
like ambrosia.³

3. An allusion to the Nō play *Hachi no ki* (Dwarf Tree), in which a destitute warrior is rewarded for loyalty by a high-ranking lord traveling incognito.

hisashiburi nari / hisashiburi nari; sano no uma / kanro
no yō na / mame o kui

[1029] Ah, how very uncouth,
ah, how very uncouth:

Nagi leaves left
to be swept out while she's away
at the theater.⁴

4. The leaves had fallen out of the backing of her mirror as she made herself up to go to the theater.

jitaraku na koto / jitaraku na koto; nagi no ha o / shibai
no rusu ni / hakidasare

[1030] Ah, how very uncouth,
ah, how very uncouth:

As he's eating,
the workman sprinkles complaints
like seasoning.

jidaraku na koto / jidaraku na koto; shigotoshi no /
meshi wa kogoto o / sai ni shite

1031. [1771]

He's entirely tired out,
he's entirely tired out:

Popular doctor—
but not one of his neighbors
wants his services.

kutabirenikeri / kutabirenikeri; hayariisha / kinjō de
tanomu / mono de nashi

1032. [1782]

Just a little out of place,
just a little out of place:

Exchanging smiles,
the physician and the priest
pass each other.

asamashii koto / asamashii koto; nikoniko to / isha to
shukke ga / surichigai

1033. [1782]

My, but you speak the truth,
my, but you speak the truth:

Out of ten of us,
nine will be "the old lady"—
that's life for a woman.

hon no koto nari / hon no koto nari; jūnin ga / kunin
shūto wa / onna nari

1034. [1796]

At the outhouse
someone cuts in, leaving me
to praise the moon.

setchin e / saki o kosarete / tsuki o home

1035. [1796]

> "Be sure to lock up
> before bed!" says the thief—
> on his way to work.

yoku shimete / nero to ii ii / nusumi ni de

1036. [1796]

> The mother-in-law
> takes revenge for her own time
> as daughter-in-law.

shūtome wa / yome no jibun no / ishugaeshi

1037. [1796]

> "Dog shit ahead!"—
> so the word gets passed on
> back down the line.

inu no kuso / dan dan ato e / iiokuri

Kyōka

1038. Hezutsu Tōsaku [1726–89]. "Blossoms at Dawn"

> "Are they blossoms
> or clouds on that mountain ridge?"
> I fight with myself—
> till the sun intervenes
> to settle the argument!

yama no ha ni / hana ja kumo ja / to arasoi no / naka e
deru hi ya / rachi o akebono

1039. Tōsaku. Written when he saw ripe grapes at
the house of a man who was also a believer

Wine being so close
　　to something quite divine,
why not join your hands
　　and pray for a cluster of grapes
　　　rich as the beads of your rosary!

butsudō ni / chikaki budō no / tanagokoro / awasete
tanome / juzu no hitofusa

1040. Akera no Kankō [1740–1800]

So strong it can help
　　a fallen chestnut get away
from a village urchin
　　running along in pursuit—
　　that's how strong the wind is!

sato no ko ni / oikakerarete / igakuri no chi o / nigema-
waru / kaze no hageshisa

1041. Kankō

The money I owe
　　is no easier to conceal
than what's behind
　　the holes and tears in my loincloth
　　at the end of the year.

shakukin mo / ima wa tsutsumu ni / tsutsumarezu /
yaburekabure no / fundoshi no kure

5. Pen name of Ōta
Nanpo.

6. An allusion to
poem 250, by Monk
Nōin.

1042. Yomo no Akara [1749–1823][5]

In Yoshiwara
　　the women are showing their wares
　　　this evening—
blossoms glowing amidst echoes
　　from the vespers bell.[6]

City folk out enjoying the cherry blossoms

yoshiwara no / yomise o haru no / yūgure wa / iriai no
kane ni / hana ya sakuran

1043. Akara

    In this world of ours
       one can no more tire of rice
         than of moonlit nights.
    Yes, that's all a body wants—
    that, and a little cash!

yo no naka wa / itsumo tsukiyo ni / kome no meshi / sate
mata mōshi / kane no hoshisa yo

1044. Akara

    To let the hours pass
       in absolute idleness—
         now, that's fun too;

> a man can't spend all his time
> looking at the blossoms!

itazura ni / suguru tsukihi mo / omoshiroshi / hana mite
bakari / kurasarenu yo wa

Kobayashi Issa (1763-1827)

Kobayashi Issa, the last great haikai poet of the Edo period, is today the most popular among the general public, where he wins praise for his optimism and poignant humor (see 1051–52, 1057). These qualities were not achieved easily. Born to a peasant family in Shinano, he lost his mother at age two, living thereafter under the eye of an abusive stepmother. In his teens he was sent off to Edo as an apprentice. Happily, that city offered much to console his loneliness. It was there that his poetic talent emerged as he studied under the master Chikua (d. 1790). After Chikua's death he succeeded him as a haikai teacher.

Between 1792 and 1798, Issa was on the road, establishing his reputation. But several years after his return to Edo, he was called back to Shinano with news of his father's illness. The old man died that summer. This ended one trial but began another, precipitated by his brother's refusal to grant him his portion of the family estate. For the next decade Issa lived an impoverished existence in Edo, estranged from his family and bitter over his losses.

In 1813 Issa's brother relented, giving Issa half his father's property. This allowed the poet to return home at last, where he married and had eight children. But even then his misfortunes continued. All of his children went to early graves and eventually his wife was taken too. He remarried in 1825, but died two years later.

Issa's life was thus replete with trials—a fact that has always been partly responsible for his reputation. In Japan he is still known as the champion of little things, from children to bugs and frogs (see 1048–50, 1060–61). But in recent years he has also come to be recognized as a contemplative poet who can be compared with Bashō (1049, 1059) and descriptive poet in the style of Buson (1045–46, 1062, in particular). At times, he even produces a scene imbued with the spirit of *sabi* (see 1054), connecting himself with the traditions of a past increasingly distant in sensibility.

The following haikai and haibun are arranged chronologically.

1045. SUMMER. [1792]

Only the pagoda
   can be seen, with Tō Temple
     in its summer grove.[1]

tō bakari / miete tōji wa / natsu kodachi

1. The pagoda of Tō Temple in Kyōto was one of the first things seen by travelers entering from the south.

1046. WINTER. [1803]

Steam from broth
   rises above a wattle fence,
  with sleet coming down.

yudejiru no / keburu kakine ya / mizore furu

1047–48. "Holy Man Tokuon." [2] [1804]

The Holy Man Tokuon made his way into the mountains as a child, and there he lived, patching leaves together for a cloak, bathing in mountain streams, bearing up against cold and heat, with only fruit and roots to stave off hunger, as he exposed his soul to pine-wind and white moonlight, tempered his skin with rain, dew, frost, and snow. This he did for all together twenty springs and autumns, all the while doing Amidist rites for the boars and gibbons. Since the Second Month of this year, he has been down from the hills, devot-

2. A monk of the day who was famous for his ascetic devotions. After years in the mountains of central Japan, he visited Kyōto in 1803 and Edo the next year.

ing himself to saving those of us still in the muddy waters of the world. How the beasts of the mountains must miss him! How hard it must have been to bid him farewell!

[1047] The holy man
          has turned away from the sight
              of cherry trees.

shōnin ni / mihanasaretaru / sakura kana

Hearing that he would be preaching at Ryōzen Temple, a great many people, high and low, gathered to hear him. I went to the hall too—for was not my passing by at a time when I could meet Tokuon the work of the gods and the buddhas? And I found that it was as people said: his manner of sitting was unusual, and his voice had the buoyancy of the wind blowing in the bamboos. Truly his was a Way encountered only in old stories. What happiness to see him right before my own eyes!

[1048] Even sparrow's mouths
          are agape in the plum trees—
              hailing Amida!3

3. *Nembutsu*, the name given to the act of invoking the name of the bodhisattva Amida.

suzumeko mo / ume ni kuchi aku / nebutsu kana

1049. SPRING. [1810]

    Blossoms at dusk—
      making the day that just passed
          seem long ago.

yūzakura / kyō mo mukashi ni / narinikeri

1050. SPRING. [1810]

Garden butterfly:
baby crawls up, it flies off—
crawls up, it flies off.

niwa no chō / ko ga haeba tobi / haeba tobu

1051. "Chasing a Thief." [1810]

A fortyish man—who knows where he came from
—was wandering along by the back gates of some
houses in the country when he glanced over a fence
and saw an old robe hung out to dry. Quick as a
kite after prey, he plucked it up, hid it in his own
robe, and made off. But men came running from
the fields, not about to let him get away with it,
and soon caught him. They bound both his arms
to a five-foot length of bamboo just like that priest
who killed the birds.[4] Then they wrapped anything
they could find around his arms and hung things
from his neck—the sash he'd taken, even a ham-
mer—and sang, "Take him, anyone who claims
him!" while beating a drum and ringing a bell just
as they would in sending off [Yakugami] the god of
disease. Finally, they chased him down into a river-
bed and let him go. It was so much fun watching it
all that I forgot about the gravity of his crime.

> Along they go
>   chasing a bumbling thief
>   out of town.

gyōgyōshi / heta nusubito o / hayasuran

4. An allusion to a
story in *Tsurezure-
gusa* (Essays in Idle-
ness; 1330–31) about a
worldly priest who sets
a trap for birds and
then kills them—only
to be similarly pun-
ished by his neighbors.

1052. "Stricken Mute." [1810]

On the first day of the Eighth Lunar Month, I was suddenly stricken with an illness that left me unable to speak. I beckoned everyone, and asked for warm water, just like a mute. Now, I had heard that mutes could not become buddhas because they cannot intone the holy name.[5] I didn't need to worry about that, but while I was in this world I at least wanted to be as I had always been.

5. The savior Amida was believed to guarantee salvation to all who invoked his name.

> What frustration:
> even the wild geese call freely
>   to one another!

modokashi ya / kari wa jiyu ni / tomo o yobu

1053. MISCELLANEOUS. [1811]

> The moon, the blossoms—
> forty-nine years I've wasted
>   walking beneath them!

tsuki hana ya / yonjūkunen no / mudaaruki

1054. AUTUMN. [1811]

> Autumn night—
> a hole in my paper door
>   whistling away.

aki no yo ya / shōji no ana ga / fue o fuku

1055–56. "The Suffering of a Cherry Tree." [1812]

21st. Went with Zuisai to visit Mikawa-bō at his cottage.[6] Passing by the fields of Naoki, heard that the cherry tree there had just that morning been sold into Yoshiwara for the Snake Festival.[7] So even plants have to suffer the pains of this world![8] This is the sort of time when "blossoms shed tears."[9] Indeed, how sad the blossoms must be!

[1055]   Over the place
    where blossoms were dug up
      blows the wind.

hana horishi / ato o obaete / kaze no fuku

[1056]   Blossoms appeared—
    to be dug up on the spot
      with the cherry tree.

hana saku to / sugu ni horaruru / sakura kana

1057. SUMMER. [1813]

    Cicadas drone—
    as if to make my house
      into a rock![10]

semi naku ya / waga ya mo ishi ni / naru yō ni

1058. SPRING. [1814]

    Snow starts melting
      and the village overflows—
    with children.

yuki tokete / mura ippai no / kodomo kana

6.   Zuisai was the pen name of Natsume Seibi (d. 1816), a haikai poet; Mikawa-bō has not been identified.

7.   A festival held on the third day of the Third Month; live cherry trees were brought in and transplanted for decoration. The daughters of the down-and-out were often sold into prostitution in Yoshiwara, the pleasure quarter of Edo.

8.   *Kukai*, the suffering people go through in the world.

9.   Lines from "Spring View," by the Chinese poet Du Fu (712–70).

10.   An allusion to Bashō's haiku on the cicadas at Ryūshakuji (poem 840).

1059. AUTUMN. [1814]

Lightning flashes,
throwing light on those who cringe
at the thought of death.

inazuma o / abisekakeru ya / shinigirai

11. Referring to fights
between male frogs
during mating season.

1060. SPRING. Watching frogs fight.[11] [1816]

You, skinny frog—
don't go giving up just yet.
Issa's here!

yasegaeru / makeru na issa / kore ni ari

1061. SUMMER. [1818]

Hold on! Don't hit him!
—that fly praying with his hands,
praying with his feet.[12]

12. The fly seems to
be offering prayers.

yare utsu na / hae ga te o suri / ashi o suru

1062. AUTUMN. [1819]

Distant mountains
are reflected in the eye
of a dragonfly.

tōyama ga / medama ni utsuru / tombō kana

Monk Ryōkan (1758-1831)

While Issa pursued his career in Edo and on the road, one of his finest contemporaries was living a simpler life in faraway Echigo. Like Issa, this man, known to history as the Zen Monk Ryōkan, was born in the provinces; but instead of going to the great cities to make a name for himself, he spent almost all of his seventy-four years near his birthplace.

Things could have been otherwise: for Ryōkan was born into a well-to-do country family, was given a good education for a man of his day, and might have succeeded to the office of village headman or perhaps found other ways to please his father, a sometime student of the art who would doubtless have been happy to see his son become a haikai poet and teacher. But from the beginning Ryōkan was a bookish sort with no interest in money or politics; these he left to a younger brother while he pursued his studies and eventually became a Zen monk. Unlike many wearing priestly robes, he was serious about his devotions—although of course in a madcap way appropriate to his Zen beliefs. For a time he studied at a temple some distance from his hometown; then he spent some years on the road, visiting Kyōto, among other places. In the end, however, he decided to pursue his way in his own town, on the cold shores of the Japan Sea, where he stayed in a number of huts, affiliated with various temples and patrons. Among other things, this lifestyle kept him aloof from the schools and factions of the cities that consumed the time and energies of so many other poets.

The persona Ryōkan adopts in his poems is not unfamiliar to students of Zen. Sometimes playing the hermit (poems 1063, 1065, 1070, 1076–77, 1081) or teacher (1075, 1078), sometimes the idler (1068–69) or fool (1071, 1073), he is always careful to appear at his ease—an old man doing his own thing, in the manner of Ikkyū. But in his poems, his education shows, whether in the rhetorical ease of his Chinese lyrics, in the allusions (see 1067, 1072, 1075) and deliberate archaisms (1068, 1073) of his uta, or in his deft handling of haiku topics. Like Issa, his focus is often on the small things of the world; and like other uta poets of the time, he was influenced by his reading of *Man'yōshū*. These influences, along with his tempera-

Monk Ryōkan's self-portrait

ment, give his work a buoyancy of spirit that keeps it free of sentimentality or self-pity.

1063. *Long Winter Night*

It's all I think of: of when I was young,
reading books in the empty temple hall—
refilling the lamp again and again with oil,
never lamenting the long winter night.

1064. *Dream Dialogue*

Out begging food, I came into town at morning,
and on the road met an old man I used to know.
He asked me: "What you up to these days,
living on top of that peak, in white clouds?"[1]
I asked him: "What you up to these days,
getting old down here in the red dust?"[2]
We were about to reply, but we'd said nothing
when the dream was broken by the Fifth
    Night Bell.[3]

1. Referring to the life of a reclusive monk.

2. Referring to the worldly atmosphere of the city.

3. Rung at four o'clock each morning.

1065. *Empty Begging Bowl*

In the blue heavens, cold geese calling.
On the empty hills, leaves flying.
Day is darkening over the smoky village road.
Alone, I hold my empty bowl, going home.

1066. *Bashō*

Before this old man, there was never an old man;
after this old man, there's never again been an
    old man.
Old Man Bashō, ah, Old Man Bashō—
since long ago, how you've made people
    praise you!

1067.

     Although unworthy,
       I put the robes of the Law
         upon my body;
       sitting here, looking sometimes
         at mountain cherry blossoms.[4]

ōkenaku / nori no koromo o / mi ni matoi / suwarite
mitari / yamazakura kana

4. An allusion to
poem 509, by Arch-
bishop Jien.

1068.

     In my hut of grass
       I stretch my legs out full length—
     and ah, what a joy
         to hear mountain paddy frogs
           singing in mountain paddies!

kusa no io ni / ashi sashinobete / oyamada no / yamada
no kawazu / kiku ga tanoshisa

1069.

Underneath the trees
in a grove around the shrine,
tossing a ball
back and forth with village kids—
that's how I spent my day!

kono miya no / mori no shita ni / kodomora to / temari
tsukitsutsu / kurashinuru kana

1070.

Over my coal fire
I clasp stretched hands together,
counting up the days—
discovering that already
the Tenth Month has gone by.

uzumibi ni / te tazusawarite / kazoureba / mutsuki mo
sude ni / kurenikeru kana

1071.

So what if people
say I'm being foolish;
still in the morning
I'll make my way into the weeds—
going wherever I please.

ada nari to / hito wa iu to mo / asajihara / asa wake-
yukan / omou kata ni wa

1072.

Out of loneliness
I went out of my hut of grass
and gazed out—
at waves of leaves on rice plants
bending in the autumn wind.[5]

5. An allusive varia-
tion on poem 484, by
Monk Ryōzen.

sabishisa ni / kusa no iori o / idete mireba / inaba oshi-
nami / akikaze zo fuku

1073.

> Fair are the breezes;
> clear is the gleam of the moon.
> So, come along, then!
> Let's dance the night away—
> a memory for old age!

kaze wa kiyoshi / tsuki wa sayakeshi / iza tomo ni / odori
akasan / oi no nagori ni

1074.

> How one autumn night
> we chatted in a brush hut
> till the hour was late—
> now is that the sort of thing
> a man could ever forget?

aki no yo no / sayo fukuru made / shiba no to ni / kata-
rishi koto o / itsu ka wasuren

1075.

> Our life in this world—
> to what shall I compare it?
> It's like an echo
> resounding through the mountains
> and off into empty sky.[6]

6. An allusion to
poem 57, by Sami
Mansei.

yo no naka wa / nani ni tatoen / yamabiko no / kotauru
koe no / munashiki ga goto

1076.

> If anyone asks,
> "How's that recluse?" I answer:

If the rain falls
from the far sky, let it rain!
If the wind blows, let it blow!

suteshi mi o / ika ni to towaba / hisakata no / ame furaba
fure / kaze fukaba fuke

1077.

It's not as if
I have decided not to mix
in the world of men;
but just that I am better
at playing by myself!

yo no naka ni / majiranu to ni wa / aranedomo / hitori
asobi zo / ware wa masareru

1078.

The way breath goes out,
and then again breath comes in:
know this as a sign
that this world we live in
never comes to an end.

izuru iki / mata iru iki wa / yo no naka no / tsukisenu
koto no / tameshi to zo shire

1079. Written after thieves had broken into his hut

At least the robbers
left this one thing behind—
moon in my window.

nusubito ni / torinokosareshi / mado no tsuki

1080.

> A bush warbler—
> and not one of a hundred men
> even knows it's there.

uguisu ya / hyakunin nagara / ki ga tsukazu

1081.

> On a summer night
> I began counting up fleas—
> then a new day dawned.

natsu no yo ya / nomi o kazoete / akashikeri

1082.

> River in winter.
> From high on a peak above,
> a hawk is glaring.

fuyukawa ya / mine yori taka no / niramikeri

Uta of the Late Edo Period

Ryōkan was not the first Edo poet to reclaim the uta as a poetic vehicle. That distinction goes instead to the scholars of the National Studies Movement involved in research into *Man'yōshū* and other ancient texts—men such as Kamo no Mabuchi (1697–1769) and Motoori Norinaga (1730–1801), both remembered now primarily for their rediscovery of the Japanese past as represented in the classics of the Nara and Heian periods.

What characterizes the uta of these writers, too, is an attempt to breathe new life into the genre through the use of the vocabulary, rhetoric, and themes of the early and "pristine" eras of Japanese literary history, as a famous poem by Mabuchi makes clear (1083). Poems such as Mabuchi's, in a lofty style that shunned the more gentle rhythms of intervening eras in favor of the more masculine cadences of *Man'yōshū*, could not but have a great impact on poets of the day—even a hermit like Ryōkan, who knew enough of the National Studies Movement to develop a taste for Man'yō diction, if nothing else. In similar ways, men like Mabuchi can be said to have set the stage for the development of uta during the remainder of the Edo period. Some poets disagreed with their approach, of course; but even those who did not openly follow Mabuchi's lead seem to have been influenced by his emphasis on a more direct approach to poetic statement.

Four of these poets are represented here. The first, Tayasu Munetake (1715–71), was a son of the shogun Tokugawa Yoshimune (1684–1751), who studied with Mabuchi and supported his cause in the highest circles. As one might expect from a man of that background, there is a strong moralistic strain in many of his poems; but he produced fine nature poetry that shows Mabuchi's influence as well.

Ozawa Roan (1723–1801), by contrast, was no ally of Mabuchi and his disciples. He began his career studying with the head of the Reizei family and then went on to create a style of his own, one that he claimed was based on a respect less for *Man'yōshū* than for Ki no Tsurayuki and *Kokinshū*. His poems, however, reveal a debt to his contemporaries in numerous ways, not the least being his focus on immediate experience and contemporary subject matter.

Kagawa Kageki (1768–1843) also criticized the National Studies poets, identifying Roan as his teacher. And he was somewhat more successful in creating a style based on the courtly themes of Ki no Tsurayuki. Avoiding Mabuchi's archaisms, he relied instead on timeworn images of the court anthologies for his effects. Ironically, however, he often seems most powerful when he speaks in a direct voice.

The most interesting of these four poets is Tachibana Akemi (1812–68), another participant in the National Studies Movement. Born into the family of a paper merchant in the provinces, he went to Kyōto to study under a prominent scholar in his early twenties and then continued his studies back home. There he earned a reputation as a scholar in his own right. He was also known as a patriotic poet, but most modern critics reserve their highest praise for his poems that employ the direct style in observations of everyday life. Among uta poets, he is the one poet who ranks with Ryōkan as a master of haikai powers of observation within the conventions of the uta form.

Kamo no Mabuchi

1083.

> On an autumn night
>   the high plain of heaven shines
> brightly, brightly
>   with moonbeams that illumine
> wild geese crying out in flight.

aki no yo no / hogara hogara to / ama no hara / teru
tsukikage ni / kari nakiwataru

Tayasu Munetake

1084.

> Not a trace of mud,
>   nor even a wave disturbs
>   this coursing stream
>   that draws into its current
>   even one ignorant as I.

nigori naku / nami sae mo naku / yuku mizu wa / mono
shiranu ware mo / uzumikeru ka mo

1085. "Autumn's Beginning"

> A gust of wind
>   strums the strings of my zither[1]
>   as it passes by—

1. The Japanese koto.

a sign bearing tidings
of the coming of autumn.

koto no o o / sawataru kaze no / hibikasu ni / aki sari
kinu to / ima wa shirushi mo

1086. "Charcoal Kiln"

With no snowfall yet,
there is nothing but the smoke
from a charcoal kiln
to behold in the winter trees
that line the mountainside.

yuki madaki / fuyuki no yama wa / sumigama no / keburi
narade wa / miraku mono nashi

2. *Herasagi*, a water
bird known for its
large, clownish bill.

1087. "Spoonbill"[2]

The man who does nothing
but let the world pass him by
is inferior
even to a spoonbill
foraging idly for his food.

mono mo nasade / yo ni furu hito wa / herasagi no /
munaasari su ni / nao otorikeri

Ozawa Roan

1088. AUTUMN. Written when he was looking out
on the landscape at Uzumasa

At Uzumasa
the wind roars down toward me
through the dense woods—
striking a fearsome note
on an evening in autumn.[3]

3. An allusion to
poem 316, by Saigyō.

uzumasa no / fukaki hayashi o / hibikikuru / kaze no to
sugoki / aki no yūgure

1089.

> All by itself
>   the moon hangs in the heavens,
> shining with such force
>   that it pierces the hard earth
>   with its penetrating light.

tsuki hitori / ame ni kakarite / aragane no / tsuchi mo
tōrete / teru hikari kana

1090. An expression of concern written when
he heard men and women of the area had
gathered to consider what to do against the
drought

> With the earth cracked
>   by sunlight that has showered
>   our people in heat,
> I pray for just enough rain
>   to dry their tear-drenched sleeves.

tsuchi sakete / teru hi ni nureshi / tami no sode / kawaku
bakari no / ame mo furanan

1091. At hearthside, lamenting the years

> Poking at the coals,
> I stir up old memories
>   that make the past year
> seem like the vanishing warmth
>   of the fire in my hearth.

kakiokoshi / omoi kaeseba / uzumibi no / kieshi ni nitaru /
hitotoshi no ato

Kagawa Kageki

1092. SUMMER. "Love Seen in Summer"

My secret spying
     through the cracks in her fence
is impeded now
     by thick growth on the bamboo
     that tells us summer has come.

hito shirenu / waga kaimami mo / wakatake no / shigemi
ni sawaru / natsu wa kinikeri

1093. MISCELLANEOUS. Topic unknown

It was in lamplight
     that I was reading my book—
or so I had thought
     when I saw a page turn white
     with the start of a new day.

tomoshibi no / kage nite miru to / omou ma ni / fumi no
ue shiroku / yo wa akenikeri

1094. A haikai uta. "Selling Blackwood"

"Buy some, buy some now—
buy some firewood for your wife
     to make your dinner.
I've a long way to go back
     to Ōhara Village."

mese ya mese / yūge no tsumagi / hayaku mese / kaerusa
tōshi / ōhara no sato

1095. LOVE. Topic unknown

On the mountain ridge
     I see the Pleiades twinkling—

the only sign
   that the hour has grown late
   at the height of summer.[4]

yama no ha ni / subaru kagayaku / minazuki no / kono yo
wa itaku / fukenikerashi na

4. Subaru, the Pleia-
des, is a constellation
visible on the horizon
late at night in mid-
summer.

1096. LOVE. Topic unknown

When a blast of wind
   blows down from the mountain
      in the evening light—
that's when my heart is pierced
   with longing for the one I love.

yamaoroshi / hi mo yūkage ni / fuku toki zo / shimijimi
hito wa / koishikarikeru

Tachibana Akemi

1097. "Rice Planting"

Bent toward the earth,
   scores of women planting rice
      stand in a row—
with broad hats and long sleeves
   both dangling in the mud.

utsufushi ni / ōku no ueme / tachinarabi / kasa mo tamoto
mo / doro ni sashiiru

1098. "On the Road in the Rain"

After the rainfall,
   a man struggles through the mud
      on Otsu Road.
"Say, I have a horse for hire—
   won't you use him, traveler?"

ame fureba / doro fuminazumu / ōtsu michi / ware ni uma ari / mesanu tabibito

5. From a sequence of fifty-one poems, all beginning with the phrase *tanoshimi wa* ("How pleasant it is") and all dealing with the private life.

1099–1103. From *Poems for Solitary Pleasure*[5]

[1099] How pleasant it is—
when I can spend idle time
thinking about
anything that comes to mind,
puffing on my pipe.

tanoshimi wa / kokoro ni ukabu / hakanagoto / omoi-tsuzukete / tabako suu toki

[1100] How pleasant it is—
when I meet an acquaintance
after a long time
and we stop to talk together
about the past, the present.

tanoshimi wa / monoshiribito ni / mare ni aite / inishie ima o / katariau toki

[1101] How pleasant it is—
when I can bring home a fish
for the kids' dinner,
and they say, "Delicious! Delicious!,"
as we eat it together.

tanoshimi wa / mare ni uo nite / kora mina ga / umashi umashi to / iite kuu toki

[1102] How pleasant it is—
when I'm reading through a book
at my leisure
and see there a person
who is exactly like me.

tanoshimi wa / sozoro yomiyuku / fumi no naka ni / ware to hitoshiki / hito o mishi toki

[1103] How pleasant it is—
    when someone I don't like
       comes to visit
    but before much time has passed
       just gets up and goes home.

tanoshimi wa / iya naru hito no / kitarishi ga / nagaku mo
orade / kaerikeru toki

1104. "Tired of Sleeping Alone"

    Hearing the report
       of bullets fired from muskets,
    I find myself
       trembling as I ask people,
    "Any word of my husband?"

hi ni hajiku / tama no otozure / ozuozu mo / waga se no
yukue / hito ni towaruru

1105. "Tired of Sleeping Alone"

    Since you went away
       with your halberd in your hand,
    it's been three long years—
       yet I have not opened my jewel box
       for even a single day.[6]

hoko torite / kimi yukishi yori / toshi mitose / heredo
kushige o / akeshi hi wa nashi

6. In other words, as a sign of devotion the woman has not put on makeup during the three years her man has been away.

The
Modern Age

To characterize the changes in poetry that accompanied Japan's transition from feudalism to modern democracy is no easy task. One way to summarize the matter, however, is to say that whereas earlier poets from Hitomaro to Saigyō and Bashō were influenced only by their forebears in China and Japan, the poets of the modern world have also learned much from traditions their ancestors knew nothing about—namely, the traditions of Dante, Shakespeare, Villon, Wordsworth, and a host of other Western poets too numerous to mention.

Under these new influences, many poets turned to the imported genre of "free verse" as a way to express the values of an age that was open to new ideas and ways of expression. In this way, they created forms suited to an audience that was more free-spirited and, in time, better educated than any in the past. Yet it is a tribute to the resilience of the old forms that they have not died out. Even today, thousands of haiku are published each year; and the same is true of tanka. While those who write in the older forms may not represent the mainstream of modern Japanese poetry, they clearly constitute a strong minority that keeps old traditions alive in a country now renowned for its dedication to what is new.

Modern Haiku

When the Edo period came to an abrupt end with the forced entry of Commodore Perry's ships into Uraga Harbor, the culture of Japan was changed forever. Soon horses and palanquins gave way to rickshas and trains; old-style kimonos yielded to English tweeds; the principles of Confucian education were replaced by a new spirit of scientific inquiry and pragmatism.

Surrounded by such changes, poetry could not remain unaffected. Before long, young men and women were experimenting with modes of free verse learned from Europe, which set them to writing about subjects—from sexual liberation to politics—that even the most open-minded of medieval poets would have considered taboo. Yet the old traditions did survive, attracting some of the finest talents of the day. A case in point is Masaoka Shiki (1867–1902), a young man from Matsuyama on the island of Shikoku who came to Tokyo to study in his teens, then withdrew from school to become first a newspaper reporter and subsequently the leader of a group of young people working toward the reform of traditional poetry. A lucid thinker and indefatigable campaigner, Shiki stated clearly his goals: to break with the old schools that had made the art of haikai too conventional for too long; to rethink history in a way that showed the limitations of a "nature" poet like Bashō (Shiki favored Buson as more "humanistic"); to liberate poets from concepts of decorum that seemed irrelevant in the modern age; and to stress direct statement of emotion through new, vibrant imagery. As a way to set his work apart from that of older schools, he referred to it as "haiku." Sadly, he died of tuberculosis at the young age of thirty-five. But the poems below show that he was able to realize his ambitions remarkably well, employing images that are indeed new, and in ways that evoke emotions with great subtlety.

When Shiki died in 1902, he left behind many disciples and a magazine, *Hototogisu* (Cuckoo), that became an institution. In the years after his death, the group split into two factions. One remained closer to Shiki's expressed goals; the other wanted to go farther than their teacher had, eventually doing away with the traditional 5-7-5 syllable count and even the "season words" that had always been central to the identity of the form. These two factions remain even today.

Masaoka Shiki

The most prominent of the conservative poets was Takahama Kyoshi (1874–1959), another man from Matsuyama, who became the editor of *Hototogisu* on Shiki's death and went on to lead the strongest school of haiku for the next six decades. His style is fairly straightforward—especially in comparison with that of his rival Kawahigashi Hekigodō (1873–1937), another native of Matsuyama, who was more adventuresome as both man and poet. Unlike Kyoshi, who remained in the mainstream of poetry his entire life and gained prominence and wealth as a publisher, Hekigodō was always an independent figure, and he paid the price for his independence in isolation.

Understandably, it was Kyoshi who attracted more students, literally thousands of them over the years. But it is one of Hekigodō's students—Ogiwara Seisensui (1884–1976)—who represents the most interesting developments in the haiku form. Perhaps more than any other's, his works make us ask whether poems so unbound from the formal strictures of traditional haiku can be called haiku at all.

Masaoka Shiki

1106. SPRING

> I get myself shaved—
> on a day when Ueno's bell
> is muffled by haze.

hige soru ya / ueno no kane no / kasumu hi ni

1107. SUMMER

> My summer jacket
>   seems to want to fly away
>   and leave me behind.

natsu haori / ware o hanarete / toban to su

1108. SUMMER

> A field of graves—
> gravestones low to the ground,
> grass growing high.

hakahara ya / haka hikuku shite / kusa shigeru

1109. AUTUMN

> Eating an apple
>   as I sit before peonies—
> that's how I'll die.

ringo kuute / botan no mae ni / shinan kana

1110. AUTUMN

> Over railroad tracks
>   wild geese go by, flying low
>   on a moonlit night.

kisha michi ni / hikuku kari tobu / tsukiyo kana

1111. WINTER

Me here in my bed,
with snow all around the house—
all I think about.[1]

yuki no ie ni / nete iru to omou / bakari nite

1. This and the next poem were written in 1896, when Shiki was confined to his bed by the illness that would take his life several years later.

1112. WINTER

Time and time again,
"How deep is the snow now?"
—I keep on asking.

ikutabi mo / yuki no fukasa o / tazunekeri

Takahama Kyoshi

1113. SPRING

Playing poem cards,
they're all so beautiful—
bent on winning.[2]

karuta toru / mina utsukushiku / makemajiku

2. Referring to a New Year's game in which players try to match the lower halves of the poems of *One Hundred Poems by One Hundred Poets* to the upper halves, which are read aloud by a moderator.

1114. SPRING

Onto the rain porch
from somewhere outside it comes—
a fallen petal.[3]

nure'en ni / izuku to mo naki / rakka kana

3. "Rain porch" translates *nure'en*, a narrow veranda running below the rain shutters.

1115. SUMMER

The snake flees away—
but those eyes that stared at me
stay there in the grass.

hebi nigete / ware o mishi me no / kusa ni nokoru

1116. AUTUMN

Beneath the autumn
sky—a field chrysanthemum
missing petals.

shūten no / moto ni nogiku no / kaben kaku

1117. AUTUMN

I put something down—
and at that place emerges
an autumn shadow.

mono okeba / soko ni umarenu / aki no kage

1118. WINTER

At the cold's height
I go to see a sick friend—
and learn that he's died.

daikan ya / mimai ni ikeba / shinde ori

Kawahigashi Hekigodō

1119. SPRING

Off in the distance, a tall tree
with summer near,

standing there
—amidst folds of roofs.

tōku takaki ki / natsu chikaki / tateri / tatamu yane ni

1120. SPRING

After provoking the bees in their nest,
I throw the pole aside.

su no hachi okoraseshi / sao o sutetari

1121. SPRING/SUMMER [Written when his daughter
graduated from elementary school]

Gripping a graduation certificate,
covered with sweat,
standing here facing me.

sotsugyō shōsho o nigiri / asebamite / ware ni mukaitachi

1122. SUMMER

Until I swatted that fly
the fly swatter never existed.

hae utsu made / haetataki nakarishi

1123. WINTER

A duck—its prickly plucked flesh now visible.

kamo mushiru hada arawaruru

The Modern Age

Ogiwara Seisensui

1124.

Lined up neatly, they make lines—
all of them the graves of soldiers.

tadashiku retsu o nasu / mina sotsu no haka narikeri

1125.

The aged shadow of a peddler,
in evening light, reaching its full stature.

monouri no oishi kage / yūhi ni nobikiritari

1126.

I carry Mother on my back
into the winter sun, and set her down.

haha o ōte kite / fuyuhi no en ni sueru

1127.

Among the insects crying, insects crying.

mushi naku naka ni mushi naku

Modern Tanka

It is only fitting that an anthology of traditional Japanese poetry should end where it began—with the uta, albeit in its modern incarnation. For just as the tradition of Bashō and Buson continues in Japan today, so does the tradition of Yakamochi and Teika. To distinguish it from its ancestors, the modern form is generally referred to as "tanka"—an old term, to be sure, but one that has in time taken on a modern ring. Its practitioners, too, have attempted to make their genre new.

One of the first of these reformers was Ochiai Naobumi (1861–1903), a man trained in the National Studies school who took it as his goal to create a revolution of sensibility among contemporary poets in the old form. Although his own poems fall short of his own ideals, Naobumi recognized new talent and gave it encouragement with the support of his own publishing house. Eventually this effort led to the emergence of Yosano Akiko (1878–1942), a truly new poet whose passionate and often sexually explicit love poems caused a sensation in their time. With her poetry we confront the persona of Komachi unbound.

While Akiko was writing her love poems, another reformer was opening new territory as well—the renegade Masaoka Shiki (1867–1902), who during the last years of his life devoted much of his time to tanka reform. In typical fashion, he began with an attack—on Tsurayuki, *Kokinshū*, and all that could be identified with the conventions of the court tradition. His models were the "masculine" *Man'yōshū* poets and Minamoto no Sanetomo. Yet what is most attractive about his own poems is his evocation of subjective states, particularly those relating to his own physical decline. For this reason, he is still today regarded as a Keatsian figure among his countrymen.

For all their revolutionary ideas, neither Akiko nor Shiki went so far as to reject the basic form of the tanka. This was left to Ishikawa Takuboku (1886–1912), a participant in Akiko's Romantic movement who went on to be associated with the naturalistic novelists that so dominated the literary world of the early 1900's. His three-line tanka (the name is retained because Takuboku preserves the thirty-one syllable count) represent perhaps the most fundamental change in the form of the tanka to take place in its long history. This change in sensibility is reflected in his themes as well.

Yet Takuboku's attempt to move the old form in a new direction ultimately failed—or, led in the direction of free verse, which amounted to the same thing in historical terms. Instead, the new generation of tanka poets settled for a compromise, represented by Saitō Mokichi (1882–1953), a poet who can be considered the heir of Shiki. With his work, the tradition of lyrical, descriptive poetry begun by poets a millennium before asserts itself once again.

Ochiai Naobumi

1128.

> Ruler in hand,
> a little girl came outside
>   to measure its depth—
> flakes of delicate spring snow
> clinging to her long sleeves.

kazashi mote / fukasa hakarishi / komusume no / tamoto
ni tsukinu / haru no awayuki

1129.

> The melancholy
>   of rain showers heard in bed
>   at break of day—
> something those not in love
> must know nothing about.

akatsuki no / neya no shigure no / awaresa mo / koi senu
hito wa / shirazu ya aruramu

1130.

When blossoms appeared
on bush clover in the morning,
when blossoms scattered
from bush clover in the evening—
I was thinking only of you.

hagi no hana / sakishi ashita mo / hagi no hana / chirishi
yūbe mo / kimi o koso omoe

Yosano Akiko

1131.

Not even once
have you touched my soft flesh,
coursing with hot blood.
Don't you feel a bit lonesome,
you—always preaching your way?[1]

yawahada no / atsuki chishio ni / fure mo mide / sabishi-
karazu ya / michi o toku kimi

1. Like most of
Akiko's poems trans-
lated here, this was ad-
dressed to her husband
Tekkan (1873–1935),
himself an avant-garde
poet, who was fond
of preaching about his
own "way."

1132.

At a flute's sound,
the priest's hand hesitates
over the *Lotus*;[2]
and look at how he knits his brow—
being still so very young.

fue no oto ni / hokkekyō utsusu / te o todome / hisomeshi
mayu yo / mada urawakaki

2. *The Lotus Sutra*,
most prominent of all
the Buddhist sutras
in Japan.

1133.

Ah, that noontime
  when at the house a plum fell
    onto my koto,
while out by the clear stream
  you were intoning poems!

koto no ue ni / ume no mi otsuru / yado no hiru yo / chi-
kaki shimizu ni / uta suzuru kimi

1134.

Ah, my black hair,
  the thousand strands of my hair,
    my tangled hair:
my thoughts entangled as well
  in the tangle of my thoughts.

kurokami no / sensuji no kami no / midaregami / katsu
omoi midare / omoi midaruru

1135.

Must you lecture me?
Must you expound your way?
Enlighten me?
Put your karma away now—
I offer you hot blood.

isamemasu ka / michi tokimasu ka / satoshimasu ka /
sukuse no yoso ni / chi o meshimase na

1136.

"The springtime is so short,
  and who ever heard of a life
    that lasts forever?"
So I said, and filled his hands
  with the power of my breasts.

haru mijikashi / nani ni fumetsu no / inochi zo to / chikara
aru chibusa o / te ni sagurasenu

1137.

> Of the way—say nothing.
> Of the future—think nothing.
> Of fame—ask nothing.
> Now I see just you and me—
> one loving, the other loving back.

michi o iwazu / nochi o omowazu / na o towazu / koko ni
koikou / kimi to ware to miru

Masaoka Shiki

1138.

> I dozed off, until
>   awakened from a painful dream
>   by yet more pain;
>   wiping away the sweat,
>   I send rose petals scattering.

utatane no / utata kurushiki / yume samete / ase fuki
oreba / bara no hana chiru

1139.

> Nothing is left now
>   of the man I used to see—
> so utter his decline.
> The face of the man in the mirror
>   is streaming with tears.

mukashi mishi / omokage mo arazu / otoroete / kagami
no hito no / horohoro to naku

1140.

> Under the heavens
> of distant America
> it was created:
> this game of baseball
> I never tire of watching.

hisakata no / amerikabito no / hajimenishi / besuboru wa /
miredo akanu ka mo

1141.

> After a wind storm
> that toppled the enclosing wall
> of the house out back—
> a young girl eating breakfast
> comes clearly into view.

nowaki shite / hei taoretaru / ura no ie ni / wakaki onna
no / asage suru miyu

3. The personal
poetry anthology of
Minamoto no Sane-
tomo (1192–1219).

1142. Reading *Kinkaishū*[3]

> After Hitomaro
> who is there that can be called
> a true *uta* poet?
> The Barbarian-subduer
> Minamoto no Sanetomo!

hitomaro no / nochi no utayomi wa / tare ka aran / seiitai
shōgun / minamoto no sanetomo

1143.

> There in their vase,
> the plumes of wisteria
> are so short
> that they cannot span the distance
> to the straw mat here below.

kame ni sasu / fuji no hanabusa / mijikakereba / tatami no
ue ni / todokazarikeri

1144.

> I think to myself
>   about making a trellis
>   to hold evening faces—
>   but, alas, this life of mine
>   will never last till autumn.

yūgao no / tana tsukuran to / omoedomo / aki machi-
gatenu / waga inochi kamo

1145.

> The new green growth
>   stands out on the young pines
> as a long day
>   gives in to evening's advance—
> sending my fever up again.

wakamatsu no / medachi no midori / nagaki hi o / yūkata
makete / netsu idenikeri

Ishikawa Takuboku

1146.

> In the Eastern Sea, on a little island, on a beach, on white sand,
> I drench myself with tears,
>   playing with a crab.

tōkai no kojima no iso no shirasuna ni / ware naki-
nurete / kani to tawamuru

1147.

> Ah, the sadness of this lifeless sand.
> Softly it sifts
> down through the fingers of my clenched hands.

inochi naki suna no kanashisa yo / sara sara to / nigireba
yubi no aida yori otsu

1148.

> Just in fun I took up Mother on my back—
> but she was so light that I broke down and cried
> before I could take three steps.

tawamure ni haha o seoite / sono amari karoki ni nakite /
sanbo ayumazu

1149.

> First in hushed tones—then their talk gets louder.
> A pistol shot rings out;
> a life comes to an end.

kosokoso sono hanashi ga yagate takakunari / pisutoru
narite / jinsei owaru

1150.

> I keep on working,
> and keep on working, but still life gets no easier.
> Blankly I stare at my hands.

hatarakedo / hatarakedo nao waga kurashi raku ni nara-
zari / jitto te o miru

1151.

> I breathe in and out,
> and from my chest comes a sound—
> a sound more forlorn than a blast of storm wind.

iki sureba / mune no naka nite naru oto ari / kogarashi
yori mo sabishiki sono oto

1152.

> Putting pressure on my aching tooth,
> I saw the sun shine red, bright red,
> rising up before me from the midst of the winter fog.

itamu ha o osaetsutsu / hi ga akaaka to / fuyu no moya
no naka ni noboru o mitari

1153.

> Leaning against the hospital window,
> I gaze out at the people
> as they go walking by, so full of vigor.

byōin no mado ni yoritsutsu / iroiro no hito no / genki ni
aruku o nagamu

Saitō Mokichi

1154.

> A bunch of hens
>   are scratching about in the sand,
> while silently
>   a razor sharpener
>   passes by and away.

mendorira / suna abi itare / hissori to / kamisoritogibito
wa / sugiyukinikeri

1155.

> In hushed silence
> I lie here by my mother
> as she faces death—
> and hear frogs from far paddies
> echoing through the heavens.

shi ni chikaki / haha ni soine no / shinshin to / tōda no
kawazu / ten ni kikoyuru

1156.

> Off to the east,
> a new day will be dawning
> —with a boy here
> whistling in a high thin tone
> as he goes walking by.

hingashi wa / akebono naramu / hosohoso to / kuchibue
fukite / iku dōji ari

1157.

> As I look now
> at Gauguin's Self-Portrait
> I remember
> when I was in Michinoku—
> that day I killed a silkworm.

gōgan no / jigazō mireba / michinoku ni / yamako koro-
shishi / sono hi omōyu

Reference Material

Supplementary Notes

1. MYS 1: ko mo yo / miko mochi / fukushi mo yo / mibukushi mochi / kono oka ni / na tsumasu ko / ie norase / na norasane / soramitsu / yamato no kuni wa / oshinabete / ware koso ore / shikinabete / ware koso ore / ware kosoba / norame / ie o mo na o mo

2. MYS 2: yamato ni wa / murayama aredo / toriyorou / ama no kaguyama / noboritachi / kunimi o sureba / kunihara wa / keburi tachitatsu / unahara wa / kamame tachitatsu / umashi kuni zo / akizushima / yamato no kuni wa

3. MYS 16: fuyukomori / haru sarikureba / nakazu arishi / tori mo kinakinu / sakazu arishi / hana mo sakeredo / yama o shigemi / irite mo torazu / kusa fukami / torite mo mizu / akiyama no / ko no ha o mite wa / momichi o ba / torite zo shinou / aoki o ba / okite zo nageku / soko shi urameshi / akiyama ware wa

4. MYS 25: miyoshino no / mimiga no mine ni / toki naku zo / yuki wa furikeru / ma naku zo / ame wa furikeru / sono yuki no / toki naki ga goto / sono ame no / ma naki ga goto / kuma mo ochizu / omoitsutsu zo koshi / sono yamamichi o

5. Emperor Tenji moved his official residence from the Yamato plain to the southern tip of Lake Biwa in 667, there establishing his Ōtsu Palace in a new city commonly referred to as the Ōmi capital (modern Ōtsu City, east of Kyōto). Upon Tenji's death in 671, Emperor Temmu (d. 686; r. 673–86), after defeating Tenji's successor in a war referred to as the Jinshin Disturbance, moved the capital back to its traditional site in Asuka.

6. MYS 29: tamatasuki / unebi no yama no / kashihara no / hijiri no miyo yu / aremashishi / kami no kotogoto / tsuga no ki no / iya tsugitsugi ni / ame no shita / shirashimeshishi o / sora ni mitsu / yamato o okite / aoniyoshi / narayama o koe / ikasama ni / omōshimese ka / amazakaru / hina ni wa aredo / iwabashiru / ōmi no kuni no / sasanami no / ōtsu no miya ni / ame no shita / shirashimeshikemu / sumeroki no / kami no mikoto no / ōmiya wa / koko to kikedomo / ōtono wa / koko to iedomo / haru kusa no / shigeku oitaru / kasumi tatsu / haruhi no kireru / momoshiki no / ōmiyatokoro / mireba kanashi mo

7. MYS 36: yasumishishi / waga ōkimi no / kikoshimesu / ame no shita ni / kuni wa shi mo / sawa ni aredomo / yamakawa no / kiyoki kōchi to / mikokoro o / yoshino no kuni no / hana jirau / akizu no nohe ni / miya-

bashira / futoshikimaseba / momoshiki no / ōmiyabito wa / fune namete / asakawa wataru / funakioi / yūkawa wataru / kono kawa no / tayuru koto naku / kono yama no / iya takashirasu / mina sosogu / taki no miyako wa / miredo akanu ka mo

8. MYS 38: yasumishishi / waga ōkimi / kamu nagara / kamusabi sesu to / yoshinogawa / tagitsu kōchi ni / takadono o / takashirimashite / noboritachi / kunimi o seseba / tatanaharu / aokakiyama / yamatsumi no / matsuru mitsuki to / harube wa / hanakazashi mochi / aki tateba / momiji kazaseri / yukisou / kawa no kami mo / ōmike ni / tsukaematsuru to / kamitsuse ni / ukawa o tachi / shimotsuse ni / sada sashiwatasu / yama kawa mo / yorite tsukauru / kami no miyo ka mo

9. MYS 135: tsuno sahau / iwami no umi no / koto saeku / kara no saki naru / ikuri ni zo / fukamiru ouru / ariso ni zo / tamamo wa ouru / tamamo nasu / nabikineshi ko o / fukamiru no / fukamete omoedo / saneshi yo wa / ikuda mo arazu / hau tsuta no / wakare shi kureba / kimo mukau / kokoro o itami / omoitsutsu / kaerimi suredo / ōbune no / watari no yama no / momijiba no / chiri no magai ni / imo ga sode / saya ni mo miezu / tsumagomoru / yakami no yama no / kumoma yori / watarau tsuki no / oshikedomo / kakuroikureba / amatsutau / irihi sashinure / masurao to / omoeru ware mo / shikitae no / koromo no sode wa / tōrite nurenu

10. MYS 196: tobu tori no / asuka no kawa no / kamitsuse ni / iwabashi watashi / shimotsuse ni / uchihashi watasu / iwabashi ni / oinabikeru / tamamo mo zo / tayureba ouru / uchihashi ni / oioireru / kawamo mo zo / karureba hayuru / nani shi ka mo / waga ōkimi no / tataseba / tamamo no mokoro / koyaseba / kawamo no gotoku / nabikaishi / yoroshiki kimi ga / asamiya o / wasuretamau ya / yūmiya o / somukitamau ya / utsusomi to / omoishi toki ni / haruhe wa / hana orikazashi / aki tateba / momiji momijiba kazashi / shikitae no / sode tazusawari / kagami nasu / miredomo akazu / mochizuki no / iya mezurashimi / omōshishi / kimi to tokidoki / idemashite / asobitamaishi / mikemukau / kinoe no miya o / tokomiya to / sadametamaite / ajisawau / megoto mo taenu / shikarekamo / aya ni kanashimi / nuedori no / katakoizuma / asadori no / kayowasu kimi ga / natsukusa no / omoishinaete / yūtsuzu no / ka yuki kaku yuki / ōbune no / tayutau mireba / nagusamuru / kokoro mo arazu / soko yue ni / semu sube shire ya / oto nomi mo / na nomi mo taezu / ame tsuchi no / iya tōnagaku / shinoiyukamu / mina ni kakaseru / asukagawa / yorozuyo made ni / hashiki ya shi / waga ōkimi no / katami ka koko o

11. MYS 220: tamamo yoshi / sanuki no kuni wa / kuni kara ka / miredomo akanu / kamu kara ka / kokoda tōtoki / ametsuchi / hitsuki to tomo ni / tariyukamu / kami no miomo to / tsugikitaru / naka no minato yu / fune ukete / waga kogikureba / tokitsu kaze / kumoi ni fuku ni / oki mireba / toinami tachi / he mireba / shiranami sawaku / isanatori / umi o kashikomi / yuku fune no / kaji hikiorite / ochichochi no / shima wa ōkedo /

naguwashi / samine no shima no / arisomo ni / iorite mireba / nami no
oto no / shigeki hamahe o / shikitae no / makura ni nashite / aratoko ni /
korofusu kimi ga / ie shiraba / yukite mo tsugemu / tsuma shiraba / ki mo
towamashi o / tamahoko no / michi dani shirazu / ohohoshiku / machi ka
kou ramu / hashiki tsumara wa

12. MYS 320: ame tsuchi no / wakareshi toki yu / kamu sabite / takaku tōtoki /
suruga naru / fuji no takane o / ama no hara / furisake mireba / wataru
hi no / kage mo kakurai / teru tsuki no / hikari mo miezu / shirakumo
mo / iyuki habakari / tokijiku zo / yuki wa furikeru / kataritsugi / iitsugi
yukamu / fuji no takane wa

13. MYS 931: yasumishishi / waga ōkimi wa / miyoshino no / akizu no ono
no / nonohe ni wa / tomi sueokite / miyama ni wa / ime tatewatashi /
asagari ni / shishi fumiokoshi / yūgari ni / tori fumitate / uma namete /
mikari zo tatasu / haru no shigeno ni

14. MYS 808: yo no naka no / sube naki mono wa / toshitsuki wa / nagaruru
gotoshi / toritsutsuki / oikuru mono wa / momokusa ni / semeyorikitaru /
otomera ga / otomesabisu to / karatama o / tamoto ni makashi / yochikora
to / te tazusawarite / asobikemu / toki no sakari o / todomikane / sugu-
shiyaritsure / mina no wata / kaguroki kami ni / itsu no ma ka / shimo no
furikemu / kurenai no / omote no ue ni / izuku yu ka / shiwa ga kitarishi /
masurao no / otokosabisu to / tsurugitachi / koshi ni torihaki / satsuyumi
o / tanigirimochite / akagoma ni / shitsukura uchi oki / hainorite / asobi-
arukishi / yo no naka ya / tsune ni arikeru / otomera ga / sanasu itato
o / oshihiraki / itadoriyorite / matamade no / tamade sashikae / saneshi yo
no / ikuda mo araneba / tatsukazue / koshi ni taganete / ka yukeba / hito ni
itowae / kaku yukeba / hito ni nikumae / oyoshio wa / kaku nomi narashi /
tamakiwaru / inochi oshikedo / semu sube mo nashi

15. MYS 896: kaze majiri / ame furu yo no / ame majiri / yuki furu yo wa /
sube mo naku / samuku shi areba / katashio o / toritsuzushiroi / kasu-
yuzake / uchisusuroite / shiwabukai / hana bishibishi ni / shika to aranu /
hige kakinadete / are o okite / hito wa araji to / hokoroedo / samuku
shi areba / asabusuma / hikikagafuri / nunokatakinu / ari no kotogoto /
kisoedomo / samuki yo sura o / ware yori mo / mazushiki hito no / chichi
haha wa / uekoyuramu / me kodomo wa / kōkōnakuramu / kono toki wa /
ika ni shitsutsu ka / na ga yo wa wataru; ame tsuchi wa / hiroshi to
iedo / a ga tame wa / saku ya narinuru / hitsuki wa / akashi to iedo / a
ga tame wa / teri ya tamawanu / hito mina ka / a nomi ya shikaru /
wakuraba ni / hito to wa aru o / hitonami ni / are mo tsukuru o / wata mo
naki / nunokatakinu no / miru no goto / wawakesagareru / kakau nomi /
kata ni uchikake / fuseio no / mageio no uchi ni / hitatsuchi ni / wara
tokishikite / chichi haha wa / makura no kata ni / me kodomo wa / ato
no kata ni / kakumiite / ureesamayoi / kamado ni wa / hoke fukitatezu /
koshiki ni wa / kumo no su kakite / iikashiku / koto mo wasurete /
nuedori no / nodoyoi oru ni / itonokite / mijikaki mono o / hashi kiru

to / ieru ga gotoku / shimoto toru / satoosa ga koe wa / neyado made / kitachiyobainu / kaku bakari / sube naki mono ka / yo no naka no michi

16. MYS 909: yo no hito no / tōtobinegau / nanakusa no / takara mo ware wa / nani semu ni / waga naka no / umareidetaru / shiratama no / a ga ko furuhi wa / akahoshi no / akuru ashita wa / shikitae no tokonohe sarazu / tateredomo / oredomo / tomo ni tawabure / yūtsuzu no / yūbe ni nareba / iza neyo to / te o tazusawari / chichi haha mo / ue wa na sagari / sakikusa no / naka ni o nemu to / utsukushiku / shi ga kataraeba / itsu shika mo / hito to nariidete / ashikeku mo / yokeku mo mimu to / ōbune no / omoi tanomu ni / omowanu ni / yokoshimakaze no / nifufuka ni / ōikitareba / semu sube no / tadoki o shirani / shirotae no / tasuki o kake / masokagami / te ni torimochite / amatsukami / augikoinomi / kuni-tsukami / fushite nukatsuki / kakarazu mo / kakari mo / kami no ma ni ma ni to / tachiazari / ware koinomedo / shimashiku mo / yokeku wa nashi ni / yakuyaku ni / katachi kuzuhori / asana sana / iu koto yami / tamakiwaru / inochi taenure / tachiodori / ashi surisakebi / fushi augi / mune uchinageki / te ni moteru / a ga ko tobashitsu / yo no naka no michi

17. MYS 1751: shirakumo no / tatsuta no yama no / taki no ue no / ogura no mine ni / sakioiru / sakura no hana wa / yama takami / kaze shi yamaneba / harusame no / tsugiteshifureba / hotsue wa / chirisuginikeri / shizue ni / nokoreru hana wa / shimashiku wa / chiri na magai so / kusamakura / tabiyuku kimi ga / kaerikuru made

18. MYS 1789: hito to naru / koto wa kataki o / wakuraba ni / nareru a ga mi wa / shi ni mo iki mo / kimi ga ma ni ma to / omoitsutsu / arishi aida ni / utsusemi no / yo no hito nareba / ōkimi no / mikoto kashikomi / amazakaru / hina osame ni to / asatori no / asadachishitsutsu / muratori no / muradachiinaba / tomariite / are wa koimu na / mizu hisa naraba

19. MYS 469: waga yado ni / hana zo sakitaru / so o miredo / kokoro mo yukazu / hashikiyashi / imo ga ariseba / mikamo nasu / futari narabi i / taorite mo / misemashi mono o / utsusemi no / kareru mi ni areba / tsuyushimo no / kenuru ga gotoku / ashihiki no / yamaji o sashite / irihi nasu / kakurinishikaba / soko omou ni / mune koso itaki / ii mo ezu / nazuke mo shirazu / ato mo naki / yo no naka ni areba / semu sube mo nashi

20. MYS 4184: ame tsuchi no / tōki hajime yo / yo no naka wa / tsune naki mono to / kataritsugi / nagaraekitare / ama no hara / furisakemireba / teru tsuki mo / michikake shikeri / ashihiki no / yama no konure mo / haru sareba / hana sakinioi / akizukeba / tsuyu shimo oite / kaze majiri / momiji chirikeri / utsusemi mo / kaku nomi narashi / kurenai no / iro mo utsuroi / nubatama no / kurokami kawari / asa no emi / yūbe kawarai / fuku kaze no / mienu ga gotoku / yuku mizu no / toma-ranu / gotoku / tsune mo naku / utsurou mireba / niwatazumi / nagaruru namida / todomekanetsu mo

21. At the beginning of each emperor's reign, young, unmarried women were called from among the members of the imperial family to serve as

chief priestesses in the Shinto shrines at Ise and Kamo. Legend identifies this particular woman as one who served during the reign of Emperor Seiwa, but the story probably has no basis in fact. Likewise, the poem attributed to her may well be the work of someone else, perhaps even Narihira himself.

22. shoku KKS 270 (Narihira): Headnote: Topic unknown. "On a summer day / that stretches out with no end, / I gaze afar— / and for no special reason / find myself feeling forlorn" (kuregataki / natsu no higurashi / nagamureba / sono koto to naku / mono zo kanashiki).

23. SIS 205 (anon.): Headnote: Topic unknown. "No visitor / accompanies the winds that blow / from Storm Mountain— / making the pine cricket's voice / seem somehow more forlorn" (tou hito mo / ima wa arashi no / yamakaze ni / hito matsumushi no / koe zo kanashiki).

24. KKS 689 (anon.): Headnote: Topic unknown. "Tonight again, / will she spread her robe alone / on her straw mattress, / the Maiden of Uji Bridge, / who waits for me to come?" (samushiro ni / koromo katashiki / koyoi mo ya / ware o matsuramu / uji no hashihime).

25. KKS 283 (anon.): Headnote: Topic unknown. "A confused array / of red leaves in the current / of Tatsuta River. Were I to cross, I would break / the fabric of a rich brocade" (tatsutagawa / momiji midarete / nagarumeri / wataraba nishiki / naka ya taenamu). KKS 284 (anon.): Headnote: Topic unknown. "Red leaves are flowing / in the Tatsuta River. / On the mountain / of Mimuro in Kannabi / showers must be falling" (tatsutagawa / momiji nagaru / kannabi no / mimuro no yama ni / shigure furu rashi).

26. KKS 250 (Yasuhide): Headnote: From a contest at the home of Prince Koresada. "Every grass and tree / has a color of its own, / but for the blossoms / out on the waves of the sea / there is no such thing as autumn" (kusa mo ki mo / iro kawaredomo / watatsuumi no / nami no hana ni zo / aki nakarikeru).

27. KKS 770 (Archbishop Henjō): Headnote: Topic unknown. "Now even the path / leading up to my house / has gone to ruin— / while I have waited in vain / for one who no longer cares" (waga yado wa / michi mo naki made / arenikeri / tsurenaki hito o / matsu to seshi ma ni).

28. KKS 362 (Sakanoue Korenori): Headnote: Written on a screen depicting the four seasons set behind the guest of honor when the Principal Handmaid held a celebration marking the fortieth year of the Major Captain of the Right. "Even in autumn / no new colors appear / on Evergreen Hill— / but for red leaves from elsewhere / lent by the passing wind" (aki kuredo / iro mo kawaranu / tokiwayama / yoso no momiji o / kaze zo kashikeru).

29. KKS 1077 (anon.): Headnote: A sacred song. "Back in the mountains / hailstorms must be raging: / for in the foothills / the leaves on the vines / are of a crimson hue" (miyama ni wa / arare fururashi / toyama naru / masaki no kazura / irozukinikeri).

30. SKKS 55 (Ōe no Chisato): Written after Karyō's poem on a spring night from *Wen xuan*, "Not clear, but not dark—the hazy moon." "Not truly shining / and yet not clouded over— / nothing can compare / with the hazy moon / on a night in spring" (teri mo sezu / kumori mo hatenu / haru no yo no / oborozukiyo ni / shiku mono zo naki).

31. MYS 265 (Naga Okimaro): "Ah, how hard it is / to be caught in this driving rain / —for at Miwa Point, / in the fields around Sano Ford / there's no house to be found" (kurushiki mo / furikuru ame ka / miwanosaki / sano no watari ni / ie mo aranaku ni).

32. MYS 3182 (anon.): "When we parted, / how I hated to separate / our sleeves of white hemp— / but with thoughts in turmoil, / still I let him go away" (shirotae no / sode no wakare wa / oshikedomo / omoimidarete / yurushitsuru ka mo).

33. SIS 646 (anon.): Headnote: Topic unknown. "What am I to do / to forget even a moment? / For while I have life, / this is a world in which / I will surely see him again" (ika ni shite / shibashi wasuremu / inochi dani / araba au yo no / ari mo koso sure).

34. KKS 484 (anon.): Headnote: Topic unknown. "As evening falls, I muse while looking out / at banners of cloud— / thinking of the one I love, / who is distant as the sky" (yūgure wa / kumo no hatate ni / mono zo omou / amatsusora naru / hito o kou tote).

35. KKS 243 (Ariwara no Muneyana): Headnote: A poem for the Empress's Contest, held during the reign of the Kampyō Emperor. "Are they the sleeves / of grasses in the autumn fields / —those miscanthus plumes / looking so like girls beckoning / with their colorful sleeves?" (aki no no no / kusa no tamoto ka / hanasusuki / ho ni idete maneku / sode to miyuramu).

36. Headnote to GSIS 939: "Once when she was talking with Major Counselor Yukinari he said that he had to leave because of an Imperial Abstinence and then rushed off. The next morning he sent a note saying how sorry he was that the rooster had called him home, to which she replied that the rooster must have been the one that called at Han Gu Gate. Then he wrote back that instead it had been at the Gate at Meeting Hill." Han Gu Gate was the site of an incident in ancient Chinese history when a fleeing minister had one of his men imitate a cock's crow, which fooled the wardens of the barrier into opening the way for free passage—even though it was the dead of night. Yukinari's reference to the gate at Meeting Hill has obvious erotic connotations, which it is the task of Shōnagon's poem to deny.

37. Headnote to SZS 1026: "When his son, the priest Kōkaku, had been passed over several times for appointment as Lecturer for the Vimalakirti Service, Mototoshi made a request to the Hosshōji Lay Monk and Former Chancellor Tadamichi, who replied that he could be depended upon more than the moxa plants 'on the fields of Shimeji.' But again that year Kōkaku was passed over, and Mototoshi sent this poem to

Tadamichi." Tadamichi's allusion is to a poem (SKKS 1197) in which Kannon vows to stay reliable even against the heat of all the moxa "on the fields of Shimeji."

38. GSIS 827 (Minamoto no Shigeyuki): Headnote: Topic unknown. "As wet as the sleeves / of fishers after their work / at Matsushima, / on the beach of Oshima— / so wet have my sleeves become" (matsushima ya / oshima no iso ni / asari seshi / ama no sode koso / kaku wa nureshi ka).

39. MYS 935 (Kasa no Kanamura): The relevant lines are: "At Awaji Isle, / on the bay at Matsho, / they cut jeweled seaweed / on the beach at morn; / they burn seaweed for salt / on the beach at eve . . ." (awajishima / matsuho no ura ni / asanagi ni / tamamo karitsutsu / yūnagi ni / moshio yakitsutsu).

40. GSIS 231 (Minamoto no Yoritsuna): Headnote: Written on the topic "Taking the Night Air and Feeling as If Autumn Had Come," at the home of Lord Toshitsuna. "As day nears its end / with a breeze rustling oak leaves / in the summer hills, / this year once again / I feel as if it were autumn" (natsuyama no / nara no ha soyogu / yūgure wa / kotoshi mo aki no / kokochi koso sure). SKKS 1375 (anon.): Headnote: A love poem. "As those around me / do their ablutions in the wind / off Nara Stream, / I am praying only / for my secret love not to end" (misogi suru / nara no ogawa no / kawakaze ni / inori zo wataru / shita ni taeji to).

41. SIS 139 (Tsurayuki): Headnote: Written on a standing screen during the Engi era. "In the whispering / of leaves rustling on the reeds: / thus does the coming / of the wind in autumn / first make itself known to men" (ogi no ha no / soyogu oto koso / akikaze no / hito ni shiraruru / hajime narikere).

42. KKS 1091 (anon.): Headnote: A Michinoku song. "You, attendants— have your lord put on his hat. / For on Miyagi Moor / the dew falling from the trees / is more numerous than raindrops" (misaburai / mikasa to mōse / miyagino no / ko no shita tsuyu wa / ame ni masareri).

43. WRS 605 (Bao Rong): "At his temple in the fields, I visit a monk—then go home bathed in moonlight; / in a fragrant grove, I enjoy my friend— then get drunk and sleep among the flowers."

44. From *San ti shi* (Qin Xi): *Poem on the Mountain Cottage of Taoist Zhang.* "Great stones and drooping vines are his only home; looking behind, you can still see him in the flowers of the five boughs. / Among the pines all is still, with no fire, no smoke; for sustenance he takes a clump of morning haze."

45. SKKS 1635 (Go-Toba): Headnote: On the topic "Mountains" from the Sumiyoshi Poem Contest. "That in this world / there is a Way to be made / even through the tangles / of thickets in the mountains: / this is what I would proclaim" (okuyama no / odoro ga shita mo / fumiwakete / michi aru yo zo to / hito ni shirasen).

46. SZS 36 (Minamoto no Toshiyori): Headnote: Written on the topic "Returning Geese" for a hundred-poem sequence at the time of Retired

Emperor Horikawa. "When springtime arrives / our thoughts rise to pathways / up above the clouds / where the geese always tell us / the time to depart has come" (haru kureba / tanomu no kari mo / ima wa tote / kaeru kumoji ni / omoitatsu nari).

47. SKKS 182 (Princess Shikishi): Headnote: Written at the [Kamo] shrine, when she was serving as Virgin. "Could I forget this / —the dew of a hazy daybreak / when with hollyhocks / I make myself a grass pillow / for a brief night in the fields?" (wasureme ya / aoi o kusa ni / hikimusubi / karine no nobe no / tsuyu no akebono).

48. SKKS 58 (Monk Jakuren): Headnote: From a hundred-poem sequence poem contest at the home of the Regent-Chancellor. " 'The time has come,' / the geese cry as they leave paddies, / lamenting as they go / beneath a hazy moon / in the sky at break of day" (ima wa tote / tanomu no kari mo / uchiwabinu / oborozukiyo no / akebono no sora).

49. GSS 1083 (Narihira): Headnote: Written when he was tired of the world. " 'That's enough!' I say, / tired of the ways of the world / —and go off to find / a lodging in the mountains / to make a living cutting firewood" (sumiwabinu / ima wa kagiri to / yamazato ni / tsumagi koru beki / yado motometemu).

50. SKKS 1560 (Shunzei): Headnote: Presented on being asked for a hundred-poem sequence when he was long past eighty years old. "The place I have marked / seems to say the time has come— / this autumn mountain / where the pine cricket calls out / from a patch of wormwood" (shimeokite / ima ya to omou / akiyama no / yomogi ga moto ni / matsumushi no naku).

51. The official Yan Zilin, a friend of Emperor Guang Wu Di of the Later Han dynasty, abandoned life in the capital to become a farmer-hermit, thereby proving the degree of his resolve to live the reclusive life.

52. SKKS 565 (Hōribe no Narimochi): Headnote: On the subject "Fallen Leaves," from the *Kasuga Shrine Poem Contest.* "The winter comes / and lays the hillsides bare / after the leaves— / with even the pines left behind / looking lonely on the peaks" (fuyu no kite / yama mo arawa ni / ko no ha furi / nokoru matsu sae / mine sabishiki).

53. SKKS 82 (Ietaka): Headnote: On the idea of an outing in the fields, for a contest of hundred-poem sequences at the home of the Regent-Chancellor. "My friends and I / have wandered in no sure direction, / and now day is ending. / O warbler in the fields, may we / stay tonight beneath some bough? (omou dochi / soko to mo shirazu / yukikurenu / hana no yadori kase / nobe no uguisu).

54. KKS 221 (anon.): Headnote: Topic unknown. "They must be the tears / shed by wild geese whose cries I heard / as they crossed the sky— / these dewdrops on bush clover / by the hut where I muse alone" (nakiwataru / kari no namida ya / ochitsuramu / mono omou yado no / hagi no ue no tsuyu).

55. GSS 1195–96: Headnote: When Komachi went to Isonokami Temple on pilgrimage, she decided to spend the night and then visit the temple the next day since it was near dark when she arrived. Learning that Henjō was in the temple at the time, she wanted to get to know him, and sent this. "If I spend the night / sleeping on this bed of stones, / I will be so cold! / Won't you lend this traveler / the use of your robes of moss?" (iwa no ue ni / tabine o sureba / ito samushi / koke no koromo o / ware ni kasanan). [Reply] Ah, but the robes / of one who has left the world / are not thick enough / to provide you any warmth— / unless we sleep together!" (yo o somuku / koke no koromo wa / tada hitoe / kasaneba utoshi / iza futari nen).

56. KKS 832 (Kamutsuke no Mineo): Headnote: Composed after the burial of the Horikawa Chancellor at Fukakusa. "You cherry trees / in the fields of Fukakusa— / if you have a heart, / this year please dye your blossoms / the color of black charcoal (fukakusa no / nobe no sakura shi / kokoro araba / kotoshi bakari wa / sumizome ni sake).

57. SANKS 370 (Saigyō): "The way the clouds / descend from high above / from time to time: / as if to hang decorations / all around the moon (nakanaka ni / tokidoki kumo no / kakaru koso / tsuki o motenasu / kazari narikere).

Abbreviations

Poems in imperial collections are cited in the usual style, by their numbers. Poems in other collections are cited by volume (where relevant) and number or page number (e.g., NKBZ, 46, no. 177; FS, p. 154).

BRC	*Buson renga chūshaku*, ed. Nomura Kazumi. 1975.
BZ	*[Kōhon] Bashō zenshū*, comp. Komiya Toyotaka et al. 10 vols. 1962–69.
CKS	*Chikuba kyōginshū*. In vol. 77 of SNKS.
CS	*[Kōhon] Chikurinshō*, ed. Hoshika Muneichi. 1937.
CSES	*Chōshū eisō*. In vol. 3 of SKKT.
FGS	*Fūgashū*. In vol. 1 of SKKT.
FS	*Fude no susabi*, ed. Kidō Saizō. *Rengaron shū III*. 1985. Vol. 12 of *Chūsei no bungaku* series.
GBT	*Gendai bungaku taikei*. 69 vols. 1963–68.
GMS	*Gendai meika sen*, comp. Kubota Masabumi. 1976.
GNBT	*Gendai nihon bungaku taikei*. 97 vols. 1970–73.
GSIS	*Goshūishū*. In vol. 1 of SKKT.
GSS	*Gosenshū*. In vol. 1 of SKKT.
GYS	*Gyokuyōshū*. In vol. 1 of SKKT.
HY	*Haifū yanagidaru*. In vol. 63 of SNKS.
ITS	*Inu tsukubashū, kenkyū to shohon*, ed. Fukui Kyūzō. 1948.
IZ	*Issa zenshū*, ed. Kobayashi Keiichirō et al. 9 vols. 1976–79.
KB	*Kanke bunsō*. In vol. 72 of NKBT.
KCS	*Kyōchūshō*. In vol. 17 of ZGR.
KH	*Kindai haiku*, ed. Kanda Hideo and Kusumoto Kenkichi. 1965. *Kindai bungaku chūshaku taikei* series.
KHT	*Koten haibungaku taikei*, ed. Hisamatsu Sen'ichi and Imoto Nōichi. 15 vols. 1971–72.
KJ	*Kojiki*. Poems indexed in vol. 5 of SKKT.
KKS	*Kokinshū*. In vol. 1 of SKKT.
KM	*Shinkei kushū koke mushiro*. In Noguchi Eiichi and Yokoyama Shigeru, eds., *Shinkei shū, ronshū*. 1946.
KS	*Kinkaishū*. In vol. 4 of SKKT.
KSNKB	*Kenkyū shiryō nihon koten bungaku*, ed. Kubota Jun et al. 12 vols., 1 supp. 1983–84.
KYS	*Kin'yōshū*. In vol. 1 of SKKT.
MS	*Moritake senku chū*, ed. Iida Shōichi. 1977.

MSa	*Minase sangin hyakuin.* In vol. 39 of NKBT.
MYS	*Man'yōshū.* In vol. 2 of SKKT.
NGBZ	*Nihon gendai bungaku zenshū,* ed. Itō Sei. 108 vols. 1960–69.
NKBT	*Nihon koten bungaku taikei,* ed. Takagi Ichinosuke et al. 102 vols. 1957–68.
NKBZ	*Nihon koten bungaku zenshū,* ed. Akiyama Ken et al. 51 vols. 1970–76.
NKDBT	*Nihon kindai bungaku taikei,* ed. Itō Sei et al. 60 vols. 1969–75.
NST	*Nihon shisō taikei,* ed. Hayashiya Tatsusaburō et al. 67 vols. 1970–82.
RBUA	*Roppyaku-ban uta-awase.* In vol. 5 of SKKT.
RZ	*Ryōkan zenshū,* ed. Ōshima Kasoku. 1959.
SanKS	*Sankashū.* In vol. 3 of SKKT.
SBKS	*Shibakusa.* In *Shinkei sakuhin shū,* ed. Yokoyama Shigeru. 1972.
SCSS	*Shin chokusenshū.* In vol. 1 of SKKT.
SG	*Sasamegoto.* In vol. 66 of NKBT.
SGS	*Shūi gusō.* In vol. 3 of SKKT.
SGYS	*Shingyokushū.* In *Shinkei sakuhin shū,* ed. Yokoyama Shigeru. 1972.
shokuGSS	*Shoku gosenshū.* In vol. 1 of SKKT.
shokuKKS	*Shoku kokinshū.* In vol. 1 of SKKT.
shokuSS	*Shoku sōanshū.* In vol. 4 of SKKT.
SIS	*Shūishū.* In vol. 1 of SKKT.
SK	*Sōkonshū.* In vol. 5 of SKST.
SKKS	*Shin kokinshû.* In vol. 1 of SKKT.
SKKT	*[Shinpen] kokka taikan,* ed. Taniyama Shigeru et al. 10 vols. 1983–92.
SKS	*Shikashū.* In vol. 1 of SKKT.
SKST	*Shikashū taisei,* ed. Wakashi Kenkyū-kai. 8 vols. 1973–76.
SMS	*Shunzei no musume shū.* In vol. 4 of SKKT.
SNKS	*Shinchō nihon koten shūsei.* 97 vols. 1976–.
SNS	*Shikishi naishinnō shū.* In vol. 4 of SKKT.
SS	*Sōanshū.* In vol. 4 of SKKT.
SSEK	*Shōgetsu shōtetsu eiga.* In vol. 5 of SKST.
SSZS	*Sōtō zensho.* 20 vols. 1929–38.
STS	*Shinsen tsukubashū,* ed. Kaneko Kinjirō and Yokoyama Shigeru. 1970.
SYS	*[Sone no] Yoshitada shū.* In vol. 3 of SKKT.
SZ	*Shiki zenshū,* comp. Masaoka Tadasaburō. 25 vols. 1975–78.
SZS	*Senzaishū.* In vol. 1 of SKKT.
TK	*Tsukikusa.* In vol. 5 of SKST.
TS	*Tsukubashū,* ed. Fukui Kyūzō. 2 vols. 1948–51. *Nihon koten zensho* series.
TTHS	*Tametada-ke godo hyakushu.* In vol. 4 of SKKT.
UB	*Uraba.* In *Sōgi kushū,* ed. Ijichi Tetsuo and Kaneko Kinjirō. 1977.

WB　　　*Wakuraba*. In *Sōgi kushū*, ed. Ijichi Tetsuo and Kaneko
　　　　　Kinjirō. 1977.
WG　　　*Wasuregusa*. In *Sōgi kushū*, ed. Ijichi Tetsuo and Kaneko
　　　　　Kinjirō. 1977.
WRS　　*Wakan rōeishū*. In vol. 2 of SKKT.
ZGR　　*Zoku gunsho ruijū*, ed. Hanawa Hokiichi and Hanawa Tadatomi.
　　　　　71 vols. 1923–30.
ZHS　　*Zenrin hōwashū*, comp. Takegasa San. 1927.

Sources of Poems

112	KKS 616	157	GSS 1356	202	SKS 76
113	KKS 645	158	SIS 1006	203	SKS 82
114	KKS 646	159	GSS 57	204	SKKS 495
115	KKS 747	160	SIS 479	205	SYS 175
116	KKS 784	161	KB 483	206	SIS 1342
117	KKS 785	162	KB 490	207	GSIS 13
118	KKS 861	163	KKS 2	208	GSIS 102
119	KKS 884	164	KKS 9	209	GSIS 317
120	KKS 971	165	KKS 22	210	GSIS 568
121	KKS 972	166	KKS 49	211	GSIS 573
122	KKS 552	167	KKS 117	212	GSIS 711
123	KKS 556	168	KKS 124	213	GSIS 755
124	KKS 557	169	KKS 260	214	GSIS 920
125	KKS 623	170	KKS 279	215	GSIS 999
126	KKS 635	171	KKS 404	216	GSIS 1008
127	KKS 657	172	KKS 471	217	GSIS 1162
128	KKS 658	173	KKS 475	218	SKS 158
129	KKS 797	174	KKS 605	219	SKS 254
130	KKS 938	175	KKS 838	220	SZS 247
131	KKS 1030	176	KKS 851	221	GYS 1467
132	KKS 27	177	GSS 434	222	WRS 27
133	KKS 165	178	SIS 64	223	WRS 28 (KKS 41)
134	KKS 248	179	SIS 224	224	WRS 50
135	KKS 348	180	KKS 86	225	WRS 53
136	KKS 394	181	KKS 87	226	WRS 54
137	KKS 106	182	KKS 88	227	WRS 56 (KKS 134)
138	KKS 139	183	KKS 89	228	WRS 57 (SIS 77)
139	KKS 145	184	KKS 90	229	WRS 199
140	KKS 317	185	KKS 91	230	WRS 200
141	KKS 489	186	KKS 92	231	WRS 436
142	KKS 547	187	KKS 93	232	WRS 438
143	KKS 647	188	KKS 94	233	WRS 555
144	KKS 659	189	KKS 95	234	WRS 559
145	KKS 708	190	KKS 96	235	WRS 563 (KKS 944)
146	KKS 712	191	KKS 97	236	WRS 624
147	KKS 795	192	KKS 98	237	WRS 628
148	KKS 818	193	KKS 99	238	WRS 629
149	KKS 933	194	KKS 100	239	WRS 630 (KKS 56)
150	KKS 1023	195	KKS 101	240	WRS 741
151	KKS 1027	196	KKS 102	241	WRS 745
152	KKS 1057	197	KKS 103	242	WRS 749 (SIS 991)
153	KB 161	198	KKS 104	243	WRS 780
154	KB 247	199	KKS 105	244	WRS 782
155	KB 257	200	GSIS 273	245	WRS 787(KKS 611)
156	KB 274	201	GSIS 775	246	WRS 788 (SIS 848)

247	GSIS 43	304	SKKS 938	349	SCSS 16
248	GSIS 384	305	SKKS 1099	350	Shokukks 147
249	GSIS 518	306	SKKS 1536	351	GYS 239
250	SKKS 116	307	SKKS 1613	352	GYS 1256
251	KYS 145	308	SKKS 1615	353	FGS 402
252	KYS 150	309	SKKS 1619	354	SNS 77
253	KYS 239	310	SKKS 1751	355	SNS 127
254	KYS 595	311	Sanks 77	356	SNS 166
255	SZS 202	312	Sanks 139	357	SNS 186
256	SZS 340	313	Sanks 362	358	SNS 187
257–		314	Sanks 496	359	SKKS 2
70	SKKT, 4	315	Sanks 766	360	SKKS 361
271	TTHS 51	316	Sanks 848	361	SKKS 515
272	CSES 165	317	Sanks 907	362	SKKS 516
273	SZS 259	318	Sanks 937	363	SKKS 517
274	SZS 443	319	Sanks 1318	364	SKKS 518
275	SZS 897	320	Sanks 1474	365	SKKS 519
276	SKKS 114	321	Sanks 1502	366	SKKS 520
277	SKKS 201	322	Sanks 1551	367	SKKS 521
278	SKKS 291	323	SKKS 169	368	SKKS 522
279	SKKS 631	324	SKKS 361	369	SKKS 523
280	SKKS 677	325	SKKS 1938	370	SKKS 524
281	SKKS 706	326	RBUA 348	371	SKKS 525
282	SKKS 796	327	SKKS 258	372	SKKS 526
283	SKKS 1107	328	SKKS 580	373	SKKS 527
284	SKKS 1232	329	SKKS 679	374	SKKS 528
285	SKKS 1389	330	SKKS 1782	375	SKKS 529
286	SKKS 1468	331	SKKS 1	376	SKKS 530
287	SKKS 1561	332	SKKS 147	377	SKKS 531
288	SKKS 1845	333	SKKS 393	378	SKKS 532
289	SKKS 1846	334	SKKS 1601	379	SKKS 533
290	SCSS 57	335	SKKS 37	380	SKKS 534
291	SZS 69	336	SKKS 246	381	SKKS 535
292	SZS 875	337	SKKS 595	382	SKKS 536
293	SKKS 7	338	SCSS 197	383	SKKS 537
294	SKKS 86	339	SKKS 1081	384	SKKS 538
295	SKKS 262	340	SKKS 1136	385	SKKS 539
296	SKKS 299	341	SMS 71	386	SGS 2286
297	SKKS 362	342	SMS 113	387	SGS 176
298	SKKS 448	343	SKKS 3	388	SGS 268
299	SKKS 472	344	SKKS 149	389	SGS 391
300	SKKS 570	345	SKKS 1035	390	SGS 810
301	SKKS 603	346	SKKS 1309	391	SGS 846
302	SKKS 625	347	SKKS 1329	392	SGS 876
303	SKKS 627	348	SKKS 1969	393	SKKS 38

394	SKKS 40	436	KKS 249	481	SZS 964
395	SKKS 44	437	KKS 193	482	GSIS 860
396	SKKS 63	438	KKS 420	483	GSIS 366
397	SKKS 363	439	GSS 700	484	GSIS 333
398	SKKS 420	440	SIS 1128	485	KYS 173
399	SKKS 671	441	SKKS 996	486	KYS 469
400	SKKS 953	442	KKS 315	487	GSIS 120
401	SKKS 1142	443	KKS 27	488	SZS 708
402	SKKS 1206	444	KKS 625	489	SZS 1026
403	SKKS 1336	445	KKS 325	490	SKS 382
404	SKKS 1390	446	KKS 303	491	SKS 229
405	SCSS 256	447	KKS 84	492	KYS 270
406	SCSS 744	448	KKS 909	493	SKKS 413
407	ShokuGSS 757	449	KKS 42	494	SZS 802
408	FGS 964	450	KKS 166	495	SZS 161
409	SGS 2069	451	GSS 308	496	SZS 818
410	SGS 2190	452	SIS 870	497	SZS 1151
411	TS 110	453	GSS 577	498	SKKS 1843
412	TS 461	454	SIS 622	499	SZS 766
413	TS 600	455	SIS 621	500	SZS 929
414	TS 860	456	GSIS 770	501	SKKS 491
415–		457	SIS 710	502	SZS 807
514	SKKT, 5, pp.	458	SIS 678	503	SKKS 1034
	933–34	459	SIS 950	504	SZS 886
415	GSS 302	460	SKKS 1071	505	SKKS 518
416	SKKS 175	461	SIS 140	506	SZS 760
417	SIS 778	462	SKS 211	507	SCSS 525
418	SKKS 675	463	SKS 225	508	SKKS 483
419	KKS 215	464	GSIS 669	509	SZS 1137
420	SKKS 620	465	GSIS 612	510	SCSS 1052
421	KKS 406	466	GSIS 672	511	SCSS 849
422	KKS 983	467	SIS 912	512	SCSS 192
423	KKS 113	468	SKKS 1149	513	ShokuGSS 1202
424	GSS 1089	469	SIS 449	514	ShokuGSS 1205
425	KKS 407	470	GSIS 763	515	KS 312
426	KKS 872	471	SKKS 1499	516	KS 348
427	GSS 76	472	GSIS 709	517	KS 378
428	KKS 724	473	GSIS 680	518	KS 592
429	KKS 21	474	KYS 550	519	KS 593
430	KKS 365	475	SKS 29	520	KS 594
431	KKS 294	476	GSIS 939	521	KS 653
432	KKS 559	477	GSIS 750	522	KS 697
433	SKKS 1049	478	SZS 420	523	KS 706
434	GSS 960	479	GSIS 815	524	KS 708
435	KKS 691	480	KYS 521	525	KS 710

526	GYS 83	581	NKBT, 89, p. 63	626	CS 3330
527	GYS 419	582	NKBT, 89, p. 73	627	CS 1258
528	GYS 1142	583	NKBT, 89, p. 83	628	CS 1272
529	GYS 1367	584	NKBT, 89, p. 87	629	CS 1454
530	GYS 1381	585	NKBT, 89, p. 92	630	CS 2024
531	GYS 1683	586	NKBT, 89, p. 96	631	CS 2170
532	GYS 2095	587	NKBT, 89, p. 95	632	CS 2618
533	FGS 27	588	NKBT, 89, p. 101	633	STS 156
534	FGS 804	589	KSNKB, 11, p. 61	634	STS 270
535	FGS 1687	590	KSNKB, 11, p. 61	635	STS 318
536	GYS 2179	591	NKBT, 89, p. 123	636	STS 706
537	GYS 2180	592	NKBT, 89, p. 122	637	STS 1584
538	FGS 391	593	NKBT, 89, p. 117	638	STS 1586
539	FGS 1214	594	ZGR, 12, p. 392	639	STS 2913
540	GYS 924	595	ZGR, 12, p. 392	640	STS 3026
541	GYS 1407	596	TS 149	641	STS 3056
542	FGS 199	597	TS 1363	642	SGYS 1627
543	SS 346	598	TS 97	643	KM 2088
544	SS 382	599	TS 389	644	CS 3278
545	SS 395	600	TS 561	645	CS 3372
546	SS 843	601	TS 631	646	STS 3800
547	SS 957	602	TS 960	647	STS 3803
548	SS 1372	603	TS 1415	648	SBKS 385
549	Shokuss 230	604	TS 1553	649	SGYS 726
550	TS 374	605	FS, p. 154	650	STS 544
551	TS 443	606	SG, p. 166	651	STS 736
552	TS 1204	607	TS 2062	652	STS 1089
553	SG, p. 165	608	TS 2091	653	STS 3010
554	FGS 1227	609	TS 2116	654	STS 3024
555	FGS 1228	610	SK 1974	655	STS 3424
556	FGS 1229	611	SK 2622	656	STS 3580
	(MYS 2602)	612	SK 2674	657	WG 840
557	FGS 1230	613	SK 3098	658	WB 210
	(MYS 2592)	614	SG, p. 118	659	WB 212
558	FGS 1231	615	SK 3986	660	ZGR, 17, p. 1238
	(MYS 2703)	616	SK 4443	661	STS 3801
559–		617	SK 7784	662	WB 1662
73	FGS 1232–46	618	TK 273	663	UB 131
574	SSZS, 2: 189	619	SSEK 164	664	UB 178
575	SSZS, 2: 191	620	CS 678	665	UB 260
576	SSZS, 2: 191	621	STS 904	666–	
577	SSZS, 2: 190	622	STS 1417	765	NKBT, 39, pp.
578	NKBT, 89: 55	623	STS 2219		345–66
579	FGS 2063	624	STS 3110	766	NKBT, 89, p. 148
580	FGS 2076	625	FS, p. 173	767	NST, 16, no. 117

768	ZHS, p. 73	818	BZ, 6, p. 136	914	NKBZ, 32, p. 362
769	NST, 16, no. 879	819	BZ, 6, p. 19	915	BZ, 3, p. 230
770	NST, 16, no. 543	820	BZ, 1, p. 208	916	BZ, 3, p. 329
771	NST, 16, no. 512	821–		917	NKBT, 92, no. 303
772	NKBT, 89, p. 159	26	BZ, 3, p. 85	918	NKBZ, 42,
773	NKBT, 89, p. 160	827	BZ, 1, p. 232		no. 227
774	ZGR, 13, p. 160	828	BZ, 1, p. 246	919	KHT, 6, p. 272
775	ZGR, 13, p. 173	829	BZ, 1, p. 260	920	NKBT, 92, no. 319
776	CKS 86	830	BZ, 1, p. 263	921	NKBT, 92, no. 321
777	CKS 148	831	BZ, 6, p. 32	922	NKBT, 92, no. 325
778	CKS 212	832	BZ, 6, p. 33	923	NKBT, 92, no. 332
779	CKS 228	833	BZ, 1, p. 297	924	NKBT, 92, no. 343
780	CKS 244	834	BZ, 1, p. 298	925	NKBZ, 32, p. 454
781	ITS 22	835	BZ, 6, p. 53	926	NKBZ, 32, p. 480
782	ITS 40	836	BZ, 1, p. 406	927	NKBT, 92, no. 378
783	ITS 44	837	BZ, 1, p. 434	928	NKBT, 92, no. 380
784	ITS 55	838	BZ, 2, p. 924	929	NKBT, 92, no. 386
785	ITS 102	839	BZ, 1, p. 513	930	NKBZ, 42, no. 269
786	ITS 106	840	BZ, 1, p. 520	931	NKBZ, 42, no. 271
787	ITS 199	841	BZ, 1, p. 531	932	NKBT, 66, p. 342
788	ITS 207	842	BZ, 6, p. 85	933	NKBT, 92, no. 400
789	ITS 326	843	BZ, 1, p. 573	934	NKBT, 92, no. 402
790	ITS 353	844	BZ, 1, p. 588	935	NKBT, 92, no. 414
791	ITS 367	845	BZ, 1, p. 597	936	NKBZ, 42, no. 290
792	NKBZ, 32, p. 223	846	BZ, 2, p. 615	937	NKBT, 66, p. 315
793	NKBZ, 32, p. 240	847	BZ, 2, p. 634	938	BZ, 4, p. 260
794	MS 330	848	BZ, 2, p. 635	939	BZ, 4, p. 262
795	MS 421	849	BZ, 6, p. 105	940	NKBT, 92, no. 504
796	NKBZ, 42, no. 10	850	BZ, 2, p. 644	941	NKBT, 92, no. 505
797	NKBZ, 42, no. 11	851	BZ, 2, p. 646	942	KHT, 6, p. 281
798	NKBZ, 32, p. 288	852–		943	NKBT, 92, no. 514
799	NKBZ, 32, p. 294	59	BZ, 4, p. 233	944	NKBT, 92, no. 520
800	NKBZ, 42, no. 12	860	BZ, 2, p. 827	945	NKBT, 92, no. 522
801	NKBZ, 42, no. 20	861	BZ, 6, p. 117	946	NKBT, 92, no. 361
802	NKBZ, 42, no. 21	862	BZ, 2, p. 781	947	NKBT, 92, no. 366
803–		863	BZ, 2, p. 841	948	NKBT, 92, no. 369
10	NKBZ, 32, pp.	864–		949	BZ, 5, p. 131
	317–18	72	BZ, 5, p. 219	950	BZ, 5, p. 146
811	NKBZ, 42, no. 93	873	BZ, 2, p. 868	951	NKBT, 92, no. 437
812	NKBZ, 42, no. 99	874	BZ, 2, p. 879	952	NKBT, 92, no. 443
813	BZ, 1, p. 85	875	BZ, 2, p. 884	953	NKBT, 92, no. 446
814	BZ, 1, p. 106	876	BZ, 2, p. 976	954	NKBT, 92, no. 591
815	BZ, 1, p. 116	877	BZ, 2, p. 911	955	NKBT, 92, no. 594
816	BZ, 1, p. 133	878–		956	NKBT, 92, no. 598
817	BZ, 1, p. 149	913	NKBZ, 32, pp.	957	NKBT, 92, no. 559
			463–74		

958	NKBZ, 42, no. 377	1003	NKBT, 92, no. 720	1053	IZ, 1, p. 743
959	NKBZ, 42, no. 387	1004	NKBT, 92, no. 732	1054	IZ, 1, p. 445
960	KHT, 12, no. 33	1005	NKBT, 92, no. 889	1055–	
961	KHT, 12, no. 38	1006	NKBZ, 42, no. 842	6	IZ, 5, p. 126
962	KHT, 12, p. 321	1007	NKBZ, 42, no. 505	1057	IZ, 1, p. 383
963	KHT, 12, no. 150	1008	NKBT, 92, no. 672	1058	IZ, 1, p. 95
964	KHT, 12, no. 245	1009	NKBZ, 42, no. 513	1059	IZ, 1, p. 484
965	KHT, 12, no. 277	1010	NKBT, 92, no. 682	1060	IZ, 1, p. 161
966	KHT, 12, no. 326	1011	NKBT, 92, no. 684	1061	IZ, 1, p. 375
967	BRC, p. 91	1012	NKBT, 92, no. 851	1062	IZ, 1, p. 542
968	KHT, 12, no. 423	1013	NKBT, 92, no. 858	1063	RZ, p. 128
969	BRC, p. 126	1014	NKBZ, 42, no. 802	1064	RZ, p. 70
970	BRC, p. 129	1015	NKBT, 92, no. 867	1065	RZ, p. 127
971	BRC, p. 153	1016	NKBT, 92, no. 870	1066	RZ, p. 183
972	KHT, 12, no. 610	1017	NKBZ, 46, no. 57	1067	RZ, p. 324
973	KHT, 12, no. 806	1018	NKBZ, 46, no. 91	1068	RZ, p. 329
974	KHT, 12, no. 879	1019	NKBZ, 46, no. 99	1069	RZ, p. 330
975	KHT, 12, no. 887	1020	NKBZ, 46, no. 177	1070	RZ, p. 332
976	KHT, 12, no. 890	1021	NKBZ, 46, no. 178	1071	RZ, p. 343
977	KHT, 12, no. 1080	1022	NKBZ, 46, no. 403	1072	RZ, p. 349
978	KHT, 12, no. 1277	1023	NKBZ, 46, no. 500	1073	RZ, p. 350
979	KHT, 12, no. 1507	1024–		1074	RZ, p. 364
980	KHT, 12, no. 1526	30	HY 606–12	1075	RZ, p. 391
981	BRC, p. 291	1031	NKBZ, 46, no. 698	1076	RZ, p. 397
982	BRC, p. 298	1032	NKBZ, 46, no. 778	1077	RZ, p. 400
983	KHT, 12, no. 1738	1033	NKBZ, 46, no. 787	1078	RZ, p. 408
984	KHT, 12, no. 1743	1034	NKBT, 57, p. 223	1079	RZ, p. 448
985	KHT, 12, no. 1906	1035	NKBT, 57, p. 262	1080	RZ, p. 450
986	KHT, 12, no. 1940	1036	NKBT, 57, p. 263	1081	RZ, p. 450
987	KHT, 12, no. 1947	1037	NKBT, 57, p. 264	1082	RZ, p. 452
988	KHT, 12, no. 2022	1038	NKBZ, 46, no. 78	1083	NKBT, 93, p. 75
989	KHT, 12, no. 2220	1039	NKBZ, 46, no. 108	1084	NKBT, 93, p. 137
990	KHT, 12, no. 2355	1040	NKBZ, 46, no. 127	1085	NKBT, 93, p. 149
991	KHT, 12, no. 2475	1041	NKBZ, 46, no. 130	1086	NKBT, 93, p. 159
992	KHT, 12, no. 2560	1042	NKBZ, 46, no. 39	1087	NKBT, 93, p. 173
993	KHT, 12, no. 2669	1043	NKBZ, 46, no. 55	1088	NKBT, 93, p. 282
994	KHT, 12, no. 2815	1044	NKBZ, 46, no. 73	1089	NKBT, 93, p. 283
995	KHT, 12, no. 2832	1045	IZ, 1, p. 419	1090	NKBT, 93, p. 288
996	KHT, 12, p. 336	1046	IZ, 1, p. 650	1091	NKBT, 93, p. 291
997	NKBT, 92, no. 691	1047–		1092	NKBT, 93, p. 361
998	NKBT, 92, no. 696	8	IZ, 2, p. 200	1093	NKBT, 93, p. 364
999	NKBT, 92, no. 703	1049	IZ, 1, p. 227	1094	NKBT, 93, p. 378
1000	KHT, 13, p. 400	1050	IZ, 1, p. 175	1095	NKBT, 93, p. 384
1001	NKBZ, 42, no. 552	1051	IZ, 2, p. 572	1096	NKBT, 93, p. 391
1002	KHT, 13, p. 401	1052	IZ, 5, p. 148	1097	NKBT, 93, p. 400

1098	NKBT, 93, p. 408	1120	NKDBT, 56, p. 131	1139	GNBT, 10, p. 163
1099–		1121	NKDBT, 56, p. 135	1140	GMS, p. 72
1103	NKBT, 93, pp. 428–31	1122	NGBZ, 25, p. 299	1141	GMS, p. 72
		1123	NKDBT, 56, p. 133	1142	NKDBT, 16, p. 107
1104	NKBT, 93, p. 439	1124	NKDBT, 56, p. 168	1143	NKDBT, 16, p. 125
1105	NKBT, 93, p. 439	1125	GBT, 69, p. 80	1144	NKDBT, 16, p. 129
1106	SZ, 3, p. 442	1126	NKDBT, 56, p. 183	1145	NKDBT, 16, p. 129
1107	SZ, 2, p. 227	1127	NKDBT, 56, p. 185	1146	NKDBT, 23, p. 57
1108	SZ, 2, p. 513	1128	GMS, p. 9	1147	NKDBT, 23, p. 58
1109	SZ, 3, p. 275	1129	GMS, p. 10	1148	NKDBT, 23, p. 59
1110	SZ, 2, p. 559	1130	GMS, p. 11	1149	NKDBT, 23, p. 73
1111	SZ, 2, p. 610	1131	NKDBT, 17, p. 54	1150	NKDBT, 23, p. 77
1112	SZ, 2, p. 610	1132	NKDBT, 17, p. 69	1151	NKDBT, 23, p. 170
1113	KH, p. 216	1133	NKDBT, 17, p. 71	1152	NKDBT, 23, p. 171
1114	KH, p. 80	1134	NKDBT, 17, p. 90	1153	NKDBT, 23, p. 190
1115	KH, p. 87	1135	NKDBT, 17, p. 95	1154	NKDBT, 43, p. 53
1116	KH, p. 91	1136	NKDBT, 17, p. 101	1155	NKDBT, 43, p. 61
1117	KH, p. 217	1137	NKDBT, 17, p. 105	1156	NKDBT, 43, p. 77
1118	GNBT, 19, p. 33	1138	GNBT, 10, p. 164	1157	NKDBT, 43, p. 87
1119	NKDBT, 56, p. 127				

Glossary of Important Place-Names

ADANO; ADA NO ŌNO; ADA MOOR. Located in central Yamato (modern Nara Prefecture), along the Yoshino River near the modern city of Gojō. Often associated with ephemerality in the poetic mind because one character read ada means "transient."

AKASHI NO URA; AKASHI BAY. Small bay on the coast of ancient Harima Province (modern Hyōgo Prefecture), just across from the northern tip of Awaji Isle. Since the time of Hitomaro, who wrote a poem about a "boat fading behind the isles" off Akashi (poem 35), the bay has been associated with the sadness of parting. In addition, it is important as the place where Genji spent the last year of his exile and met the Akashi Monk and his daughter; she later bore Genji a daughter who went on to become empress.

AKIZU. Lit., "Dragon-fly Fields," a name whose source is attributed to an incident in which Emperor Yūryaku was saved from a hostile horsefly by a dragonfly. Located in the mountains of Yoshino. Following Hitomaro (MYS 336), later poets nearly always prefaced it with the pillow-word hana jirau, "where flowers scatter."

AMA NO HASHIDATE; HEAVEN'S LADDER. Pine-lined sandspit in Miyatsu Harbor, Miyatsu City (modern Kyōto Municipality)

AMA NO KAGUYAMA; KAGU'S HEAVENLY HILL. One of Yamato's most majestic peaks, located just to the east of the site of the old capital of Fujiwara Kyō (modern Nara Prefecture, near Sakurai City). Ama no, meaning "of heaven," is a pillow word for Kaguyama, carrying with it the idea that the mountain came "from heaven" quite literally in the Age of the Gods. As in MYS 2 by Emperor Jōmei (see poem 5), the mountain is often alluded to in poems of praise for the nation, acting as a symbol of the majestic beauty of the Yamato plain and its people.

ARASHIYAMA; STORM MOUNTAIN. Mountain on the Ōi River in the Saga area, just northwest of Kyōto. Famous for the beauty of its cherry blossoms and autumn leaves.

ARIMA HILL. Mountain in Settsu Province (modern Hyōgo Prefecture, Arima District), just inland from Ashiya (modern Hyōgo Prefecture)

ASHIYA. Coastal area in Settsu Province (modern Hyōgo Prefecture)

ASUKA. Area in central Yamato (modern Nara Prefecture, between Sakurai and Kashihara cities) where the capital was located for some decades of the 5th and 6th centuries. Known for its gentle landscapes and smoothly flowing streams and rivers.

ASUKAGAWA; THE RIVER ASUKA; TOMORROW RIVER. River with headwaters near Inabuchi Mountain that flows through the site of the old capital of Fujiwara Kyō and then on to the northwest, eventually joining the Yamato River. An anonymous poem (KKS 933; poem 149) capitalized on the pun inherent in its name—the sound asu meaning "tomorrow"—and used it as a symbol of the mutability so well symbolized by the changing "pools" and "shallows" of the river's flow. Since then, even the most casual mention of the Asuka has brought with it the idea of "change as swift as a river's current."

AUSAKA; MEETING HILL. Site of important barrier in Ōmi Province (modern Mie Prefecture), in modern Ōtsu City, located on a major road leading east. Associated in the poetic mind with travel, parting, and meeting.

AWAJI ISLE. Large island located at the east end of the Inland Sea

AYUCHIGATA. Located on the coast of Owari Province (modern Aiichi Prefecture) near modern Nagoya City

AZUMA; THE EAST COUNTRY. Name given to the eastern provinces—first referring to those east of the Ausaka Barrier, then to those east of Hakone

BITTER HILLS, see UJIYAMA

CAPE KARASAKI, see KARASAKI

CATHAY, see KARA NO KUNI

CHIKUZEN PROVINCE. Classical name for what is now the western half of Fukuoka Prefecture

CROSSING MOUNTAIN, see WATARI NO YAMA

DAZAIFU. Site of government offices of Tsukushi in northern Kyūshū (modern Fukuoka Prefecture), first established in the 7th century and continuing on in various forms throughout the classical and medieval periods. Important literary center in the early 8th century, when Ōtomo no Tabito served as governor-general there. Also famous as the place where the broken-hearted Sugawara no Michizane died in the equivalent of exile in 903.

DEEP GRASS, see FUKAKUSA

EAST COUNTRY, see AZUMA

EASTERN HILLS, see HIGASHIYAMA

EASTERN SEA; TŌKAI. Sea along the coast of the eastern provinces

ECHIGO PROVINCE. Classical name for what is now Niigata Prefecture

ECHIZEN PROVINCE. Classical name for what are now the eastern districts of Fukui Prefecture

EDO. Modern Tōkyō. Capital of the nation from 1603 to 1868 and a major cultural and commercial center.

ETCHŪ PROVINCE. Classical name for what is now Toyama Prefecture

FUJI; FUJI NO YAMA; FUJISAN; MOUNT FUJI. Most famous of all Japan's many volcanic peaks, located on the border between the ancient provinces of Kai and Suruga (modern Yamanashi and Shizuoka prefectures). In early poetry, as seen most conspicuously in Akahito's paean to the mountain (MYS 317–18; poems 36–37), Fuji was often treated as a symbol of steadfastness specifically associated with the gods—a place always snow-capped and thus beyond the reach of time. This treatment continued into the Edo period, but was supplemented with poems focusing on the smoke that occasionally rose from the peak (it erupted most violently in the 9th century and in 1707) as symbolic of the fickleness and uncertainty of human passion.

FUKAGAWA. District of Edo (modern Tōkyō)

FUKAKUSA. Located in the Fushimi area, south of Kyōto. Associated in the poetic mind with the plaintive cry of the quail since the mid-9th century, when Narihira exchanged poems with a lover living there (KKS 971–72; poems 120–21).

FUKIAGE NO HAMA; WINDBLOWN STRAND. Located at the mouth of the Ki River, in Kii Province (modern Wakayama City, Wakayama Prefecture)

FURU WATERFALL. Located in Yamato Province (modern Nara Prefecture), in what is now Tenri City

FUSHIMI HILLS. Area just south of Kyōto known for its pastoral beauty

FUWA NO SEKI; FUWA GATEHOUSE. Ancient sekisho, or barrier, set up in Mino (modern Gifu Prefecture, Fuwa-gun) in 675 by Emperor Temmu and destroyed just over a century later. Alluded to as a symbol of the vanity of human ambition in poems by Go-Kyōgoku Yoshitsune (SKKS 1601; poem 334) and later writers.

HAHASO GROVES; HAHASO NO MORI. Located near the headwaters of the Izumi River in Yamashiro Province (modern Sōraku-gun, Kyōto Municipality). Noted for its autumn leaves.

HAKONE. Mountainous area in Sagami Province (modern Kanagawa Prefecture) on the western border of the Kantō plain

HARIMA PROVINCE. Classical name for what is now the southern half of Hyōgo Prefecture

HASA. Located somewhere in Yamato Province (Nara Prefecture), probably near what is now Kashihara City

HASE; HATSUSE. Located in Yamato Province (modern Sakurai City, Nara Prefecture). Site of a famous temple dedicated to the bodhisattva Kannon.

HEAVEN'S LADDER, see AMA NO HASHIDATE

HIEI, see MOUNT HIEI

HIGASHIYAMA. Mountains that border Kyōto on the east. Site of many temples and shrines.

IBUKI, see MOUNT IBUKI

IGA PROVINCE. Classical name for what is now the western corner of Mie Prefecture

IKAZUCHIYAMA; IKAZUCHI NO OKA; IKAZUCHI HILL; THUNDER HILL. Small hill in the Asuka area (the central area of modern Nara Prefecture)

IKOMA MOUNTAIN. Located on the border between Yamato and Kawachi provinces (modern Ōsaka City and Nara Prefecture)

IKUNO. Located in Tamba Province (modern Kyōto Municipality)

IMIZUGAWA; IMIZU RIVER. River in ancient Etchū (modern Toyama Prefecture)

INA. Name given the moorlands along the Ina River in Settsu Province (modern Ōsaka City). Famous for their fields of dwarf bamboo.

INABA PROVINCE. Classical name for what is now the eastern half of Tottori Prefecture

INLAND SEA; SETONAIKAI. Name for the sea between Honshū, Shikoku, and Kyūshū

IRO BEACH. Located in Echizen Province (modern Fukui Prefecture) near modern Tsuruga City

ISE PROVINCE. Classical name for what are now the eastern districts of Mie Prefecture

IWAMI PROVINCE. Classical name for what is now the western half of Shimane Prefecture

IWAMI NO UMI; IWAMI SEA. Japan Sea off the coast of ancient Iwami (the western part of modern Shimane Prefecture)

IWASE MOOR. Precise location unknown, but probably in Etchū Province (modern Toyama Prefecture), near the modern city of Takaoka

IZU. Famous peninsula south of modern Tōkyō (eastern Shizuoka Prefecture)

IZU SEA. Sea off the eastern coast of the Izu Peninsula

IZUMI RIVER. Ancient name for the Kizu River

IZUMO. Classical name for what is now the eastern third of Shimane Prefecture

IZUMO POINT. Located on the coast of Echigo Province (modern Niigata Prefecture) southwest of Niigata City

JAPAN SEA; NIHONKAI. Sea between Japan, North China, and Korea

JEWEL POINT; SAKITAMA NO TSU. Located on a river in Musashi (modern Saitama Prefecture)

KAGA PROVINCE. Classical name for what are now the southwestern districts of Ishikawa Prefecture

KAGU'S HEAVENLY HILL; KAGUYAMA, see AMA NO KAGUYAMA

KAMAKURA. Located just south of Tōkyō. Capital of the shogunal government from 1185 to 1333 and a major center of Buddhism.

KAMO SHRINE. Name for two important Shinto shrines located just north of Kyōto

KAMOYAMA; KAMO HILL. Precise location unknown, but located somewhere in Iwami (the western part of modern Shimane Prefecture)

KANNABI NO MIMURO. Lit., "The Mountain Where the God Dwells." Located in Yamato Province (modern Nara Prefecture) in what is now Ikoma-gun.

KARA NO KUNI; CATHAY. Old name for China, "The Tang Kingdom." In poetry, used in contrast to Japan, often connoting what is "strange" and "foreign," or, in love poems, "distant" and "unapproachable."

KARASAKI; CAPE KARASAKI. Located on the southern tip of Lake Biwa (modern Shiga Prefecture). See also ŌMI, ŌTSU, and SHIGA. Not to be confused with Kara no Saki (the Cape of Kara).

KARA NO SAKI. Precise location unknown, but located somewhere on the coast of the Japan Sea in modern Shimane Prefecture

KASHIHARA. Purported site of the capital of Emperor Jimmu, the legendary first Japanese sovereign. Located in Yamato Province (modern Nara Prefecture)

between the three great peaks of central Yamato—Unebiyama, Miminashi-yama, and Kaguyama.

KASUGA; KASUGANO; KASUGA FIELDS. Area on the eastern border of Heijō/Nara (now part of Nara City). Associated in the poetic mind with new greens and spreading haze, both harbingers of spring.

KATANO MOOR. Name given to moorlands in Kawachi Province (now in Hira-kata, Ōsaka Municipality). Famous as hunting grounds.

KATSUNO; TAKASHIMA NO KATSUNO NO HARA. Moorlands located on the east shore of Lake Biwa near modern Takashima-gun

KEHI. Located on the west coast of Awaji Isle

KIBUNE SHRINE. Located in Kurama, just north of Kyōto

KOSHI. Name for ancient Echizen, Noto, Kaga, Etchū, and Echigo provinces (modern prefectures of Fukui, Ishikawa, Toyama, and Niigata). Famous in poetry for its heavy snow and for the great peak of Shirayama—"White Mountain" (now called Hakusan; located on the border between modern Gifu and Ishikawa prefectures).

KUROUSHIGATA; KUROUSHI STRAND. Located on the coast of Kii Province (modern Wakayama Prefecture) just south of modern Wakayama City

LAKE BIWA. Lake north of Kyōto, in ancient Ōmi Province (modern Shiga Prefecture). Also known as Niho no Umi, "The Sea of Grebes," and the Ōmi Sea.

LAND OF TSU. Settsu Province, the classical name for what is now the western section of Hyōgo Prefecture

MATSUO BEACH. Located on the northern tip of Awaji Isle

MATSUYAMA. City in ancient Iyo Province (modern Ehime Prefecture)

MEETING HILL, see AUSAKA

MICHINOKU. Ancient name for Mutsu Province, which made up most of later Iwaki, Iwashiro, Rikuzen, Rikuchū, and Mutsu provinces (modern Fuku-shima, Miyagi, Iwate, and Aomori prefectures)

MIKA MOOR. Area in Sōraku-gun, Kyōto Municipality

MIKAWA PROVINCE. Classical name for what are now the eastern districts of Aichi Prefecture

MIMIGA NO MINE; MIMIGA PEAK. One of the mountains of the Yoshino area. Precise location unknown.

MIMURO, see KANNABI NO MIMURO

MINA RIVER; MINA NO KAWA. River with headwaters near Mount Tsukuba in Hitachi that flows into Sakuragawa, emptying into Kasumigaura Lake

MINASE. Area along the Minase River, a tributary of the Yodo River that runs through Settsu Province (modern Mishima-gun, Ōsaka Municipality). Site of a pleasure palace erected by Retired Emperor Go-Toba.

MINO PROVINCE. Classical name for what are now the southwestern districts of Gifu Prefecture

MIWA MOUNTAIN. Mountain in Yamato Province (modern Nara Prefecture). Famous for its cryptomeria. Later the location of a prominent market town.

MIYAGINO; MIYAGI MOOR. Located in ancient Michinoku (modern Sendai City, Miyagi Prefecture)

MIYANOTAKI. Lit., "Palace Waterfall." Located on the Yoshino River in Yamato (Nara Prefecture)

MIYOSHINO; FAIR YOSHINO, see YOSHINO

MOGAMI RIVER. River running into the sea near Sakata City in ancient Dewa (modern Yamagata Prefecture)

MORUYAMA; MOUNT MORU. Located in ancient Ōmi (Shiga Prefecture)

MOUNT HIEI. Name given to the mountains just northeast of Kyōto. Site of Tendai's Enryakuji monastery

MOUNT HIRA. Mountain rising on western banks of Lake Biwa in Ōmi Province (modern Shiga Prefecture)

MOUNT IBUKI. Mountain on the border between the ancient provinces of Ōmi and Mino (modern Shiga and Gifu prefectures)

MOUNT INABA. Mountain in Inaba Province (modern Tottori Prefecture, Iwasa-gun)

MOUNT MIKASA. Mountain in Yamato Province (now in Nara City) near Kasuga

MOUNT MIMURO, see KANNABI NO MIMURO

MOUNT MIWA, see MIWA MOUNTAIN

MUSASHINO; MUSASHI MOORS. Area just northwest of modern Tōkyō (Saitama Prefecture) famous for its tall grasses and autumn winds

NAGASAKI. City in Hizen Province (modern Nagasaki Prefecture). Site of Dutch settlement during Edo period and therefore associated with Christianity and Western learning.

NAKAMURA. Town in Ise Province (modern Mie Prefecture)

NAKA NO MINATO; NAKA HARBOR. Harbor on the coast of Sanuki (modern Kagawa Prefecture) near the modern town of Kanakura

NANAO. Fishing village located on the Noto Peninsula, Noto Province (modern Ishikawa Prefecture)

NANIWA; NANIWAE; NANIWAGATA. Inlet on the coast of ancient Settsu (modern Ōsaka City). Famous from very early on for its reeds, which formed the basic material for literally thousands of poems over the centuries—the most famous of all being SKKS 625, by Monk Saigyō (see poem 302) and an earlier work praising the spring scenery of the place—GSIS 43, by Monk Nōin (poem 247).

NARA. Area around the city of Heijō (modern Nara City). Capital from 710 to 784 and thereafter an important agricultural area and religious center by virtue of the great institutions located in or near it—including the great temples Kōfukuji, Tōdaiji, Yakushiji, and Hōryūji, and the Kasuga Shrine. Often prefaced with the pillow-word aoniyoshi, a term of praise describing its "rich blue earth."

NASU MOOR. Moorlands in Shimotsuke Province (modern Tochigi Prefecture). Famous for their shino, or "bamboo grass."

NIHO NO UMI, see LAKE BIWA

NŌTO PROVINCE. Classical name for what is now the northern tip of Ishikawa Prefecture

OE. Mountain in Tamba Province (modern Kyōto Municipality)

OFFERING HILL, see TAMUKEYAMA

OGURA NO MINE; PEAK OF OGURA. One of the peaks of the Tatsuta area, famous for the beauty of its autumn foliage and its spring blossoms

ŌHARA. Village in Yamashiro Province (now Kyōto Municipality)

ŌI RIVER. River running by Arashiyama in the Saga area of Yamashiro (modern Kyōto Municipality). Famous for its fireflies and cormorant fishing.

OJIMA. One of the islands of Matsushima in Michinoku (modern Miyagi Prefecture)

OKI ISLANDS. Located off the coast of Izumo Province (modern Shimane Prefecture). Place of exile.

ŌMI. Classical name for the province (modern Shiga Prefecture) surrounding Lake Biwa, where the imperial capital was located from 667 to 671. See also ŌTSU, SHIGA.

ŌMI SEA, see LAKE BIWA

ONO. Area in Yamashiro, north of Kyōto. Noted for its autumn leaves and as a place for collecting firewood.

ŌTSU. Located at the southern tip of Lake Biwa. Site of the national capital from 667 to 671. See also ŌMI, SHIGA.

OWARI PROVINCE. Classical name for what is now the western portion of Aiichi Prefecture

PINE MOUNTAIN IN SUE, see SUE NO MATSUYAMA

RIVER ASUKA, see ASUKAGAWA

RIVER UJI, see UJIGAWA

SADO ISLE. Large island off the coast of Echigo Province (modern Niigata Prefecture). Place of exile noted for its rugged aspect.

SAHOGAWA; SAHO RIVER. A river with headwaters near Kasuga Mountain in Yamato (near modern Nara City) that flows south, eventually joining the Yamato River. In poetry, associated with plovers because of a famous poem by Yakamochi (MYS 715; see poem 93); also associated with river mist and river wind.

SAKAMOTO. Town located at the eastern foot of Mount Hiei in Ōmi Province (now in Ōtsu City, modern Shiga Prefecture). Site of Enryakuji monastery and the Hie Shrine.

SAKITAMA NO TSU; JEWEL POINT. Located on a river in Musashi (modern Saitama Prefecture)

SAKURADA. Lit., "Blossom Paddies." Located in Owari Province (modern Aiichi Prefecture), in modern Nagoya City.

SAMINE NO SHIMA; SAMINE ISLAND. Now called Shamine Island. One of the small islands off the coast of Sanuki Province (modern Kagawa Prefecture).

SANO FORD; SANO NO WATARI. An area along the Ki River in Kii Province (modern Wakayama), southeast of Miwa Point. The word watari probably meant "area" (atari), but poets took it to mean "ford."

SANUKI; LAND OF SANUKI. Name for what is now Kagawa Prefecture. Known for its rugged coastline and many small islands, as memorialized in Hitomaro's famous poem "On seeing a dead man among the rocks at Samine Island in Sanuki" (MYS 220–21; see poems 26–28).

SAO MOUNTAIN. Located east of Heijō Kyō in Yamato Province (modern Nara Prefecture). Noted for its autumn leaves and as the residence of Saohime, the Princess of Spring.

SASANAMI, see SHIGA

SEA OF GREBES, see LAKE BIWA

SETTSU PROVINCE. Classical name for what is now the western section of Hyōgo Prefecture. Also known as the Land of Tsu and Tsu Province.

SHIGA. Northern section of the old capital at Ōmi, on the southern tip of Lake Biwa. Often prefaced with the pillow-word sasanami no—the name of a place on the nearby lakeshore and also a descriptive term meaning "rippling waves." Beginning with Hitomaro's lament in MYS 29–31 (poems 12–14), the site of the old capital generally called forth nostalgic sentiments from poets. See also ŌMI, ŌTSU.

SHIGA MOUNTAIN ROAD. Road from north Shirakawa district of Kyōto through Jizō Valley to Shiga Village, site of an important temple in classical times

SHIMABARA. Important entertainment district in Kyōto

SHIMŌSA PROVINCE. Classical name for what is now the northernmost part of Chiba Prefecture

SHINANO PROVINCE. Classical name for what is now Nagano Prefecture

SHIRAKAWA BARRIER. Barrier on the border between Shimotsuke Province and Michinoku (located in modern Shirakawa City, Fukushima Prefecture) that served as gateway to the frontier in ancient times

STORM MOUNTAIN, see ARASHIYAMA

SUE NO MATSUYAMA; PINE MOUNTAIN IN SUE. Precise location unknown, but probably in Michinoku on the coast near modern Taga City (modern Miyagi Prefecture)

SUMA; SUMA BAY. Coastal area in Settsu (modern Hyōgo Prefecture) noted for its rugged beauty. First place of exile for Genji, before he moved down the coast to Akashi.

SUMIDAGAWA; SUMIDA RIVER. Major river running between Musashi and Shimōsa province, and later through the city of Edo

SUMINOE; SUMIYOSHI. Coastal area between Naniwa and Sakai in Settsu Province (modern Ōsaka Municipality). Site of Sumiyoshi Shrine, whose deity was the patron god of poets. Noted for its venerable pines.

SURUGA PROVINCE. Classical name for what is now the central portion of Shizuoka Prefecture

SUZUKA MOUNTAIN. Located on the border of Ise, Iga, and Ōmi provinces (modern Mie and Shiga prefectures). Famous for its showers and autumn leaves.

SUZUKA RIVER. River forming the border between Ōmi and Ise provinces (modern Shiga and Mie prefectures), running from Ise to Kyōto

TAGO NO URA; TAGO BAY. Bay on the coast of Suruga (modern Shizuoka Prefecture), on the western side of Mount Fuji

TAKA. Located in Yamashiro (modern Kyōto Municipality), modern Tsutsugi-gun

TAKASAGO. Coastal area in Harima Province (modern Hyōgo Prefecture) at the mouth of the Kako River. Site of famous Shinto shrine noted for the beauty of its surrounding pines, which are "twins" with those of the Sumiyoshi Shrine across the bay.

TAKASHI NO HAMA; TAKASHI STRAND. Coastal area in Izumi Province (modern Sakai City, Ōsaka Municipality)

TAKASHIMA NO KATSUNO NO HARA; FIELDS OF KATSUNO IN TAKASHIMA. Moorlands located on the east shore of Lake Biwa (modern Shiga Prefecture) near modern Takashima-gun

TAMAKAWA VILLAGE. Name of at least six villages in different areas of Japan. The one alluded to by Shunzei in SZS 443 (poem 274) is probably Tamakawa in Noda, modern Miyagi Prefecture.

TAMUKEYAMA; OFFERING HILL. Name given to various mountains prayed to by travelers for safety on the road

TANGO PROVINCE. Classical name for what is now the northernmost portion of Kyōto Municipality

TATSUTA. Mountainous area in Ikoma-gun (modern Nara Prefecture), between ancient Nara and Naniwa. Famous in poetry for its autumn leaves and cherry blossoms.

TATSUTA RIVER. A river running from Ikoma Mountain through the Tatsuta area of Yamato Province (modern Nara Prefecture)

THUNDER HILL, see IKAZUCHIYAMA

TOBA. Village in the Fushimi area of Ōmi Province (modern Mie Prefecture)

TŌKAI; EASTERN SEA. Sea along the coast of the eastern provinces

TOMO NO URA; TOMO BAY. Located on the coast of Bingo (modern Hiroshima Prefecture) near modern Fukuyama

TOMORROW RIVER, see ASUKAGAWA

TORIBE HILL. Moorlands in the Higashiyama area of Kyōto, at the foot of Amidaka Peak in Yamashiro (modern Kyōto Municipality). Famous for its cremation grounds and cemeteries.

TOSA PROVINCE. Classical name for what is now Kōchi Prefecture

TSUKUBA PEAK. One of the great peaks of the East Country, located in Hitachi Province (modern Ibaraki Prefecture). Revered especially by poets of linked verse, which was sometimes called Tsukuba no michi, or "the Way of Tsukuba," because it was there in ancient times that the first linked verse was composed by deities.

TSU PROVINCE. Settsu Province, the classical name for what is now the western section of Hyōgo Prefecture

UENO. 1: district of Edo (modern Tōkyō). 2: a town in Iga Province (modern Mie Prefecture) known as the birthplace of Matsuo Bashō.

UJI RIVER; UJIGAWA. River that runs through the Fushimi area south of Kyōto to eventually join the Yodo. Famous for its autumn leaves and fishing weirs.

UJIYAMA; BITTER HILLS. Mountainous area south of Kyōto. Associated with bitter feelings because its name involves a partial homophone with the word ushi, "bitter," or "painful."

UNEBIYAMA; MOUNT UNEBI. One of central Yamato's famous peaks, located just to the west of the site of the old capital of Fujiwara Kyō (modern Nara Prefecture, new Sakurai City)

UZUMASA. Area near Kyōto (now Kadano-gun, Kyōto Municipality)

WAKA NO URA; WAKA BAY. Bay in Kii (modern Wakayama Prefecture) just south of Wakayama City. Early poems like Akahito's MYS 924 (poem 38), which described cranes flying over the reeds there, connected those two images with the place ever after. And because the name is homophonous with waka, "Japanese poetry," it is often used to refer to the poetic tradition.

WATARI NO YAMA; CROSSING MOUNTAIN. Precise location unknown, but probably near the mouth of the Gō River in central Iwami (the western part of modern Shimane Prefecture)

WHEN-SEE RIVER; see IZUMI RIVER

WINDBLOWN STRAND, see FUKIAGE NO HAMA

YAKAMI NO YAMA; YAKAMI. Located in Iwami near Gōzu City (modern Shimane Prefecture)

YAMADA MOOR. Located outside Ise Shrine in Ise Province (modern Mie Prefecture)

YAMASHIRO. Name of the ancient province that encompassed Heian Kyō—the capital at Kyōto

YAMATO. Early name (mid-4th and 5th centuries) for the first unified Japanese state, the center of which was located in the Yamato area (modern Nara Prefecture); later, the name of the province encompassing most of the same area. Consisting of broad plains ideal for rice culture, the northern part of the area was the site for many early capitals, the last being the city of Nara itself, which served that function from 710 to 784. By contrast, the southern regions of Yamato were dominated by the mountainous terrain of Yoshino. In poetry, the name Yamato is generally used to mean the Japanese nation, Yamato koto no ha ("leaf-words of Yamato") being a euphemism for Japanese poetry.

YODO. Town situated at the confluence of the Kamo, Kizu, and Katsura rivers in the Fushimi area of Yamashiro Province (modern Kyōto Municipality). A thriving commercial center from the medieval period on.

YOSHINO. Mountainous region in central and southern Yamato Province (modern Nara Prefecture). Famous for its rugged peaks, swift streams, cherry blossoms, and autumn leaves. The site of a number of famous temples.

YOSHINOGAWA; YOSHINO RIVER. River running through the valleys of the Yoshino area, eventually joining the great Ki River, which flows into the sea at Waka Bay in Kii (modern Wakayama). Known for its clear water and pastoral beauty.

YOSHIWARA. Chief entertainment district of Edo

YURA BAR. Name given to the straits between the mouth of the Ki River in Kii Province (modern Wakayama Prefecture) and Awaji Isle

Select Bibliography

TRANSLATIONS

General

Bownas, Geoffrey, and Anthony Thwaite. 1964. *The Penguin Book of Japanese Verse*. Baltimore: Penguin Books.

Keene, Donald, comp. and ed. 1955. *Anthology of Japanese Literature: Earliest Era to Mid-Nineteenth Century*. New York: Grove Press.

Miner, Earl. 1969. *Japanese Poetic Diaries*. Berkeley: University of California Press.

Rexroth, Kenneth. 1976. *One Hundred More Poems from the Japanese*. New York: New Directions.

———. 1964. *One Hundred Poems from the Japanese*. New York: New Directions.

Rexroth, Kenneth, and Atsumi Ikuko. 1977. *The Burning Heart: Women Poets of Japan*. New York: Seabury Press.

Sato, Hiroaki, and Burton Watson. 1981. *From the Country of Eight Islands: An Anthology of Japanese Poetry*. Seattle: University of Washington Press.

Waley, Arthur. 1919. *Japanese Poetry: The 'Uta.'* Honolulu: University Press of Hawaii.

Watson, Burton. 1975–76. *Japanese Literature in Chinese*. New York: Columbia University Press.

The Ancient Age

Brannen, Noah, and William Elliot. 1969. *Festive Wine: Ancient Japanese Poems from the Kinkafu*. New York: Walker/Weatherhill.

Levy, Ian Hideo. 1981– . *The Ten Thousand Leaves: A Translation of the Man'yōshū, Japan's Premier Anthology of Classical Poetry*. 4 vols. projected; 1 to date. Princeton, N.J.: Princeton University Press.

Miller, Roy Andrew. 1975. *The Footprints of the Buddha: An Eighth-Century Old Japanese Poetic Sequence*. New Haven, Conn.: American Oriental Society.

Nippon Gakujutsu Shinkōkai, ed. [1940] 1968. *The Man'yōshū: One Thousand Poems Selected and Translated from the Japanese*. New York: Columbia University Press.

Philippi, Donald L. 1968. *This Wine of Peace, This Wine of Laughter: A Complete Anthology of Japan's Earliest Songs*. New York: Mushinsha/Grossman.

———. 1965. *Kojiki*. Tokyo: Tokyo University Press.

Wright, Harold. 1979. *Ten Thousand Leaves: Love Poems from the Man'yōshū.* Boulder, Colo.: Shambala.

Yasuda, Kenneth. 1960. *Land of the Reed Plains: Ancient Japanese Lyrics from the Man'yōshū.* Rutland, Vt.: Tuttle.

The Classical Age

Bowring, Richard. 1982. *Murasaki Shikibu: Her Diary and Poetic Memoirs.* Princeton, N.J.: Princeton University Press.

Cranston, Edwin R. 1969. *The Izumi Shikibu Diary: A Romance of the Heian Court.* Cambridge, Mass.: Harvard University Press.

Harries, Phillip Tudor. 1980. *The Poetic Memoirs of Lady Daibu.* Stanford, Calif.: Stanford University Press.

Hirshfield, Jane, with Mariko Aratani. 1988. *The Ink Dark Moon: Love Poems by Ono no Komachi and Izumi Shikibu.* New York: Scribner's.

McCullough, Helen Craig. 1985. *Kokin Wakashū: The First Imperial Anthology of Japanese Poetry, with 'Tosa Nikki' and 'Shinsen Waka.'* Stanford, Calif.: Stanford University Press.

————. 1967. *Tales of Ise: Lyrical Episodes from Tenth-Century Japan.* Stanford: Stanford University Press.

Moriguchi Yasuhiko and David Jenkins. 1990. *The Dance of the Dust on the Rafters: Selections from Ryojinhisho.* Seattle, Wash.: Broken Moon Press.

Rodd, Laurel Rasplica, with Mary Catherine Henkenius. 1984. *Kokinshū: A Collection of Poems Ancient and Modern.* Princeton, N.J.: Princeton University Press.

Seidensticker, Edward G. 1976. *The Tale of Genji.* 2 vols. New York: Knopf.

Tahara, Mildred. 1980. *Tales of Yamato: A Tenth-Century Poem Tale.* Honolulu: University Press of Hawaii.

Teele, Nicholas J. 1976. "Rules for Poetic Elegance: Fujiwara no Kintō's *Shinsen Zuinō* and *Waka Kuhon,*" *Monumenta Nipponica,* 31.2 (Summer): 145–64.

Videen, Susan Downing. 1989. *Tales of Heichū.* Cambridge, Mass.: Harvard University Press.

The Early Medieval Age

Brower, Robert H. 1987. "The Foremost Style of Poetic Composition: Fujiwara Tameie's *Eiga no Ittei,*" *Monumenta Nipponica,* 42.4 (Winter): 391–429.

————. 1985. "Fujiwara Teika's *Maigetsushō,*" *Monumenta Nipponica,* 40.4 (Winter): 399–425.

————. 1978. *Fujiwara Teika's Hundred-Poem Sequence of the Shōji Era, 1200.* Tokyo: Sophia University.

————. 1972. "'Ex-Emperor Go-Toba's Secret Teachings': *Go-Toba no In Gokuden,*" *Harvard Journal of Asiatic Studies,* 32: 3–70.

Brower, Robert H., and Earl Miner. 1967. *Fujiwara Teika's Superior Poems of Our Time.* Stanford, Calif.: Stanford University Press.

Galt, Tom. 1982. *The Little Treasury of One Hundred People, One Poem Each.* Princeton, N.J.: Princeton University Press.

Huey, Robert N. 1987. "The Kingyoku Poetry Contest," *Monumenta Nipponica*, 42.3 (Autumn): 299–330.

Huey, Robert N., and Susan Matisoff. 1985. "Lord Tamekane's Notes on Poetry: *Tamekane-kyō Wakashō*," *Monumenta Nipponica*, 40.2 (Summer): 127–46.

Lafleur, William. 1978. *Mirror for the Moon: A Selection of Poems by Saigyō.* New York: New Directions.

Marra, Michele. 1984. "*Mumyōzōshi*, Introduction and Translation" (3 parts), *Monumenta Nipponica*, 39.2 (Summer): 115–45; 39.3 (Autumn): 281–305; 39.4 (Winter): 409–34.

Sato, Hiroaki. 1973. *Poems of Princess Shikishi.* Hanover, N.H.: Granite Publications.

The Late Medieval Age

Brazell, Karen. 1980. "Blossoms: A Medieval Song," *Journal of Japanese Studies*, 6.2 (Summer): 243–66.

Carter, Steven D. 1989. *Waiting for the Wind: Thirty-Six Poets of Japan's Late Medieval Age.* New York: Columbia University Press.

————. 1987. "Sōgi in the East Country, *Shirakawa Kikō*," *Monumenta Nipponica*, 42.2 (Summer): 167–209.

————. 1983. "Rules, Rules, and More Rules: Shōhaku's *Renga* Rulebook of 1501," *Harvard Journal of Asiatic Studies*, 43.2 (Dec.): 581–642.

Hirota, Dennis. 1977. "In Practice of the Way: Sasamegoto, an Instruction Book in Linked Verse," *Chanoyu Quarterly*, 19: 23–46.

Pollack, David. 1985. *Zen Poems of the Five Mountains.* New York: Crossroad Publishing Company; Decatur, Ga.: Scholar's Press.

Ury, Marian. 1977. *Poems of the Five Mountains: An Introduction to the Literature of the Zen Monasteries.* Tokyo: Mushinsha.

The Early Modern Age

Blyth, R. H. 1961. *Edo Satirical Verse Anthologies.* Tokyo: Hokuseido.

————. 1949–52. *Haiku.* 4 vols. Tokyo: Hokuseido.

Britton, Dorothy. 1980. *A Haiku Journey: Bashō's Narrow Road to a Far Province.* Tokyo: Kodansha International.

Corman, Cid, and Kamaike Susumu. 1968. *Back Roads to Far Towns: Bashō's Oku no Hosomichi.* New York: Grossman.

Henderson, Harold G. 1958. *An Introduction to Haiku: An Anthology of Poems and Poets from Bashō to Shiki.* Garden City, N.Y.: Doubleday Anchor Books.

Huey, Robert N. 1984. "Journal of My Father's Last Days: Issa's *Chichi no Shūen no Ki*," *Monumenta Nipponica*, 39.1 (Spring): 25–54.

Keene, Donald. 1971. "Bashō's Journal of 1684," in Keene, *Landscapes and Portraits: Appreciations of Japanese Culture*, pp. 94–108. Tokyo: Kodansha International.

———. 1971. "Bashō's Journey to Sarashina," in Keene, *Landscapes and Portraits: Appreciations of Japanese Culture*, pp. 109–30. Tokyo: Kodansha International.

Mackenzie, Lewis. 1957. *The Autumn Wind: A Selection of Poems of Issa.* Tokyo: Kodansha International.

Maeda, Cana. 1973. *Monkey's Raincoat.* New York: Grossman.

Mayhew, Lenore. 1985. *Monkey's Raincoat: Linked Poetry of the Bashō School, with Haiku Selections.* Rutland, Vt.: Tuttle.

Miner, Earl, and Hiroko Odagiri. 1981. *The Monkey's Straw Raincoat and Other Poetry of the Bashō School.* Princeton, N.J.: Princeton University Press.

Sato, Hiroaki. 1983. *One Hundred Frogs: From Renga to Haiku to English.* New York: Weatherhill.

Sawa, Yuki, and Edith M. Shiffert. 1978. *Haiku Master Buson.* San Francisco: Heian International.

Stryk, Lucien. 1985. *On Love and Barley: Haiku of Bashō.* New York: Penguin Books.

Terasaki, Etsuko. 1976. "*Hatsushigure*: A Linked Verse Series by Bashō and His Disciples," *Harvard Journal of Asiatic Studies*, 36: 204–39.

Watson, Burton. 1990. *Kanshi: The Poetry of Ishikawa Jozan and Other Edo-Period Poets.* San Francisco: North Point Press.

———. 1983. *Grass Hill: Poems and Prose by the Japanese Monk Gensei.* New York: Columbia University Press.

———. 1971. *Ryōkan, Zen Monk-Poet of Japan.* New York: Columbia University Press.

Yuasa, Nobuyuki. 1981. *The Zen Poems of Ryōkan.* Princeton, N.J.: Princeton University Press.

———. 1966. *The Narrow Road to the Deep North and Other Travel Sketches.* Baltimore: Penguin Books.

———. 1960. *The Year of My Life: A Translation of Issa's Oraga Haru.* Berkeley: University of California Press.

The Modern Age

Beichman-Yamamoto, Janine. 1975. "Masaoka Shiki's *A Drop of Ink*," *Monumenta Nipponica*, 30.3 (Autumn): 291–315.

Heinrich, Amy Vladeck. 1978. "My Mother Is Dying: Saitō Mokichi's '*Shinitamau Haha*,'" *Monumenta Nipponica*, 33.4 (Winter): 407–39.

Ishikawa, Takuboku. 1977. *Sad Toys*, tr. Sanford Goldstein and Seishi Shinoda. West Lafayette, Ind.: Purdue University Press.

———. 1966. *Poems to Eat*, tr. Carl Sesar. Tokyo: Kodansha International.

Ueda, Makoto. 1976. *Modern Japanese Haiku: An Anthology.* Tokyo: Tokyo University Press.

Yosano Akiko. 1971. *Tangled Hair: Selected Tanka from "Midaregami,"* tr. Sanford Goldstein and Shinoda Seishi. Lafayette, Ind.: Purdue University Studies.

STUDIES

General

Brower, Robert H. 1983. "Waka," in *Kodansha Encyclopedia of Japan,* vol. 8: 201–17. Tokyo: Kodansha International.

Brower, Robert H., and Earl Miner. 1961. *Japanese Court Poetry.* Stanford, Calif.: Stanford University Press.

————. 1957. "Formative Elements in the Japanese Poetic Tradition," *Journal of Asian Studies,* 16 (August): 503–27.

Cranston, Edwin A. 1975. "The Dark Path: Images of Longing in Japanese Love Poetry," *Harvard Journal of Asiatic Studies,* 35: 60–100.

Keene, Donald. 1988. *The Pleasures of Japanese Literature.* New York: Columbia University Press.

————. 1955. *Japanese Literature: An Introduction for Western Readers.* New York: Grove Press.

Konishi, Jin'ichi. 1984–. *A History of Japanese Literature.* 5 vols. projected; 2 to date. Princeton, N.J.: Princeton University Press.

————. 1958. "Association and Progression: Principles of Integration in Anthologies and Sequences of Japanese Court Poetry, A.D. 900–1350" (tr. Robert H. Brower and Earl Miner), *Harvard Journal of Asiatic Studies,* 21: 67–127.

Lafleur, William R. 1983. *The Karma of Words: Buddhism and the Literary Arts in Medieval Japan.* Berkeley: University of California Press.

Miner, Earl. 1973. "Toward a New Conception of Classical Japanese Poetics," in The Japan P.E.N. Club, ed., *Studies in Japanese Culture,* vol. 1: 99–113.

————. 1969. *Japanese Poetic Diaries.* Berkeley: University of California Press.

————. 1968. *An Introduction to Japanese Court Poetry.* Stanford, Calif.: Stanford University Press.

Miner, Earl, Hiroko Odagiri, and Robert Morrell. 1985. *The Princeton Companion to Classical Japanese Literature.* Princeton, N.J.: Princeton University Press.

Pollack, David. 1986. *The Fracture of Meaning: Japan's Synthesis of China from the Eighth Through the Eighteenth Centuries.* Princeton, N.J.: Princeton University Press.

Ueda, Makoto. 1967. *Literary and Art Theories in Japan.* Cleveland: Press of Case Western Reserve University.

The Ancient Age

Cranston, Edwin A. 1983. "Man'yōshū," in *Kodansha Encyclopedia of Japan*,
vol. 5: 103–11. Tokyo: Kodansha International.

————. 1973. "The River Valley as *Locus Amoenus* in Man'yō Poetry," in The
Japan P.E.N. Club, ed., *Studies in Japanese Culture*, vol. 1: 14–37.

————. 1971. "Water Plant Imagery in *Man'yōshū*," *Harvard Journal of Asi-
atic Studies*, 31: 137–78.

Doe, Paula. 1982. *A Warbler's Song in the Dusk: The Life and Works of Ōtomo
no Yakamochi (718–785)*. Berkeley: University of California Press.

Ebersole, Gary L. 1989. *Ritual Poetry and the Politics of Death in Early Japan*.
Princeton, N.J.: Princeton University Press.

Levy, Ian Hideo. 1984. *Hitomaro and the Birth of Japanese Lyricism*. Princeton,
N.J.: Princeton University Press.

Miller, Roy Andrew. 1981. "The Lost Poetic Sequence of the Priest Manzei,"
Monumenta Nipponica, 36.2 (Summer): 133–72.

The Classical Age

Cranston, Edwin A. 1970. "The Poetry of Izumi Shikibu," *Monumenta Nip-
ponica*, 25.1 (Spring): 1–11.

Harries, Phillip T. 1980. "Personal Poetry Collections: Their Origin and Devel-
opment Through the Heian Period," *Monumenta Nipponica*, 35.3 (Autumn):
297–317.

Heinrich, Amy Vladeck. 1982. "*Blown in Flurries*: The Role of the Poetry in
'Ukifune'," in Andrew Pekarik, ed., *Ukifune: Love in The Tale of Genji*, pp.
153–71. New York: Columbia University Press.

Konishi, Jin'ichi. 1978. "The Genesis of the *Kokinshū* Style" (tr. Helen C.
McCullough), *Harvard Journal of Asiatic Studies*, 38: 61–170.

McCullough, Helen Craig. 1985. *Brocade by Night: 'Kokin Wakashū' and the
Court Style in Japanese Classical Poetry*. Stanford, Calif.: Stanford Univer-
sity Press.

Morrell, Robert E. 1973. "The Buddhist Poetry in the *Goshūishū*," *Monumenta
Nipponica*, 28.1 (Spring): 87–100.

Ramirez-Christensen, Esperanza. 1982. "The Operation of the Lyrical Mode in
the *Genji Monogatari*," in Andrew Pekarik, ed., *Ukifune: Love in The Tale
of Genji*, pp. 21–61. New York: Columbia University Press.

Wagner, James G. 1976. "The *Kenreimon'in Ukyō no Daibu Shū*," *Monumenta
Nipponica*, 31.1 (Spring): 1–27.

Wixted, John Timothy. 1983. "The *Kokinshū* Prefaces: Another Perspective,"
Harvard Journal of Asiatic Studies, 43.1 (June): 215–38.

Yung-Hee, Kwon. 1986. "The Emperor's Songs: Emperor Go-Shirakawa and
Ryōjin Hishō Kudenshū," *Monumenta Nipponica*, 41.3 (Autumn): 261–98.

————. 1986. "Voices from the Periphery: Love Songs in *Ryōjin Hishō*,"
Monumenta Nipponica, 41.1 (Spring): 1–20.

The Early Medieval Age

Lafleur, William R. 1973–74. "Saigyō and the Buddhist Value of Nature," (2 parts), *History of Religions*, 13.2 (Nov.): 93–128; 13.3 (Feb.): 227–48.

Plutschow, Herbert Eugen. 1979. "Two Conversations of Saigyō and Their Significance in the History of Medieval Japanese Poetry," *Asiatische Studien/Etudes Asiatiques*, 33.1: 1–8.

Royston, Clifton. 1974. "Utaawase Judgments as Poetry Criticism," *Journal of Asian Studies*, 34.1 (Nov.): 98–108.

Shirane, Haruo. 1990. "Lyricism and Intertextuality: An Approach to Shunzei's Poetics," *Harvard Journal of Asiatic Studies*, 50.1 (Summer): 71–85.

The Late Medieval Age

Arntzen, Sonja. 1986. *Ikkyū and The Crazy Cloud Anthology*. Tokyo: Tokyo University Press.

Carter, Steven D. 1988. "Mixing Memories: Linked Verse and the Fragmentation of the Court Heritage," *Harvard Journal of Asiatic Studies*, 48.1 (June): 5–45.

———. 1987. *The Road to Komatsubara: A Classical Reading of the Renga Hyakuin*. Cambridge, Mass.: Harvard University Press.

———. 1984. "A Lesson in Failure: Linked-Verse Contests in Medieval Japan," *Journal of the American Oriental Society*, 104.4: 727–37.

———. 1983. *Three Poets at Yuyama*. Berkeley, Calif.: Institute of East Asian Studies.

———. 1981. "*Waka* in the Age of *Renga*," *Monumenta Nipponica*, 36.4 (Winter): 425–44.

Ebersole, Gary L. 1983. "The Buddhist Ritual Use of Linked Poetry in Medieval Japan," *Eastern Buddhist*, 16.2, n.s. (Autumn): 50–71.

Keene, Donald. 1981. "Jōha, a Sixteenth-Century Poet of Linked Verse," in George Elison and Bardwell Smith, eds., *Warlords, Artists, and Commoners: Japan in the Sixteenth Century*, pp. 113–32. Honolulu: University Press of Hawaii.

———. 1977. "The Comic Tradition in Renga," in John Whitney Hall and Toyoda Takeshi, eds., *Japan in the Muromachi Age*, pp. 241–77. Berkeley: University of California Press.

Konishi, Jin'ichi. 1975. "The Art of Renga" (tr. Karen Brazell and Lewis Cook), *Journal of Japanese Studies*, 21.1 (Winter): 33–61.

Miner, Earl. 1979. *Japanese Linked Poetry: An Account with Translations of Renga and Haikai Sequences*. Princeton, N.J.: Princeton University Press.

The Early Modern Age

Blyth, R. H. 1964. *A History of Haiku*. Tokyo: Hokuseido.

Hibbett, Howard S. 1960–61. "The Japanese Comic Linked Verse Tradition," *Harvard Journal of Asiatic Studies*, 23: 76–92.

Keene, Donald. 1976. *World Within Walls: Japanese Literature of the Pre-Modern Era, 1600–1868.* New York: Holt, Rinehart and Winston.

Ueda, Makoto. 1970. *Matsuo Bashō.* New York: Twayne Publishers.

Yasuda, Kenneth. 1957. *The Japanese Haiku, Its Essential Nature, History, and Possibilities in English, with Selected Examples.* Rutland, Vt.: Tuttle.

The Modern Age

Beichman, Janine. 1982. *Masaoka Shiki.* New York: Twayne.

Brower, Robert H. 1971. "Masaoka Shiki and Tanka Reform," in Donald H. Shively, ed., *Tradition and Modernization in Japanese Culture*, pp. 379–418. Princeton, N.J.: Princeton University Press.

Keene, Donald. 1984. *Dawn to the West: Japanese Literature in the Modern Era*, vol. 2: *Poetry, Drama, and Criticism.* New York: Holt, Rinehart and Winston.

Morris, Mark. 1984–85. "Buson and Shiki" (2 parts), *Harvard Journal of Asiatic Studies*, 44.2 (Dec.): 381–425; 45.1 (June): 256–319.

Sources of Illustrations

Index of Poets

In this index all numbers are poem numbers unless otherwise indicated. The supplementary notes on pages 459–67 are cited as "s.n."

Index of First Lines

In this index all numbers are poem numbers unless otherwise indicated. The supplementary notes on pages 459–67 are cited as "s.n."

Library of Congress Cataloging-in-Publication Data

Traditional Japanese poetry: an anthology / translated,
with an introduction, by Steven D. Carter.
   p.   cm.
Includes bibliographical references and index.
ISBN 0-8047-1562-9 (cl.): ISBN 0-8047-2212-9 (pbk.)
   1. Japanese poetry—Translations into English.
2. English poetry—Translations from Japanese.
I. Carter, Steven D.
PL782.E3T7   1991
895.6'1008—dc20   90-26365
                                     CIP

♾ This book is printed on acid-free paper